ASIAN AMERICAN POLITICAL PARTICIPATION

ASIAN AMERICAN POLITICAL PARTICIPATION

Emerging Constituents
and Their Political
Identities

Janelle Wong
S. Karthick Ramakrishnan
Taeku Lee
Jane Junn

Russell Sage Foundation
New York

The Russell Sage Foundation

The Russell Sage Foundation, one of the oldest of America's general purpose foundations, was established in 1907 by Mrs. Margaret Olivia Sage for "the improvement of social and living conditions in the United States." The Foundation seeks to fulfill this mandate by fostering the development and dissemination of knowledge about the country's political, social, and economic problems. While the Foundation endeavors to assure the accuracy and objectivity of each book it publishes, the conclusions and interpretations in Russell Sage Foundation publications are those of the authors and not of the Foundation, its Trustees, or its staff. Publication by Russell Sage, therefore, does not imply Foundation endorsement.

Library of Congress Cataloging-in-Publication Data

Asian American political participation : emerging constituents and their political identities / Janelle Wong ... [et al.].
    p. cm.
Includes bibliographical references and index.
    ISBN 978-0-87154-962-4 (pbk. : alk. paper) — ISBN 978-1-61044-755-3
(ebook)   1. Asian Americans—Politics and government.   I. Wong, Janelle.
    E184.A75A841445 2011
    323.1195'073—dc23   2011022380

Text design by Genna Patacsil.

RUSSELL SAGE FOUNDATION
112 East 64th Street, New York, New York 10065
10 9 8 7 6 5 4 3 2 1

To the 5,159 Americans of Asian descent who shared
their time and thoughts about politics with us

Contents

About the Authors |

JANELLE WONG is associate professor of political science and American studies and ethnicity at the University of Southern California and director of the Institute of Public Service at Seattle University.

S. KARTHICK RAMAKRISHNAN is associate professor of political science at the University of California, Riverside.

TAEKU LEE is professor of political science and law at the University of California, Berkeley.

JANE JUNN is professor of political science at the University of Southern California.

Acknowledgments

THANK YOU. Xie xie. Nanri. Komapsumnida.

Over the past six years we have faced the challenging—yet extremely rewarding—project of conducting a large-scale, multilanguage political survey of Asian Americans, and then writing a book about it. Perhaps the most challenging task, however, is to come up with a set of acknowledgments that do justice to the many debts we have collectively accumulated over the course of this project.

This project started innocently enough, as a series of informal one-on-one and one-on-two conversations that began in late 2005. We had just put the finishing touches on a book on immigrant political participation edited by Taeku, Karthick, and Ricardo Ramirez, and news was buzzing in our ears about the Latino National Survey that was being conducted by a "dream team" of six very accomplished scholars in Latino politics. It had been fifteen years since a comparable survey of Latino politics had taken place, and it was exciting to see momentum building again for a new explosion of studies on Latino politics.

We dared to think that perhaps the moment was ripe to try something similar for Asian Americans. Certainly, Asian Americans had a lot of catching up to do with respect to Latinos in terms of their numbers and political sway. Latinos were increasingly being recognized as an important electoral constituency in many states, and became the country's largest minority group in 2003. Still, we felt that important developments were under way for Asian Americans—in terms of their population growth, their dispersal to suburbs and new metro areas, and their growing political clout in several states and cities—that demanded a nationally representative survey of Asian Americans in politics.

Recognizing the need for a survey of Asian American politics, though important, was only the beginning of what we ultimately had to do to bring this project to fruition. It was the summer of 2006 by the time we had solidified commitments from the four of us, and we had less than two years to get the planning, fundraising, bidding, design, and implementation in place for our pre-election survey in 2008. There were many moments when we did not think we were going to make it, either because of setbacks in our funding requests or in the vagaries of keeping four professors and, by extension, their entire families, synchronized and focused around a project whose ultimate payoff was years in the offing.

We are listed in reverse alphabetical order on the cover, but the book represents a truly collaborative effort in terms of research and writing. Writing a book is never easy, but along the way we encountered several unexpected rewards. We started this journey as academic colleagues, but got to know each other on a more personal level. A project such as this requires almost constant communication, and so we began to share in the rhythms of each other's lives. Calls and meetings revolved around class schedules, deadlines for other projects, and various academic commitments, but also family trips, celebrations, home repairs, visits to doctors, and life events big and small. Thankfully, our family members gave us considerable leeway—for dozens of late-night planning calls, frantic revisions to proposals before their deadlines, and much more—and we remain forever indebted to them.

It is customary to thank family members last in the course of other acknowledgements, but their patience and support was vital to the success of this project. This is especially so in our case, given that the survey and this book were conducted over a six-year period that involved five house moves, three cross-country treks, the births of three babies, and five more children growing up too quickly before our eyes. We just can't say thank you enough to our loving, understanding, and supportive partners and children: David, Evan, and Mariana; Brinda, Omji, and Millan; Shirley, Ella, and Linus; David, Eve, and Juliet.

We have also relied on the support of many other families, whether foundations, community organizations, fellow scholars, or our home institutions. An early grant from the James Irvine Foundation, and a subsequent large grant from the Russell Sage Foundation, came at a critical time during this project, when we were unsure whether we would be able to pull off a national survey prior to the 2008 presidential election. Generous grants from the Eagleton Institute of Politics and the Carnegie Corporation of New York also helped extend the scope and reach of our project. Special thanks to Eric Wanner and Aixa Cintrón-Vélez of the Russell Sage Foundation, Amy Dominguez-Arms of the James Irvine Foundation, Ruth Mandel of the Eagleton Institute of Politics, and Geraldine Mannion of the Carnegie Corporation of New York.

One of the important goals of the National Asian American Survey was to help inform public debate and news coverage of Asian Americans during the 2008 presidential election. In trying to do so, we benefited greatly from the input and collaboration of numerous community partners, including APIAVote, the Congressional Asian Pacific American Caucus, National Council of Asian Pacific Americans, the Asian Pacific American Legal Center, Leadership Education for Asian Pacifics, the Asian American Justice Center, and the Orange County Asian and Pacific Islander Alliance. We give special thanks to Christine Chen of Strategic Alliance, who worked tirelessly to get our proposals and subsequent survey reports to organizations and individuals doing important policy work in the Asian American community.

We are also grateful to the following scholars for their expert advice on various aspects of the survey enterprise: Matt Barreto (University of Washington), Elena Erosheva (University of Washington), Luis Fraga (University of Washington), Rodney Hero (Notre Dame), Charles Hirschman (University of Washington), Vincent Hutchings (University of Michigan), Dan Ichinose (APALC), Martin Iguchi (RAND Corporation), Michael Jones-Correa (Cornell University), James Lai (Santa Clara University), Pei-Te Lien (UC Santa Barbara), John Mollenkopf (Graduate Center, City University of New York), Susan Pinkus (*Los Angeles Times*), Ninez Ponce (UCLA), Gary Segura (Stanford), and David Takeuchi (University of Washington). More generally, for the book, we have also benefited from conversations with long-time friends and colleagues, including Irene Bloemraad (UC Berkeley), Cathy Cohen and Michael Dawson (University of Chicago), Rodolfo de la Garza (Columbia), Ann Lin (University of Michigan), Natalie Masuoka (Tufts University), Paul Ong (UCLA), Ricardo Ramirez (Notre Dame), and Robert Shapiro (Columbia).

Writing a foundational book on Asian American political participation, based on a nationally representative sample of citizens as well as noncitizens, has long been a central goal of our project. We thank Suzanne Nichols, publications director at the Russell Sage Foundation, for consistently seeing the value for such a book, and for guiding it through various stages of revision and preparation. The press is an invaluable resource for scholarship on race and immigration in the United States, and we are thrilled to be a part of a large and important corpus of work from the Russell Sage Foundation. We also benefited from the three anonymous reviews for this publication, and our book has improved tremendously from revisions that drew on the reviewers' comments.

For research assistance, we thank Dana Brown, Ming Hsu Chen, Nicole Fox, Anna Junn Murphy, Loan K. Le, Míchel Martinez, Catherine Ngo, and Tom Wong. David Silver (UCLA) and David Crow (UC Riverside) provided important assistance with the creation of survey weights, and helped us think through our sample design in critical and important ways.

We would also be remiss if we did not thank our various institutional homes for their encouragement and support for this project, including our departments at Rutgers, UC Berkeley, UC Riverside, and the University of Southern California. Special thanks also to seminar participants at the Institute for Governmental Studies at UC Berkeley, conference attendees at the American Political Science Association and the Midwest Political Science Association, and to various participants in the Politics of Race, Immigration, and Ethnicity Consortium (PRIEC).

The interviews were conducted by Interviewing Services of America, Inc. (ISA) of Van Nuys, California, under the supervision of Francine Cafarchia, Martin Magaña, and Mike Vanacore. We also benefited from the involvement and expertise of scores of individuals who were involved in fielding the survey. Without their efforts, our survey would not have been possible in the ambitious three-month time frame that we had set out for completing the data collection. Instead of having the field staff listed as anonymous voices that get only passing recognition, we acknowledge each of them individually by their first names: supervisors Claudia, Jennifer, Liana, Azalia, Daniel, Frank, Sam, Christal, Corlis, Helen, and Miguel; and interviewers Addam, Advent, Alfredo, Andrew, Angelica, Anh, Anita, Ann, Annet, Annie, Antwanette, Arnette, Ashley, Astrid, Audrea, Audrey, Aulbonie, Berenice, Boyd, Bryan, Byung, Carlos, Carolina, Cham, Charlotte, Charmaigne, Chau, Chris, Christopher, Chuan, Corlis, Cui, Cynthena, Cynthia B., Cynthia C., Damein, Debra, Deshawn, Devin, Dexter, Diane, Dolores, Domingo, Donald P., Donald R., Dong, Donitia, Eddiemar, Edward, Elva, Erick, Estela, Estrella, Eufrocino, F.A., Felicia, Fernando, Fumiko, Gerrick, Gilbert, Gloria, Guo, Gustavo, Hae, Hang, Hawk, Helen C., Helen M., Henry, Hien, Hieu, Hui, Ian, Irene, Irma, James, Jaqueline, Jason, Jawed, Jay, Jayne, Jean, Jestine, Jewell, Jihan, Jing, Johanna, Johnny, Juanita, Judy, Julie, Julita, Karen, Katherine, Kathryn, Kaylee, Ke-Hui, Kelly, Khoa, Kuei-Yu, Kum, Kun, Kyong, Ladonna, Lamberto, Laura, Lavon, Leilani, Li, Lily, Linda, Lisa, Lizette, Lo, Luevnia, Luz, Marites, Marleen, Mary C., Mary G., Melissa, Melojane, Mia, Michael, Michelle B., Michelle L., Michelle R., Milton, Misty, Mitchell, Monica L., Monica M., Moti, Nadyne, Naho, Naira, Nancy H., Nancy M., Nancy T., Nathaniel, Natividad, Nelly, Ngoc-Diep, Nhuan, Noelle, Oanh, Omar, Patricia, Peter, Ping, Portia, Renato, Richard C., Richard M., Ron, Rose, Ryan, Ryna, Sandra, Sang, Saolele, Sara A., Sara S., Selene, Sephora, Shenay, Shirley, Shu, Shun, Soledad, Stacy, Steven H., Steven Z., Susan, Sylvia, Terry, Thanh, Thanh, Theresa, Thieu, Thuong, Trevor, Tricia, Vanessa, Vincent, Vivian, William, Xianbi, Yaguang, Yanzhen, Yi, Yingjuan, Young, and Yun. Thank you all.

Despite the legions of individuals who helped us along the way, we bear responsibility for any errors that may be contained in this work. We remain excited and hopeful at the prospects for greater political participation among Asian Americans, and greater attention to the needs, interests, and concerns of this fast-growing constituency.

Seattle, Washington
Riverside, California
Berkeley, California
Los Angeles, California

Chapter 1 | Making Visible: Political Participation

IN THE SPRING of 2008, Asian American voters were showered with attention for the first time in a presidential election year, as Hillary Clinton and Barack Obama scrambled for voters after the initial set of caucuses and primaries in Iowa, New Hampshire, South Carolina, and Nevada. With the consequences of Super Tuesday far from certain, and with every delegate potentially important on the road to secure the Democratic nomination, the Clinton and Obama campaigns pressed their case to various constituencies. For the first time, this included a significant number of Asian Americans. Clinton drew endorsements from several Asian American elected officials and sought to build on her formidable fundraising operation in New York, which included prominent Asian Americans. At the same time, Barack Obama highlighted his childhood roots in Hawaii and enlisted the support of his family members, including his Indonesian American sister Maya Soetoro-Ng and her Chinese American husband, Konrad Ng. With a trove of Asian American voters in Super Tuesday states such as New York and California, and more in subsequent states, such as Washington and Virginia, the campaigns were paying attention to Asian American voters as never before.

As a consequence, the political news media also began to draw attention to the role of Asian American voters. The attention was not entirely flattering, however. One of the main storylines that emerged was the strong level of support Asian Americans gave to Hillary Clinton over Barack Obama. In California, for example, the National Election Pool found that Clinton won more than 70 percent of the Asian American vote, much more than the 67 percent among Latinos, and the 56 percent among white women (National Election Pool 2008). Similar results held true in Super Tuesday states, such as New York, leading many news commentators to attribute the support to racial prejudice against black candidates (Cullen 2008; Ramakrishnan et al. 2009).

However, these media-sponsored polls were problematic. Perhaps most basically, they did not include questions on factors such as name recognition for Clinton versus Obama and voters' attitudes toward the Bill Clinton presidency (which was reported to have largely been beneficial to the livelihoods of Latinos and Asian Americans). By reporting only the top-line numbers, the polls did not provide a clear signal about whether people were voting for Clinton or against Obama. The problems in the National Election Pool were even more acute for Asian Americans for two significant reasons: the survey was conducted only in English and Spanish and included only about 150 respondents in California, thus failing to take into account the number of respondents necessary to cover the significant national-origin diversity within the Asian American community. Despite these problems, news stories in *Time* magazine, on CNN, and from other sources argued that Obama "had an Asian problem," and that he needed to overcome racial prejudice among Asian Americans to win their vote (Cullen 2008; Tuchman 2008). The political story was too appealing to be dethroned by the lack of good data.

It is in this context that we were planning a national political survey of Asian Americans. We had conceived of the idea in early 2006, and, by the time Super Tuesday rolled around, we were well on our way to raising funds for a nationally representative survey of Asian American politics. As our pre-election survey showed, and as various exit polls later corroborated, race-based considerations played only a minor role in the voting behavior of Asian Americans during the presidential primaries and the general election of 2008 (Ramakrishnan et al. 2009). Indeed, Obama enjoyed a level of Asian American support significantly higher than any earlier Democratic presidential candidate (see chapter 4).

What our data highlighted, and what motivated the writing of this book, is the desire to provide a more definitive account of Asian American politics than what exists today. Before the 2008 National Asian American Survey (NAAS), no nationally representative survey had focused on the political behavior and attitudes of Asian Americans and the factors that intervene between immigration, citizenship, voting, and other political activities. Given this lack of data, one of the primary tasks in this book is to lay out a careful descriptive analysis of Asian American political participation as seen through five broad sets of factors: immigrant socialization, residential contexts, party socialization, racial identification, and civic association. At the same time, we also engage with several important theoretical questions about the determinants of political participation among Asian Americans, and what the answers indicate about the importance of socioeconomic status, national origin, party mobilization, and racial identification in shaping political behavior. Before delving into the analysis, however, it is important to address a few basic questions, including: Who are Asian Americans? Why it is important to draw scholarly attention and analysis to political participation among Asian Americans?

IMPORTANT QUESTIONS IN ASIAN AMERICAN POLITICAL BEHAVIOR

The anecdote with which we began this book—of a misreading of Asian American opinion toward Obama during the 2008 presidential election—suggests that the place of Asian Americans in the American political system remains unclear to most Americans, including many news organizations. Perhaps this should not be surprising. Asian Americans constitute about 5 percent of the U.S. resident population, a relatively small group today when compared with other racial-ethnic groups such as whites and African Americans. Internal diversity within the group—along the lines of national origin, language, religion, immigrant generation, and socioeconomic status—also poses a challenge to those trying to assess the political position of Asian Americans as a whole.

And yet, we argue that there are good reasons to pay closer attention to this group when it comes to U.S. politics. First, according to the U.S. Census, Americans of Asian and Pacific Islander heritage have been one of the fastest-growing populations over the last several decades. In 1960, there were fewer than 1 million Asian Americans in the country, less than .5 percent of the total population. By July 2008, the Asian American population had grown to 15.3 million, about 5 percent of the total. This explosive growth is expected to continue, census projections suggesting 44.4 million Asian Americans by 2060, or slightly more than 10 percent of the expected total population of 432 million Americans that year.[1] In a democratic system in which numbers matter, this kind of population growth may very likely translate into increased political influence for Asian Americans.

Because Asian Americans exhibit patterns of concentrated geographic settlement in particular regions, some places in the United States have already seen the growing political influence of the group. According to the 2008 American Community Survey, nearly one in two Asian Americans (48 percent) live in the western region of the United States, the Pacific seaboard states (including Alaska and Hawaii) accounting for about 43 percent of the national Asian American and Pacific Islander population. California has by far the largest Asian American population, accounting for one-third of the national total, and adding New York and Texas covers nearly half (48 percent). In fact, it is estimated that Asian Americans now make up a larger proportion of California's registered voter population than African Americans do. Although Latinos are even more concentrated in particular states (California, Texas, and Florida accounting for 56 percent of the national Latino population), the geographic concentration of Asian Americans is considerably higher than the residential concentration of blacks and whites, where the top three states of residence account for 22 percent and 20 percent, respectively, of each group's national population.

In high Asian American concentration states such as Hawaii, California, and New York, Asian American political power is no longer a matter of long-term speculation, but a present-day reality. For example, Asian Americans in 2008 accounted for twenty-four of fifty-one state house representatives in Hawaii, and eight of eighty assembly seats in California. Asian Americans have also enjoyed some success in winning statewide offices in these high-concentration states, from U.S. senators to governors and attorneys general, although the examples of governors Jindal (R-LA), Haley (R-SC), and Locke (D-WA) show that the appeal of Asian American candidates extends to areas of smaller concentrations as well. Finally, at the local level, Asian Americans have served as council members in major cities such as New York, Los Angeles, Houston, Boston, San Francisco, Oakland, and Seattle.

Despite their high levels of geographic concentration relative to whites and blacks, Asian Americans are now becoming increasingly geographically dispersed. This dispersion is evident at region, state, county, and municipality levels. By region, the Asian American population grew by an impressive 57 percent in the West between 1990 and 2000, but somewhat modestly in comparison with the 79 percent in the Northeast, 84 percent in the Midwest, and 107 percent in the South. Between the 1990 and 2000 censuses, the Asian American population more than doubled in nineteen states, which continue to be high growth areas. Indeed, data from the American Community Survey indicates that between 2000 and 2008, the Asian American population grew by more than 30 percent in most states, with higher than 50 percent growth in such politically important states such as Florida and Texas (figure 1.1). In 2000, seventy-one counties had Asian American populations that were more than 5 percent of the resident population. By 2008, the American Community Survey indicated that the number had risen to ninety-two. Even more congressional districts have Asian American and Pacific Islander residents above the 5 percent threshold (103 of 435). When the unit of analysis is the city or municipality, the number of places with significant Asian American populations shoots up to nearly six hundred. Hence, as their numbers grow in places considered competitive battleground states in presidential elections, Asian Americans may become a critical constituency in national politics as well.

Of course, political power is not based only on the number of residents.

Figure 1.1   Growth in Asian American Population, 2000 to 2008

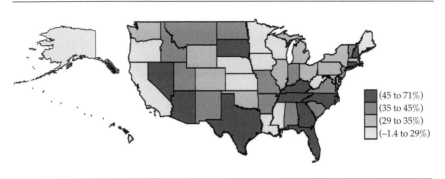

(45 to 71%)
(35 to 45%)
(29 to 35%)
(−1.4 to 29%)

Source: Authors' figure based on data from U.S. Census Bureau (2000, 2008a).

For a group to exert influence in American politics, it must show that the individuals who contribute to those numbers actually participate in the political system. The central question at the foreground of this book, then, is perhaps one that is central to the study of any group-based population in a representative democracy: Who among this group participates in the political process, and why?

For the population of Asians in America, these bedrock questions have a particular force that emerges from the mismatch between the high average economic and education achievement of the Asian American community and its correspondingly modest levels of political activity. As figure 1.2 indicates, higher group levels of educational attainment do not demonstrate a strong correspondence with higher levels of formal aspects of political participation, such as registration and voting. Among adult citizens, Asian Americans and Latinos have similar rates of voting participation, but vastly different levels of educational achievement. The lack of correspondence between group-level educational attainment and voting rates is evident not only in comparisons between Asian Americans and members of other racial and ethnic groups, but also in comparisons across national origin groups for Asian Americans. For instance, among adult citizens, Asian Indians are nearly three times as likely as their Vietnamese counterparts to have a college degree (74 percent versus 26 percent) but only marginally more likely to have voted in 2008 (66 percent versus 62 percent). Similarly, Chinese Americans are slightly more likely than Filipino Americans to have completed a college degree, but less likely to have voted in 2008.

This lack of linear correspondence, at least as a first-order association, between education and voting can also be shown using other measures of

Figure 1.2   Voting and Educational Attainment Among Adult Citizens

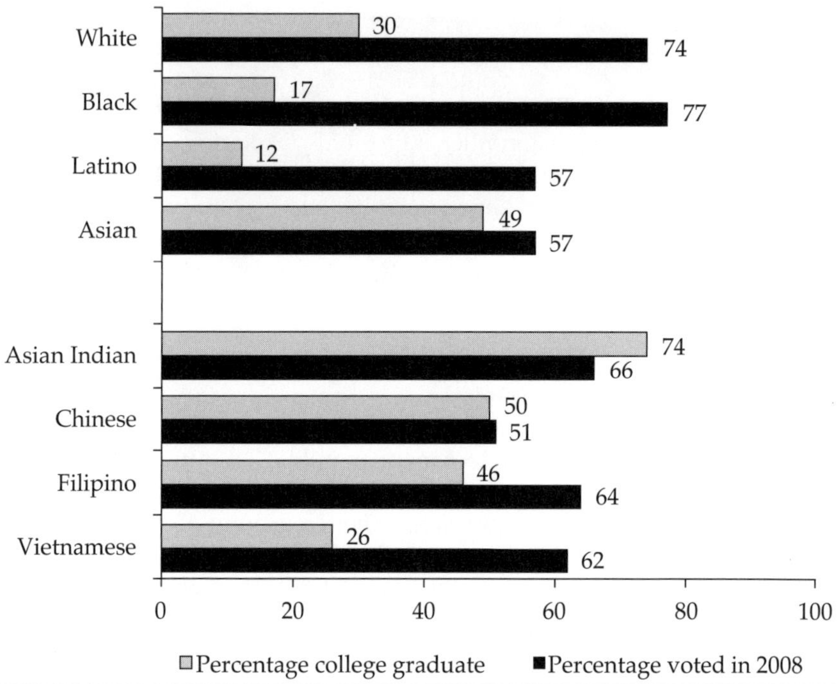

Horizontal bar chart. Each category shows two bars: "Percentage college graduate" and "Percentage voted in 2008."

- White: college graduate 30, voted 74
- Black: college graduate 17, voted 77
- Latino: college graduate 12, voted 57
- Asian: college graduate 49, voted 57
- Asian Indian: college graduate 74, voted 66
- Chinese: college graduate 50, voted 51
- Filipino: college graduate 46, voted 64
- Vietnamese: college graduate 26, voted 62

x-axis: 0, 20, 40, 60, 80, 100

☐ Percentage college graduate   ■ Percentage voted in 2008

Source: Authors' compilation of data from the 2008 Current Population Survey Voter Supplement (U.S. Census Bureau 2008b).

socioeconomic resources and of political participation. The finding rubs against one of the most robust results in political behavior research: namely, that high levels of socioeconomic resources go hand in hand with high rates of voting and other forms of political participation (Verba and Nie 1972; Verba, Nie, and Kim 1978; Rosenstone and Hansen 1993; Verba, Schlozman, and Brady 1995). To put this in context, the conventional view today is that political participation is the result of at least three factors: having the means, being properly motivated, and being mobilized to act. As one set of scholars puts it, "individuals may choose not to participate because they can't, because they don't want to, or because nobody asked" (Verba, Schlozman, and Brady 1995, 15). The means of participation here range from individual-level resources, such as time, money, civic skills, and political knowledge, to institutional rules, such as voter eligibility requirements, in-language ballots, redistricting, and vote-recording technologies. Although a resource like education is perhaps most intuitively linked to the resource-based roots of participation, it clearly also redounds to how incentivized people are to vote and whether they are recruited to do so. In the ensuing sections, then, we seek to better understand why high levels of socioeconomic resources appear not to engender correspondingly high levels of political engagement for Asian Americans by specifying five pathways to participation that take into account the distinct characteristics of the Asian American population.

Figure 1.2 also suggests another important corollary question: the extent to which national origin plays an important role in shaping Asian American political behavior. Given the relatively high proportion of first-generation immigrants, one might expect national origin differences to remain a powerful determinant of Asian American political behavior. Thus, for instance, a recent Indian immigrant who has voted in several elections before coming to the United States may be better informed about the role of political parties in the United States than a recent immigrant from the People's Republic of China. National-origin differences are also evident in party identification and presidential vote choice, Vietnamese Americans leaning heavily toward the Republican Party and Republican candidates, and Japanese Americans and Indian Americans favoring Democrats. At the same time, there may be reasons to think that national-origin differences fade away as immigrants spend more time in the United States, confront common hurdles such as racial discrimination, and receive messages about a pan-ethnic racial identity from community organizations, schools, and various government agencies (Espiritu 1993). Indeed, we find from the National Asian American Survey that, when we move from the first generation to subsequent generations, national origin differences begin to fade for a wide variety of political outcomes (see chapter 8). Furthermore, even in instances when national-origin differences are important, they are often attributable to other factors, such as group variations in rates of English proficiency, educational attainment, and experiences with racial discrimination.

Finally, an important background question that may arise in the examination of Asian American politics is one that arises in any study of political behavior: Why does it matter? Why does it matter if some groups are more likely to vote in elections than others, or if some groups are more likely to make campaign contributions than others? The United States, as a growing chorus of political scientists have shown, is a place where political participation is polarized and unequal (Jacobs and Skocpol 2005; Hacker 2006; Bartels 2008; McCarty 2006; Gelman 2008). The normative grounds for concern here are obvious enough. As Sidney Verba argues, "of the various ways in which U.S. citizens can be unequal, political inequality is one of the most significant and troubling . . . one of the bedrock principles in a democracy is the equal consideration of the preferences of all citizens" (2003, 663). Moreover, political activity and the attendant claims to social membership that accompany it, are central to a full and flourishing conception of citizenship itself (Kymlicka and Norman 1994; Bosniak 1999).

Empirically, research has revealed several important reasons to pay attention to group disparities in political participation. For instance, higher turnout may alter election outcomes, though studies suggest that this is more likely in local than in statewide elections (Hajnal and Trounstine 2005; Citrin, Schickler, and Sides 2003). More important, however, several studies indicate that elected officials are more likely to be responsive to the interests of those active in politics than those who are not (Griffin and Newman 2005, 2008; Bartels 2008). This is true even for U.S. senators, who are elected only once every six years and are presumably more insulated from electoral influence than state and local representatives. Additionally, the dynamics of political mobilization may reproduce inequalities in representation over time, because political parties and campaigns pay far more attention to those who have participated in past elections than those who have not, and as those who are contacted by political parties and campaigns continue to participate at higher levels than those who are not contacted (Rosenstone and Hansen 1993; Ramirez and Wong 2006). Recurring cycles of differential participation and mobilization can thus perpetuate a form of American democracy characterized by unequal representation, and research on lower participation and lower mobilization among Asian Americans suggests that they are at an unequal political footing with respect to other racial and ethnic groups in the United States (Uhlaner, Cain, and Kiewiet 1989; Junn 1999; Ramakrishnan 2005; Wong 2006). That is, to the extent that political participation is a primary vehicle for the representation of policy preferences, groups that do not participate at high rates will be systematically disadvantaged. This is true across groups, but also within heterogeneous pan-ethnic groups, such as Asian Americans.

To better understand Asian American political participation, we must contextualize their political involvement. For example, we might look to the past and consider the extent to which institutions that have historically played an instrumental role in the integration and incorporation of immigrants from multiple shores and whether they continue to play this role today. In the portrayal of many historians, the late nineteenth and early twentieth centuries in America were a golden age of sorts for newcomers and their offspring (Dahl 1961; Allswang 1977; Archdeacon 1983).[2] In the political realm, this period is especially notable—if only in our collective memory—for representing an American archetype of inclusion into a pluralist political system through the rough and tumble of street-level party competition, with ward bosses and precinct captains deploying favor and coercion to impress upon immigrants what it meant to be a

Democrat or a Republican. Although most scholars continue to see partisan attachments as a defining political identity for Americans, many scholars of immigrant incorporation conclude that today's political parties are far more selective in their inclusion of new Americans into the political process. What role, then, do institutions like parties and other forms of organizational life in civil society like unions, places of worship, community organizations, and ethnic media play in the politicization of Asian Americans?

We might also look to the present and consider the current role of Asian American voters in the terrain of electoral competition in America. From the standpoint of race relations, for instance, we might inquire about the extent to which President Barack Obama's race factored into the Asian American vote in the 2008 primaries and general election. As noted at the outset of this book, many observers were surprised by the overwhelming support among Asian Americans for Hillary Clinton over Barack Obama, and did not have the benefit of survey data to realize that racial attitudes actually played only a marginal role in the voting decisions of Asian Americans. Or, we might look to the future and consider the extent to which the dramatic demographic transformation of American society is likely to engender a similarly dramatic political transformation of electoral competition in America. Social demographers foretell a near future in this century in which whites will no longer be a majority of the population and, soon thereafter, of the electorate. The U.S. population will, simultaneously as well, continue to grow in its proportion of immigrants and their offspring and in its proportion who claim multiple racial and ethnic heritages. How will the current configuration of America's ethnoracial categories survive this metamorphosis and what political implications follow?

WHO ARE ASIAN AMERICANS?

Who are Asian Americans and are they a meaningful category when it comes to U.S. politics? This question underlies much of Asian American politics and is one we engage with throughout this book. In particular, our analysis highlights the ways in which the community shares patterns as a group and how their political participation varies according to internal group variations. This approach allows us to assess points of convergence and divergence in the group's political participation. We discuss how members of the group are similar and different in how they engage with the political system, and we suggest potential building blocks for political community based on patterns of political participation.

It is true that Asian Americans are remarkably diverse in terms of ethnicity, national origin, language, religion, cultural orientation, socioeconomic status, and immigration histories. Focusing on regions and countries of origin alone, Asian Americans have shifted from a population of primarily working-age men from China and Japan in 1900 to a considerably more diverse population today in terms of national origin, gender, class background, and modes of entry into the United States. The U.S. Census Bureau's system of racial classification reflects this growing diversity, from the addition of Chinese in 1870 and Japanese in 1890, to the addition of Filipinos and Hawaiians in 1910, and Hindus and Koreans in 1920 (Minnesota Population Center 2011). Indeed, the Census Bureau did not group these various national origins under the same category until 1990, when it included ten options under the umbrella of Asian or Pacific Islander (API). Many Native Hawaiian and Pacific Islander activists then pushed for a separate racial category, which the Census Bureau granted in 2000. Today, according to various federal government agencies, the term Asian refers to individuals with origins in the Far East, Southeast Asia, or Indian subcontinent and to individuals who self-identify racially as Asian Indian, Chinese, Filipino, Korean, Japanese, Vietnamese, or Other Asian, including Asians of Burmese, Cambodian, Hmong, Laotian, Pakistani, and Thai origin. Starting with the 2000 census, after consultation with relevant community organizations, the federal government began to group Native Hawaiians and Pacific Islanders in a separate category. Of course, census definitions shift over time and reflect changing popular and scientific notions of race and ethnicity (Omi and Winant 1994).

Asian Americans in the United States today are thus very much a moving target in terms of their geographic location and ethnic composition. However, certain common characteristics and dynamics unify this diverse group of residents and, we believe, warrant treating it, at times, as a meaningful pan-ethnic category, Asian Americans. First, Asian Americans share a history of racial exclusion from naturalization in the United States (Ngai 2004). Thus, even though Asian immigrants and native-born Asian Americans were classified variously as Chinese, Filipino, Hindu, and so on, and even though popular notions of race from the early 1900s viewed Asians as belonging to two or more racial stocks, Asian immigrants were nevertheless treated the same when it came to eligibility for naturalization. As the U.S. Supreme Court ruled in two separate decisions (Takao Ozawa v. U.S., 260 U.S. 178 1922; United States v. Bhagat Singh Thind, 261 U.S. 204 1923), Asians were neither white nor Caucasian, and thus could not gain citizenship through naturalization. Not until the 1950s were most Asian immigrants granted the right to naturalize as citizens of the United States. Because they occupied a racial hinterland outside the traditional formation of Caucasian-white,

Figure 1.3   Legal Permanent Residents

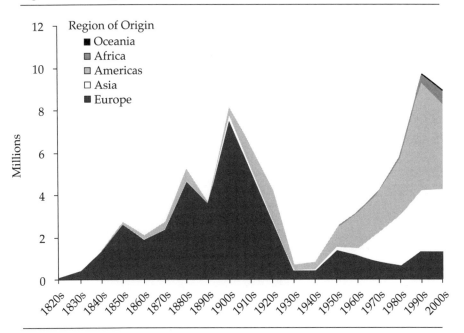

Source: Authors' compilation based on data from U.S. Citizenship and Immigration Services (2009b).

Negro-black, and American Indian, Asian Americans from various national origins found themselves politically disenfranchised until the second half of the twentieth century.

Apart from having a common history of political disadvantage for much of the last century, two other important characteristics unify most Asian Americans: they are the most heavily immigrant group among the five major racial and ethnic groups in the United States at the beginning of the twenty-first century and are also among the most highly educated. Both characteristics stem from the liberalization of immigration laws starting in 1965, as the United States dramatically raised quotas on migration and emphasized professional skills and family reunification as important considerations for permanent resident applications. As figure 1.3 indicates, the Immigration and Nationality Act of 1965 had a profound effect on the national origin mix of immigrants to the United States. Whereas before World War II most migrants to the United States came from Europe, immigrants in the past four decades have predominantly come from Latin America and Asia. As a result, the foreign-born account for a very high proportion of Asian American residents (67 percent) when compared with whites (4 percent), blacks (8 percent), and even Latinos (40 percent), who had a sizable population of native-born citizens before the rise in immigration after 1965.

For Asian Americans, the expansion of professional visas after 1965 also coincided with policies in Asian countries that produced a surplus of skilled labor relative to the needs of centrally managed national economies (Bhagwati and Hamada 1974; Khadria 1999). As a consequence, most of the Asian immigrants who came to the United States after 1965 tended to be highly skilled, though significant numbers of migrants who came through refugee provisions and family reunification were less likely to be college educated. Despite the bimodal distribution of Asian Americans according to various indicators of resources and socioeconomic status, Asian Americans nevertheless enjoy higher-than-average levels of income and educational attainment when compared with any other group of Americans classified by race. According to the most recent American Community Survey (ACS) data, about 50 percent of the Asian American (Asian alone) population age twenty-five and older had a bachelor's degree or higher, versus roughly 31 percent of whites, 18 percent of blacks, and 13 percent of Latinos. Similarly, the proportion of households living under the poverty line in 2008 was 8 percent for Asian Americans, 6 percent for whites, 21 percent for African Americans, and 19 percent for Latinos (U.S. Census Bureau 2008a). As several studies have shown, however, the relative economic gains of Asian Americans have not automatically led to more social and political resources in American society (Tuan 1998; Junn 2008). Instead, the association of Asian Americans as "perpetual foreigners," combined with the high proportion of Asian Americans who are first- and second-generation immigrants, has produced a situation where they are seen as outsiders to the sociopolitical system, though occupying relatively high-status positions in the labor force when compared with Latinos and African Americans (Kim 1999).

In this book, we use the terms Asian and Asian Americans interchangeably and frequently, with a broader understanding of their meanings than might be implied by our reference to particular census categories. We use both as covering terms for the diverse populations represented in the 2008 National Asian American Survey without intending to imply either wrongful judgments about proper membership in the United States when we use Asian or incorrect assumptions about the nativity of our sample when we use Asian American. (See appendix A for a more detailed discussion of Asian and Asian American as socially and politically constructed racial categories.)

BUILDING ON RESEARCH
OF ASIAN AMERICANS

This book is based on a new, original survey of Asian American political attitudes and behavior. Much of the data we have relied on in the past for statements about Asian American citizens and voters are important, but limited in several ways. The Current Population Survey (CPS), which is a standard reference on voter registration and turnout across racial and ethnic groups, conducts its interviews only in English and Spanish. Various exit polls from organizations such as the Asian American Legal Defense and Education Fund (AALDEF) have interviews in various Asian languages, but are limited in that they survey only voters in heavily Asian precincts. Thus the perspectives of nonvoters and noncitizens, and the factors that intervene between immigration, citizenship, voting, and other political activities, are rendered invisible. Finally, studies of Asian Americans, such as the Pilot National Asian American Political Survey (PNAAPS), have had an impressive set of questions and a mix of citizens and noncitizens, but drew only on Asian Americans in major metropolitan areas. A nationally representative survey of Asian Americans, citizens as well as noncitizens, with support in the major Asian languages, was still lacking.

The survey we conducted between August and October 2008 addresses many of these problems. The NAAS involved 5,159 interviews of the six major national-origin groups that together account for 85 percent of the Asian American population. The survey was drawn from a nationally representative sample of Asian American residents, with oversamples in new immigrant destinations, such as Houston, Texas, and in particular states like New Jersey. Interviews were conducted in eight languages, including English, and included many questions on political attitudes, political and civic behavior, immigrant socialization, and racial identification. Many of these questions are comparable to those in other concurrent data collections, such as the American National Election Study, which had oversamples of more than five hundred African Americans and Latinos, whereas others are uniquely designed to capture the political dynamics of a highly immigrant community with significant diversity in national origin, region of settlement, and English proficiency.

A number of surveys have been conducted on reasonably large samples of Asian American respondents, but generally fall into one of three groupings, each with different limitations. The first are a set of geographically specific samples that do not offer broad coverage of the national Asian American population: the Los Angeles Study of Urban Inequality, the Immigrant Second Generation in Metropolitan New York project, and the University of Massachusetts–Boston Institute of Asian American Studies Polls. Next are media polls that include a limited set of explanatory variables and are therefore not well suited for in-depth research: the *Los Angeles Times*'s polls of Chinese, Filipino, Korean, and Vietnamese Americans in the 1990s; and the Kaiser Family Foundation's surveys with the *Washington Post* in 1995 and 2001 and the *San Jose Mercury News* in 2004. Last are exit poll data limited both in terms of the small number of questions included in the survey instrument, and by their sampling frames: the Voter News Service/National Election Pool exit polls and Asian-specific exit polls by Asian Pacific American Legal Center, Asian American Legal Defense and Education Fund, Chinese American Voters Education Committee, and other advocacy organizations. Furthermore, in many of these cases, the approaches to sampling the Asian American population fall shy of being representative because they rely exclusively on listed surname frames, English-only interviews, and selection on either one or only a few national origin and ethnic groups.

The most significant scholarly effort thus far to study Asian American political behavior is the Pilot National Asian American Political Survey (PNAAPS) of 2001 (Lien, Conway, and Wong 2004). PNAAPS surveyed 1,218 Asian Americans living in the metropolitan statistical areas (MSAs) with the largest concentrations of Asian Americans in the United States: New York, Los Angeles, San Francisco, Honolulu, and Chicago. Because Asian Americans tend to live in urban areas on the east and west coasts, this method yielded a sample representing 40 percent of the Asian American population. However, the validity and utility of inferences were limited by sample size for particular national groups and the heavy reliance on Asian Americans living in large central cities.

Since the 2001 PNAAPS, one other important effort focused on the political opinions of Asian Americans: the National Poll of Asian Pacific Islanders (NPAPI) on the 2004 election. The NPAPI interviewed 1,004 Asian American registered voters who were identified as likely voters in the 2004 presidential election. This approach was useful for understanding the potential influence of Asian Americans in that election, but tells us far less about the barriers Asian Americans face in terms of democratic participation (such as becoming citizens and registered voters), the key political interests and priorities that characterize the community as a whole, or the future political potential of noncitizens and those not registered to vote. The inferences that can be drawn from a survey that screens for likely voters, furthermore, depends on what factors are taken into consideration in constructing the likely voter screen. Neither of these studies included a large enough sample to allow for meaningful analysis within specific ethnic subgroup and national origin.

THE 2008 NATIONAL
ASIAN AMERICAN SURVEY

To address these multiple limitations of previous efforts and, more generally, to advance our understanding of this emerging population, we undertook the most comprehensive survey to date of the civic and political life of Asians in the United States. The National Asian American Survey represents the fruits of our labors and serves as our primary source of data for this book's effort to answer long-standing questions about the relationship between individual-level resources, political partisanship, ethnic and racial identity, immigrant assimilation, social capital, and structural context and political engagement. The NAAS is a dataset of 5,159 completed interviews conducted over roughly ten weeks before the 2008 election and includes large numbers of respondents from the six largest Asian national-origin groups: Asian Indians, Chinese, Filipinos, Japanese, Koreans, and Vietnamese. Surveys were conducted by telephone between August 18 and October 29, 2008. The NAAS includes adults in the United States who identify any family background from countries in Asia, exclusive of those classified as the Middle East.[3] Survey interviews were conducted in eight languages based on the interviewee's preference—English, Cantonese, Mandarin, Korean, Vietnamese, Tagalog, Japanese, and Hindi—and yielded sample sizes of at least five hundred adult residents for Asian Americans in the six largest national-origin groups. The final breakdown was 1,350 Chinese, 1,150 Asian Indian, 719 Vietnamese, 614 Korean, 603 Filipino, and 541 Japanese, and an additional 182 either from other countries in Asia or who identify as multiracial or multiethnic.[4] Overall, 40 percent of our sample chose English as their preferred language for the interview. We weight our sample, using a raking procedure, to reflect the balance of gender, nativity, citizenship status, and educational attainment of the six largest national-origin groups in the United States, as well as the proportion of these groups within each state. More details about our sample design and weights are provided in appendix F.

Before discussing our survey questionnaire, we address our primary choice in drawing our samples by national origin or ethnoracial classification, and their relationship to the larger body of scholarship on Asian immigrants and Asian Americans more generally. As we shall see in chapter 2, there are many good reasons to do so, from the perspective of Asian American histories that vary by national origin, as well as census categories and immigration policies that continue to differentiate Asians on the basis of national origin. Additionally, several decades of scholarship on Asian Americans suggest that examining national-origin differences is critical to a thorough understanding of the community (Zhou and Xiong 2005). In fact, with more than twenty-four national-origin groups included under the Asian American umbrella since 1990, every major textbook on Asian Americans testifies that national-origin diversity is a central feature of contemporary Asian America (Kitano and Daniels 1995; Zhou and Gatewood 2000; Võ and Bonus 2002; Min 2005a). Min Zhou and James Gatewood, for example, claim that "national origins evoke drastic differences in homeland cultures, such as languages, religions, foodways, and customs; histories of international relations, contexts of emigration; reception in the host society; and adaptation patterns" (2000, 19). In addition, they write that "panethnicity accounts for neither regional or national differences nor for the historical legacies of intergroup conflicts . . . the Asian American community today is, and continues to be, marked by tremendous diversity in the era of high immigration" (27).

Still, by presenting our findings in a manner that highlights national origins, we remain cautious about unintentionally reifying national origin categories or privileging national origin differences over other internal distinctions, such as class, gender, religion, and nativity. Like race, national origin categories do not represent inherent biological, geographic, or even cultural divisions between groups of people, but instead reflect a complex social, historical, and political process that distinguishes people based on the meanings attributed to their geographic origins, phenotypic characteristics, language background, and a host of other features or experiences (see appendix A). Our measure of national origins does not speak to these complex processes. However, we find important distinctions between national-origin groups (even crudely measured), and thus disaggregate the sample according to group and report on relevant differences between particular groups.

Questionnaire

The 2008 NAAS was a comprehensive interview that included questions about political behavior and attitudes as well as personal experiences in immigration to the United States. Its length and complexity is less than in-person social and political surveys such as the American National Election Study and the General Social Survey, and is comparable to the Latino National Survey of 2005–2006. The overall length of interview was about twenty-nine minutes, with English-language interviews taking a little longer than twenty-six minutes and Asian-language interviews taking thirty-two. Our response rates are in line with typical telephone surveys: 47 percent of those we reached agreed to take the survey, making for a 12 percent rate of all valid numbers dialed.

The interview began with screening questions that allowed respondents to interview in the language of their choice and allowed us to meet our sampling targets, for example, by ethnic-national origin groups and county of residence. To obtain an adequate representation of multiracial Americans of Asian ancestry, we added two follow-up screening questions to our racial identifier.

The main body of the instrument is composed of modules that allow us to gain a better sense of respondents' national origins and experiences with migration; media use and political priorities; political participation and candidate evaluations; issue orientations, party identification, and political ideology; racial-ethnic identification and inter- or intragroup relations; and civic engagement. The questionnaire ends with standard demographic measures of individual-level characteristics on education, income, home ownership, length of residence, and other items known to influence voting and other forms of political participation such as mass media consumption. The full text of our survey instrument—including details of question wording, question order, and randomization among response categories—is included in appendix B.

THE NATIONAL ASIAN AMERICAN SURVEY AND POLITICAL PARTICIPATION

The NAAS study is at its heart a study of Asian American political participation. But what is political participation? Sidney Verba and Norman Nie introduced a classic formulation of political participation in their seminal work *Participation in America: Political Democracy and Social Equality* (1972). Political participation, according to this account, is "activities by private citizens that are more or less directly aimed at influencing the selection of governmental personnel and/or the actions they take" (2–3). This definition, the authors admit, is "broader than some, narrower than others." The breadth here is in the openness to multiple modes of influence on democratic decision-making. The narrowness is in the emphasis on "acts that aim at *influencing* the government, either by affecting the *choice* of government personnel or by affecting the *choices made by* government personnel" (1972, 3, emphasis in original). What is excluded by this definition, then, are participatory acts aimed at expressing generalized support for an existing political regime. Although this distinction, wrought in a previous era of authoritarian regimes and Cold War politics, is a meaningful way of excluding symbolic gestures of legitimation, the realm of participatory democracy has changed profoundly in the last four decades.

Specifically, although we continue to use this general definition in the pages that follow, we note important shifts in the way political scientists conceive of what is political and what counts as influence. On the former, there has been a durable shift away from thinking about politics as a closed system in which participation is compartmentalized as inputs into the electoral process and governance is compartmentalized as outputs from political institutions, government agencies, and the public policy-making process (Easton 1965). To wit, there is a broader embrace of multiple modalities of participation and a range of inputs from ritualized participation to shared governance. In parallel with these "changing boundaries of the political" (Maier 1987, 2), there has been a shift away from viewing civil society as a hermetically distinct sphere of social interaction from the state. In its place, there is a growing awareness of the potential for positive-sum interactions between civil society and the state and a heightened scrutiny of civic engagement and civil society organizations as important pathways into the political process (Evans 1997). These arc not just theoretical conceits, but shifts in thinking that reflect changes on the ground in the modes of political participation that are deployed and in the linkages between participatory acts in the civic and political realms. In this book, then, we make more inclusive allowances for indirect affects on political choices and policies and for activities at a range of levels of collective decision-making, from national to local to community to transnational.

How, then, do private political actors strive to help shape the actors and acts of government? The 2008 NAAS asks its respondents about a broad range of participatory acts. Table 1.1 shows the basic frequency of responses on thirteen items. Some, like registering to vote, self-reported voting in past elections, vote intentions, and political talk, have a high incidence rate. Others, like campaigning, protesting, and actively taking part in the politics of one's country of origin, are far less common. Additionally, differences between ethnic-national origin groups in their partiality for particular modes of participation are numerous. For example, Japanese Americans are the likeliest group to be registered to vote and to report voting; Asian Indians are especially likely to report engaging with others in their community on some common problem; Koreans are the likeliest to report following politics online; and Vietnamese tend to engage in protest politics far more frequently than other groups.

Although the thirteen participatory acts presented in table 1.1 capture meaningful variation in the range of ways that citizens and noncitizens can make their druthers known on political matters, we focus on a select

Table 1.1 Frequency of Participatory Acts

	Asian Indian	Chinese	Filipino	Japanese	Korean	Vietnamese	Total
Registered to vote	43	52	61	63	49	60	54
Voted in 2004	33	39	48	55	37	51	42
Voted in 2008 primaries	42	45	53	53	35	39	45
Vote intention in 2008*	76	67	69	82	84	80	74
Talk with family or friends	71	71	63	72	73	58	68
Worked for campaign	3	3	5	4	3	3	3
Contributed money	12	11	17	18	11	7	13
Contacted politician	11	9	13	10	5	5	9
Community work	27	19	23	17	18	21	21
Online participation	13	14	11	5	17	7	12
Protest activity	4	4	4	3	3	8	4
2006 immigration marches	0.3	0.7	0.8	0.4	1.5	1.6	0.8
Home country politics	5	5	4	1	1	2	4

Source: Authors' compilation of data from the 2008 National Asian American Survey (Ramakrishnan et al. 2011).
Note: All numbers are in percentages.
* Registered voters who reported being "absolutely" certain they would vote in the November elections.

subset of these in our subsequent analysis. Trying to be comprehensive here would simply yield an indigestible hodgepodge of empirical findings. Which, then, among these multiple modes are most likely to shed light on the nature and dynamics of Asian American political engagement? Sidney Verba and Victor Nie argued, on theoretical grounds, that there are four distinct modes of participation: voting, campaigning, group work to address some community problem, and particularized contacting of elected or public officials (1972). There are, however, a number of reasons to dispute that these are the only four distinctive modes of participation (Rusk 1976; Rosenstone and Hansen 1993). In particular, arguments that protest politics, interest group participation, and making monetary contributions are all equally distinct as a mode of doing politics are persuasive.

FIVE ACTS OF PARTICIPATION

In this book, we concentrate on five key participatory acts as our dependent variables: voting, political donations, contacting government officials, working with others in one's community to solve a problem, and protest. There are a number of ways to think about these distinctive acts of political participation, in terms of their inputs and outputs as well as the context of the engagement as an individual- or group-based activity. Voting, contacting, contributing, protesting, and community participation take place in different settings, the first three in greater isolation—the voting booth, composing a letter or making a call, and writing a check—than either protest or community activity. Both protest and community activity by definition involve other people and usually local settings. Although voting, contacting, and contributing can also be at the local level, they often have a federal or national political focus, particularly within respect to U.S. presidential elections. Interaction with other people and institutions differs in important ways.

In terms of participatory inputs (Verba and Nie 1972), distinctive political acts require greater and different types of resources. Contacting public officials in the United States is done in English, whether one writes a letter, sends an email message, or telephones. Asian Americans with limited English-language ability or those less comfortable communicating in a second language will be at a systematic disadvantage and require stronger mobilization efforts and motivation. Making contributions to candidates or political groups requires discretionary income, and the activities that make up the voting measure are encouraged by partisan affiliation and political party mobilization, both more likely to be held among native-born Asian Americans and naturalized citizens who have lived longer in the United States. Alternatively, protesting and working with others in the community are encouraged by strong associations with like-minded individuals and mobilization through other community-based organizations. These activities do not require English or U.S. national institutions, therefore reducing the assimilation barriers to entry.

The five acts of participation are distinctive in a second way in terms of the outputs that they deliver. As other scholars of political participation have duly noted, voting, though a blunt instrument, is nevertheless among the most powerful motivators of responsiveness among elected officials. Power of the franchise and the voting booth among Asian Americans are among the more important aspects of influence and representation. Contacting and contributing provide more direct and precise information to elected officials than voting, but the important takeaway is that these acts are directed at traditional structures of democratic governance. They are system-directed and aimed at making policy and party changes within the constraints of democratic institutions as they currently exist. On the other hand, protest and community activity are less constrained, both in terms of the amount and type of information communicated, as well as with respect to audience. Often considered weapons of the weak, group-based collective behavior such as these are well suited as challenges to the existing political agenda and structure of democratic institutions. In this sense, the political output of protest and community activity is more information-rich and potentially more transformative.

To summarize, then, participation can be classified along several dimensions of difference. As Margaret Conway (2000) notes, some are active (going door-to-door to register voters) and others are passive (watching the State of the Union address on television); some are conventional (voting) and others are unconventional or radical (burning military draft cards); some are symbolic (singing the national anthem) and others are instrumental (writing one's representative about a local zoning matter). Across the spectrum of participatory acts we examine in this book are a range of distinct relationships between political subjects and the state. Voting embodies the minimal expectations of citizenship and is necessary to the legitimacy and proper functioning of a representative democracy. Monetary contributions to campaigns and candidates and contacting government officials capture two distinct particularistic expressions of preference intensity and, more controversially, a greater demand for gaining access and particularistic benefits. Protest politics and community work push the boundaries of the political beyond formalized channels of political input and enlist more lateral modes of collective engagement.[5] We describe each of these five acts in greater detail in the following sections, and provide a basis for comparing the participation of Asian Americans with members of other racial and ethnic groups in the 2008 American National Election Studies (ANES).

Voting

Voting is considered a key indicator of the health and democratic character of a political system. Although a large body of literature questions whether voting constitutes rational political behavior given that it is unlikely that any individual's vote will determine the outcome of an election, democratic theory posits that voting in regular elections provides a critical mechanism for holding elected officials accountable to the will and policy choices of the people. And it remains true that voting constitutes the most common type of political participation in the United States. When it comes to making group comparisons on voting, however, it is important not to focus on just one particular election since regular voters may have missed their chance to participate for various idiosyncratic reasons. Thus, most polling organizations create a "likely voter" index based on an individual's voter registration status and past voting history. We follow a similar convention here when we report out our voting statistics: we rely on a factor scale of voting based on registration status, voting in the 2004 presidential election, voting in the 2008 primaries, and intention to vote in the 2008 presidential election; and we weight the results to reflect the participation rates as reported by the Current Population Survey Voter Supplement in 2008.[6] We have already seen how Asian American participation compares to those of other racial and ethnic groups in the Current Population Survey, with Asian Americans tied with Latinos at 57 percent, and lagging behind whites at 74 percent and African Americans at 77 percent.

Political Donations

As the costs of running for elective office or ballot proposition campaigns rise, political donations have become a more important political activity (Abramowitz 1988; Coleman and Manna 2000; Gimpel, Lee, and Kaminski 2006). In fact, according to John Coleman and Paul Manna, campaign spending may be beneficial to democratic participation: "Campaign spending increases knowledge of and affect toward the candidates, improves the public's ability to place candidates on ideology and issue scales, and encourages certainty about those placements" (2000, 757). Yet campaign spending may also transform economic inequalities into political inequalities, because those with more resources have greater access to elected officials than those of relatively modest means (Gimpel, Lee, and Kaminski 2006).

Finally, the study of campaign contribution activity is arguably of central importance to Asian American participation for several reasons.

Table 1.2   Rates Of Political Participation

	Asians	Whites	Blacks	Latinos
Campaign work	3	4	6	4
Contribute	13	13	8	5
Contact	9	21	11	9
Community work	21	30	27	21

Source: Authors' compilation of data from the 2008 National Asian American Survey (Ramakrishnan et al. 2011).
Note: Data on whites, African Americans, and Latinos for campaigning, contributions, contact, and community work for these groups are from the 2008 National Election Study. The 2008 ANES contains only thirty-five Asian American respondents, with no interviews in Asian languages. The ANES also does not include a measure of protest politics comparable to the NAAS item. Figures are in percentages.

First, that Asian Americans are a highly dispersed population with considerable socioeconomic resources suggests that making campaign contributions may be a more effective way of gaining political access than relying primarily on votes. Furthermore, the controversy surrounding the political contributions to the 1996 Clinton-Gore campaign from three individuals with connections to the Chinese government, and the subsequent media frenzy and scrutiny over contributions from all Asian Americans, directed a large spotlight on an emerging trend in political participation among Asian Americans (Lee 2000). Subsequent studies of Asian American participation have also focused on contribution activity, to show that such scandals may have been responsible for a shift in campaign contributions away from presidential candidates and toward Asian American candidates from across the country (Cho 2002). As we can see from table 1.2, however, the contribution rate of Asian Americans remain on par with the contribution activity of whites, despite the fact that Asian American citizens have, on average, higher levels of household income.

Contacting Government Officials

Contacting a government official constitutes a direct attempt to influence political representatives and policy outcomes. Constituents send letters to express deeply felt policy positions (Lee 2002) or to request assistance on personal matters related to government bureaucracies or agencies. Research on Congress and public policy also suggest that elected officials pay far greater attention to correspondence from constituents, especially when it takes the form of individual letters or personal phone calls, than they do to mass mailing campaigns or even individual votes. This is especially so when it comes to the day-to-day policymaking that occurs in between election years.

Yet contacting a government official requires familiarity with the political system and the ability to navigate political offices and bureaucracies. It also often requires strong English-language skills, both in terms of speaking and writing formal letters. As such, we believe it is important to examine this activity among Asian Americans, who, as a predominantly immigrant group, may be less familiar with the U.S. political system and demonstrate lower levels of English-language proficiency. What is noteworthy from our comparison of racial groups in table 1.2 is that for whites, a higher propensity to contribute money is coupled with a higher propensity to contact elected and other public officials. For Asian Americans, however, there is no such correspondence. Where 21 percent of whites report contacting officials, only 9 percent of Asians do so, the low incidence for Asians being quite similar to that for African Americans (11 percent) and Latinos (9 percent).[7]

Community Activism

Research has shown that working with others to solve a community problem is one of the most popular non-voting activities among Asian Americans (Lien, Conway, and Wong 2004). Although Asian Americans may join a group to tackle a local community issue without the direct intention of influencing elected officials or national policy, we believe that this form of participation is both political and important. First, working with others to solve a community problem is likely to build the civic skills identified as crucial to longer-term political engagement (Verba, Schlozman, and Brady 1995). Second, this form of political participation allows both citizens and noncitizens to influence local political and community structures. Finally, working with others to solve a community problem may provide Asian Americans a measure of political influence at the local level that, because of their relatively small share of the national population, may be difficult to achieve at the state or national level. As table 1.2 indicates, however, this is another type of political activity in which Asian Americans lag significantly behind whites and African Americans, and are on par with Latinos.

Protest Activity

We include protest activity as a measure of political participation because it allows us to examine behavior that often is outside of the traditional boundaries of the political system. Protests often challenge core aspects of the political system itself (Meyer 2007). For a group made up largely of immigrants, many of whom may not be citizens, protest may be one of the most visible political activities available. Thus, for example, hundreds of thousands of immigrants gained national attention for marching and demonstrating for immigrant rights and comprehensive immigration reform in the spring of 2006. Thus, because it is less traditional and may draw both citizens and noncitizens alike, we focus on protest activity as a critical measure of political participation in the chapters that follow. Our data indicate that 4 percent of Asian Americans have taken part in a protest in the previous twelve months. Although the American National Election Studies do not include comparable measures of protest activity, data from the 1990 Citizen Participation Study show that 5 percent of whites, 9 percent of African Americans, and 4 percent of Latinos engaged in protest activity in the two years before the survey. More recent studies of the 2006 immigration rallies suggest that Latino protest activity may have been higher, although since 2007 it has diminished considerably (Voss and Bloemraad 2010).

WHAT EXPLAINS PARTICIPATION?

Several decades ago, political scientists asked who votes and who participates in various types of political activities beyond voting. One of the most consistent answers to have emerged from the literature is that those with higher levels of socioeconomic status (often measured as educational attainment and income) are the ones most likely to get involved in politics. In 1972, Sidney Verba and Norman Nie declared in their pioneering study of civic and political participation that "citizens of higher social and economic status participate more in politics. This generalization has been confirmed many times in many nations" (17). Subsequent research on what is often referred to as the standard socioeconomic model of political participation has since confirmed the validity of this statement, not only in the general population but also among immigrants and members of racial and ethnic minorities (Wolfinger and Rosenstone 1980; Rosenstone and Hansen 1993; Verba, Schlozman, and Brady 1995; Ramakrishnan 2005). For Asian Americans, this is true not only in studies that use large-scale national data such as the Current Population Survey Voter Supplement, but also in smaller studies that rely on surveys of Asian Americans from several states and metropolitan areas (Ramakrishnan 2005; Lien 1997; Lien, Conway, and Wong 2004). That is, at the individual level, greater levels of education or income translate into more political participation. The consensus seems to be that higher education leads to greater participation, whether through acquiring political skills or connections to social networks that foster mobilization (Rosenstone and Hansen 1993; Nie, Junn, and Stehlik-Barry 1996). The effects of income are also significant, though their magnitudes have generally been weaker than in the case of education, especially for immigrants and members of racial and ethnic minorities (Wolfinger and Rosenstone 1980; Ramakrishnan 2005).[8]

When studying political participation it is important to keep in mind that the standard socioeconomic model has never been as simple as it might at first sound. When Verba and Nie first introduced the model in *Participation in America* (1972), they took care to explain that resources such as income, education, and occupation are only a baseline for understanding participation. They also considered other factors such as race, organizational membership, party affiliation, community context, and political beliefs to be important influences on political participation. Raymond Wolfinger and Steven Rosenstone give greater weight to income, occupation, and education as critical determinants of political participation (namely voting). But they, too, put forth a theory that leaves room for other influences on political participation, such as institutional barriers to voting. Finally, Sidney Verba, Kay Lehman Schlozman, and Henry Brady (1995) emphasize income as one of the most important determinants of political involvement, but also underscore the extent to which variables such as organizational membership and mobilization stand out as critical influences on political participation as well. Thus, the most prominent studies of socioeconomic status and political participation highlight the link between resources and political participation, but resources are defined broadly, and encompass much more than educational achievement and family income (Verba and Nie 1972; Verba, Nie, and Kim 1978; Wolfinger and Rosenstone 1980; Rosenstone and Hansen 1993; Verba, Schlozman, and Brady 1995). We adopt a similarly broad view of resources here.

Second, the degree to which socioeconomic resources match up to political participation depends a great deal on the unit of analysis: the individual or the group. This is particularly important to consider when considering differences in participation across racial and ethnic groups. In the decades following the publication of *Participation in America*, a host of studies grappled with the fact that African American voting was higher than expected based on SES models, given the group's relatively low levels of education, income, and homeownership with respect to whites (Shingles 1981; Bobo and Gilliam 1990; Leighley and Vedlitz 1999; Alex-Assensoh and Assensoh 2001). Even when socioeconomic factors mattered for participation within the group, other factors—such as group consciousness, feelings of political empowerment, and links to social movements and community organizations—helped diminish the role of lowering black voter turnout vis-à-vis whites. For Latinos, too, studies have shown that factors such as group consciousness and living in places characterized by high levels of political threat or high levels of political empowerment help push voter turnout higher than one might expect, based on socioeconomic resources alone (Pantoja, Ramirez, and Segura 2001; Ramakrishnan and Espenshade 2001; Barreto, Segura, and Woods 2004; Stokes 2003).

For Asian Americans, the puzzle with respect to socioeconomic models of voting is the opposite one—the group's lower levels of participation despite relatively high levels of education and income. The surprisingly lower level of participation among Asian Americans has been noted nearly as long as the higher level of participation among blacks (Brackman and Erie 1995; Nakanishi 1986, 1991; Uhlaner, Cain, and Kiewiet 1989; Leighley and Vedlitz 1999; Cho 1999; Lien et al. 2001; Lien 2001, 1997, 2004a; Lien, Conway, and Wong 2004). For example, in one of the earliest studies of Asian American political participation, Carole Uhlaner and her colleagues stated that the "the high level of education among Asians does not translate into activity" (1989, 212). Nearly fifteen years later, Andrew Aoki and Don Nakanishi described the puzzle similarly: "APA voting rates have remained low. . . . This seems particularly curious given their high median socioeconomic measures" (2001, 607–8). Consistent with these observations, Phil Kasinitz and his colleagues report in their study of first- and second-generation immigrants in New York City that some groups participate in politics at much higher rates than one would expect based on the group's average income and education levels, and others at much lower rates (2008).

It is critical to emphasize that those concerned with the puzzle of political participation for Asian Americans or other immigrant groups focus on the racial or ethnic group as a the unit of analysis. At the individual level, we expect to see a link between socioeconomic status and political participation more in line with that predicted by Verba and Nie and more recent studies (compare Lien, Conway, and Wong 2004; Ramakrishnan 2005). However, because Asian Americans as a group exhibit high levels of education and, relative to whites and blacks, low levels of political participation, we also take seriously Aoki and Okiyoshi Takeda's imperative to "take into account other factors that might mitigate the effects of education and income on Asian Americans' participation" (63).

Our analysis, then, builds on this literature. In addition to the standard focus on socioeconomic resources and key demographic traits such as age and gender, we identify five factors that potentially influence the political participation of Asian Americans: immigrant socialization; residential contexts; party identification, mobilization, and political orientation; racial identity formation; and membership and involvement in civic associations (see figure 1.4).

Figure 1.4   Explaining Asian American Political Participation

```
                    ┌──────────────┐  ┌──────────────┐
                    │ Sociopolitical│  │    Party     │
                    │   contexts   │  │identification│
                    │  (chapter 3) │  │  (chapter 4) │
                    └──────────────┘  └──────────────┘
 ┌──────────────┐                                      ┌──────────────┐
 │  Immigrant-  │                                      │    Racial    │
 │related factors│                                     │identification│
 │  (chapter 2) │                                      │  (chapter 5) │
 └──────────────┘                                      └──────────────┘
                          ┌────────────────┐
                          │     Asian      │
                          │    American    │
 ┌──────────────┐         │   political    │         ┌──────────────┐
 │     Age,     │         │  participation │         │ Religion and │
 │  education,  │         │                │         │     civic    │
 │  resources   │         └────────────────┘         │  engagement  │
 └──────────────┘                                    │  (chapter 6) │
                                                     └──────────────┘
```

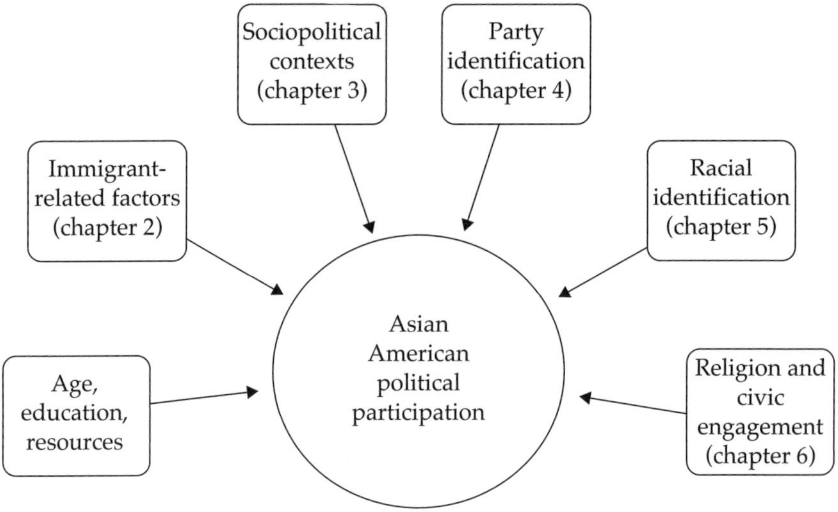

Source: Authors' compilation.

Immigrant Socialization

Immigrant socialization is critical because Asian Americans are predominantly a population of immigrants and their offspring. Based on the 2004 American Community Survey, nearly two in three Asians in America (65 percent) are foreign-born, and roughly 90 percent are either immigrants or their offspring. Thus, unlike most native-born Americans who acquire partisan habits through their parents and civic skills in their K–12 education and other institutional venues, Asian immigrants and their offspring are less likely to be fully socialized into American political life. It is little surprise, then, that previous studies have shown that factors related to immigrant socialization such as nativity, immigrant generation, length of stay in the United States, English-language skills, and citizenship status are significant predictors of Asian American political participation (Lien 1994; Cho 1999; Wong 2000; Lien, Conway, and Wong 2004; Ramakrishnan 2005). Thus, one potential explanation for the patterns of political participation we observe among Asian Americans is that different ethnoracial groups may vary in the extent to which they are socialized into the political arena.

Residential Contexts and Political Geography

A growing and robust literature finds that a broad range of political out-comes—from racial attitudes to voting behavior to hate crimes—are shaped by the context in which a person lives (Key 1949; Huckfeldt and Sprague 1992; Cohen and Dawson 1993; Green, Strolovich, and Wong 1998; Oliver and Mendelberg 2000; Hajnal 2001; Oliver and Wong 2003; Gay 2001, 2004). The range of structural contexts that shape one's politics are diverse, including demographic (absolute numbers of each racial-ethnic group, population growth, racial balance), social (organizational density, network ties, hyper-segregation), economic (poverty rates, tax base, skills mismatch), and political contexts (party competition, regime type, electoral rules). Indeed, all previously articulated explanations of Asian American political engagement are tested with self-reported obser-vations at the individual level. And yet these individuals are embedded in structural contexts that mediate the impact of various explanations for immigrant political incorporation and political engagement. Devoid of the actually lived contexts in which political parties get out votes, social-izing experiences transpire, identities are formed, civic ties are forged, and so on, such individual-level explanations alone provide too little in-ferential leverage to fully explain Asian American underparticipation. Our second explanation argues that variation in Asian American partici-pation is largely a function of how social and political processes occur at an aggregate geographic level, and not at the individual level.

Party Identification

In the political science literature, the psychological attachment individu-als have to one of the two major political parties is a ubiquitous and piv-otal factor in defining a person's politics (Campbell et al. 1960; Miller and Shanks 1996; Green, Palmquist, and Schickler 2002). Alan Gerber and Donald Green write, "In the field of public opinion and electoral behavior, no explanatory variable is more pervasive than party identification" (1998, 794). Kinder and Sanders describe party identification as "the sin-gle most important determinant of individual voting decisions" (1985, 686). Despite this primacy of place of partisanship, research shows a plu-rality (and, in some surveys, majority) of Asian Americans have no rela-tionship to a political party, choosing either to identify as an independent or otherwise refusing to self-identify with any partisan category (Lien, Conway, and Wong 2004; Hajnal and Lee 2006). In addition to weaker party identification, research has also shown weaker mobilization efforts by political parties and campaigns, due variously to the lack the organizational capacity, cultural literacy, institutional incentives, and perhaps even political will to shepherd Asian Americans into the political system (Kim 2007; Wong 2006). Thus, factors related to political parties give us an important set of hypotheses: Asian Americans vary in their participation based on how strongly they hold any party identification, and perhaps relatedly, based on whether parties have sought to mobilize them.

Racial Identity Formation

Our account of immigrant socialization highlights the roles that mainstream political institutions and social processes of acculturation play in engaging Asian Americans. Underlying these accounts is a lively debate over whether and how immigrants assimilate into their newfound societies, ranging from the view that immigrants are assimilated and incorporated in an invariant, linear process across time and generations (Gordon 1964; Dahl 1961; Alba and Nee 2003), to the view that this process of assimilation and incorporation is conspicuously bumpier and more segmented, especially for racialized present-day minorities like Latinos and Asian Americans (Glazer and Moynihan 1963; Tuan 1998; Ortiz and Telles 2008; Portes and Zhou 1993; Jiménez 2010). In the latter case, the formation of a sense of racial-ethnic identity constitutes a fourth potential pathway to political engagement.

Here, Asian Americans are commonly viewed as a single group for purposes of bureaucratic classification (Omi and Winant 1994), but the activation of this identity in politics varies across historical, institutional, and spatial contexts (Espiritu 1993; Okamoto 2003, 2006). Specifically, there are two ways in which racial identity formation might help explain Asian American political engagement. If the process of racialization is driven by discrimination, social isolation, or other exclusionary processes, the processes that shape Asian Americans' sense of groupness may also shape a sense of political alienation, distrust, and inefficacy, all to the detriment of political engagement. Alternatively, group consciousness may in theory work for Asian Americans as it does for African Americans in enabling and empowering participation (Miller et al. 1981; Dawson 1994; Chong and Rogers 2005; Lien, Conway, and Wong 2004), but the conditions to sustain such an authorized sense of groupness may not yet exist for Asian Americans. Therefore, by our fourth hypothesis, Asian Americans vary in their participation based on the extent to which they identify as a racial or ethnic group, the extent to which they feel that they share political interests with each other and with other racial and ethnic groups, and the extent to which they see discrimination as a problem that requires political action.

Involvement in Secular and Religious Organizations

In the absence of a demonstrable role of parties in the incorporation of Asian Americans, and given the overwhelming numbers who do not think in U.S. partisan terms, one place scholars have increasingly turned to is civic institutions and civil society (Ecklund and Park 2005; Ramakrishnan and Viramontes 2006; Wong 2006; Ecklund 2006). The logic and attraction behind looking here is quite clear. Civic institutions like labor unions, social service organizations, ethnic associations, and religious institutions should serve as a mediating influence. Secular and religious organizations may bridge between Asian American newcomers and politics writ large in the United States. Political philosophers and empirical political scientists alike view civic engagement, volunteerism, and associated networks of belonging as vehicles to develop key civic skills, like political communication and organizing, and to nurture a sense of social trust and psychological engagement and efficacy in the realm of public affairs (Pateman 1970; Verba, Schlozman, and Brady 1995; Skocpol and Fiorina 1999a, 1999b; Putnam 2000; Macedo 2005). By these accounts, then, Asian American participation in politics varies according to their engagement in religious and civic life and the degree to which civic institutions mobilize them to participate in the political sphere.

CENTRAL RESEARCH QUESTIONS AND PLAN OF THE BOOK

The central research questions we address in this book are why some Asian Americans participate and others do not, and why they get involved more in some types of activities than in others. We argue that immigrant socialization; residential contexts; party identification, mobilization, and political orientation; racial identity formation; and membership and involvement in civic associations all contribute to political participation among Asian Americans. We engage this question by leveraging the diversity within the Asian American population. That is, we observe that some Asian Americans participate more than others and we seek to better understand why differences in political participation exist within the community.

Do the pathways to participation we identify operate differently across distinct segments of the population? To get a better handle on this question, we first provide a deep exploration of each of these pathways. Chapters 2 through 6 each begin by laying out the relationship between a set of descriptive traits of individual survey respondents, including national origin, citizenship, generation of migration, class, gender, age, educational attainment, region, and the pathway of interest—that is, immigrant socialization, residential contexts, party identification, mobilization, and political orientation, racial identity formation, and membership and involvement in civic associations. We then introduce a more complex modeling of the relationship of these descriptive traits to the pathway of interest.[9] Finally, we link the pathway of interest to variations in political participation, the key dependent variables using descriptive statistics.

The research that forms the basis for these chapters compels us to confront a much broader question. Given the tremendous internal diversity that characterizes those that fall under the Asian American rubric, why study the group as a whole at all? Should we aggregate under a single racial banner those who differ so greatly in terms of national origin, socioeconomic status, language, religion, generation, and a host of other demographic, economic, and social dimensions? This question has implications for how we understand the role of groups in American politics, particularly groups defined in racial terms. The very nature of this research, a study of Asian American political attitudes and behavior, assumes that the category of Asian American has some meaning in the U.S. political system. In the pages that follow, we return to this theme both explicitly and implicitly. In fact, by taking a careful, systematic look at the political participation of those who identify themselves as somehow Asian or with one of many national origin groups, we provide new information about the degree to which the diverse members of this group are similar or different when it comes to their political activity and, to a more limited extent, their political orientations.

In chapter 7, we bring together the different pathways to political participation examined in the previous five chapters, and draw attention to the major findings that emerge from a statistical analysis that controls for various factors simultaneously. In addition to figuring out which variables emerge as consistently important to political participation, we focus on three narratives that arise from the multivariate results: the extent to which civic and political resources may compensate for group advantages or disadvantages in socioeconomic status, the extent to which political behavior among Asian Americans conforms to standard models of immigrant assimilation or newer models of group racialization, and whether religious diversity among Asian Americans has any significant consequence for political behavior. In chapter 8, we conclude by reflecting on the future of Asian Americans as a political group, drawing attention to the small but growing group of super-participants. We also assess our empirical findings in light of key questions about the extent to which Asian Americans constitute a coherent or meaningful category in terms of their participation in American politics. Finally, we project the future of Asian American participation in the decades to come, and point to opportunities for political parties and other institutions to mobilize and gain the allegiance of Asian American voters.

Chapter 2 | Settling In: Immigrant Adaptation

ALTHOUGH PEOPLE FROM Asia began to settle in the United States in significant numbers in the mid-1800s, the majority of the population today is foreign-born. In fact, of the five major racial and ethnic groups enumerated by the U.S. Census, Asian Americans are the most heavily immigrant. Data from the 2007 American Community Survey indicate that fully 67 percent of Asian Americans are born outside the United States (table 2.1). By contrast, only 40 percent of Latino residents (adults and children) and a scant 8 percent of African Americans, 5 percent of Native Americans, and 4 percent of whites are foreign-born.[1] The foreign-born account for an even greater share of Asian Americans when one considers the adult population alone (80 percent), far surpassing the proportion of first-generation Latino adults. It stands to reason, then, that factors related to immigrant socialization—such as national origin, citizenship status, and language use—are central to the study of political and civic participation among Asian Americans, and arguably more so than for any other major racial and ethnic group in the United States.

As noted in chapter 1, for most Americans, the road to political action is built from three central influences: resources, psychological engagement with politics, and networks of recruitment toward participation (Verba and Nie 1972; Wolfinger and Rosenstone 1980; Leighley and Nagler 1992; Verba, Schlozman, and Brady 1995). But for Asian Americans, and other populations that include a large proportion of immigrants, a greater range of factors specific to the experience of immigration and adaptation to the United States may be at play. If we apply the standard model of political participation to Asian Americans, we emerge with only a partial explanation of why they do or do not take part in the American political sphere.

The gap here between conventional accounts of political engagement and the empirical patterns found among Asian Americans is filled in the

34

Table 2.1   Proportion Foreign-Born, 2008 American Community
Survey

	Asian	American Indian	Black	Hispanic	White Non-Hispanic
Adults	80	9	10	53	5
All residents	67	7	8	38	4

Source: Authors' compilation based on data from the 2008 American Community Survey (U.S. Census Bureau 2008a).
Note: Rates are in percentages.

first instance by noting that immigrants rarely come to a new host society as fully formed and well-adapted political selves. Long-term experience with the American political system may be critical to whether the triumvirate of predisposing factors in the standard model of political participation—means, motivation, and mobilization networks—exert an effect. As Wendy Tam Cho argued in a relatively early study of Asian American political participation, traditional theories of political participation fail to account for the fact that as the country becomes more diverse, so must theories of political participation (1999). In other words, a one-size fits all model of political participation does not recognize that multiple channels of socialization toward participation exist. Cho pays particular attention to the mediating influences of foreign-born status and language barriers to participation. She finds that though differences in education and income did not explain a gap in voting participation between whites and Asian Americans, rates were roughly equal across groups once she accounted for foreign-born status and English-language proficiency.

Other studies of Asian American political participation also make a persuasive case for extending the conventional account of political participation to better fit the unique immigration-related experiences of the population at this point in time (Cain, Kiewiet, and Uhlaner 1991; Lien 1994, 2001; Junn 1999; Ramakrishnan and Espenshade 2001; Lien, Conway, and Wong 2004; Ramakrishnan 2005; Stoll and Wong 2007). These studies follow the lead of earlier studies of immigrant adaptation in other disciplines. For instance, economists have long studied outcomes such as occupational mobility across national-origin groups and immigrant generations (Chiswick 1977; Borjas 1987, 1999), sociologists have examined varying trajectories in educational outcomes and socioeconomic status across national-origin groups (Portes and Zhou 1993; Alba and Nee 2003), and demographers have examined differences in health outcomes and fertility behavior between immigrants (Guendelman et al. 1990; Kahn 1994).

Some of the more pressing debates and questions in these fields include the extent to which the model of straight-line assimilation accounts for intergenerational outcomes across immigrant groups, the reasons some groups may experience second-generation declines in socioeconomic status and health outcomes, and the extent to which home-country ties remain relevant to ethnic identification, civic behavior, and remittance activity. For Asian immigrants, scholars have attempted to answer similar questions relating to how time in the United States, home-country characteristics, and host-country settlement contexts explain variations in political outcomes such as voting (Ramakrishnan 2005).

The study of immigrant socialization into politics also recalls the long scholarly tradition in political science on the socialization experiences of children and youth into patterns of party identification, political attitudes, and political behavior. The term *political socialization*, according to Fred Greenstein (1970), entered the lexicon of political science more or less impromptu, in a 1954 essay by Seymour Martin Lipset in the inaugural edition of *The Handbook of Social Psychology* (1954). It then reappeared with greater purpose and precision in Herbert Hyman's *Political Socialization* (1959). Hyman's work, together with several subsequent influential works that explicitly incorporated socialization into their theoretical frameworks (Almond 1963; Easton 1965), spawned a wave of interest in the role of formative experiences and social learning on one's political attitudes and behavior. This was especially so in the case of longitudinal and intergenerational studies of political behavior, which noted the critical importance of parents' political orientations, civic experiences in high school and college, and salient moments in American political history for particular age cohorts (Jennings and Niemi 1968, 1981; Sigel 1970; Jennings, Stoker, and Bowers 2009).

This literature is certainly important to our understanding of Asian American political participation as we explore the role of parental socialization in party identification in chapter 4. At the same time, we also believe that any thorough study of Asian American political engagement needs to begin with a consideration of what it means to be an immigrant (as is the case for roughly two of every three Asians in America) or what it means to be the child of an immigrant. This directs us to reconsider political socialization through the lens of immigration. For adult immigrants, socialization cannot be presumed to be a by-product of being born and raised in the United States. For immigrants who settled in America as children and for children of immigrants, the experience of socialization to norms and practices in a non-U.S. context are likely to linger given the long-standing (if debated) effects of intergenerational transmission of political beliefs and values from parents to their offspring.

By extending the range of potential influences on Asian American political participation, we do not mean to imply that the population is static, or that foreign-born status, citizenship, or other characteristics constitute enduring or permanent forces on the group's political involvement. As the population changes, we expect that the influences on Asian American political involvement will change as well. As we will see, however, nativity, length of residence, and other variables related to immigrant socialization continue to exert a visible impact on the contemporary community.

NATIONAL ORIGIN

Asian American immigrants hail from many nations. Much scholarship on Asian Americans, in fact, is organized around the thorough study of the defining particularities of single national-origin groups. Moreover, where the research purports to speak about Asian Americans writ large, a preponderance of the attention is directed toward the histories and experiences of particular national-origin groups. The prevailing practice, in a sense, is to read the Asian American experience as a compendium of individual, ethnic, national-origin experiences. In acknowledging this prevailing practice, we begin our examination of the immigrant socialization of Asian Americans by parsing our analysis by the six main ethnic-national-origin groups that comprise the Asian American population in the 2008 NAAS.

This analytic choice, however, is not meant merely to adhere to custom or, perhaps worse yet, naturalize or reify multiple Asian national-origin exceptionalisms. We believe, rather, that there are sensible analytic grounds to start with national-origin differences. One may be tempted to think of such differences as being grounded in socially real foundations such as linguistic differences or racial phenotype, rather than official constructions of race and ethnicity in the United States through various government policies and administrative practices. However, many Asian immigrants may share a national origin without sharing a language (Indian immigrants, for example), and differences in racial phenotype among those who self-identify as Indian, Chinese, and the like may be significant.

A more logical basis for taking national origin as an important way to differentiate Asian Americans may lie in the way they have been categorized with respect to immigration policy, citizenship rules, and social classification. For instance, the census question on race provides an Asian category with several national-origin options, such as Asian Indian, Chinese, and Filipino. These classifications are collected and provide the basis for public policymaking and implementation for the Equal Employment Opportunity Commission, statewide electoral redistricting offices, and countless other federal, state, and local agency activities. Census categories can also have a powerful impact on other data collection efforts as social scientists use population statistics reported by the U.S. Census Bureau to compare with their own findings to weight individual-level data.

These national-origin groupings have also been decisive in shaping the history of Asians in America. As Mae Ngai has shown in her study on the role of the state in shaping the boundaries and meanings of citizenship, the census classifications play a significant role, not only in how various government agencies classify the foreign born, but also in the ways members of civil society perceive and treat immigrants and their descendants (2004). Further, for much of this country's history, national origin played a pivotal role in determining who was eligible for admission into the country and qualified for citizenship. Political inclusion was limited to free white persons (Jacobson 1998). Asian immigrants were the primary targets of national origin discrimination, beginning with the Chinese Exclusion Act of 1882. Later, the 1924 National Origins Act, which created a permanent quota system that favored those from western European nations, essentially shut off most immigration from other Asian countries for more than forty years. The United States has had a checkerboard history of immigration laws and practices pertaining to specific countries of origin in Asia, each of which has left an indelible mark on generational patterns, areas of settlement, and trajectories of mobilization among Asian Americans in the United States.

The power of ethnoracial classification is apparent, not only in the contours of official government policies relating to enumeration and immigration, but also through the reinforcement of such frameworks through social interactions. Thus, for instance, the one-drop rule to classify all those with black ancestry as nonwhite was not only part of official government classification through the mid-1900s, it was also reinforced through the understandings and practices of black and white communities alike. For Asian Americans, in particular, the power of official government classification has meant that many Asian Americans self-identify with a national origin group more often than with other ethnic or racial labels (see chapter 5). Also, immigrants from places like Lebanon and Iraq do not consider themselves Asian American, even though they come from countries in Asia (Omi 1997; Abdulrahim 2009). The power of these official classifications can thus be felt not only directly but also indirectly, by shaping the common sense understandings of race in America by relating it to national origin and ethnicity (Omi and Winant 1994).

Thus, in attempting to understand the creation of Asian American communities in the United States today, it is important to recognize the diverse Asian national origins of the community and to examine the varying histories of these groups.[2] At the same time, we argue that variations in Asian Americans political participation cannot be understood on the basis of national origin differences alone. Other factors related to immigrant socialization play as important a role in shaping the Asian American community and, in many respects, experiences of migration bind the diverse members of the group across national origin, economic position, and generation. A typical recent immigrant from mainland China must spend a number of years in the United States and become a citizen before she will be able to vote. The third-generation granddaughter of Japanese immigrants does not need to naturalize to vote, but her participation in politics may still be connected to the immigration experience of Japanese Americans more generally. Her motivation to vote or to take part in politics by organizing a community event may be the knowledge that her grandparents were denied the right to naturalize because they were non-white "strangers from a different shore" (Takaki 1989).

SIX NATIONAL-ORIGIN GROUPS AND THEIR HISTORIES

In our survey, we gave priority to the six largest Asian national-origin groups in the United States. As table 2.2 indicates, these six groups account for more than 85 percent of the adult Asian American population in the United States.[3] The concentration of Asian Americans in a few national-origin groups is even more remarkable when looking at the top three groups (Chinese, Indian, and Filipino), which account for 61 percent of Asian American adults. By contrast, groups like Cambodians, Hmong, and Pakistanis, though including well over half a million adult residents combined, account for only 1 or 2 percent each. It is quite possible that, in a few decades, Cambodians and Hmong will outnumber those of Japanese origin living in the United States. For now, however, Japanese Americans remain a numerically significant group, with a long-standing pattern of settlement in the United States. As we shall see in this and in subsequent chapters, Japanese Americans also differ from many other Asian American groups on such matters as party identification and civic participation.

CHINESE AMERICANS

Chinese Americans are, at nearly 3 million, the largest Asian ethnoracial group in the United States. The number is even larger if one includes Taiwanese immigrants and the number who identify as Chinese in combination with other races (bringing the total to about 3.4 million in 2007).[4] Chi-

Table 2.2   Asian Americans by National Origin

	2008	Percentage of Total in 2008	2000
Total	13,413,976		10,474,184
Chinese	2,998,849	22%	2,445,363
Asian Indian	2,495,998	19	1,718,778
Filipino	2,425,697	18	1,908,125
Vietnamese	1,431,980	11	1,169,672
Korean	1,344,267	10	1,099,422
Japanese	710,063	5.3	852,237
Pakistani	280,726	2.1	164,628
Cambodian	186,068	1.4	183,769
Hmong	171,316	1.3	174,712
Laotian	159,347	1.2	179,103
Thai	139,208	1.0	120,918
Bangladeshi	88,212	0.7	46,905
Taiwanese	78,934	0.6	132,144
Indonesian	51,148	0.4	44,186
Sri Lankan	29,607	0.2	21,364
Malaysian	12,506	0.1	15,029
Other Asian	577,081	4.3	31,383
Other Asian, not specified	232,969	1.7	166,446

Source: Authors' compilation of data from the 2000 Census (U.S. Census Bureau 2000) and the 2008 American Community Survey (U.S. Census Bureau 2008a).

nese Americans have gained some prominence in American politics as well. In his first year in office, President Obama nominated Chinese American Nobel prize winner Steven Chu to be his secretary of energy and former governor of Washington, Gary Locke, to be his secretary of commerce.

Chinese immigration to the United States can be traced to the late 1840s. In that era, social, economic, and political turmoil in China provided the push factors toward immigration to the United States. The earliest traveled to Hawaii to work on sugar plantations, and their successors to the continental United States soon after the discovery of gold in California in 1849 (Takaki 1989). Following the Gold Rush, the building of the transcontinental railroad drew more than 10,000 Chinese workers to perform backbreaking labor, often high in the mountains, for much lower wages than their white counterparts (Chan 1991, 29). In the 1870s, the anti-Chinese movement gained momentum as organizations formed in California to urge employers not to hire Chinese labor and to encourage boycotts of Chinese merchants (Perea 2000, 375). White labor groups justified the movement's goals by painting Chinese workers as racially unfit for the American workforce, uncivilized, and even animal-like. Still, until the 1900s, California remained home to a majority of Chinese immigrants. In 1900, almost 46,000 Chinese lived in California (mostly working as miners) and nearly 90,000 lived across the United States (Chan 1991, 28). Chinese immigration was curtailed severely by the Chinese Exclusion Acts of the 1880s and 1890s and the creation of the Asiatic barred zone in 1917. By this time, however, a good number of Chinese were established in businesses beyond mining and railroad work, including laundries, groceries, restaurants, and domestic service. A merchant class had also developed to serve Chinese workers in these industries.

Although the Chinese have a long history in the United States, immigrants make up about half of the contemporary Chinese population, which thus includes both people whose families settled in the United States many generations ago as well as a large number of newcomers. Many immigrants from China who have arrived since 1965 are professionals, but the group includes a substantial proportion of people who struggle at the bottom rungs of the labor force in restaurants, garment factories, and other low-wage occupations.

Because many of the original immigrants from China were from poor rural backgrounds, their relatives who arrived as part of the family-reunification program since 1965 were likely to come from similar circumstances. Nevertheless, a growing number of immigrants were professionals allowed to immigrate under the professional visa provisions of the 1965 law. Between 1965 and 1975, almost half of all immigrants from China were professionals such as scientists, doctors, and engineers, and this trend toward professional occupational status in the migrant stream continues today (Takaki 1995, 44). However, as for other Asian immigrant groups, the continuing priority given to family reunification visas has meant that professional immigrants have been able to sponsor relatives who may vary in their educational attainment and professional skills (Kwong 1996). We might expect that class distinctions among Chinese Americans would play out in the political sphere as well. For example, well-to-do Chinese Americans are probably more likely to be targeted for campaign donations than those at the bottom of the economic ladder. Finally, the past two decades of political turmoil and rapid urbanization in China have led to further diversification of the Chinese immigrant community, not only along lines of socioeconomic status, but also political ideology and homeland regions.

This diversity within the Chinese community affects internal political coalition-building. A vivid example is the tensions in New York's Chinatown between recent immigrants from Fujian province and more established Chinese immigrant residents from other southern provinces in China. As Jane Lii of the *New York Times* reported, many Fujianese arrive in New York with few economic resources and are channeled into the lowest-paying sectors of the Chinatown job market. More established Chinese residents in the neighborhood hold negative stereotypes regarding Fujianese immigrants, accusing them of drug trafficking, gang membership, and crime ("Chinatown: Latest Wave of Immigrants Is Splitting Chinatown," June 12, 1994, C-6). The longtime residents also accuse the Fujianese of taking over parts of the neighborhood, especially along East Broadway, where they have established restaurants, businesses, and Fujianese-serving social service agencies and advocacy organizations ("Lower Manhattan: A New Attraction on Tourist Maps: Chinatown East?" December 18, 1994, C-6).

Political divisions also exacerbate the uneasy relationship between older and newer Chinese immigrants. Many Cantonese immigrants tend to support the Taiwanese nationalist movement, whereas Fujianese immigrants are often sympathetic to the mainland communist government (Lii, "Latest Wave of Immigrants Is Splitting Chinatown," June 12, 1994). Organization leaders express uncertainty about how the diversity will affect the community's future development. One long-time leader noted, "In my day, we had Toishanese and Toishanese, and now we have everybody. Nowadays, the faces are all different. I mean we have northern faces, and the food. It's wonderful. An amazing explosion. And we have Fukianese [Fujianese] with their associations. There are going to be a lot of differences, and I don't know if that will be better or worse, because it may end up splitting us, which is even worse" (quoted in Wong 2006, 30).

Thus, politics in the Chinese American community is a complicated affair, influenced by cleavages—sometimes cross-cutting, sometimes reinforcing—along lines of region, class, homeland politics, and immigrant generation (Toyota 2010).

Despite these challenges, Chinese Americans have been relatively successful among the various Asian American groups in terms of their representation in federal and state government. For instance, in 2010, two Chinese Americans served in the U.S. Congress (David Wu, D-OR, and Judy Chu, D-CA), two in cabinet positions (Steven Chu in the Department of Energy and Gary Locke in the Department of Commerce), and two in prominent White House staff positions (Christina Tchen as director of the White House Office of Public Engagement and Chris Lu as cabinet secretary). Fifty-five Chinese Americans served as elected officials at various levels of government at the time our survey was conducted, second only to the fifty-nine Japanese Americans (Lai and Nakanishi 2007). These included representatives in states with large Chinese American populations such as California and New York, but also in those with smaller concentrations, including Georgia, Maryland, and Connecticut.

ASIAN INDIANS

Seeking escape from British colonialism and famine, immigrants from India began to arrive on the West Coast in the late 1800s after their initial migration to Hong Kong and Canada. The vast majority of these early immigrants came from the Punjab region and practiced Sikhism. Early ethnographic studies concluded that most of these immigrants were unskilled laborers and agricultural workers. About 25 percent arrived from other parts of India, including Gujarat, Oudh, and Bengal (Sheth 1995, 171). Some of these immigrants settled on the East Coast, and worked as merchants or middle-class professionals. Further, Asian Indian immigrants as a whole were more disproportionately male than any other Asian migrant group. According to Ronald Takaki, fewer than 1 percent of Asian Indian immigrants during this period were women (1989, 62).

Although many Sikh immigrants in California bought farms and married Mexican American women,[5] a significant contingent of immigrants were keen to overthrow British colonialism in India. Organizing under the banner of the Gadar Party, a group of revolutionaries sought assistance from Germany in 1915 to fight the British presence in India. This led to the arrests and prosecution of several Indians and German consulate officials in the Hindu German Conspiracy Trial of 1917 (Dignan 1971). The growing unease with Indian immigration, among other factors, prompted Congress to pass the Immigration Act of 1917 (also known as the Asiatic Barred Zone Act), which excluded migration from countries in a zone ranging from Turkey to Indonesia. However, more than a thousand students from India were allowed to immigrate after the 1917 legislation had passed, although the Immigration Act of 1924 finally excluded all Asians from immigrating to the United States (Takaki 1989).

The Immigration and Nationality Act of 1965, which opened the U.S. immigration doors after a four-decade hiatus, was significant in two respects: it abolished discrimination on the basis of race and national origin for purposes of admission, and it formalized three major categories that remain the basis of our immigration system today: family reunification, professional skills, and refugee provisions. As Ted Kennedy, one of the major backers of the bill in the U.S. Senate, noted, Congress passed the bill because it "recognized the need to facilitate the reunion of families long separated by the rigidities and strictures of the national-origins system, to encourage the entry of persons with professional ability and skills especially advantageous to our developing society, and to include a continuing authority in basic law for the admission of refugees" (Kennedy 1966).

Before the passage of the 1965 Immigration and Nationality Act, fewer than 1 percent of all Asian Americans in the United States were of Indian origin, with estimates ranging from 6,500 to 8,000 (Takaki 1989; Sheth 1995). But passage of the act prompted a second (and much larger) wave of immigration from India. The law laid the foundation for a bifurcation in the skills mix of immigrants to the United States because professional visa categories favored those with higher levels of education, and family reunification visas tended to provide a greater mix of skilled and un-skilled labor. The professional visa provisions of the 1965 act, combined with the Indian government's controlled economy under import substitution, created a surplus of high-skilled college graduates eager to find work in the United States (Bhagwati and Hamada 1974; Khadria 1999). At the same time, family reunification and asylum provisions led to the migration of less-skilled immigrants bound for work in small shops and restaurants, although access to dense social networks have enabled many of these immigrants to pool resources to own motels and retail enterprises (Takaki 1995; Varadarajan 1999).

In the past decade, the immigration of Indian professionals to the United States has skyrocketed, increasing the overall population from 1.7 million in 2000 to nearly 2.5 million in 2008. The foundation for this change can be found in the 1990 Immigration Reform and Control Act, which created a temporary visa category (H-1B) with an annual cap of 65,000, and allowed these workers to petition for permanent resident status during their stay in the United States. Subsequent changes—such as exemptions granted to universities and government research laboratories, the demand for thousands of foreign technology workers during the Y2K problem and the dot-com boom, the lifting of the H-1B cap to 195,000 between 2001 and 2003, and continuing links between U.S. corporations and off-shore enterprises in India—all led to a marked increase in the issuance of H-1B visas. Official statistics indicate that H-1B visas have increased dramatically in the past two decades, from below 65,000 annually in the mid-1990s to well above 200,000 today (U.S. General Accounting Office 2000; U.S. Citizenship and Immigration Services 2009a). Indians have been the primary beneficiaries of the H-1B program: in 2008, for instance, India accounted for 54 percent of the 276,252 petitions approved and China for 9 percent.

These changes have several implications for the Asian Indian (or Indian American) population in the United States. It has the highest earnings and average household income, among the highest growth rate of any immigrant group since 2000, and is the most recently arrived population among the six major Asian national-origin groups (U.S. Census Bureau 2008a). Indian American organizations thus tend to be more heavily focused on home country politics and home-region activities than other Asian American groups, and domestic-focused organizations tend towards advocating for the interests of particular occupations such as doctors and motel owners (Mishra 2009; Sheth 1995; Varadarajan 1999).

By some measures, Indian Americans have a long history of representation in U.S. politics. From 1957 to 1963, Dalip Singh Saund, a Sikh Indian from southern California, served as the first Asian American member of the U.S. House of Representatives. Like Saund, recent Indian American elected officials have needed to reach far beyond the Indian or even Asian community for support. In the past decade, Indian Americans have won office in predominantly white districts in states such as Georgia, Ohio, and Iowa. Commenting on this trend in 2007, an Indian American community leader from New York City noted the cross-over appeal to non-Asian constituencies:

> Now we have a young man from Louisiana (Bobby Jindal) and we have four or five assemblymen from different states—New Jersey, Maryland, Minnesota, Wisconsin, etc. . . . we have won elections from areas where there are very few Indians. They (South Asians–Indian Americans) could do it because they are educated people. Take an example of Louisiana—there are not too many Indians there, there is no support for Indians there. Similarly, the assemblyman from New Jersey is not from a constituency with a high number of Indians. If he can win from a non-Indian community to state assembly, the people who really work hard and have the same goal to get what they want, I think they can get it. (Mishra 2009, 108)

Despite these recent advances, Indian Americans lag significantly behind other Asian American groups in terms of their representation in elected office, most likely due to their more recent migration history to the United States. In 2008, eighteen Indian Americans held elected office at various levels, versus fifty-nine Japanese Americans, fifty-five Chinese Americans, and forty-one Filipino Americans (Lai and Nakanishi 2007). As of 2010, no Indian American had served as a cabinet member in the White House, and no Indian Americans other than Dilip Singh Saund (1957–1963) and Bobby Jindal (2005–2008) had been elected to the U.S. House of Representatives.

FILIPINO AMERICANS

The very earliest Asian settlements in the United States can be traced to the mid-1700s, when sailors from the Philippines arrived on Spanish ships that were part of the Manila-Acapulco galleon trade. They debarked on

Mexico's west coast and eventually settled in Louisiana (Okihiro 2001). The first major wave of Filipinos, however, did not arrive until the early 1900s, after the United States annexed the Philippines following the Spanish-American War of 1898.

Like the Japanese and Chinese, Filipinos initially migrated to the United States as agricultural laborers. By the late 1920s, Filipinos constituted the largest ethnic group working on sugar plantations in Hawaii. Eventually they were recruited into domestic service and service-industry jobs as bellhops, waiters, cooks, doormen, and janitors (Chan 1991). On the U.S. mainland, the number of Filipinos grew from 6,000 to more than 45,000 in the 1930s, and settled not only on the West Coast, but also in Michigan, Illinois, Kansas, Montana, and Idaho. Takaki reports that in 1930, 25 percent of Filipinos in the continental United States worked in service industries and 9 percent in Alaskan salmon fisheries. The majority, however, worked in agriculture.

Filipino migrants were distinct from other contemporary Asian settlers because they arrived as subjects of a territory administered by the United States, and not as immigrants from another sovereign country. They were thus able to organize strikes without fear of reprisal and deportation. They were also familiar with Western religions, in that 90 percent were Catholic as the result of hundreds of years of Spanish colonial rule on the islands (Takaki 1989). However, labor difficulties and nativist reactions in the United States made life difficult for Filipinos, and reduced the flow of U.S. immigrants. The passage of the Tydings-McDuffie Act in 1924 establishing Filipino independence, the Filipino Repatriation Act of 1935, and the Great Depression all contributed to the return of thousands back to the Philippines (Takaki 1989; Ngai 2004).

Filipino migration did not rebound until the passage of the 1965 Immigration Act. The migrant flow arriving in the late 1960s was dramatically different from the first wave in terms of class and occupational status. Most post-1965 migrants were from urban rather than rural areas and arrived as professionals rather than unskilled laborers. Immigration from the Philippines has remained robust. As of 2010, about half of all Filipinos were foreign-born. The Filipino community includes a large number of undocumented immigrants, and some struggle economically, such as veterans who fought with American troops in World War II but received U.S. veterans' benefits only in 2009 (De la Cruz and Agbayani-Siewert 2003). Over the past three decades, however, thousands of Filipino professionals have migrated to the United States. Starting in the 1970s, the United States recruited a large number of Filipino nurses and doctors to compensate for domestic labor shortages. Takaki reports that in the 1970s "one-fifth of the 20,000 nurses who graduated from school in the Philippines came to the United States" and that "the flow of Filipino doctors has been even

greater" (1989, 60). Finally, one vestige of the colonial relationship between the Philippines and the United States is that many residents in the
former U.S. territory speak English. As a result, schools in the United
States continued to recruit teachers from the Philippines until the late
2000s (De la Cruz and Agbayani-Siewert 2003). Thus, like Indian Americans, the Filipino population in the United States continues to grow at a
rapid pace, from 1.9 million in 2000 to more than 2.4 million in 2008.[6]

Filipino Americans have made notable strides in some areas of American politics. In 2008, forty-one were elected officials, from city council to
the U.S. House of Representatives (Lai and Nakanishi 2007). Most in federal and state offices, however, were concentrated in Hawaii. In California, which is home to the highest Filipino American population, no Filipino American had been elected to the state's legislature or to the U.S.
Congress as of 2010. This lack of political success is all the more remarkable given that Filipino Americans and Chinese Americans are the largest
two Asian American groups in the state, four times larger than Japanese
Americans and twice as large as Vietnamese Americans, who have both
gained representation.

JAPANESE AMERICANS

The initiation of immigration from Japan to the United States can be said
to have started with Commander Matthew Perry's forced opening of the
Tokugawa Empire in 1854. However, significant migration from Japan to
Hawaii and the mainland United States did not occur until 1890, when
thousands began work in agriculture (Chan 1991).[7] From the late 1800s
until the 1920s, approximately 400,000 Japanese immigrated to the West
Coast and Hawaii, mostly as contract laborers recruited to work on sugar
plantations and at other commercial agriculture ventures. In 1913, California passed its first Alien Land Law, which prohibited those ineligible for
citizenship (Japanese immigrants) from owning land. Thus, the Japanese
community invested heavily in tenant farming. In tandem with the United
States' involvement in World War I, Japanese tenant farmers were producing much of the consumer agriculture for California, including 90 percent
of all celery, asparagus, onions, tomatoes, berries, and cantaloupes and 50
percent of all seeds for the state. A fair number of Japanese Americans
(from 12,000 to 15,000) also entered domestic service during this period
(Chan 1991, 40). Japanese immigration came to a halt in 1924 with the passage of the National Origins Act, which effectively ended migration from
Asia. Still, the Japanese immigrants who arrived before 1924 continued to
work on farms, and eventually many saved up enough funds to lease
small plots of land themselves.

Diplomatic relations between the U.S. and Japan have long shaped Japanese immigration and political incorporation patterns. At the end of the nineteenth century, Japan was the only Asian country recognized by the United States as a rising force in world politics. Despite local anxiety over Japanese migration among the U.S. population, the federal government took pains not to offend Japanese leaders. For example, although migration from China was banned outright in the Chinese Exclusion Acts, the U.S. government reached a gentleman's agreement in 1907 whereby the Japanese government agreed that it would not issue passports to its citizens for travel to the United States. U.S.-Japan relations disintegrated in December 1941 after Japan bombed the Pearl Harbor naval base in Hawaii and the United States declared war on Japan. The same month, President Roosevelt signed an executive order that led to the internment of 120,000 Japanese immigrants and Japanese American citizens. The internment shaped Japanese American politics for the decades to follow. The first generation (Issei), who had once been strike leaders on sugar plantations and founded vibrant ethnic associations, were for the most part hesitant to take a visible role in American politics after the war ended. However, for the second (Nisei) and third generations (Sansei), largely professional and highly educated, the Asian American movement and fight for reparations after internment deepened their sense of ethnic identity and increased their prominence in American politics (Chan 1991; Takezawa 2000). Partly as a result of such sustained activism, many Japanese Americans ran for elected office and, by 2008, the majority of Asian American elected officials were of Japanese descent.

After World War II, immigration from Japan rose and remained steady at its present rate of about 5,000 per year (Toji 2003, 75). Although the Japanese population increased consistently between World War II and 2000, immigration from Japan has leveled off relative to other Asian groups. Japanese were once the largest Asian-origin group in the United States, making up more than 50 percent of all Asian-origin people in 1960 (Takaki 1995, 36). Today, however, they are the sixth-largest group and account for just over 5 percent (table 2.2).

At least four important characteristics distinguish Japanese Americans from other Asian national-origin groups. First, the Japanese population includes a larger proportion of second-, third-, and later generation people than other groups. Relatedly, the proportion of elderly among Japanese Americans (22 percent) is also much higher than among other Asian American groups (8 percent), and the number of Japanese Americans has actually declined since 2000 due to lower rates of immigration and higher rates of mortality. Moreover, the Japanese-origin population in the United States has the second-highest average income of any racial or national-origin group in the United States, second only to Asian Indians and higher than non-Hispanic whites (U.S. Census Bureau 2008a). Although many immigrants migrate to the United States to escape poverty in their countries of origin, contemporary Japanese immigrants come from an advanced industrialized economy. Japanese immigrants to the United States since 1945 have also come from the oldest constitutional democracy in Asia, although one-party rule was the norm until 2007. Finally, it is unclear at the time of this writing whether emigration from Japan will increase in the aftermath of the 2011 earthquake and tsunami. On the one hand, the destabilization of the Japanese economy and infrastructure may prompt many working-age Japanese to seek jobs in other countries. At the same time, reconstruction needs in Japan may compel many Japanese to remain in their country and fill the jobs necessary for an economic recovery.

When it comes to political participation, Japanese Americans have high rates of citizenship, though this is largely because more than half of the population (57 percent) is U.S.-born. Among the foreign-born, however, only 29 percent were naturalized as U.S. citizens in 2007, the lowest rate of naturalization among the six major Asian American groups (U.S. Census Bureau 2008a). Still, many factors continue to make Japanese Americans important to the politics of Asian America today, including the long history of Japanese migration to the United States, the early creation of organizations like the Japanese American Citizens League, and the long-standing movement seeking redress for internment. Consequently, Japanese Americans hold the highest number of elected offices among the various Asian American groups—fifty-nine at the time of our survey in 2008 (Lai and Nakanishi 2007). These included 44 percent of all state representatives, 42 percent of all state senators, three of the six Asian American members in the U.S. House of Representatives, and the long-serving senator from Hawaii, Daniel Inouye (1963 to the present).

KOREAN AMERICANS

In contrast to Asians from China, the Philippines, and Japan, the history of mass emigration from Korea to the United States is a relatively recent phenomenon. At the same time, Koreans have been in America for well over a century. The first Koreans to traverse the Pacific were reform-minded exiles like Suh Jae-pil who came to San Francisco in 1885. Suh, who legally changed his name to Philip Jaison, is easily the most celebrated of this pioneering group. Among his many notable accomplishments, Suh was the first Korean who naturalized as a U.S. citizen, was the first to receive a medical degree, established the first modern newspaper in Korea (*The Independent*), and continued his lifelong struggle for Korean independence on multiple fronts.

Increasing but still small numbers of Koreans continued to trickle in into the early 1900s as political exiles, students, and then laborers. In 1903, the first mass migration of Koreans began with labor emigrants to sugar plantations in Hawaii. Many of these early emigrants left Korea because of the 1901 famine and the generally harsh economic conditions in Korea. Then, just as quickly as labor-based immigration to Hawaii began, in 1905 it abruptly came to a halt. In those two years, some 7,226 Koreans left their homeland for Hawaii (Yu 1977). The Korean Foreign Ministry stopped issuing passports to its citizens on its own accord at the same time that the Japanese government pressured U.S. authorities to restrict immigration from Korea, fearing economic competition between Japanese and Korean immigrants in Hawaii. By 1907, a further presidential decree from Theodore Roosevelt prohibited emigration from Hawaii to the U.S. mainland, after some 2,000 Koreans left Hawaii for San Francisco and beyond (Min 1995).

These pioneer Korean immigrant laborers were more urban and more Christian than their Chinese, Filipino, and Japanese counterparts. Pyong Gap Min reports that fully 40 percent of early Korean immigrants were Christians (1995), and Eui-Young Yu that more than 80 percent were male (1977). After the series of restrictionist immigration policies and presidential decrees of the late nineteenth and early twentieth centuries, Korean immigration came in one of two forms. From 1910 until 1924, when the National Origins (Reed-Johnson) Act was passed, more than a thousand picture brides entered the United States (mostly to Hawaii) to partner with Korean bachelor immigrants. At roughly the same time, a somewhat smaller contingent of Korean students, intellectuals, and political exiles (from the Japanese occupation) also came to the United States. Then, between 1924 and the Korean War period, emigration from Korea to the United States effectively ended.

The influx of Koreans resumed with some momentum after the Korean War, as war brides and war orphans began to come to the United States in significant numbers. As with other Asian immigrants, the number of Koreans skyrocketed after the passage of the 1965 Immigration and Nationality (Hart-Cellar) Act. The 1960 census reported a Korean-origin population of 25,000; by 2000, this figure had exploded to more than a million (see table 2.2). In the 2006 and 2008 American Community Surveys, the estimated Korean American population is somewhere between 1.3 million and 1.5 million, depending on whether multiracial Americans with some Korean heritage are included or excluded from the tally. In contrast to Indians and Filipinos, who have continued to see high rates of immigration to the United States since 2000, the growth of the Korean American population appears to have slowed considerably in the last two decades. During the 1970s, about 267,000 Koreans immigrated to the United States, followed by another 338,000 in the 1980s. In the 1990s, however, the number decreased to 164,000, and recent estimates show that Korean immigrants are on pace to add another 200,000 immigrants during the first decade of this century (U.S. Citizenship and Immigration Services 2009b).

As with Indian immigrants, the post-1965 wave of Korean immigrants tends to be college-educated and middle-class. Many were professional and technical workers in Korea who left the country beginning in the 1970s. Although the Korean economy grew rapidly in that decade, the country was also notable for its hard-line control over the economy and society, and the government outlawed labor strikes and imposed restrictions on farmed goods. Consequently, many farmers abandoned agriculture and contributed to rapid population growth in major Korean cities. Urban jobs became scarce, creating a push factor toward immigration to the United States. As Takaki notes, more than 13,000 Korean medical professionals arrived in the United States between 1965 and 1977 (1995, 69).

After coming to the United States, many Korean professionals encountered discrimination and licensing restrictions. Some of these professionals turned to self-employment in small businesses. Thus, by 1990, 25 percent of southern California liquor-grocery stores and 60 percent of New York City green grocery stores were Korean-owned (Min 1995, 210). The prominent role of Koreans in shops in urban areas has led to heightened targeting and visibility in American urban and racial politics. Before 1981, African American communities organized several boycotts against Korean-owned stores in New York and Los Angeles. Similar conflicts have taken place in every city Korean Americans have settled in large numbers. Most dramatically, in 1992, more than 2,300 Korean-owned stores in Los Angeles were burned or looted by black and Latino residents during the civil unrest that followed the Rodney King trial verdict (Kitano and Daniels 1995).

Although prominent Korean Americans, such as former Congressman Jay Kim (R-CA) have served in office, analysis of data on Asian American elected officials shows proportionately fewer Korean Americans have held office compared with other groups. Of course, this is partly because Korean Americans are a smaller group than either Chinese Americans or Filipino Americans. Many more Japanese Americans than Korean Americans are elected officials, however, even though Japanese Americans are a relatively small group in the population. Furthermore, the rate of naturalization among Korean Americans (53 percent in 2008) is significantly lower than for Vietnamese (72 percent) and Filipinos (63 percent), and slightly lower than the average for Asian immigrants (56 percent).[8] Still, their mobilization in response to consumer boycotts and communal violence has made the group more attentive and involved in politics than one might expect given some of these demographic disadvantages (Min 1995). Indeed, during the spring of 2006 when marches defending immigrant rights took place across the country, Korean American organizations and individuals played an important role in building coalitions with Latino groups, and were exceptions to the more general rule of nonparticipation by Asian Americans (Lee 2006).

VIETNAMESE AMERICANS

Before the 1965 Immigration and Nationality Act, fewer than a thousand Vietnamese lived in the United States, and most were students, diplomats, and language teachers (Takaki 1995, 95). With the American withdrawal from Vietnam and the fall of Saigon in 1975, more than 130,000 Vietnamese refugees were admitted into the United States (Kitano and Daniels 1995). Many, up to 60,000, had left Vietnam in crowded boats with the hopes of being rescued in the open sea by the U.S. Navy. The first wave was well educated, and a majority spoke English because they were from Saigon and other urban areas in Vietnam. Another large wave began in 1978, when large numbers fled the country in small, overcrowded boats after a period of brutal reforms that included mass relocations, the closing of ethnic Chinese businesses, and the torture of dissidents. Many languished in camps in Thailand for years before they were able to travel to the United States, Australia, Canada, and France.

Between 1979 and 1980, almost 90,000 Vietnamese arrived in the United States. Harry Kitano and Roger Daniels report that "in all, from April 1975 to September 1984, more than 700,000 Southeast Asians were admitted to the United States" (1995, 150). Professionals constituted only part of this second wave of refugees. Others included fishermen, farmers, and shopkeepers. In 1982, the United States negotiated an agreement with the Vietnamese government to allow 20,000 Vietnamese per year to reunite with family members who had already immigrated to the United States (Takaki 1995, 106). By 2000, Vietnamese Americans were the fourth-largest Asian American group in the United States, and their numbers have grown at a rate comparable to Korean Americans, from about 1.2 million in 2000 to more than 1.4 million in 2008.

When it comes to their reception in the United States, what sets Vietnamese Americans apart from other Asian groups today is the extent to which they have received support from the federal government. From 1975 to 1986, the U.S. government provided $5 billion dollars to refugee assistance programs, many of the funds flowing to Vietnamese and other Southeast Asian populations in the United States (Rumbaut 1995, 235). In coordination with church groups and other nonprofit organizations, the United States sought to settle Vietnamese refugees throughout the country. This policy of dispersal was intended to relieve the social services burden on any particular city. One study found, for instance, that Vietnamese refugees were settled in 813 zip code areas, across every U.S. state (Baker and North 1984). Eventually, however, the group sought shared community with family and friends, and re-migrated to places like northern Orange County in California, San Diego, San Jose, and Houston. At the same time, significant pockets of Vietnamese American settlement are established in states like Louisiana, Mississippi, Arkansas, and Oklahoma (Rumbaut 1995).

Compared with their Chinese and Filipino counterparts, Vietnamese immigrants have much more recently arrived and have fewer economic resources. In 1990, 25 percent of all Vietnamese-origin people in the United States, versus 14 percent of the Asian-origin population as a whole, were living in poverty (Chuong and Ta 2003). Vietnamese also lagged behind other Asians in education and income. Since then, Vietnamese have made great gains in all of these areas (Zhou and Bankston 1998), but gaps in socioeconomic status remain. Our analysis of American Community Survey data from 2006 and 2008 reveals that 49 percent of Vietnamese Americans age twenty-five and older have a high school degree or more, versus 71 percent among all other groups, and that they earn more than $13,000 less on average among men and about $7,500 less among women.

Because most Vietnamese immigrants arrived in the United States as political refugees with no intention of returning permanently to their country of origin, it is not surprising that they have high rates of citizenship. Their naturalization patterns and migration experiences parallel those of Cuban migrants. Also like their Cuban American counterparts, Vietnamese tend to be the most Republican-leaning of any Asian American group, an orientation attributed to a strong anticommunist strain within the community. However, some evidence indicates that identification with the Republican Party has declined over time, especially among the second and third generation (Collet and Seldon 2003). Vietnamese Americans have also gained footholds in local political office the way that Cuban Americans did in the 1980s. Thus, for instance, Orange County, California, has long been a hotbed of Vietnamese American activism and in the past decade has seen several members elected to city councils, and one to the state assembly. The first Vietnamese-origin representative in the U.S. House was Republican Joseph Cao, who was elected in 2008 from a predominantly Democratic (and African American) district in Louisiana, though it seems that more stable bases for future representation are Orange County, California, and the city of San Jose.

PARTICIPATION BY NATIONAL ORIGIN

The story of Asian America is thus comprised of several overlapping stories. Even though the six Asian-origin groups had varying start-and-stop points in the early history of migration to the United States, and even though contemporary Asian immigrants may vary significantly in their occupational skills, religious affiliation, and language spoken at home, key similarities remain. Perhaps most notably, immigrants from these countries are still enumerated as Asian in the decennial census and by various state and federal government institutions, and these official classifications have been reinforced through important social institutions and processes such as news coverage in mainstream and ethnic media, the activities of civil rights organizations, and the policies and practices of colleges and universities (Espiritu 1992; Ngai 2004; Omi and Winant 1994; Wei 1993). Furthermore, important common developments among contemporary Asian immigrants—from occupational mobility and educational attainment in the United States to patterns of intergenerational cultural transmission and health behaviors—underscore these groups' relation to one other as collectively distinct from other racial-ethnic groups, such as Latinos and African Americans (Omi and Winant 1994; Collier and Mahon 1993). And as we shall see in the rest of this chapter and in the chapters that follow, numerous aspects of Asian American political behavior and explanatory models of political behavior make their common study possible and important. These include not only social indicators, such as educational attainment and ethnic media consumption, but also political indicators, such as party identification and membership in civic organizations. Indeed, one could argue that these alternative ways of systematically cutting, conceptualizing, and operationalizing differences in national origin are more important than taking countries of origin as given (Ramakrishnan 2005).

And yet our initial foray into the examination of Asian American political participation must begin with what is taken as given, and the answer must therefore take national-origin differences in citizenship acquisition and political participation as a starting point. In table 2.3, we present variation across the six major national origin groups on citizenship rates and voting in recent elections as reported by respondents in the National Asian American Survey (and weighted to be representative of the national Asian American population).[9] As we can see, differences by national origin among Asian Americans are significant. Vietnamese Americans have the highest rates of citizenship: more than three in four adults are citizens. This rate is even higher than for Japanese Americans, who are most likely to have citizenship by virtue of birthplace. At the low end are Asian Indi-

Table 2.3   Citizenship and Voting Rates

	Citizen	November 2004*	November 2004**	2008 Primaries*	2008 Primaries**
Asian Indian	49	65	33	42	18
Chinese	67	57	39	45	23
Filipino	72	65	48	53	32
Japanese	70	79	55	54	34
Korean	61	60	37	35	17
Vietnamese	76	68	51	39	23
Total	64	65	45	46	24

Source: Authors' compilation of data from the 2008 National Asian American Survey (Ramakrishnan et al. 2011).
Note: Rates are in percentages. Unless otherwise specified, we report tabulated findings from the National Asian American Survey weighted by national origin, state of settlement, education, gender, nativity, and years in the United States as indicated in the 2006–2008 American Community Survey.
* adult citizens; ** all adults.

ans, who are generally much more recently arrived in the United States than the rest of the Asian American population (for more on length of stay, see table 2.6).

Beyond the initial step of citizenship, we see that significant gaps remain with respect to political participation. Thus, a very high proportion of Japanese American citizens report that they voted in the George W. Bush and John Kerry election of 2004 (79 percent), whereas only 57 percent of Chinese Americans and 60 percent of Korean Americans did so. Indian Americans, who had the lowest rates of citizenship, voted in line with the Asian American adult average of 65 percent.

In addition to voting rates among adult Asian American citizens, we also examined voting rates among all adult citizens—both to see whether group advantages in citizenship are canceled by disadvantages in voting among citizens, but also to give an overall, basic impression of how much voice Asian American adults have in presidential elections. Even here, we see significant national-origin differences, with only about a third of Indian American and Korean American adults having a say in the 2004 presidential election, but more than half of Japanese Americans and Vietnamese Americans doing so. Finally, only 24 percent of Asian American adults, and only 46 percent of those eligible to vote, participated in the 2008 presidential primaries. The national-origin differences here are similar to 2004, with one notable exception: Vietnamese Americans were among those least likely to participate. Such a finding can be explained by a confluence of three factors: the strong Republican identification among Vietnamese

Americans (see chapter 4), the lack of a competitive Republican primary after John McCain's insurmountable lead after the Super Tuesday primaries on February 5, 2008, and that Vietnamese Americans were more likely to live in a post–Super Tuesday state (34 percent) than other Asian American citizens (28 percent).

Although it may be interesting to pay attention to the dynamics of particular elections and how participation rates may vary, it is also important to be able to come up with a more general pattern of voting participation across groups that is not subject to the vagaries of a particular context. It is also important, when looking at the political participation of Asian Americans, to go beyond voting in presidential elections and to compare groups on other important aspects of political participation, such as making campaign contributions and getting in touch with government officials. As we noted in chapter 1, we created a likely voter model based on registration status, voting in 2004 and in the 2008 primaries, and intention to vote in the 2008 general election, and created a 0–1 scale based on actual turnout as reported in the 2008 Current Population Survey Voter Supplement. Based on this model (table 2.4), we see that the summary voting rate for Japanese American citizens is quite high (65 percent), but low for Chinese Americans (39 percent) and Korean Americans (40 percent). The results are similar when we examine participation among all Asian American adults, although lower rates of citizenship among Indian Americans makes their voting rates the lowest.

Table 2.4 also enables us to examine national-origin differences in activities other than voting. Using all adults as the eligible population, we find that participation in activities such as contributing to political campaigns (13 percent) and contacting government officials (9 percent) is much lower for Asian American adults than voting is, even when using the lower estimate of voting among all resident adults. When it comes to political contributions, Japanese and Filipino Americans are the most likely to participate, and Vietnamese Americans the least likely. As one might imagine, differences in socioeconomic status may be driving this finding. This is a possibility we test for in our final chapter, where we present group differences after controlling for socioeconomics status and a host of other factors. For now, however, when political candidates and party organizations look out at the Asian American population they are much less likely to see Vietnamese Americans as contributors than to encounter them as voters.

The survey results on political participation also reveal some important differences for activities beyond voting. Indian Americans may have the lowest rates of citizenship among the six largest Asian American groups, but they have relatively high rates of contact with government officials.

Table 2.4   Political Participation and National Origin

	Likely Voter*	Likely Voter	Political Contributor	Contact Government Officials	Protester	Community Activist
Asian						
Indian	47	23	12	11	4	27
Chinese	39	26	11	9	4	19
Filipino	47	34	17	13	4	23
Japanese	65	45	18	10	3	17
Korean	40	24	11	5	3	18
Vietnamese	48	36	7	5	8	21
Total	45	30	13	9	4	21

Source: Authors's compilation of data from the 2008 National Asian American Survey (Ramakrishnan et al. 2011).
Note: Rates are in percentages.
*Among adult citizens

On this measure, Filipino Americans have the highest rates of participation (13 percent), and Korean and Vietnamese Americans the lowest (5 percent each). When it comes to protest activity, Vietnamese Americans are twice as likely to participate as all other Asian American groups. This finding, based on our nationally representative sample of Vietnamese Americans, confirms what one might expect from news reports of protest activity in Vietnamese American enclaves related to U.S. foreign policy toward Vietnam and intracommunity conflicts. Prominent recent examples of large-scale Vietnamese American protests include the successful efforts to shut down an art exhibit on communist art in Orange County, California, in January 2009, and a months-long protest and recall attempt against City Councilwoman Madison Nguyen in March 2008 for proposing to name a Vietnamese area in San Jose as Saigon Business District instead of the more traditional—and apparently more anticommunist—label of Little Saigon (Tran 2008; Sahagun and Tran 2009). Finally, when it comes to working with others in your community to solve a problem, Indian Americans were the most likely to have reported such participation in the previous twelve months (27 percent), and Japanese Americans and Korean Americans the least likely.

Thus we see that voting and other types of political participation vary dramatically with national origin. As we outline in the introductory chapter, we attribute these differences to socioeconomic differences, but also contend that immigrant socialization, political and geographic context, party identification, racial identity, and civic engagement help shape the

Figure 2.1   Systematic Assessments of Immigrant Socialization in Relationship to Political Participation

National Origin

Citizenship status
Immigrant generation (first, second, third and higher)
Length of stay in the United States
Language-related factors (English proficiency, ethnic news consumption, bilingual voting materials)
Transnational activities (contact, remittances, voting)
Opportunity costs of work (use of extra time)

Source: Authors' compilation.

varying political trajectories of these groups. We devote systematic attention to each of these factors in the rest of this book, and begin with different measurements of immigrant socialization in the United States.

Research suggests that variables related to immigrant socialization will exert great influence on the political participation of Asian Americans (Cain, Kiewiet, and Uhlaner 1991; Lien 1994, 2001; Cho 1999; Junn 1999; Ramakrishnan and Espenshade 2001; Lien, Conway, and Wong 2004; Ramakrishnan 2005; Wong, Lien, and Conway 2005). In particular, previous studies highlight six broad aspects of immigrant socialization that we consider paramount to understanding Asian American political participation (figure 2.1). These include the attention to the now-standard set of factors such as immigrant generation, immigrant length of residence in the United States, citizenship status, language-related factors, and transnational attachments (Lee, Ramakrishnan, and Ramírez 2006), as well as some new considerations on the opportunity cost of participation that may be particularly relevant for immigrants.

CITIZENSHIP STATUS

Perhaps most obvious, citizenship is critical. With a few exceptions like local elections in Takoma Park, Maryland, since 1992 and school board elections in Chicago since 2007, noncitizens cannot vote in the United States (Hayduk 2006; Huang 2007). Even beyond voting, however, we may expect citizens to have higher rates of political participation than noncitizens. In contrast to native-born Asian Americans, gaining legal rights as a citizen of the United States for the foreign-born structures the relationship of the individual to the state. Not only are naturalized citizens able to vote in federal elections, they also have priority in current U.S. immigration policy for family reunification. Beyond the right to vote, being a citizen places the individual in a distinctive position from those who are not by increasing the incentives to participate in political activities, at the same time reducing the barriers to participation. For example, contacting a government official carries more weight from a citizen than a person—even a lawful permanent resident—who cannot vote for or against that politician in an election. Similarly, contributing money to a campaign or organization is easier and potentially more efficacious for citizens than noncitizens, especially given the high level of scrutiny given to contributions by noncitizens, especially Asian immigrants, during the 1996 and 2008 presidential campaigns (Lee 2000; Nicholas and Hamburger 2007).[10] At the same time, the two other political activities we address—protesting and working with others in the community—are not mediated in the same way by citizenship as the system-directed activities of voting, contacting, and making contributions. Instead, both protesting and community-based work do not require a formal principal-agent relationship with the government. Although citizenship may offer additional avenues for working with others in the community in particular, protesting has frequently been the province of disenfranchised populations. Thus, we would expect the importance of citizenship to vary by political activity (for a broader notion of citizenship, see Bloemraad 2006; Reed-Danahay and Brettell 2008).

How do Asian American groups vary in terms of their citizenship status? About two-thirds of Asian American adults are U.S. citizens, but, as we saw in table 2.3, differences across ethnoracial groups are considerable. For instance, Asian Indians have the lowest rates of citizenship (49 percent among adults), and Vietnamese Americans the highest (76 percent). Given the centrality of citizenship to voting, the extent to which Asian American groups may have political voice through the ballot box is limited by the prevalence of noncitizenship within the group. Thus, for instance, voting rates among Indian Americans adult citizens was on par with the Asian American average during the 2008 presidential primaries (42 percent), but Indian Americans had considerably lower rates of participation among all adult residents (18 percent).

How might citizenship relate to political acts beyond voting? Research suggests that citizenship status is a critical factor to consider when it comes to participation well beyond voting (compare Bloemraad 2006). In figure 2.2, we present the results for our four major nonvoting activities based on citizenship status. As we can see, citizens are more than three

Figure 2.2   Political Participation by Citizenship Status

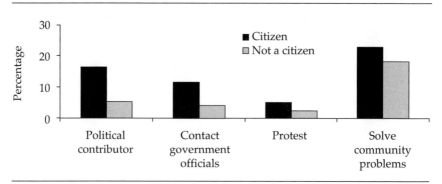

Source: Authors' compilation of data from the 2008 National Asian American Survey (Ramakrishnan et al. 2011).

times as likely as noncitizens to contribute money to politics (16 percent versus 5 percent), and also three times as likely to contact a government official (12 percent versus 4 percent). Even for protest activity and community activism, citizens are more likely to participate than noncitizens, though the differences are smaller (5 percent versus 2 percent for protests, and 23 percent versus 18 percent for solving community problems). Thus the participation advantage among citizens extends well beyond voting, where it is formally required.

IMMIGRANT GENERATIONS

As we have seen, the generational mix of immigrants for any national-origin group has been shaped by two major factors: changes in U.S. immigration policy over time and the political and economic histories of countries of origin. For example, with rapid expansion of the Japanese economy after World War II, fewer push factors propelled Japanese Americans to emigrate to the United States. Japanese immigration did not come to a halt, but leveled off and remained steady, whereas immigration from other parts of Asia increased dramatically (Toji 2003). Thus Japanese Americans in the NAAS sample are the least likely to be in the first immigrant generation (40 percent), and most likely to be among those who have been in the United States for three or more generations. By contrast, the demand for professional labor in the United States after the 1960s (doctors, engineers, and nurses) coincided with a surplus of professional labor and heavy government regulation of industry in countries such as

Table 2.5   Mix of Immigrant Generations

	Asian Indian	Chinese	Filipino	Japanese	Korean	Vietnamese	Total
First	93	82	78	40	86	89	81
Second	5	13	20	34	12	9	14
Third and higher	1	5	2	26	2	2	5

Source: Authors' compilation of data from the 2008 National Asian American Survey (Ramakrishnan et al. 2011).
Note: Rates are in percentages.

India, the Philippines, and China. This brain drain of professionals continued through the early twenty-first century, but was also accompanied by the arrival of immigrants sponsored by family reunification visas. Finally, hundreds of thousands of refugees arrived from Southeast Asia starting in the mid-1970s. Thus, with the exception of Japanese Americans, the pattern of immigration flows since 1965 have produced a population of Asian Americans, and Asian American adults in particular, who are heavily first-generation immigrant (table 2.5).

The role of immigrant generation, or a group's generational status, has received a great deal of treatment in the literature on immigration (see, for example, Kasinitz et al. 2008) and is implicit in many studies of immigrant political incorporation. Most notably, theories of assimilation, based on the great wave of European immigration at the turn into the twentieth century, assert that with each subsequent generation of immigrants born in the United States, an immigrant group's economic status will improve, as will its degree of social and political integration (Handlin 1951; Dahl 1961). More recently, scholars have questioned the applicability of the classic assimilation model to contemporary immigrants from Asia and Latin America (Gans 1992; Portes and Zhou 1993; Alba and Nee 1997, 2003). Karthick Ramakrishnan and Thomas Espenshade present one of the most comprehensive investigations of immigrant generation and voting to date (2001). Using data from the Current Population Surveys from the mid-1990s, they find that with each generation in the United States, voting increases for Asian Americans. Interestingly, this straight-line relationship between generation and voter turnout does not hold for other groups. The authors argue that, unlike white Americans, for whom barriers to social acceptance and participation may disappear after the first generation, second-generation Asian Americans may continue to encounter racial discrimination and thus be less likely to participate than second-generation whites.

Figure 2.3   Political Participation by Immigrant Generation

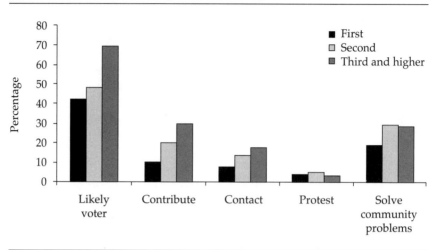

Source: Authors' compilation of data from the 2008 National Asian American Survey (Ramakrishnan et al. 2011).
Note: The likely voter figures are for adult citizens only.

Does this straight-line relationship between immigrant generation and political participation still hold for Asian Americans today, and does it apply across different types of political activities beyond voting? In figure 2.3, we present differences in political participation by immigrant generation, and find that the straight-line story still applies when it comes to voting participation. Second-generation Asian Americans are only slightly more likely to vote than those in the first generation (48 percent versus 42 percent), and significantly less likely than those in the third generation and higher (69 percent). A similar pattern holds for contacting government officials and for contributing to politics, where 10 percent of first-generation adults gave to political campaigns, compared with 20 percent of those in the second generation and 30 percent of those in the third generation and higher. Finally, there is no clear generational pattern for protest activity and, in the case of working collectively to solve community problems, the second generation is on par with those in the third generation and higher.

Thus we see that generational patterns in voting are consistent across many political activities in that first-generation immigrants are less likely to participate than those in the third generation and higher. We find that significant gaps remain between second-generation Asian Americans and those in higher generations when it comes to voting and contributing to politics. One notable exception is protest activity, which is a relatively low-frequency activity among Asian Americans (about 4 percent overall). We are, however, presenting bivariate differences in participation. Factors such as age and homeownership may thus actually underlie some of these differences, particularly those between second- and third-generation immigrants. We explore this possibility in greater detail in chapter 7, where we examine the explanatory strength of various factors in a multivariate regression.

LENGTH OF STAY IN THE UNITED STATES

In addition to immigrant generation, another important time-based factor in immigrant socialization is the number of years in the host country. Countless studies in fields ranging from economics and sociology to public health, epidemiology, and geography have paid attention to time in the United States as a critical factor that shapes immigrant outcomes. Thus, for instance, scholars have debated whether immigrants working in ethnic enclave economies have occupational mobility (Portes and Bach 1985; Sanders and Nee 1987), and whether immigrants continue to move from central cities to suburbs the longer they stay in the United States (Park 1925; Massey and Denton 1992; Allen and Turner 1996; Frasure and Jones-Correa 2010). Regardless of whether scholars subscribe to models of immigrant assimilation, racialization, or segmented assimilation, length of stay plays an important role in empirical assessments of how immigrants are faring in the United States (Myers 2007).

Within political science, many studies have considered the role of length of residence in shaping immigrant political incorporation, and of Asian Americans in particular (Uhlaner, Cain, and Kiewiet 1989; Cain, Kiewiet, and Uhlaner 1991; Wong 2000; Ramakrishnan and Espenshade 2001; Lien, Conway, and Wong 2004; Ramakrishnan 2005; Wong 2006). These studies find that length of residence exerts a powerful force on the political attitudes and behaviors, some suggesting that length of residence serves as a proxy for exposure to the U.S. political system and "greater contacts with, and stronger commitments to, the mainstream political system" (Ramakrishnan and Espenshade 2001, 877). In the National Asian American Survey, we asked foreign-born respondents to identify the year they first came to the United States. We had valid responses for 94 percent of our foreign-born respondents, which we then used to produce sample weights that approximate the duration of stay among Asian immigrants as reported by the American Community Survey.

As we can see from table 2.6, Asian Americans as a whole are a remarkably recently arrived population. More than half of the foreign-born

Table 2.6   Length of Stay in the United States

Decade of Entry	Asian Indian	Chinese	Filipino	Japanese	Korean	Vietnamese	Total
2000s	31	20	18	36	21	12	22
1990s	35	30	27	20	23	40	31
1980s	20	28	28	12	30	29	26
1970s	11	13	18	12	22	18	15
1960s	3	5	7	10	4	1	4
1950s	<1	1	1	9	1	<1	1
Before 1950	<1	1	1	1	<1	<1	<1

Source: Authors' compilation of data from the 2006 to 2008 American Community Survey Public Use Microdata (U.S. Census Bureau 2008c).
Note: Rates are in percentages.

arrived after 1990. Even among Filipino and Korean immigrants, those who came after 1990 account for about 45 percent of the total. Still, the data also reveal some important variation across groups. Although fewer than 2 percent of today's Vietnamese immigrants and 4 percent of Indian immigrants came before 1970, 20 percent of Japanese and 9 percent of Filipino immigrants did so. Another important difference is that Indian immigrants are much more likely to be represented among recent arrivals, nearly two-thirds having arrived since 1990. These patterns make sense given the groups' varying histories of migration noted earlier in this chapter.

How does length of stay relate to political participation among Asian Americans? First, U.S. naturalization policy enforces a three- to five-year waiting period before immigrants are eligible to apply for citizenship. As such, it is perhaps no surprise that the association between length of stay and naturalization is fairly tight, because citizens are much more likely than noncitizens to be long-term residents (table 2.7).

Because voting in most U.S. elections requires citizenship, we would expect that length of stay would also exhibit a strong relationship with voting. The results from our survey indicate that this is indeed the case (figure 2.4). The chances of being a likely voter go from 0 percent among the most recent arrivals (up to four years) to 37 percent among those in the United States for fifteen to twenty-four years, and 53 percent for those who have lived here for twenty-five years or more. Furthermore, length of residence is also tied to other types of political participation, such as contributing to a campaign, contacting an official, and community activism. Because these activities do not require citizenship for participation, it is

Table 2.7   Length of Stay Among Citizens and Noncitizens

	Noncitizens	Citizens	Total
Zero to four years	14	0	5
Five to fouteen years	54	10	25
Fifteen to twenty-four years	22	28	26
Twenty-five years or more	8	33	25
Native-born	1	29	19

Source: Authors' compilation of data from the 2008 National Asian American Survey (Ramakrishnan et al. 2011).
Note: Rates are in percentages.

unlikely that length of residence is a mere stand-in for citizens versus noncitizens. What the data suggest, and what we explore later in this book, is that length of stay may be significantly related to factors such as party identification and political information, which in turn play a significant role in shaping political participation. Finally, we see that political protest activity is more common among more recent residents than among long-term residents. This suggests that the issues underlying such protests, and perhaps the settlement patterns of recent versus established immigrants, makes these protests more relevant to the former than the latter.

LANGUAGE-RELATED FACTORS

Given that Asian Americans are the racial group with the highest proportion of foreign-born residents, the role of language use and language proficiency are potentially very important. Our analysis of the 2006–2008 American Community Survey indicates that 75 percent of Asian American adults speak a language other than English at home.[11] This rate is 89 percent among foreign-born adults and a nontrivial 31 percent among native-born adults. Language is also an important consideration in election administration, because the Voting Rights Act mandates language assistance in jurisdictions where more than 5 percent of the voting-age population, or more than 10,000 residents in a particular language group, is limited-English proficient (U.S. Department of Justice 2010). Finally, the use of non-English languages is also an important feature of electoral campaigns, as candidate organizations, interest groups, and news media all try to inform and mobilize voters in various languages. In this section, we focus on three language-related factors and their relationship to political participation: English-language proficiency, ethnic media consumption, and bilingual ballot materials.

Figure 2.4   Political Participation by Length of Stay

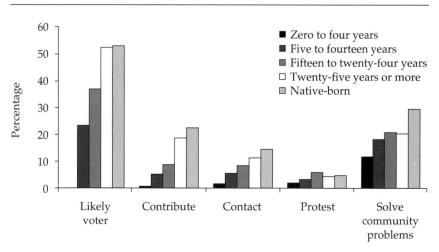

Source: Authors' compilation of data from the 2008 National Asian American Survey (Ramakrishnan et al. 2011).

ENGLISH-LANGUAGE PROFICIENCY

Whether an immigrant is proficient in English is likely to affect their inter-action with and participation in the political system. Wendy Cho's re-search suggests that "lack of English proficiency increases the costs asso-ciated with voting by exaggerating the associated bureaucratic hurdles. And again, socialization processes are certainly affected when one can only receive information in a language other than English" (1999, 1144). In an early study of Asian Americans in California, Carole Uhlaner and col-leagues found that even after taking length of resident into account, Asian Americans who were not English-dominant voted at lower rates than those who spoke English regularly (1989, 208). Since then, several other studies have identified lack of English proficiency as a potential barrier to political participation among Asian Americans. A study in Texas found a positive association between English-language proficiency and a range of political activities beyond voting (Leighley and Vedlitz 1999). Wendy Cho (1999) and Jan Leighley and Arnold Vedlitz's (1999) studies used English-language proficiency as a primary measure of immigrant adaptation. Later studies, some of which included a wider array of immigrant adapta-tion variables, found a weaker association (Lien 1997; Wong, Lien, and Conway 2005).

Focusing on English-language use and proficiency allows us to identify important differences in language capacity across national-origin groups.[12] Table 2.8 shows that English-language proficiency varies widely by national origin among the respondents in our sample. More than 85 percent of Asian Indian (95 percent), Filipino (88 percent), and Japanese (96 percent) respondents claimed to speak English very well or elected to take the survey in English. By contrast, just 42 percent of Vietnamese and 48 percent of Korean respondents did so.

Turning next to the association between English-language proficiency and political participation (figure 2.5), we see that the relationship is fairly consistent. In terms of voting and most other types of political activities, participation increases with English-language proficiency. The one exception, however, is protest activity: consistent with the finding that protesting bears a weak relationships to factors like immigrant generation and duration of stay in the United States, we find no clear or significant relationship between protesting and English proficiency. Finally, we found no significant differences in participation between those who took the survey in English and those who responded in an Asian language and reported high levels of English proficiency.[13]

ETHNIC NEWS CONSUMPTION

The importance of language is not just related to how well an Asian American may speak English or an Asian language.[14] It also matters how they use English or Asian languages in settings that may be relevant to political participation. One important setting is the ways in which residents receive political news. Research suggests that receiving political information through newspapers may bear a stronger relationship to political participation than receiving political information primarily through television (Eveland and Scheufele 2000). Some evidence, from studies of Latino political behavior, also indicates that consumption of ethnic-language media makes a difference on matters ranging from decisions to naturalize to voter turnout and vote choice (Oberholzer-Gee and Waldfogel 2006; DeFrancesco Soto and Merolla 2006; Abrajano 2005; Felix, Gonzalez, and Ramirez 2008).

In our survey, we asked respondents whether they received political information from radio, television, newspapers, and Internet sources. After each question, we also asked whether the source was in English, an Asian language, or both. We present the distribution of news sources on political information in table 2.9, which indicates that television is by far the most frequently cited source of political information among Asian Americans, followed by newspapers, Internet sources, and radio. These

Table 2.8 English-Speaking Proficiency Among U.S. Citizens

	Asian Indian	Chinese	Filipino	Japanese	Korean	Vietnamese	Total
Not at all	1	5	0	0	6	4	3
Just a little	3	16	5	4	29	25	13
Pretty well	2	13	7	1	16	28	11
Very well	3	12	2	2	10	18	8
English-language interview*	92	54	86	94	38	24	65

Source: Authors' compilation of data from the 2008 National Asian American Survey (Ramakrishnan et al. 2011).
Note: Rates are in percentages.
*Questions on English proficiency were only asked of those interviewed in an Asian language.

Figure 2.5   Political Participation by English Proficiency, Among U.S. Citizens

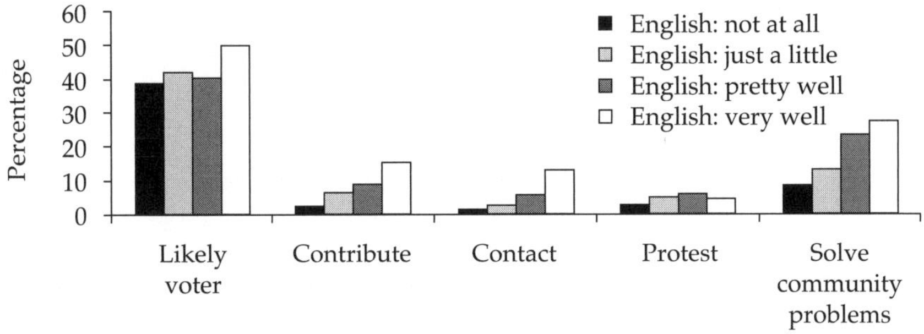

Source: Authors' compilation of data from the 2008 National Asian American Survey (Ramakrishnan et al. 2011).

rates are considerably higher than those found in surveys such as the Pew Internet & American Life Project (Smith 2009), though the data are not fully comparable because the Pew survey limits the number of responses to two sources. Thus, for instance, the 2008 Pew survey found that 77 percent of Americans relied on television for political news, and 28 percent of adults relied on newspapers, 26 percent on the Internet, and 13 percent on radio. Still, if we look at the ratio of news sources cited in the Pew study and the National Asian American Survey, we find that Asian Americans are significantly more likely to rely on newspapers and radio than the general population is.[15]

Table 2.9   Media Sources of Political Information

	Television	Newspaper	Internet	Radio
Asian Indian	84	48	60	38
Chinese	85	74	57	53
Filipino	84	60	40	37
Japanese	83	71	45	34
Korean	84	67	60	46
Vietnamese	88	68	42	57
Total	85	65	52	45

Source: Authors' compilation of data from the 2008 National Asian American Survey (Ramakrishnan et al. 2011).
Note: Rates are in percentages.

We also see some variations across national-origin groups. For example, Asian Indians and Koreans are much more likely to turn to the Internet (60 percent) for political information than Filipinos (40 percent) and Vietnamese Americans (42 percent). By contrast, consumption of radio news is much higher among Vietnamese and Chinese Americans than it is for other Asian American groups. Finally, the results in table 2.8 also allow us to assess whether the relative importance of news sources varies by national origin. Thus, for instance, although the same proportion of Indian and Korean American respondents receive political news from Internet sources, Indians are more likely to rely on such sources relative to radio and newspapers than Koreans are. Overall, however, the general pattern—of television as the most frequent source, followed by newspapers, Internet, and the radio—holds for most national-origin groups. In addition to the Internet for Asian Indians, the only other important exception is that Vietnamese Americans are much more likely to listen to political news on the radio (57 percent) than to read it on a computer (42 percent).

Given the academic literature on ethnic media use, the extent to which Asian Americans consume news in English or in an Asian language, and whether language use varies according to the news source, is important. As we can see in figure 2.6, the order of importance for Asian language media is the same as for media overall. Television is the most frequent source, 38 percent of Asian Americans getting political news from Asian language television (14 percent exclusively and 24 percent in combination with English-language sources), followed by Asian-language newspapers (35 percent), Internet sources (22 percent), and radio (20 percent). Another way to look at the data, however, is to examine the relative importance of Asian-language media to English media, by comparing the proportion of those who get news from each type of source. Viewed this way, we see that Asian-language media is much more important to political news provided in newspapers and on the radio than it is for television and the Internet.

Clearly, Asian-language media is important to the political news consumption of Asian Americans. To what extent does this importance vary across national-origin groups, and between citizens and noncitizens? It would be dizzying to present the results in figure 2.6 across subgroups. However, it is possible to come up with a summary measure of news consumption (as the number of overall sources cited), and present the proportion of those totals that relate to Asian-language news consumption (alone or in combination). As we can see from figure 2.7, this summary analysis reveals that those national-origin groups with the lowest levels of English proficiency also tend to be those who consume ethnic media the

Figure 2.6   Sources of Political Information, by Language

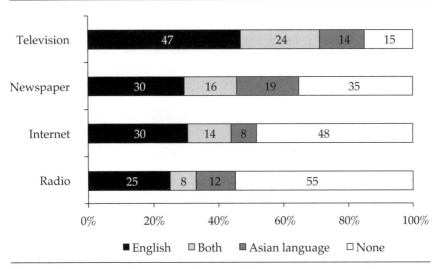

Source: Authors' compilation of data from the 2008 National Asian American Survey (Ramakrishnan et al. 2011).
Note: Includes citizens and noncitizens.

most. Thus, for instance, more than 60 percent of Chinese, Korean, and Vietnamese Americans consume ethnic media for their political news, whereas only 16 percent of Indians, 25 percent of Filipinos, and 31 percent of Japanese Americans do so. Looking next at differences by citizenship status, we see that ethnic news consumption is indeed higher among noncitizens than among citizens, but more than 40 percent of the Asian American electorate gets political information from some ethnic media source. What the final set of results in figure 2.6 suggest, however, is that this high level of ethnic news consumption among citizens is due to the behavior of naturalized citizens and not those born in the United States.

Finally, our analysis of the association between news consumption and political participation reveals some interesting patterns. The first set of rows in table 2.10 shows the relationships between news sources without respect to distinctions by language, and the second set shows the relationships for Asian-language news sources in particular. The first results indicate that watching television news is positively associated with voting and making political contributions to political campaigns, but is insignificant for other types of political activities. By contrast, getting information from newspapers and radio is positively associated with all five forms of participation. Finally, those who get political information

Figure 2.7   Ethnic Media Consumption, Proportion and Number
of Sources

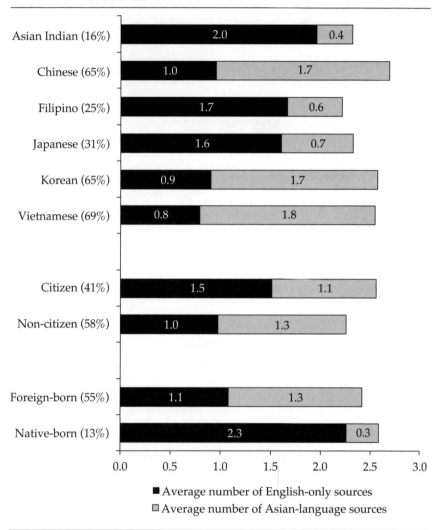

Source: Authors' compilation of data from the 2008 National Asian American Survey (Ramakrishnan et al. 2011).
Note: Proportion of ethnic news sources are indicated in parentheses.

Table 2.10   Political Participation by News Consumption, Among U.S. Citizens

	Likely Voter	Contributor	Contact	Protester	Community Activist
Television	+	+	ns	ns	ns
Newspaper	+	+	+	+	+
Internet	ns	+	+	+	+
Radio	+	+	+	+	+
Ethnic TV	—	ns	ns	ns	ns
Ethnic newspaper	—	—	—	ns	—
Ethnic internet	—	—	—	ns	ns
Ethnic radio	ns	ns	ns	+	—

Source: Authors' compilation of data from the 2008 National Asian American Survey (Ramakrishnan et al. 2011).
Note: Rows 1 through 4 show results of regression of participation variables on any media sources; rows 5 through 8 show results of regression of participation variables on ethnic media sources. ns = not significant at the .10 level or greater.

from Internet sources are more likely to participate than those who don't, and this applies for all political activities outside voting. These findings regarding news consumption, while providing an important sense of how participants and nonparticipants may vary along this dimension, do not rule out the possibility that other related factors (such as education and age) may be driving some of these apparent differences. It is not until we construct our full explanatory model in chapter 7 that we can assess whether these relationships are important in and of themselves or instead reflect the pathways through which other factors, such as age and education, operate.

Running the same analysis for Asian-language media consumption, we find that paying attention to Asian-language television is negatively associated with voting but bears no significant relationship to other types of political activities. Overall, the relationship between ethnic media consumption and participation reveals either insignificant results or negative relationships—for instance, in the case of ethnic newspapers and Internet sources. Again, we should be careful not to over interpret these results at this stage, because other factors such as nativity and language proficiency may be fundamentally driving these results. The results of various statistical regressions we present in chapter 7 help address whether ethnic news consumption continues to have a negative relationship to participation if we control for other explanatory factors.

Finally, we see that paying attention to Asian ethnic radio sources is associated with protest activity. This is interesting given the attention that Spanish-language radio has devoted to voter registration and naturalization efforts since the spring 2006 marches in favor of immigrant rights (Felix, Gonzalez, and Ramirez 2008). This may suggest that some Asian-language radio stations play a similar role, though we cannot rule out the possibility of having a spurious correlation: for instance, high rates of protest among Vietnamese Americans may be due to other underlying factors (such as refugee status, anticommunist ideology, and residence in ethnic enclaves) rather than to the higher consumption of ethnic news radio per se among Vietnamese Americans. We examine the relationship between ethnic media consumption and protest activity in the context of a multivariate regression in chapter 7, but even then, we cannot establish a clear causal relationship between the two factors.

BILINGUAL VOTING MATERIALS

Another important aspect of language use among Asian Americans is the extent to which they might find it useful to have access to ballot materials in a language other than English. Language access is an important part of election administration in the United States, as Section 203 of the Voting Rights Act mandates language assistance in jurisdictions with significant language minority populations. Areas are deemed to be covered under Section 203 if more than 5 percent of the voting-age population or more than ten thousand residents in a particular language group is limited-English proficient (U.S. Department of Justice 2010). In chapter 3, we examine the geography of language-access provision for Chinese, Tagalog, Vietnamese, Korean, and Japanese across various counties in the United States, and the extent to which the presence of such language provision makes a difference for voter turnout and other types of political participation.

Here, however, we focus on a different aspect to the story on ballot language access—namely, the extent to which Asian Americans may find such provisions useful. Research suggests that having ballot language materials in Asian languages gives voters greater access to political information (Yang and Gaines 2008; Magpantay and Yu 2005). In her 2005 testimony to the National Commission on the Voting Rights Act, Kathy Feng, former lead attorney for Voting Rights at the Asian Pacific American Legal Center in Los Angeles, described the importance of language access to political materials and ballots for Asian Americans:

Until 1999, the presence of a bilingual poll worker, or bilingual voting instructions in their poll site, was based on luck. LA County was not required to deploy bilingual poll workers in every poll site and had no good recruiting or targeting system for where to deploy its scarce bilingual resources. For the thousands of Asian American voters who did not speak English well, many of whom were first time voters, the language barrier and the punchcard voting machine prevented them from voting accurately or sometimes voting at all. (Feng 2005)

Although existing studies point to the usefulness of Asian-language ballot materials, much of the evidence is based on an examination of exit polls in covered jurisdictions, leaving unanswered the question of what proportion of Asian Americans who live in uncovered jurisdictions would nevertheless find it useful to have access to ballot materials in their Asian language. One advantage of our national survey over exit polls in urban areas is that we are much more likely to interview respondents in uncovered jurisdictions. However, the challenge is what question to ask. Based on consultations with the Asian Pacific American Legal Center in Los Angeles, we asked respondents in our Asian-language interviews the following question: "If election materials were available to you in your language, would you make use of them?"

Among those asked, we found that more than four in five adult citizens who took the survey in an Asian-language or who described themselves as demonstrating a low-level of proficiency in English (81 percent) would do so. When we expand the denominator to include all adult citizens (regardless of language of interview), we find that 28 percent would use bilingual election materials, and that such use is much greater among naturalized citizens (38 percent) than among native-born (3 percent). In line with our findings on English-language proficiency, Vietnamese (60 percent), Korean (49 percent), and Chinese Americans (37 percent) are much more likely to find such materials useful than Filipinos (11 percent), Asian Indians (7 percent), and Japanese Americans (1.5 percent). Despite some of these subgroup differences, we can say overall that the availability of ballot materials in Asian languages will likely have a salutary effect on the political participation of Asian Americans.

TRANSNATIONAL ACTIVITIES

Increasing globalization tends to strengthen bonds to the homeland. Air travel and sophisticated yet increasingly accessible communications systems such as the Internet, email, and cell phones facilitate these transnational attachments. Contemporary immigrants' linkages to their countries of origin are both strong and varied. Many return home frequently, send money, build cross-border social networks and communities, and invest in projects and property in their former hometowns. Some immigrants remain politically active in their homelands. In an age marked by rapid globalization, attention must be paid to the transnational character of migration.

Although transnational migration is a growing and robust topic in contemporary scholarship, transnationalism is not a new phenomenon: previous waves of European immigrants frequently traveled to their countries of origin (Smith and Guarnizo 1998; Morawska 2001). Early waves of Asian immigrants also maintained ties. Thus, for instance, Chinese immigrants established Gold Mountain firms in cities such as Los Angeles, Pittsburgh, New York, and Boston, operated these firms from their storefronts, and would deliver remittances and letters between Taishanese migrants in the United States and their family members in China (Hsu 2000; Wang 2001). As we noted earlier in this chapter, Korean immigrants and Indian immigrants were also actively involved in the politics of their homelands during the early part of the twentieth century, with the latter even mobilizing militarily to secure Indian independence from Great Britain.

More recent scholarship emphasizes immigrants' enduring ties to their countries of origin and their implications for political participation in the United States. Some researchers have suggested that immigrants with strong ties to their countries of origin focus on their homeland politics almost exclusively and are thus less active in American politics (Portes and Rumbaut 1996; Barone 2001). Using a survey of Asian Americans in five metropolitan areas, Pei-Te Lien, M. Margaret Conway, and Janelle Wong find that while many Asian Americans pay attention to news from Asia and maintain strong ties with family and friends in Asia, very few take part in activities dealing with politics in the country of origin after arriving in the United States, from 4 percent among Chinese and Korean respondents to 10 percent among Vietnamese (Lien, Conway, and Wong 2004). Further, despite some speculation that political involvement in homeland politics depresses political participation in the United States, they report that involvement in activities is unrelated to voting in the United States. More critically, political involvement with the home country is associated positively with participation in other types of political activities (160).

Finally, the effects of immigrant ties to their country of origin on naturalization remains an open question, as some find that it dampens naturalization (Yang 1994; Pantoja 2005), whereas others find the opposite effect (Jones-Correa 2001). Adrian Pantoja and Wong's analysis of PNAAPS data suggest that ties to the home country—political or otherwise—are not strongly associated with naturalization for Asian Americans as a whole (2009). However, for particular groups, such as Asian Indians, transnational ties may help account for lower naturalization rates, but not participation once immigrants become citizens of the United States (Mishra 2009).

Turning to the NAAS survey results, we can see that a high proportion of Asian Americans keep in touch with family and friends in their countries of origin. This is perhaps not surprising, given the high proportion of first-generation immigrants among Asian American adults. Indeed, the highest level of contact is among the most recently arrived groups, such as Asian Indians. However, contact is also high among Korean Americans, for whom immigration has slowed in the past two decades. Finally, even though many Vietnamese immigrants maintain a strong antipathy to the communist government in Vietnam, they have high rates of contact with family and friends, and the highest rate of remittances to their home countries (58 percent). Remittance activity is similar for Filipino respondents, but considerably lower for Japanese Americans and Korean Americans (17 percent). The gap between high rates of home country contact and low rates of remittances among Korean Americans is an interesting phenomenon, and future qualitative studies of Korean immigrants may shed light on why this gap is particularly wide.

Finally, we find that, consistent with past results, involvement in homeland politics is quite low compared with other types of transnational activity. Table 2.11 shows that among Asian Americans as a whole, only 4 percent report taking part in activities that deal with politics related to the country of origin. The incidence of participation is so low, however, that the only statistically significant differences are between the very low rates of participation among Japanese, Koreans, and Vietnamese on the one hand, and among Chinese and Asian Indians on the other. Additional analysis suggests somewhat lower rates of transnational participation among citizens compared with noncitizens, but the differences tend to be less dramatic than might be expected (40 percent versus 34 percent when it comes to sending money and no difference when it comes to involvement in homeland politics).

How do transnational ties relate to political participation in the United States? Here we provide a preliminary analysis of bivariate associations to answer the question of whether domestic political participation is lower among those who are involved in their home countries. Later, in chapter 7, we provide a more comprehensive analysis of whether transnational ties are associated with lower political participation in the United States. Our bivariate analysis indicates no significant relationship between sending money home and getting involved in U.S. politics. Indeed, the results indicate a weak positive association between remittance activity and U.S.-

Table 2.11 Transnational Participation

	Asian Indian	Chinese	Filipino	Japanese	Korean	Vietnamese	Total
Communicated with family and friends	87	74	67	59	82	74	75
Sent money	38	27	57	12	17	58	36
Involved in politics	5	5	4	1	1	2	4

Source: Authors' compilation of data from the 2008 National Asian American Survey (Ramakrishnan et al. 2011).
Note: Rates are in percentages.

based political participation. Turning next to home-country political activism, we do see a weak negative relationship, although for all other political activities, the relationship is stronger and in the opposite direction. Thus political contributions tend to more frequent among those who take part in homeland politics (23 percent) than those who do not (12 percent). Similarly, contacting a government official is more likely among those who take part (33 percent) than among those who do not (8 percent). Finally, those who take part in homeland politics are more than twice as likely to protest and more than three times as likely to work with others to solve a community problem. Thus those who take part in homeland politics are a very small but politically active segment of the Asian American community. This group is active in both homeland politics and U.S. politics. These findings are consistent with research on other groups as well (Levitt and Waters 2002).

OPPORTUNITY COSTS AND THE MODEL MINORITY MYTH

We have focused on factors related to immigrant socialization in this chapter, including nativity, length of residence, English proficiency, transnationalism, and the like. Although not directly related to migration, we include one final factor that often passes for conventional wisdom among elected officials, party leaders, and even many Asian American activists: that one of the primary reasons why Asian immigrants have low rates of political participation is that they are more concerned about their personal economic conditions than about collective political outcomes. As newcomers who may be facing tenuous economic prospects, they may feel pressure to devote most of their energy to work and supporting their families (Horton and Calderon 1995; Ramakrishnan 2005). Thus, an Asian immigrant may work extra hours in one job or work multiple jobs, and have no time or interest for political activities. Presumably, as they become citizens and stay longer in the United States, these immigrants may feel enough economic security to begin participating in politics. We label these explanations *economic toehold* theories of why Asian Americans may not be interested in politics.

Certain versions of the model minority myth among Asian Americans also proclaim the primacy of economic concerns over political ones, but from a different perspective. Instead of arguing that Asian immigrants are trying to maintain a toehold in a society characterized by discrimination and blocked opportunities, proponents of the model minority myth argue that Asian Americans are a unique minority group in American society because they seek economic advancement without making excessive political demands or complaining about discrimination (Pettersen 1966; Mc-Gowan and Lindgren 2006). As Frank Wu notes about the ideas underlying the model minority myth: Asian Americans do not whine about racial discrimination; they only try harder. If they are told that they have a weakness that prevents their social acceptance, they quickly agree and earnestly attempt to cure it. If they are subjected to mistreatment by their employer, they quit and establish their own company rather than protest or sue (2002, 44).

Why is the model minority stereotype a myth? First, it was seen as a vehicle for disciplining other racial minority groups, namely black Americans, and to undermine their protests against persistent racial discrimination. It also served to silence Asian Americans. The logic of the stereotype implies that racial discrimination is overcome by hard work and strong family values, rather than by protests and demands for civil rights (Kim 1999).

Scholars of Asian American studies offer additional critiques of the stereotype (compare Takaki 1989; Cheng and Yang 1996; Wu 2002; Lee 2009; Junn 2008). For example, some contend that the model minority stereotype is dehumanizing, portraying Asian Americans as robot-like strivers, concerned only with memorizing SAT practice questions. Others claim higher incomes are due to Asian Americans relative concentration in high cost-of-living cities and the fact that Asian American households tend to include more workers per household on average. Further, the stereotype assumes that success is based on cultural values, and neglects the role of U.S. immigration policy in terms of actively recruiting highly skilled workers from Asia (compare Junn 2008).

One of the most important lines of research related to the stereotype has to do with racial lumping, the tendency to group all people of Asian origin together. This tendency elides national-origin distinctions, as well as differences having to do with immigrant generation (Espiritu 1993; Omi and Winant 1994). Hence, one of the most important critiques of the stereotype is an empirical one—not all Asian American national-origin groups exhibit exceptional rates of educational and economic achievement. In fact, some groups constitute some of the least well-off in society. The model minority myth may lead policymakers to overlook lack of resources in these communities.

Perhaps the most insidious assumption embedded in the model minority myth as it relates to Asian American politics is not just that Asian Americans are successful in the labor force and other minority groups are not, but that their success has depended on avoiding explicitly political strategies to advance their group interests.

What the economic toehold theories as well the model minority myth have in common is the attention they pay to the opportunity costs of work. Under either scenario—whether to maintain stability under precarious economic and social conditions or to dramatically expand one's economic fortunes—the underlying assumption is that most of an immigrant's time is wisely spent on work and private economic benefits instead of on leisure or the acquisition of public goods.

Political science has not paid much attention to the opportunity costs of voting and other forms of political participation. In the 1970s, some studies attempted to estimate the effects of opportunity costs of work on voting, but were critiqued for their simple association of wages with opportunity costs, and for problems with estimating the benefits to participation (Frey 1971; Tollison and Willett 1973; Niemi 1976). One problem with estimating the benefits to voting is that the importance of political contests often vary according to whether the election is presidential or midterm, local or national, close contests or wide blowouts (Niemi 1976). Furthermore, a narrow cost-benefit calculation based on public goods such as election outcomes would predict very low participation because of the problem of free riding (people benefiting from the election outcome regardless of whether or not they participate). Finally, these early studies of opportunity costs were hobbled by associating the concept narrowly with wages.

We sought to avoid these two pitfalls—trying to estimate the benefits of participation, and associating opportunity costs narrowly with wages—by borrowing from some recent developments in the study of environmental recreation. As Peter Feather and Douglass Shaw note in their study of outdoor recreation, the opportunity costs of time is best measured by asking people about how they would use time, rather than estimating it from reported wages (1999). Thus they rely on a question that asks whether people would be willing to give up an hour of work for leisure time. Here we estimate the opportunity costs of work-related time by asking respondents this question: "If you had one extra hour per day, how would you spend it? For example, would you spend more time with family and friends, more time at work, or something else?" We rotated the first two categories to avoid any potential problem with response order bias. We also avoided explicitly asking about political or civic participation as an option because of various types of measurement error associated with that strategy, including overreporting of such preferences due to social desirability.[16] Because we are primarily interested in testing explanations that center on the opportunity costs of work, having only three choices of work, friends-family, and something else is sufficient.

Table 2.12 presents our findings on the opportunity costs of work and how it varies by nativity. We also present the relationships between the

Table 2.12 Use of an Extra Hour Per Day, and Its Relationship to Participation

	Total	Foreign-Born	Native-Born	Likely Voter	Contributor	Contact	Protester	Community Activist
Friends and family	62	64	63	43	11	10	4	23
Work	7	8	4	37	19	8	5	19
Something else	29	28	33	51	14	9	5	20
Don't know	2	64	63	—	—	—	—	—
Refused	0	8	4	—	—	—	—	—

Source: Authors' compilation of data from the 2008 National Asian American Survey (Ramakrishnan et al. 2011).
Note: Rates are in percentages.

use of extra time and various types of political activities. Perhaps surprisingly, given the stereotypes about Asian American workers, we find that only 7 percent of respondents indicated that they would spend more time on work, and most said that they would do so with family and friends (62 percent) or on something else (29 percent). We also find that the foreign-born are more likely to say they would spend more time at work than the native-born. These differences are statistically significant at the .001 level, but the magnitude of these differences are less dramatic than one would expect given the economic toehold hypothesis.

Finally, we see that the opportunity cost of work has its strongest effects on two activities: voting and contributing to politics. Those who would spend more time at work are indeed less likely to vote than those who would spend more time elsewhere. However, those who would spend more time at work are also more likely to contribute money to politics. One might argue that the latter finding is driven by the fact that people who would want to work more are the ones with higher wages, and thus more likely to contribute. However, we find that those in higher income brackets are less likely to spend time at work than their lower-income counterparts. A more plausible explanation seems to be that people with high opportunity costs of working are less likely to sacrifice their time for voting, but are more likely to give money for political causes. Interestingly, however, these patterns do not apply to other types of political activities such as contacting elected officials or protesting.

CONCLUSION

We began this chapter with a focus on national-origin differences within the Asian American population. Although we do find important national-origin differences in political participation, the bulk of the findings in this chapter suggest that these differences do not render the Asian American category meaningless in terms of understanding the group's participation in U.S. politics. Instead, we argue that considering the group as a whole reveals a common set of factors related to immigrant adaption and socialization that strongly influence levels and types of political engagement for Asian Americans.

In addition, past waves of scholarship posit that political participation depends in large part on socioeconomic resources, political orientations, and recruitment networks that draw individuals into the political arena. Our analysis demonstrates that though these factors may play a role in Asian American political participation, because the group is heavily immigrant, we must also look beyond the conventional influences on political participation. In particular, we contend that forces specific to the immigrant adaptation experience in the United States—nativity, length of stay, English-language proficiency and ethnic media consumption, transnational ties, and focus on economic mobility—may be as powerful, or more powerful, in shaping Asian American political participation as conventional variables like socioeconomic status. This chapter builds on research that suggests that Americans may be socialized into politics through multiple channels. For Asian Americans, the motivation to participate in politics may flow through the adaptation process and over several generations. As such, we cannot understand Asian American political participation without serious attention to the factors that affect their integration and adaptation to American society. We embark on a deeper exploration of the association between variables related to these socialization forces and political participation in chapter 7.

Immigrant adaptation factors may play an important role in facilitating the political participation of the contemporary immigrant community, but Asian Americans, and each national-origin subgroup within the Asian American community, constitute an ever-changing population. The shape of Asian American communities has long been contoured by foreign policy and immigration policy in the United States, economic and political conditions in the countries of origin, and attitudes toward Asian Americans among non-Asians in the United States. These contouring mechanisms will change, as will Asian American adaptation patterns, and both compel us to consider immigrant adaptation among Asians as an evolving process into the future.

Chapter 3 | Political Geography

POLITICS IS AN inherently spatial phenomenon. Nation-states are defined by their geographic boundaries. Electoral offices, from the Senate and the House of Representatives at the federal level to the city council, county sheriff, and district judgeships at the local level, carry jurisdictions bounded by geography. Civil wars and ethnic riots are fought over borderlands and collective remembrances of space. Voters may all share equal standing as citizens, but they can exercise their rights only in the precincts to which they have been assigned. Territoriality, in short, is conjoined to governance and governments.

In political science, the origins of scholarly attention to the effects of context are more commonly attributed to works like Harold Gosnell's field-experimental studies of political machines in Chicago (1927, 1935, 1937),[1] V. O. Key's pioneering research on spatial patterns of voting in the pre–civil rights era South (1949), and the Columbia studies of social influence in Erie, Decatur, and Elmira counties in the 1940s (Lazarsfeld, Berelson, and Gaudet 1948; Berelson, Lazarsfeld, and McPhee 1954; Katz and Lazarsfeld 1955). For reasons beyond the current scope and aim of this chapter, this salience of geographically bounded contexts in the study of political behavior receded behind the curtains by the 1960s. To some extent, this falling from favor was due to a growing partiality for generalizability—of the kind found in the survey-based behavioralist approach in *The American Voter* (Campbell et al. 1960)—and for parsimony—of the kind found in the formal, deductive approach in *An Economic Theory of Democracy* (Downs 1957). The shift away from context is also surely propelled by the methodological challenges—the perils of snowball samples, case studies, ecological inference, and the like—involved in endeavoring to study space and place with social scientific rigor.

More recently, however, scholarship on political context has revived significantly. This surge in attention to the role of political contexts has generated considerable debates over methods, and can generally be classified into four groups.

- One group consists of survey-based studies of local communities, building on methodological innovations in sampling, collection of social network data, and opportunities for longitudinal study. Robert Huckfeldt and his colleagues (Huckfeldt 1979, 1986; Huckfeldt and Sprague 1987, 1995) are the most prominent among those promoting this line of inquiry. In the area of race and ethnicity, examples of prominent recent studies taking this approach include the Multicity Study of Urban Inequality (O'Connor, Tilly, and Bobo 2003), the Moving to Opportunity (MTO) studies (Sampson, Morenoff, and Gannon-Rowley 2002; Sampson 2008), and the Children of Immigrants Longitudinal Study (Portes and Rumbaut 2001).

- Another group relies on self-reported measures of neighborhood composition and political context (MacKuen and Brown 1987; Welch et al. 2001).

- Third are studies that sample and pool data on a large number of contexts. Examples include the fifty U.S. states (Erikson, Wright, and McIver 1993; Hero 1998, 2007); electoral districts, such as the Cooperative Congressional Election Surveys (Kernell 2009); and multiple municipalities, such as the Community Benchmark Study (Putnam 2007; de Sousa Briggs 2008; Cho 2008).

- A final approach, which we propose to undertake in this chapter, entails merging geocoded contextual-level data—available in large databases like the decennial census, the Current Population Survey—with individual-level survey data (Cohen and Dawson 1993; Oliver and Mendelberg 2000; Oliver and Wong 2003; Branton and Jones 2005; Gay 2006a, 2006b; Ramakrishnan and Espenshade 2001).

As with any popular and growing line of inquiry centered on a concept, grounds for skepticism are ample. Looking ahead in this book, we note in chapter 5 the growing register of complaint against the overselling of the concept of identity. The same charge could be made of the concept of context. Across the growing body of works on context, the conceptual thickets are many and barbed. The starting point for most concerns and criticisms about research context is the unit of analysis. This varies from census blocks and tracts to zip codes, precincts, counties, metropolitan areas, media markets, legislative districts, states, and in some comparative research, nation-states themselves.

A clear consequence of this lack of consistency in the basic units of measurement is that the root mechanisms through which context influences one's politics are almost certain to differ. In fact, in approaches such as the one we pursue in this chapter, the best statistical inferences we can draw are second-order associations between patterns we find in our various contextual-level indicia and patterns we observe in our individual-level measures of political engagement. Studies of political context are much better at demonstrating *whether* space and place matter than they are at specifying *why* and *how* space and place matter. Or, put in other terms, spaces and places do not "do things" in the same way that voters vote and politicians legislate. Rather, the effects of context are always indirect and multiple. Where an Asian American settles may determine how many other Asian Americans, whites, African Americans, and Latinos live near them (and thus affect the constitution of friendship networks, coalition partners, endogamy and exogamy rates, and so on), whether local labor markets are shrinking or robust, whether bonding and bridging social capital is rife or in short supply, what civic and political institutions are present, what forms of political representation and modes of political voice are available, and so on.

How to study context and what to make of its effects are worth exploring. When it comes to understanding the political geography of Asian Americans, however, a more basic task is pressing. Given the shortage of national political data on Asian Americans, we do not yet have a comprehensive assessment of where Asian Americans live in relation to various social and political contexts, such as living in states with nonpartisan local elections, or in electoral districts with an Asian American representative. Past surveys of Asian Americans have either been confined to a few metropolitan areas, or have relied on exit polls of the Asian American population that are limited in several respects: they survey only voters (missing out on nonvoting citizens and noncitizens), they are primarily conducted in precincts with relatively high concentrations of Asian Americans, and—perhaps most important from the perspective of this chapter—they do not contain information about place of residence.

The NAAS dataset is useful for the study of contextual influences on behavior in that it includes a broad range of contextual variables—demographic, social, economic and political characteristics pegged to particular geographic units that allow for in-depth study of the interplay between context and political attitudes and behavior. As such, future studies will be able to take advantage of this collection of individual-level data on Asian American participation and extensive measures of political context to answer many of the most challenging questions raised above. Our intent here, however, is neither to oversell the findings in this chapter nor to imply that we have settled extant debates over political context—far from it. Our aims in this chapter, are far more focused. To date, few studies have been undertaken on the effects of political context on the political participation of Asian Americans beyond that of Wendy Tam Cho (Cho 1995, 2001, 2003; Gimpel, Shaw, and Cho 2006). Thus, in this chapter we aim to provide baseline information about the contexts in which Asian Americans reside and descriptive information about the basic relationship between geographic context and political participation among Asian Americans. This is admittedly a descriptive and exploratory point of departure, but also a necessary first step in any analysis of the contexts of Asian Americans politics and whether these contexts play a role in whether and when Asian Americans come to be politically engaged.

Empirically examining the geographic contexts of Asian Americans and their consequences for politics can be done a number of ways. A standard approach is to look at residential contexts. Here, the analysis begins with a choice of the basic geographic unit of analysis—most commonly, states, census regions, metropolitan areas, counties, census tracts, congressional districts, and the like. Some decision is then required on what to observe for that unit of analysis. The range here is also broad, from measures of demographic context (such as the proportion of Asian Americans living in an area, or an index of residential segregation, or some indicator of demographic change) to social or economic contexts (such as poverty rates, unemployment levels, the density of particular organizational forms, like nonprofits and churches).

Because this book is concerned with Asian American political behavior, we can also think of characterizing the Asian American population in more explicitly political ways that vary across geographically defined locales. For a given unit of analysis, we might measure the prevalence of aggregated individual-level outcomes like the proportion of registered Democrats, the incidence and magnitude of campaign contributions, and so on. We might also measure more institutionally based indicators of political representation and competition—for instance, differentiating Asian Americans according to whether they live in a district represented by an Asian American politician, whether they live in a marginal district vis-à-vis partisan competition, whether the political offices in their local area are fixed by term limits, whether in-language materials are available, whether more robust opportunities for democratic contestation like initiative and referendum politics are available, and so on.

In this chapter, we present descriptive findings for both types of contexts, given available data. Before jumping into the analysis, we remind readers that the geographic units here vary depending on the type of context being measured. For some of our contextual variables, the presence or absence of a discernible pattern between context and political engagement may be the by-product of our chosen units of analysis rather than the absence of any influences of context.

WHERE DO ASIAN AMERICANS LIVE?

Cautions against treating Asian Americans as a monolith apply not only to characteristics like national origin, language, religion, and immigrant generation (see chapter 2), but also to places of residence in the United States. For instance, if one's spatial context is politically meaningful, we might expect two Hawaii residents—one Japanese American and the other Filipino American—to have more in common politically with one another than with their co-ethnic counterparts in other states. Similarly, we might expect two Asian Americans—one Buddhist and the other Hindu—living in a new destination metropolitan area such as Fort Worth, Texas, to have a greater overlap in their politics than with their religious counterparts in traditional gateway metropolitan areas. When thinking about the national Asian American population, certain states and other geographical contexts may be more politically consequential than others.

An obvious starting point in seeking out potential connections between macro-level spatial contexts and micro-level political attitudes and behavior is to first describe where Asian Americans live. There are generally two ways to cut at geographical settlement patterns. One is to look at the distribution of the total population of Asian Americans across the country by some specified geographical unit (regions, states, metropolitan areas, for example). Another way to is to look at the concentration of Asian Americans within particular geographic or political units of interest (such as regions, states, cities, congressional districts, and wards). Each imparts a different kind of perspective on the places where Asian Americans settle, and we consider each in turn.

GEOGRAPHIC DISTRIBUTION

There are several reasons to pay attention to the geographic distribution of Asian Americans. Most important, we may find that particular patterns of Asian American behavior—from immigrant socialization to party identification and political participation—are due more to the state contexts in which Asian Americans live than to factors such as differences in national origin and educational attainment. The predominance of California and its particular array of political institutions (including nonpartisan local elections and the frequent use of the ballot initiative), suggests that state-level factors may play an important explanatory role. Another reason is

Table 3.1   Top Five States of Residence, by Group

Asian–Pacific Islander		Latino		White		Black	
California	33	California	29	California	8	New York	8
New York	9	Texas	19	New York	6	Georgia	7
Texas	6	Florida	8	Texas	6	Texas	7
Hawaii	5	New York	7	Florida	6	Florida	7
New Jersey	4	Arizona	4	Pennsylvania	5	California	6
Total	58%		67%		30%		36%

Source: Authors' compilation of data from 2008 American Community Survey (U.S. Census Bureau 2008a).
Note: The figures represent the national share of the population in each area, in percentages.

that geographic distribution plays a significant role in shaping the distribution of community organizations, ethnic media, and Asian American elected officials across the United States.

Asian Americans are among the most geographically concentrated groups in the United States. Just one state (California) accounts for 30 percent of the national population, four states (California, New York, Texas, and Hawaii) account for a majority, and adding a fifth (New Jersey) brings the total to 58 percent (see table 3.1). By contrast, California accounts for only 8 percent of whites nationally, and the top five states for just 30 percent of the white population in the United States. Similarly, the top five states account for just 36 percent of the national black population.

Only Latinos are more concentrated than Asian Americans in particular states: the top five states account for 67 percent of the national Latino population. One important contrast between Asian Americans and Latinos is that for Latinos, the correspondence between states with a large Latino population and specific ethnic-national origin groups is close: New York has a high concentration of Puerto Ricans, Florida has a high concentration of Cubans, and California and the Southwest have a high concentration of Mexicans. To an extent, this is a story of proximate borders, whether by sea or by land, for Latinos. For Asian Americans, it is more of a story about the long effects of bicoastal gateways (both literal and figurative). The presence of Texas on the list of states with a significant Asian American population is a relatively new development, which we discuss later in this chapter in our analysis of new destinations.

This contrast between Asians and Latinos is not meant to imply that there is no ethnicity-specific clustering of Asian Americans. Looking at the major national origin groups within the Asian American population, we find that some groups are much more concentrated than others. The comparisons shown in table 3.2 are too many to detail comprehensively, but several key findings are illustrative:

- Japanese Americans have the highest degree of residential concentration by state, in that nearly 75 percent of the national population live in five states, California and Hawaii themselves accounting for well over a majority of the national Japanese American population. By contrast, only 57 percent of Indian Americans and 59 percent of Korean Americans are concentrated in the top five states.

- More specifically, California is far less important to the national Indian American population (20 percent) than it is to all other groups, for which the state accounts for 30 percent or more of their various populations. For Filipinos, by contrast, California accounts for nearly half of the national population, making the political socialization and behavior of Californians crucial to our overall understanding of Filipino civic and political behavior.

- Hawaii—the state with the highest proportion of Asian Americans relative to the total state population (38 percent of Asian alone and 55 percent of Asian alone or in combination) and the second-largest state for the number of Filipinos and Japanese Americans—accounts for a relatively insignificant share of the national population for the other four national-origin groups.

The specificity of Asian ethnic-national origin populations to different states should not belie the fact that many commonalities remain. One commonality is that California, New York, New Jersey, and Texas rank in the top five states for most groups. Another is that well over a majority of each national-origin group can be found in the top five states, Japanese Americans being the most concentrated (73 percent), and Asian Indians the least (57 percent).

When thinking about the ways to characterize political participation among Asian Americans across the United States, a fifty-state strategy would prove unwieldy, in terms of both data presentation and sample size, even with a survey of more than 5,000 respondents. However, we are able to present differences in rates of citizenship and political participation by larger geographic units. In table 3.3, we present the number of Asian Americans living in each census region (West, Northeast, Midwest, South), as well as figures for two census divisions that are particularly important as new areas of settlement (the mid-Atlantic and Mountain West). What emerges from these findings is a remarkable similarity in the rates of citizenship and voting participation across regions, with one ex-

Table 3.2 Top Five States of Residence, by National Origin

Asian Indian		Chinese		Filipino		Japanese		Korean		Vietnamese	
California	20	California	40	California	48	California	35	California	32	California	40
New York	12	New York	16	Hawaii	8	Hawaii	26	New York	10	Texas	12
New Jersey	10	Texas	4	New York	5	New York	5	New Jersey	6	Washington	4
Illinois	8	New Jersey	4	Illinois	5	Washington	4	Illinois	5	Virginia	3
Texas	7	Massachusetts	4	New Jersey	5	Texas	2	Texas	5	Florida	3
Total	57%		68%		70%		73%		59%		64%

Source: Authors' compilation of data from 2008 American Community Survey (U.S. Census Bureau 2008a).
Note: The figures represent the national share of the population in each area, in percentages.

ception: the West region, where the proportion of adult citizens is 8 to 10 percentage points higher than elsewhere in the country, and where Asian American voting in the 2004 election was 7 to 10 percentage points higher than in other regions.

This Western advantage is absent, however, for other measures of participation. For instance, the rates of contributions to political campaigns are similar across regions, with the exception of the Midwest, where the contribution rates among Asian Americans (8 percent) is less than the national average (13 percent). At the same time, Asian Americans in the Midwest are also the ones most likely to work with others on solving community problems. As we shall see later in this chapter, these regional differences may indeed be due to systematic contextual factors such as the level of party competition, the prevalence of direct democracy, and the size of the Asian American population relative to other groups. At a descriptive level, however, levels of political and civic participation do indeed seem to vary by region.

GEOGRAPHIC CONCENTRATION

Tallying raw numbers of Asian Americans across states (or other contextual unit) is one way of representing the distribution of this population. Another means is to look again at the same contextual units to see where Asian Americans are most densely concentrated. By concentration, we mean a group's share of the total population of a region. Concentration does not always correspond with the size of the Asian American population because the measure depends not only on the numerator (how many Asian Americans live in the area), but also on the denominator (the area's overall population size). Thus, for instance, Yuba City in the Central Valley of California—which has had a long-standing Sikh population since the early 1900s—shows an Asian American population of about 9,000 residents in 2007. By contrast, the population in Baltimore, Maryland, is about 12,000. When it comes to population concentration, however, Asian Americans are about 15 percent of the population in Yuba City, but less than 2 percent of Baltimore. Thus we would expect Asian Americans to be more politically active in Yuba City than in Baltimore, though differences in naturalization rates across regions can add yet another layer of difference. These differences can be politically consequential, because the electoral incentives for a politician to be responsive and accountable to a particular constituency roughly correspond to that constituency's proportional size and to the competitiveness of the politician's office (Griffin 2006).

Table 3.3 Regional Distribution of Asian Americans

	Census Region				Census Division	
	Northeast	Midwest	South	West	Mid-Atlantic	Mountain West
Number of Asian American residents	3,003,418	1,822,097	3,248,302	7,398,477	1,880,292	743,963
Percentage adult citizens	47	45	47	57	48	49
Percentage eligible citizens who voted, 2004	59	58	57	67	60	57
Percentage adults who contributed to campaigns	13	8	15	13	13	11
Percentage adults who have worked on a community problem	21	27	21	21	22	21

Source: Authors' compilation of data from the 2008 American Community Survey (U.S. Census Bureau 2008a) and the 2008 National Asian American Survey (Ramakrishnan et al. 2011).

Table 3.4   Concentration of Asian American Population,
Top Ten States

	Total Population	Asian Population	Share of Resident Population	Share of Electorate (Adult Citizens)
Hawaii	1,280,273	708,074	55%	54%
California	36,418,499	4,915,229	14	12
New Jersey	8,658,668	685,068	8	6
Washington	6,453,083	505,255	8	7
New York	19,428,881	1,415,502	7	6
Nevada	2,546,235	181,002	7	6
Alaska	681,235	39,802	6	5
Maryland	5,618,250	309,358	6	4
Virginia	7,698,738	414,944	5	4
Massachusetts	6,469,770	336,803	5	4
United States	301,237,703	14,863,151	5	4

Source: Authors' compilation of data from the 2006–2008 American Community Survey (U.S. Census Bureau 2008c).

Table 3.4 presents raw population counts and the concentration of the Asian American population for the ten states with the highest Asian American proportion of the total. To draw the electoral connection here into even bolder relief, we also show the Asian American proportion of the total population of adult citizens in these states.

One state towers over the rest in this respect: more than one of every two residents of Hawaii identify as Asian American (either alone or in combination). This majority status holds even by the more restrictive focus on Asian Americans as a percentage of all adult citizens in Hawaii. The next state is California, which we saw in table 3.1 to be the most important in terms of national distribution. Roughly 14 percent (one in seven) of Californians and 12 percent (one in eight) of adult citizens in California are Asian American. The proportions drop in other states: in New Jersey, Washington, New York, and Nevada just over 7 percent of the total population identify as Asian American.

States with the largest population counts of Asian Americans are not necessarily those with the highest concentration, however. New York is home to more than 1.4 million Asian Americans, but they comprise only 7 percent of its population and only 5 percent of its citizenry. Hawaii, by contrast, has roughly half of New York's Asian American population in numbers, but a much greater concentration. Another contrast is Nevada, which has roughly the same concentration as New York, but many fewer in numbers.

A further implication from table 3.4 is that, despite the impressive growth in the total U.S. Asian American population, at the state level Asian Americans are likely to be a concentrated electoral force in only a few states. Only ten states (the ten shown in table 3.4) show a higher concentration than the national average (roughly 5 percent). In more than twenty-five states, Asian Americans make up less than 3 percent of the total population, and in more states, they make up less than 2 percent of the adult citizen population.

However, states are not the only relevant U.S. political jurisdictions: cities, counties, and congressional districts also matter. And in many of these, vote shares of 5 percent can often mean the difference between electoral victory and defeat. In table 3.5, we present places where Asian American citizens are especially politically concentrated across states, counties, congressional districts, and cities. For states and counties, the cut-point is a share of the adult citizen population that is 5 percent or greater; for congressional districts, it is at 10 percent or greater; and for cities, the cut-point is at 25 percent or greater. As we can see, the number of relevant jurisdictions grows dramatically when we look at the substate level.

Looking at counties, we find that Asian Americans constitute more than 5 percent of the adult citizen population in thirty-six counties. Not surprisingly, most of these are in Hawaii, California, New York, and New Jersey, although certain counties in Virginia (Fairfax and Loudoun) and Texas (Fort Bend) have concentrations that rival many counties in California, including Los Angeles and Contra Costa. At the congressional district level, we further find that Asian Americans are more than 5 percent of the citizen population in ninety districts and more than 10 percent in forty. They are a majority in the first congressional district of Hawaii, and more than 20 percent of the adult citizen population in ten others, nearly all of which are in California and Hawaii. The only exception here is the fifth district in New York, an area that includes the eastern parts of Queens and adjoining areas of Nassau County. In all eleven districts, the member of Congress is a Democrat, a partisan feature we will return to in chapter 4. Finally, when we go down to city politics, the ACS data show that Asian Americans are 5 percent or more of the adult citizen population in 443 cities. Table 3.6 presents the cities where Asian Americans are at least a quarter of the electorate, and these seventy-five cities are almost exclusively in California and Hawaii, with the exception of North Potomac in Maryland, Sugar Land in Texas, and Bergenfield in New Jersey.

Finally, although it is tempting to examine the political relevance of Asian American population size only with respect to the adult citizen

Table 3.5   Areas with Concentrated Adult Asian American Citizen Population

States (5%+) N=6	Hawaii (54%), California (12%), Washington (6.5%), Nevada (6.2%), New Jersey (6%), New York (5.5%)
Counties (5% +) N=36	Honolulu (HI), Santa Clara (CA), Kauai (HI), San Francisco (CA), Hawaii (HI), Maui (HI), San Mateo (CA), Alameda (CA), Queens (NY), Orange (CA), Middlesex (NJ), San Joaquin (CA), Fairfax City (VA), Fort Bend (TX), Los Angeles (CA), Solano (CA), Sacramento (CA), Contra Costa (CA), Fairfax (VA), Sutter (CA), Montgomery (MD), Somerset (NJ), Loudoun (VA), Bergen (NJ), Yolo (CA), King (WA), San Diego (CA), Howard (MD), Hudson (NJ), Fresno (CA), DuPage (IL), Gwinett (GA), Kings (NY), Collin (TX), New York (NY), Yuba (CA)
Congressional Districts (10%+) N=40 (20%+) N=11	CD-1 (HI, Abercrombie), CD-13 (CA, Stark), CD-12 (CA, Speier), CD-15 (CA, Honda), CD-2 (HI, Hirono), CD-16 (CA, Lofgren), CD-8 (CA, Pelosi), CD-29 (CA, Schiff), CD-47 (CA, Sanchez), CD-32 (CA, Chu), CD-5 (NY, Ackerman), CD-31 (CA), CD-40 (CA), CD-46 (CA), CD-42 (CA), CD-9 (CA), CD-14 (CA), CD-26 (CA), CD-7 (CA), CD-48 (CA), CD-12 (NY), CD-5 (CA), CD-51 (CA), CD-9 (NY), CD-36 (CA), CD-37 (CA), CD-38 (CA), CD-39 (CA), CD-27 (CA), CD-11 (CA), CD-50 (CA), CD-33 (CA), CD-7 (NY), CD-11 (VA), CD-6 (NY), CD-10 (CA), CD-9 (IL), CD-7 (WA), CD-8 (MD), CD-8 (NY)
Cities (25% +) N=75	Waipahu (HI), Monterey Park (CA), Pearl City (HI), Cerritos (CA), Kaluhui (HI), Rosemead (CA), Walnut (CA), Honolulu (CA), Milpitas (CA), Waimalu (HI), San Gabriel (CA), Daly City (CA), Temple City (CA), Mililani Town (HI), Alhambra (CA), Union City (CA), Rowland Heights (CA), Arcadia (CA), Westminster (CA), Cupertino (CA), Diamond Bar (CA), Hercules (CA), Hilo (Hawaii), Fremont (CA), Garden Grove (CA), Kaneohe (HI), South San Francisco (CA), Hacienda Heights (CA), Foster City (CA), Saratoga (CA), Gardena (CA), El Monte (CA), Millbrae (CA), Irvine (CA), San Jose (CA), North Potomac (MD), Fountain Valley (CA), San Francisco (CA), Sunnyvale (CA), Stanton (CA), Vineyard (CA), Newark (CA), Sugar Land (TX), Santa Clara (CA), Bergenfield borough (NJ), Alameda (CA), San Leandro (CA)

Source: Authors' compilation of data from the 2006–2008 American Community Survey (U.S. Census Bureau 2008c).
Note: Jurisdictions listed in descending order of concentration. Cities and counties where the total population is fewer than 20,000 or the Asian American population is fewer than 160 are not included.

population, in several key ways nonadults and noncitizens matter for issues of political participation and representation. As chapter 2 makes clear, noncitizens participate in various types of civic and political activities, albeit at lower rates (sometimes slightly, sometimes significantly) than naturalized citizens. All residents of the United States—adult and child, citizen and noncitizen—are counted for purposes of apportionment following the decennial federal census. For Asian Americans, this tabulation since 1868 has meant that, even when they were not eligible to naturalize, they were still counted as political subjects.[2]

Thus, if we were to look again at the places in table 3.5 where Asian Americans are a significant portion of the population and expanded the scope to include all residents, the number of states with 5 percent or more would jump from six to ten states, including Alaska, Maryland, Virginia, and Massachusetts.[3] The number of counties would expand from 36 to 92, the number of congressional districts from 91 to 103, and the number of cities from to 443 to 583.

NEW IMMIGRANT DESTINATIONS

Although the focus on geographic distribution and geographic concentration might suggest that the story of Asian American politics has a cast of a few stars (such as California, Hawaii, New York City, and the suburbs of Los Angeles) and many bit players, it would be a mistake to miss the recent and dramatic shift in this narrative. The biggest changes in the flow of immigration to the United States stem from the 1965 legislation that abolished national-origin quotas and made family reunification a significant basis of legal immigration. This change paved the way for Asians to migrate to the United States in large numbers. In the early part of this contemporary wave, immigrants from Asia went through a small number of gateway cities such as New York, Chicago, San Francisco, and Los Angeles.

In the past two decades, however, new destinations have sprung up, primarily as sources of direct migration from Asia and Latin America. Many new destinations are also significant places of remigration from large population centers (Massey 2008). Scholars of immigrant political incorporation are paying attention to these new destination areas for several reasons. Some argue that the newness of many of these settlement areas, combined with large distances to gateway cities of traditional migration, often mean fewer opportunities for participation in ethnic organizations. Instead, immigrants often participate in new organizations that cut across racial and ethnic lines, and benefit from the assistance of nonprofits such as refugee resettlement organizations and local colleges and universities (Andersen 2008). Other studies, based primarily on Latinos in new destinations, show that immigrant communities often lack political power through the ballot box, and often have to rely on bureaucratic incorporation rather than electoral mobilization (Jones-Correa 2008; Lewis and Ramakrishnan 2007; Marrow 2009).

For Asian Americans, cities such as Houston, Minneapolis, and Washington, D.C., have seen a rapid increase in the number of Asians immigrating directly to the area, whereas other places, such as Las Vegas, Nevada, and Garden Grove, California, have benefited from the internal migration of Asian Americans from other parts of the country. The rise of these new settlement areas is presented in table 3.6, which shows the distribution and concentration of the Asian American population by combined statistical areas (CSA), the most inclusive possible definition of conjoined urban-suburban settlement contexts for which the federal government collects data.[4] Many of the CSAs on this list are usual suspects, such as the greater Los Angeles, New York, and the San Francisco Bay Area. Yet the top ten also includes CSAs less commonly associated with having large Asian American populations, such as those encircling Washington, D.C., and Houston, Texas. Other important metropolitan areas with significant Asian American settlements include Dallas, Atlanta, the Twin Cities, Denver, Orlando, Raleigh-Durham, and Columbus.

There are several ways to conceive of new destinations and traditional destinations. We illustrate them using two methods: the first uses the framework pioneered by Audrey Singer and colleagues that takes into account contemporary growth trends in the total number of immigrants in a particular metropolitan area, as well as historic patterns of immigrant settlement (Singer, Hardwick, and Brettell 2008). Thus, for instance, the authors refer to established and former gateways that include *former gateways* like Baltimore and Pittsburg, *continuous gateways* like New York and Chicago, and *post–World War II gateways* like Los Angeles. On the other hand, the authors refer to twenty-first-century gateways as *emerging* (growing primarily in the past twenty-five years, such as Atlanta and Phoenix), *re-emerging* (growing again after a hiatus during the middle of the century, such as San Jose and Seattle), or *pre-emerging* (growing their immigrant populations only since the 1990s, such as Raleigh and Salt Lake City).

In our analysis, we adopt a simplified version of the six-fold framework that differentiates between former immigrant gateways, established gateways, and new gateways. We also consider an alternative measure of new destinations that focuses specifically on Asian American growth since 1990. We do so because the existing framework is primarily influenced by the settlement patterns of Latinos, who constitute nearly a majority of the foreign-born population in the United States today. Measuring the growth

Table 3.6 Asian Americans in Top Twenty Metropolitan Areas

Combined Statistical Area	Total Population	Asian American Population	Percentage Asian American	Percentage Asian American Citizens
Los Angeles–Long Beach–Riverside, CA	17,666,931	2,204,836	13%	12%
New York–Newark–Bridgeport, NY-NJ-CT-PA	22,064,411	1,964,485	9%	7%
San Jose–San Francisco–Oakland, CA	7,265,739	1,672,456	23%	21%
Washington–Baltimore–N. Virginia, DC-MD-VA-WV	8,235,781	611,444	7%	6%
Chicago–Naperville–Michigan City, IL-IN-WI	9,723,539	539,801	6%	5%
Seattle–Tacoma–Olympia, WA	4,030,692	434,828	11%	9%
Boston–Worcester–Manchester, MA-RI-NH	7,485,933	372,300	5%	4%
Houston–Baytown–Huntsville, TX	5,704,943	341,328	6%	5%
Dallas–Fort Worth, TX	6,500,787	319,618	5%	4%
Sacramento–Arden–Arcade–Yuba City, CA-NV	2,387,678	289,214	12%	11%
Philadelphia–Camden–Vineland, PA-NJ-DE-MD	6,378,898	280,263	4%	3%
Atlanta–Sandy Springs–Gainesville, GA-AL	5,597,187	239,287	4%	3%
Detroit–Warren–Flint, MI	5,390,157	193,213	4%	2%
Minneapolis–St. Paul–St. Cloud, MN-WI	3,527,009	178,876	5%	4%
Las Vegas–Paradise–Pahrump, NV	1,864,914	152,668	8%	7%
Denver–Aurora–Boulder, CO	2,985,761	117,083	4%	3%
Orlando–Deltona–Daytona Beach, FL	2,682,173	94,620	4%	3%
Fresno–Madera, CA	1,041,130	89,439	9%	8%
Raleigh–Durham–Cary, NC	1,630,204	65,143	4%	3%
Columbus–Marion–Chillicothe, OH	1,981,319	61,941	3%	2%

Source: Authors' compilation of data from the 2006–2008 American Community Survey (U.S. Census Bureau 2008c).

in the Asian American population in recent years also takes into account the native-born population, which is an increasingly important component of the Asian American electorate. In our alternative measure, we specify new Asian American destinations as those counties that were below the average population of Asian Americans in the 1990 census, but that had higher-than-average growth rates between 1990 and 2007.[5] We define traditional destinations as counties above the median population of Asian Americans in 1990, and small settlements as those below the average for Asian Americans in 1990 and with lower-than-average growth rates. Examples of counties classified as small settlements include Santa Cruz County in California and the city of Baltimore, whereas traditional destinations include Orange County in California and Cook County in Illinois (Chicago metro), and new destinations include Clark County in Nevada (Las Vegas metro) and Travis County in Texas (Austin metro).[6]

As we can see from table 3.7, the choice of framework does indeed have consequences in terms of how we see Asian American residential patterns. In the first set of columns, we see that, given the framework on new immigrant gateways by Singer and her colleagues, most Asian American adults live in traditional gateways (70 percent), followed by new gateway (25 percent) and former gateways (5 percent). In our formulation, we get roughly similar results, although the proportion of Asian Americans living in small settlements is double the figure using Singer and her colleagues' method. More important, certain counties show up in our framework as New Asian American destinations that do not appear in the Singer framework. These include places like Worcester County, Massachusetts, Snohomish County, Washington, and numerous other counties. These differences are partly because we are looking only at Asian Americans, whereas the other framework looks at all immigrants and thus is heavily swayed by the population dynamics of Latino immigrants. However, another important difference is that we measure growth at the county level, whereas the Singer framework examines growth and historical settlement patterns at the larger metropolitan level.

In both frameworks, we see that the native-born are much more likely than the foreign-born to live in traditional destinations, and that foreign-born noncitizens are the most likely to live in new immigrant gateways or new Asian American destinations.[7] However, some differences by national origin are notable. Although Filipino Americans are the most likely to live in traditional immigrant gateways (using the Singer framework), our results indicate that Japanese Americans are the most likely to live in traditional destinations for Asian American settlement. We also find that Indian Americans and Vietnamese Americans are the ones most likely to live in small Asian American settlements, whereas the Singer framework

Table 3.7 Comparing Frameworks on New Destinations in the NAAS Sample

| | Immigrant Destination Framework | | | Asian American Destination Framework | | | |
	Former Gateways	Traditional Gateways	New Gateways	Small Settlements	Traditional Destinations	New Destinations
Total	5	70	25	10	65	25
Noncitizen	7	64	29	11	56	33
Naturalized citizen	5	71	24	9	68	22
Native-born	3	79	18	9	73	17
Asian Indian	12	58	31	13	49	38
Chinese	4	75	21	7	72	21
Filipino	2	81	17	9	71	20
Japanese	3	75	22	10	75	15
Korean	6	64	29	10	65	25
Vietnamese	4	57	40	14	55	31

Source: Authors' compilation of data from the 2008 National Asian American Survey (Ramakrishnan et al. 2011).
Note: Data are weighted by nativity, length of stay in the United States, gender, and education. Rates are in percentages.

shows that Indians are far more likely than Vietnamese to live in former immigrant destinations (broadly defined).[8] As for the political implications of living in new destinations versus traditional destinations, we outline them in our discussion of factors such as political representation, electoral rules, and Asian-language assistance on ballots.

SYSTEMATIC MEASURES OF ASIAN AMERICAN POLITICAL GEOGRAPHY

The findings so far suggest several differences in the relationship between the spatial distribution of Asian Americans and political acts at the individual level. These differences should be kept firmly in mind as we move toward a more multivariate consideration of the underlying factors that precipitate or thwart participation. Asian Americans in some states (and counties) seem to participate more than other states. A possible effect of settling into a new immigrant destination also dampens participation.

For these differences, the associations between place and politics are easy to see, but the mechanisms producing these effects are far from discernible. In this last section we turn to a more explicit consideration of the institutional contexts that define the political geography of Asian Americans. We shift here from residential settlement contexts to political jurisdictions and examine their association with the five measures of political participation central to this book. Politics, as we noted at the outset of this chapter, is divided into and decided by jurisdictions—federal, regional, state, county, municipality, ward, precinct, and other governance units between and across these. To sharpen our analysis, we key in on three important ways in which jurisdictions may shape politics: political representation, political competition, and electoral rules and institutions.

POLITICAL REPRESENTATION

Research on other groups leads us to hypothesize that the political participation of Asian Americans may be shaped by whether they are represented by an Asian American elected official (also known as descriptive representation). Does descriptive representation encourage political participation among members of racial minority groups? On the one hand, it could be argued that minority representation could mobilize minority residents, providing those residents with an enhanced sense of enthusiasm for the electoral process and the ability to elect an official of their choice (Lublin 1997). On the other hand, some speculate that minority political representation, especially when tied to the creation of a majority-minority district and a "safe seat," may drive down political participation. Presumably, minorities will not turn out to vote for someone who is virtually ensured victory. The empirical evidence on this count is somewhat mixed. Descriptive representation does not always increase minority political participation, but evidence is so scant that it has a demobilizing effect. Lawrence Bobo and Frank Gilliam's early research on African American political participation and descriptive representation concludes that African Americans represented by an African American mayor were more politically active than those represented by a nonblack mayor (1990). In a study of African American congressional representatives and African American political participation, Claudine Gay reports more inconsistent results (2001). In some districts represented by an African American elected official, turnout among African Americans is quite dramatic, exceeding that of other districts by up to 26 percentage points. More often, however, African American congressional representation has little impact on African American political participation. In their groundbreaking study of descriptive representation and Latinos' political empowerment in southern California, Matt Barreto and colleagues find that descriptive representation, as it pertains to Latino majority-minority districts, is associated with higher voter turnout among Latinos (Barreto, Segura, and Woods 2004).

To our knowledge, no comprehensive study is available of Asian American political representation and its effects on Asian American political participation (Geron and Lai 2002; Cho 2002). Based on studies of African Americans and Latinos, however, we might expect that having an Asian American elected official would either boost or have no effect on Asian American political participation, but we would not expect descriptive representation to negatively affect Asian American participation. However, the context in which Asian American elected officials come to power is distinct from that of their African American and Latino counterparts. Elected representatives from the latter two groups most often find success in majority-minority districts or places where they are a very sizable minority. Because Asian Americans tend to be much more residentially dispersed than African Americans or Latinos, Asian American elected officials are most often elected in predominantly white or other non-Asian districts. As such, the dynamics shaping the relationship between Asian Americans and their Asian American elected representatives may differ from other groups and their co-ethnic representatives (Saito 1998).

For many years, the UCLA Asian American Studies Center has issued a political almanac that lists all known Asian American elected and appointed officials at the local, state, and national levels (Lai and Nakanishi

Table 3.8   Chances of Living in a Place with an Asian American
            Representative

	City Council	State Legislature	State Senate	U.S. House	U.S. Senate
All	22	17	7	8	6
Outside Hawaii	21	13	3	5	0
Outside California and Hawaii	10	5	1	1	9
Asian Indian	14	8	< 1	3	< 1
Chinese	27	19	7	8	4
Filipino	17	19	10	8	10
Japanese	33	37	26	25	26
Korean	19	13	3	6	2
Vietnamese	30	15	1	6	< 1

Source: Authors' compilation of data from the 2008 National Asian American Survey (Ramakrishnan et al. 2011).
Note: Rates are in percentages.

2007). At the time that the survey was fielded, the count numbered two U.S. senators (Dan Inouye and Daniel Akaka, both Democrats from Hawaii) and five members of the U.S. House of Representatives (Mike Honda, D-CA; Mazie Hirono, D-HI; Doris Matsu, D-CA; Bobby Scott, D-VA; and David Wu, D-OR). At the state level, the list included twenty-four state senators (eighteen in Hawaii, and the rest in Minnesota, California, Michigan, and Pennsylvania), sixty state representatives, thirty-seven mayors, and eighty-eight city council members.

We rely on the Asian American political almanac to produce a set of statistics that have never before been produced: an estimate of the proportion of Asian American adults who live in areas represented by an Asian American, and to produce this estimate at the level of city government, the state legislature, and the U.S. Congress. As we see in table 3.8, the chances of having an Asian American elected representative goes down with each succeeding level of office. Thus, for instance, 22 percent of Asian Americans are represented by an Asian American council member, 17 percent have an Asian American state representative, and 8 percent have an Asian American as their member of Congress.

Variations in the level of Asian American descriptive representation by state of residence and national origin are considerable. For instance, because Hawaii is the only state with Asian American or Pacific Islander senators, the proportion of Asian American adults with a co-ethnic senator drops to near zero when Hawaii is excluded from the analysis. Drops in the rates of descriptive representation in the U.S. House and the state legislature, once Hawaii is excluded from the analysis, are similar. The proportion of Asian Americans represented at the city level does not change, however, because the proportion of respondents from Hawaii make up just 2.3 percent of our sample. Also, when we look outside California and Hawaii—states that account for a majority of Asian American adult citizens in the country—the rates of descriptive representation fall dramatically, to 10 percent at the level of city government and 5 percent at the state legislature.

Table 3.8 also shows that the chances of being represented by an Asian American vary considerably by national origin. We can reasonably surmise that this is most likely due to variations in settlement patterns. Japanese Americans are much more likely than other groups to be concentrated in Hawaii and thus have the highest rates of descriptive representation. Asian Indians have the lowest chances of being represented by an Asian American and, as we saw in table 3.7, this is largely related to the fact that they are the ones least likely to live in areas with long-settled Asian American populations. Vietnamese Americans, by contrast, have a reasonably high likelihood of being represented by an Asian American despite the relative recency of their immigration to the United States. This is most likely a function of being concentrated in highly localized areas—such as Garden Grove and San Jose in California—that are also more generally high-density Asian American areas.

Another illuminating way to cut at these data is to look at the proportion of respondents in select geographic areas that have descriptive representation by an Asian American. Table 3.9 shows the striking difference between political representation of Asian Americans living in Hawaii and California from the rest of the nation. Nearly 80 percent of NAAS respondents from Hawaii have some form of descriptive representation by an Asian American elected official, and the likelihood is high across all levels of political office—federal, state, and city. For California, the likelihood of descriptive representation is 50 percent across the board; this likelihood, however, is most apparent at the municipal level, followed by state legislature and then Congress. By contrast, in New York and New Jersey, the two states (after California) with the largest number of respondents in the NAAS, roughly one in ten respondents is represented by an Asian American, most of this coming through seats in city councils and state legislatures.

Table 3.9 also shows an interesting gap in descriptive representation between traditional and new destinations. Across the levels of political office examined, 40 percent of NAAS respondents in traditional destinations are represented by an Asian American representative; in new desti-

Table 3.9   Political Representation by Geographic Areas

	City Offices	State Legislature	Congress	Any Representation
Hawaii	49	76	62	79
California	39	28	11	50
New Jersey	10	6	0	10
New York	11	10	0	11
Traditional destinations	33	24	9	40
Excluding California and Hawaii	18	12	0	18
New destination	6	3	1	8
Full sample	22	17	8	29

Source: Authors' compilation of data from the 2008 National Asian American Survey (Ramakrishnan et al. 2011).
Note: Rates are in percentages.

nations, the comparison figure is only 8 percent. Excluding California and Hawaii from the traditional destination states closes some of the gap between settlement areas, but not all. About 18 percent of the remaining NAAS respondents in traditional destinations still have a descriptive representative. Across all settlement areas, the likelihood of representation is highest at the local level, followed by state, then federal.

PARTY COMPETITION

In theory, political parties should demonstrate a strong interest in mobilizing minority voters in order to build winning coalitions. Samuel Huntington underscores this view of party systems writ large when he describes them as an important foundation of a stable polity, "capable of structuring the participation of new groups in politics" (1968, 401). Yet mobilization by a political party is not a given. Party competition in a particular political jurisdiction may determine the degree to which political parties and other groups attempt to mobilize potential constituents. Mobilization may in turn affect political participation (Key 1949; Schattschneider 1960). For example, Steven Rosenstone and John Mark Hansen describe the relationships between political competition, mobilization, and participation in the context of presidential elections and high-profile statewide elections: campaigns, interest groups, and the media . . . contest every inch in campaigns that stand to be decided by tenths of percentage points, and they tacitly conceded campaigns that look to be blowouts (1993, 179). Recent empirical work appears to confirm these linkages as well (Shachar and Nalebuff 1999). Scholars who study the political incorporation of contemporary minority groups suggest that, consistent with the more general scholarship on electoral competition, the role that parties play in mobilizing groups such as Asian Americans is likely to depend heavily on the extent to which local jurisdictions are politically competitive (Jones-Correa 1998; Mollenkopf, Olson, and Ross 2001; Rogers 2006; Wong 2006).

Thus we should pay close attention to party competition because it may influence Asian Americans' political participation through mobilization. Whether Asian Americans live in presidential battlegrounds may matter because parties do not need to mobilize new voters when the outcome is assured. At the same time, the effects of close presidential elections may not reach groups who have traditionally been excluded from networks of party mobilization. Thus, for groups such as Asian immigrants and black immigrants who have been shown to have less contact with party organizations (Rogers 2006; Wong 2006), the presence or absence of close electoral contests may make less of a difference in the likelihood of participation.

Measures of presidential battleground states sometimes differentiate between toss-up states where the presidential campaigns are within 5 percentage points of each other, and leaning states where the campaigns are within 10 percentage points of each other. Based on polls of the general population as identified in Real Clear Politics one month before Election Day in 2008, we identify the following states as toss-ups: Colorado, Florida, Indiana, Michigan, Nevada, New Hampshire, New Mexico, North Carolina, Ohio, and Virginia. The following additional states are marked as leaners: Georgia, Iowa, Minnesota, Missouri, Oregon, Pennsylvania, and Wisconsin. In table 3.10, we combine these states in classifying whether a state was a presidential battleground in 2008. We also examine local party competition by using the only measure available across the entire nation, which is the presidential vote share in a county. We code a county as competitive if the Republican or Democratic share of the presidential vote in the previous election was between 45 percent and 55 percent.

Party competition at the level of state politics is also an important contextual factor that could drive Asian American political mobilization and participation. State offices differ substantially in terms of partisan leaning and competition as well as the structures and strategies local parties used to mobilize the electorate (for example, Mayhew 1986). Variation across states, in particular the importance of differences in interest group activities and advertising, could prove to be an important influence on what voters in places as distinct as New Hampshire and California see during

Table 3.10   Residential Contexts of Party Competition

	Presidential Battleground	County-Level Competition
Latinos	30	
Blacks	47	
Whites	44	
Asian Americans	31	27
Asian Indian	47	27
Chinese	35	28
Filipino	17	28
Japanese	18	22
Korean	35	30
Vietnamese	27	23

Source: Authors' compilation of data from the 2008 National Asian American Survey (Ramakrishnan et al. 2011).
Note: Rates are in percentages. Our Asian American data are weighted to match the American Community Survey, producing identical results in the case of the presidential battleground column, and within two percentage points on the nonpartisan local figure (74 percent in our survey versus 76 percent in the ACS).

the course of an election (for example, Geer 2006; Goldstein 1999). Although the measures of political competition captured in the 2008 NAAS are more limited than the indicators used by scholars of campaign politics, electoral competitiveness is an important consideration as we approach the question of what influences Asian American political engagement.

What table 3.10 shows is that 31 percent of Asian American adults lived in a state that was a presidential battleground in 2008. By comparison, data from the 2008 American Community Survey reveal that 44 percent of whites and 47 percent of African Americans lived in a battleground state. Within the Asian American population, Asian Indians were among those most likely to do so (47 percent), whereas Filipinos and Japanese Americans were the least likely. These contextual variations are important because certain patterns in voter turnout may be attributed to national-origin differences but are in fact due to differences in the likelihood of residence.

Although we cannot make similar comparisons between Asian Americans and other racial and ethnic groups when it comes to party competition at the county level (given that the ACS is missing data on counties smaller than twenty thousand), we can see from our survey that a slightly smaller proportion of Asian Americans live in counties that are politically competitive (27 percent), and that the drop in competition is most notable among Indian Americans, who went from being 47 percent likely to live in a presidential battleground state to being 27 percent likely to live in a county that is politically competitive between the two major parties.

ELECTORAL RULES AND CONTEXTS

Studies of electoral rules typically focus on registration requirements, absentee or vote-by-mail ballots, at-large versus district elections, partisan and nonpartisan local elections, and direct democracy mechanisms. Do these rules affect political behavior? In fact, a host of research contends that electoral rules are a critical component of an individual's decision to take part in politics. A consistent finding in studies that analyze the effects of registration requirements, for example, is that more arduous requirements drive down voter turnout (Rosenstone and Wolfinger 1978; Hershey 2009). By contrast, the evidence linking absentee or vote-by-mail ballot options to voter participation is more mixed (Karp and Banducci 2000; Kousser and Mullin 2007). In both cases, however, it is not clear whether these ballot rules have any impact on the voting behavior of racial and ethnic minorities, including Asian Americans (Ramakrishnan 2005). Finally, it is also presumed that another important electoral context characteristic—at-large elections—dilutes minority political representation and turnout when compared with district elections, but recent research suggests that the effects of election type may be more complex. For example, Zoltan Hajnal and Jessica Trounstine find that moving from at-large to district elections increases electoral representation among blacks, but "for Latinos and Asian Americans, these institutional changes seem to offer much less hope in addressing inequalities in electoral outcomes" (2005, 526).

The use of partisan or nonpartisan local elections is another widely studied feature of the American electoral system. Nonpartisan local elections were a major plank of the Progressive Party and the larger Progressive movement during the early 1900s. Seeking to dethrone the power of urban and statewide political machines, Progressives believed that nonpartisan local elections would make voters less susceptible to the appeals of parties. They also believed that party organizations would be weakened without local bases in a federated structure. Much of the Progressive distaste for party machines also stemmed from political anxieties over the growth of immigrant political power in industrial cities, and their social and cultural influences on matters from Catholic education and alcohol consumption to socialism and political corruption (Erie 1988). Although the Progressives were successful in getting anti-machine officials elected to local offices in the Northeast and Midwest, they were not able to dethrone local political parties as effectively as in western states such as California and Oregon, where partisan local elections were banned, and voters had the chance to bypass partisan state legislatures entirely through direct democracy mechanisms such as the referendum and recall. Given this history, it is not surprising to find that most states with partisan local elections and weak direct democracy voting mechanisms are east of the Mississippi River, in states such as New York, Connecticut, and Pennsylvania, where the Progressive movement was relatively weak (International City/County Management Association 2006). The notable exception, and especially important for Asian Americans, is the high rate of partisan local elections in Hawaii.

In this section, we focus on the two latter electoral contexts—partisan and nonpartisan ballots and direct democracy mechanisms—in detailing the characteristics of residential contexts among Asian Americans. We also draw attention to the role of multilingual ballots, with studies so far producing mixed evidence regarding their effects on turnout among Asian Americans (Ramakrishnan 2005; Jones-Correa 2005). Not only are these factors commonly studied, but they may also be especially important when considering the political participation of members of racial minority groups. For example, Chandler Davidson and Luis Fraga's research suggests that nonpartisan elections exacerbate the turnout gap between whites and racial minority groups (1988). Similarly, debate is vigorous over direct democracy mechanisms and whether they exert a negative effect on minority interests and their democratic participation (Chávez 1998; Hajnal, Gerber, and Louch 2002). A second reason we focus on these two electoral context features is that they mostly vary by state, and are largely uniform within states. By contrast, the use of district versus at-large electoral systems varies considerably within a state, and there exists no comprehensive database of electoral systems across cities. Finally, the role of registration requirements and rules regarding absentee ballots have been shown to have modest or inconsistent effects with respect to voter turnout among racial and ethnic minorities, and we find that the same is true with respect to the NAAS.[9]

Nonpartisan Local Elections

A little over 75 percent of all municipal elections and half of all U.S. elections use a nonpartisan ballot (Wright 2008). This variation is important because the nonpartisan context may have a substantial effect on Asian American political behavior. Scholarship has found that nonpartisan ballots drive down political participation among the general population, especially when no significant state and federal elections are on the same ballot. Voters rely heavily on partisan cues when making vote decisions, and are less willing to turn out when there is no basis for that decision. This is especially so for low-information or low-propensity voters in local elections (Schaffner, Streb, and Wright 2001; Schaffner and Streb 2002). Even when local elections coincide with elections for state and federal offices, the absence of party cues for lower offices may lead to greater voter roll-off. That is to say, the drop in the number of people who cast valid votes for state and federal offices is greater than for local ones on the same ballot. Finally, some studies suggest that parties are less willing to expend resources mobilizing voters in nonpartisan than in partisan elections, and that nonpartisan elections lead elected officials to be less responsive to poor and working class constituents, further distancing potential voters from the polls (Wright 2008).

To what extent do Asian Americans live in places with nonpartisan local ballots? We answer that question by merging data from the American Community Survey with that on nonpartisan election structure in the ICMA's (International City/County Management Association) periodic survey of local government structures. Because the ICMA data do not cover 64 percent of the municipalities in the NAAS (and a similar proportion of respondents in the survey), we rely instead on the fact that most states converge either toward partisan local elections or nonpartisan local elections (International City/County Management Association 2006).[10] First, when comparing across racial groups, we find that Asian Americans (74 percent) are about as likely as blacks (75 percent) to live in a state that has nonpartisan local elections. They are slightly less likely to do so than whites (79 percent), and much less so than Latinos (85 percent), who are the ones most likely to live in the progressive and reform states of the Mountain West and Pacific West that eliminated partisan local elections in the early twentieth century. Variation by national-origin groups within the Asian American population is considerable, with Vietnamese Americans the most likely to live in a state with nonpartisan local elections (88 percent), Japanese Americans the least likely (64 percent), and all other groups in a range from 70 percent to 78 percent.

Direct Democracy Mechanisms

Research on direct democracy indicates that the presence of ballot initiatives often has a positive effect on voter turnout (Smith and Tolbert 2007). This is true, not only for low-information political contests such as midterm elections, but also for presidential elections, where the effects of state and local contests are less consequential to voter turnout (Tolbert and Smith 2005). The institution of ballot initiatives has also been associated

Figure 3.1   Chances of Living in a Direct Democracy State

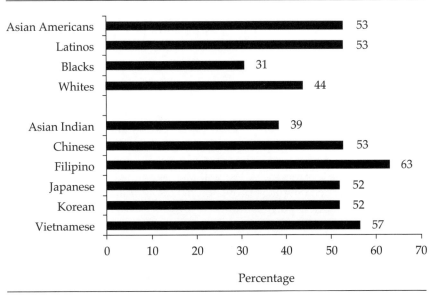

Source: Authors' compilation of data from the American Community Survey 2008 (U.S. Census Bureau 2008a).

with higher levels of political knowledge and political efficacy among voters, many of whom feel empowered to make decisions on issues of public policy rather than relying on a system of indirect representation through elected officials to make such decisions (Bowler and Donovan 2004; Smith and Tolbert 2004).

As we can see in figure 3.1, Asian Americans are just as likely as Latinos to live in a state with direct democracy mechanisms (53 percent), and much more likely to do so than African Americans (31 percent) or whites (44 percent). These gaps are largely attributable to the national distribution of Asian Americans being more heavily skewed toward California (see table 3.1). Although Latinos are slightly less likely than Asian Americans to be concentrated in California, they have settled heavily in the Mountain West states that also have strong traditions of direct democracy. By contrast, the higher distribution of whites and blacks in the South and East means that those voters are less likely to live in states with the Progressive Era legacy of the ballot initiative.

Finally, the importance of California to the direct democracy picture is evident, not only for Asian Americans overall, but also for particular Asian American groups. Indian Americans, who are among those least likely to live in California and the most likely to live on the Eastern seaboard, are also those least likely to live in a direct democracy state (39 percent). That nearly half of the Filipino population lives in California means that the group is the one most likely to live in states with ballot initiatives (63 percent).

Geography of Ballot Language Assistance

We saw in chapter 2 that language access is a potentially important factor that could engender greater political participation among Asian Americans. Here we examine the geography of language access provision for Asian Americans as it varies among Chinese, Filipino, Vietnamese, Korean, and Japanese Americans. We will also examine the extent to which the presence of such language provision makes a difference for voter turnout and other political participation.

As we have noted, language access provisions are an important part of ballot rules in the United States, with Section 203 of the Voting Rights Act mandating assistance in places with significant language minority populations. Areas are deemed to be covered under Section 203 if more than 5 percent of the voting-age population or more than 10,000 residents in a particular language group are limited-English proficient (U.S. Department of Justice 2010). The determination of covered jurisdictions occurs after each decennial Census to account for population changes (U.S. Census Bureau 2002). Currently, covered jurisdictions for Asian languages include Alaska (Kodiak Island), California (counties of Alameda, Los Angeles, Orange, San Diego, San Francisco, San Mateo, and Santa Clara), Hawaii (Honolulu and Maui), Illinois (Cook County), New York (Kings, New York, and Queens counties), Texas (Harris County), and Washington (King County).

Chinese is the language most often covered in the United States, not only in terms of the number of counties covered but also in the number of people covered (twelve counties including all the areas noted, except for Orange County, San Diego, Maui, and Kodiak Island). This is followed by Tagalog, which is covered in six jurisdictions (Kodiak, Los Angeles, San Diego, Santa Clara, Honolulu, and Maui). Vietnamese is covered in four counties (Harris, Los Angeles, Orange, and Santa Clara), Korean in three (Los Angeles, Orange, and Queens), and Japanese in two (Los Angeles and Honolulu).

Analysis of the National Asian American Survey reveals that 45 percent of Asian American adults live in an area that provides some sort of Asian-language ballot assistance, and that about 30 percent live in a place that supports two or more languages.[11] Such a statistic is important for all

Asian American voters if the mere existence of ballot language assistance points to the importance of other local factors (such as density of Asian American nonprofits and Asian language media) that may foster greater political participation. At the same time, if we want to provide a more direct measure on who might benefit from having access to such ballots, we would need to look only at those respondents in the NAAS who took the survey in a particular language that is supported in a given area. Using this criterion, we find that 61 percent of respondents interviewed in Mandarin or Cantonese live in a jurisdiction that supports those languages, and the corresponding figures are 36 percent for Vietnamese, 34 percent for Tagalog, 24 percent for Korean, and 15 percent for Japanese.

FROM CONTEXT TO PARTICIPATION

What are the relationships between these contextual-level factors and individual-level political participation? We present results from the NAAS in table 3.11. Before we launch into results, keep in mind that we are simply exploring two-way relationships and not implying a stronger degree of causal influence of political context on individual-level engagement. It is quite likely, for instance, that existing levels of higher individual-level engagement may engender greater electoral success among Asian American candidates, rather than the other way around. The analysis here is primarily descriptive and aims to cull out those contextual factors most worthy of consideration in our multivariate analysis of the factors that predispose Asian American participation.

The NAAS data show that Asian Americans living in a state with direct democracy are only very slightly more likely to be voters (47 percent) than those who do not (44 percent). Protest activity seems more common in states with direct democracy institutions, a relationship that is statistically significant at the .01 level. Although it may be tempting to conclude that the legacy of polarizing ballot propositions, especially those along racial and ethnic lines, may be responsible for this uptick, we cannot rule out the possibility that other factors (such as the greater presence of Vietnamese Americans in direct democracy states like California) are responsible. Only with a multivariate analysis can we be certain as to whether the context of direct democracy per se is responsible for these differences in participation. Finally, in our bivariate analysis, rates of political contribution or contact with government officials show no significant differences, and the proportion of Asian Americans who are community activists actually seems lower in direct democracy states.

We also find that the provision of multilingual ballots is associated with higher voter turnout among Asian Americans. This contextual factor

Table 3.11   Systematic Measures of Place and Their Relationships to
Participation

	Likely Voter	Political Contributor	Contact Government Officials	Protester	Community Activist
Direct democracy					
Yes	47	16	12	6	22
No	44	16	12	4	25
Nonpartisan local elections					
Yes	45	17	13	6	24
No	46	16	10	2	21
County party competition					
Yes	42	15	15	4	22
No	45	16	11	6	24
Ballot language assistance					
Yes	48	16	10	6	19
No	43	17	14	5	26
Represented by Asian American					
Yes	48	18	11	6	22
No	44	16	12	5	23
Areas of settlement					
New destination	39	18	15	6	25
Traditional destination	48	16	11	5	21
Small settlement	42	17	14	5	30
Traditional (excluding Hawaii, California)	39	19	15	6	25
Traditional (excluding New York)	39	19	15	7	25

Source: Authors' compilation of data from the 2008 National Asian American Survey (Ramakrishnan et al. 2011).
Note: Rates are in percentages.

also seems to make a difference for some of the other participation measures, though we do not have reasons to expect these relationships to be theoretically meaningful. Contrary to expectations, we do not find that political competition leads to higher voter turnout, whether this is measured either at the state or at the county level. Indeed, the signs are negative in both cases, and disappear in significance in a multivariate analysis that controls for national origins and some basic demographic factors. Finally, relationships between local party competition and our other measures of Asian American political participation are relatively small and inconsistent. However, there is some evidence of an association between political competition and political mobilization. Among NAAS respondents living in a battleground state, 29 percent were mobilized by a party or a candidate, compared with 25 percent of those who did not; 18 percent were mobilized by a nonparty or candidate organization, versus 14 percent not in battleground states. At the battleground county level, there is little relationship to mobilization. Finally, NAAS respondents in a state with direct democracy are very slightly (16 percent) more likely to have been mobilized by a nonpartisan, noncandidate organization than those who do not live in such a state (14 percent).

Descriptive representation seems to play a significant role in shaping voter turnout, as those living in areas with Asian American elected officials are more likely to vote and slightly more likely to contribute to campaigns. We tested for whether descriptive representation maintains a statistically significant relationship to our five political participation items of interest, controlling for a minimal set of other reasonable factors. In this case, we limit our statistical controls to four: respondents' education, sex, nativity, and years lived in the United States (if foreign-born). The results show a limited number of significant initial relationships. Descriptive representation's effects are most consistent for voting, where having some form of descriptive representation (across all levels of political office) increases one's likelihood of voting by about 5 percent. The magnitude is similar for representation in city councils and state legislatures—an estimated 49 percent of those with an Asian American representative are likely voters, versus 44 percent of those without descriptive representation at these levels. Representation in Congress yields a more modest bump up in likely voting from 44 percent to 47 percent.

Beyond voting, the effects of descriptive representation range from selective to nonexistent. There are no statistically significant effects of representation on political contributions or contacting elected officials. For protest activity, having an Asian American in one's city council leads to a greater incidence (6 percent, compared with a baseline of 4.5 percent); representation in state legislatures and in Congress, however, decreases the predicted incidence to 3 percent. Finally, having an Asian American in one's city council appears to lower the likelihood of community activism (from a baseline of 22 percent to 20 percent).

Finally, in table 3.11, geographical context is broken down by type of settlement areas. Recall that we distinguished between three types for

Asian Americans: small settlements, traditional immigrant destinations, and new destinations. The upshot of the findings on settlement types is that Asian Americans in traditional destinations are more likely than those in small settlements and new destinations to vote. This difference persists even after controlling for other individual-level demographic factors such as nativity, gender, education, and national origin. In other types of nonvoting behavior (especially making political contributions and community activism), Asian Americans in traditional destinations are less likely to be engaged. Differences, at this rough cut, between Asian Americans living in small settlements and those in new destinations are almost nonexistent.

Asian Americans in traditional destination areas in Hawaii, California, and New York seem to be more active than their traditional-destination counterparts in other states. The last two rows in table 3.11 examine respondents from traditional Asian American destinations excluding Hawaii and California, and then excluding New York. Most of the bump-up in voting rates between settlement types appears to be a difference between living in these states and living elsewhere. The other differences, however, do not change appreciably.

CONCLUSION

Geography is not a major cleavage in the Asian American community when it comes to political participation. Asian Americans in one geographic context do not appear to take part in politics in radically different ways from their counterparts elsewhere. Geographic location does matter for Asian American political engagement, but in distinctive ways for different dimensions of political context and particular types of political participation. Indeed, the effects of context are not always direct and unidirectional. Living in a battleground state or in a place with an Asian American elected official, for example, could influence political engagement indirectly through mobilization or activation of motivations associated with descriptive representation. Our conclusion, then, is that geographic diversity adds complexity to our understanding of Asian American political participation, particularly in terms of how we conceptualize these influences on political engagement. At the same time, increasing geographic diversity among Asian Americans does not seriously undermine the project of examining the group as a meaningful category in U.S. politics.

Scholars are just beginning to systematically investigate the effects of space and place for political behavior. This chapter is an important step

toward identifying potentially significant indicators of context for participation. Further tests of the importance of these contextual measures will
be undertaken in chapter 7. Next we consider the relationship between
partisan identification—one of the most widely studied antecedents of
voting behavior and political participation.

Chapter 4 | Democrat, Republican, or None of the Above?

TODAY WE CANNOT imagine electoral politics in America outside the role political parties play. Decades of research show that the political party a person identifies with remains the single most important determinant of individual vote decisions. Parties constitute key institutions through which new voters enter the political process. They also organize and simplify the decisions voters need to make, a function that should be critical for groups with less collective familiarity with the political system, such as Asian Americans.

Yet, as we show in this chapter, Asian Americans demonstrate a mixed relationship with political parties. For some, one's attachment to the Democratic or Republican Party is a defining political predisposition and a key formative influence on their political incorporation and voting behavior. Others choose to remain as political independents, free of partisan moorings. Most surprising here, however, is that the modal respondent in the NAAS does not think in partisan terms—that is, identifies neither as a Democrat, nor as a Republican, nor as an independent. In fact, as illustrated by the remarks of Slate.com writer Christopher Beam, nonpartisanship has become a defining feature of the Asian American political experience:

> Finally, as if demographics and geography and message weren't challenging enough, there is partisanship. Or, more precisely, lack thereof. African-American voters break heavily toward Democrats; Latino voters (with the exception of Cubans) are also largely Democratic. Asian-Americans, meanwhile, can't make up their minds. . . . On the national level, the most powerful groups—unions, African-Americans, evangelicals—are often the most partisan. A pandering politician wants to maximize the efficiency of his pandering. So if the strategy is to mobilize the base, it makes more sense to court

a loyal group. . . . So what are Asian-Americans planning to do about their underwhelming influence? (2008)

In the American imaginary, the late nineteenth century and early twentieth century were something of a golden age of immigration. Immigrants, mostly from eastern and southern Europe, were integrated into America's economic markets, social customs, and cultural practices within a few generations. According to conventional accounts, political parties played a crucial intermediary role in this process of incorporation:

> On a typical day in the 1890s, thousands of immigrants arrived at Ellis Island in New York. For many, learning English and acculturating to America would be the work of years, even decades. But often it would be a matter of only a few weeks or even days before they received a visit from a Tammany Hall ward heeler or before friends or family brought them along to some event at the local precinct hall. Long before many of those newcomers fully understood what it was to be American, they knew quite well what it meant to be a Democrat or a Republican. (Schier 2002, 16)

Complementing this narrative is the traditional story of the urban political machine greeting new immigrants at the docks and extending goods and favors in return for helping newcomers naturalize and become voters (Dahl 1961; Allswang 1977; Andersen 1979; Cornwell 1960; Archdeacon 1983; Sterne 2001). Kristi Andersen (1979) contends that roughly a half million to a million newcomers disembarked at Ellis Island and other points of entry each year, and to the Democratic party in particular, this group was a rich source of potential partisans whose mobilization was critical to Democratic ascendency. Although this view of the symbiotic and mostly positive relationship between parties and immigrants remains powerful, recent scholarship highlights a set of important critiques and complexities that provide a fuller account of the role of parties in bringing newcomers into the political system. Far from accepting its fate as a nation of immigrants, resistance to immigration was observed commonly at every level of government.[1] For example, Woodrow Wilson and Theodore Roosevelt, hardly allies in the realm of politics, both took negative stands against immigration. The big urban machines were motivated to mobilize immigrants not from altruism, but instead on the basis of political calculation (Erie 1988; Sterne 2001; Trounstine 2006). Thus immigrants were only mobilized by the urban machines when it was in the interests of the party. Further, not all immigrant groups from Europe were equally incorporated (Ignatiev 1995; Jacobson 1998). In fact, the willingness of party machines to incorporate new immigrants varied across historical contexts (Mayhew

1986) and with the degree of party competition in a city (Wolfinger 1965; Erie 1988). Nonparty organizations like neighborhood associations, churches, and ethnic voluntary organizations were equally vital in incorporating new immigrant groups (Sterne 2001; Oestreicher 1988; Lin 2010).

What role do parties play in the lives of immigrant dominant groups such as Asian Americans today? Contemporary scholarship tends to be pessimistic about the ability of political parties to incorporate immigrants. For the most part, scholars conclude that today's parties lack the organizational capacity, the cultural literacy, and perhaps even the political motivation to shepherd new immigrants into the political process and nurture secure attachments with a particular political party (Jones-Correa 1998; Gerstle and Mollenkopf 2001; Rogers 2006; Wong 2006; Kim 2007). As one study recounts the words of a community leader in East Los Angeles of Mexican American descent, "Stop anybody walking down the block, ask them, 'Can you please tell me where is the local chapter or the local office of the Democratic Party in your neighborhood?' Everybody will look at you with bewilderment: 'What is this crazy guy talking about?' (Wong 2006, 51).

What is described of Mexican Americans in East Los Angeles holds true of Asian Americans as well. A story for the widely read *AsianWeek* underscores the absence of the two major parties in the Asian American community during the 2008 presidential election: "Harold Pyon, the first vice chairman of the National Asian American Republican Coalition, also said that it is difficult to pin down the Asian American voter's politics. Pyon suggested that the Asian community is 'confused,' as a voting bloc courted by neither party as much as it should be—and is, therefore, less apt to feel an urgency to vote at all" (Han 2008).

Explanations for why this might be are numerous. At the institutional level, some scholars home in on the logic of party competition which renders Asian Americans as illiberal and a political hot potato (Kim 2007). Neither party, this account suggests, has an incentive to bring Asian Americans into their partisan fold because Asian Americans are viewed as outside of the traditional liberal consensus, and the association of Asian Americans with their party tarnishes the party brand and leaves the party being viewed as illiberal themselves. This account also parallels Claire Kim's (1999) theory that Asian Americans occupy a triangulated position in the U.S. racial scheme such that they are simultaneously valorized and seen as superior to African Americans in terms of social and economic acceptance and ostracized as less desirable when it comes to insider versus foreigner status. Both parties may distance themselves from Asian Americans because the group does not occupy a clear position in conventional understandings of U.S. racial politics. Janelle Wong (2006) notes that historical changes in party structure—candidate-centered politics, weakened local party organizations, selective and strategic mobilization efforts— and assumptions about the political interests and aptitude of groups like Asian Americans mean that parties will not actively mobilize members of the community (or others for that matter) in their local neighborhoods and on a sustained basis. Further, scholars and pundits contend that Asian Americans face demographic disadvantages when it comes to party mobilization. They are a relatively small population, concentrated in states that tend be reliably Democratic in presidential races, and include a large number of noncitizens ineligible to vote. From a strategic point of view, political parties may be reluctant to expend scarce resources on a small group characterized by a relatively high proportion of ineligible voters living primarily in noncompetitive states.

Is this underwhelming involvement of political parties in the everyday lives of Asian Americans also reflected in the underwhelming rates of political participation and elected representation among Asian Americans? As we have seen in previous chapters, the growing population of Asians in the United States has yet to readily translate into political power in voting booths or in the corridors of governance. Nor do the experiences of Asian Americans reflect levels of democratic inclusion and political incorporation at levels that native-born whites and African Americans experience. We noted earlier that there are several possible explanations for this democratic gap. Our focus here remains with parties and the American party system. Unlike institutionally focused studies, however, we examine what implications the less-than-complete commitments of political parties to the incorporation of immigrants has for how immigrants and their subsequent generations come to view political parties and the party system.

THEORIES OF PARTY IDENTIFICATION

How might we expect conventional theories of party identification to explain patterns of partisanship among Asian Americans? Two prominent views emerge from the literature. The first is a social psychological view developed in the 1940s and 1950s by Angus Campbell and his colleagues at the University of Michigan and is thus referred to as the Michigan school of thought. Its primary assumption is that party identification is a strong psychological attachment that is developed early in life and generally inherited from one's parents (Campbell et al. 1960; Beck and Jennings 1991; Jennings and Niemi 1991). Our attachment to a party and the party system stems from a socialization process, very similar to the way in which we adopt religious orientations. *The American Voter* (Campbell et al.

1960), considered by most to be the major source for this theory, allows that partisanship is very stable over time; partisanship better predicts vote choice than one's positions on issues or one's views of the candidates running for office; and that partisanship is an expressive act. Partisanship, according to this theory, is best conceptualized as an extension of the self or the "unmoved mover" that influences one's political attitudes and actions (Miller and Shanks 1996, 122).

A second theoretical line derives from Anthony Downs's *An Economic Theory of Democracy* (1957). The Downsian school offers a more economic model of party identification, and relies heavily on a rational choice formulation defined by information, instrumental reasoning, and self-understood interests (Fiorina 1981; Franklin and Jackson 1983; Achen 2002; Erikson, MacKuen, and Stimson 2002). Adherents of this theory contend that party identification is shaped by issues and candidates, such that the stability of partisanship varies as a function of political evaluations. This view places a great deal of emphasis on self-interest, typically measured as ideological political preference orderings—from extremely liberal to extremely conservative. As such, the expectation under this theory is that self-proclaimed liberals, more often than not, identify as Democrats, self-proclaimed conservatives align with the Republican Party, and those with more middle-of-the-road views will end up as independents.

In short, the two dominant theories of partisanship suggest rather distinct explanations for Asian American party identification. The Michigan school assumes that this develops in response to socializing experiences. For most Americans, parents are the primary socializing agents. Thus this school would expect that immigrants, as individuals less likely than the native-born to experience early socialization related to the party system, would exhibit the weakest association with the two major political parties. The Downsian model, on the other hand, would emphasize the importance of ideological commitments and issue evaluations in determining Asian American party identification.

Regardless of one's opinion about the theoretical underpinnings of partisanship, there is little dispute over how it should be conceptualized and measured. The vast majority of research in American politics assumes a linear scale of party identification, from Republicans on the political right to Democrats on the political left and independents at the midpoint. This scale is assumed to capture not only substantive distinctions between Democrats, independents, and Republicans, but partisan intensity as well (Campbell et al. 1960, 122–23). This continuum is usually operationalized by the following three items from the American National Election Studies (or some similar version of these), used in virtually every study of American voting behavior:

Q1. Generally speaking, do you usually think of yourself as a Republican, a Democrat, an independent, or what?

Q2. [If Republican or Democrat] Would you call yourself a strong (Republican/Democrat) or not a very strong (Republican/Democrat)?

Q3. [If independent] Do you think of yourself as closer to the Republican or Democratic party?

Most often, these questions are recoded into a single, unidimensional scale of seven ordered categories, such as one with strong identification at each pole (0 Democrat and 6 Republican) and then, moving inward toward the center, first moderate (1 and 5) and then weak (2, 4), with independent in the center (3).

By such coding, moderate Democrats and Republicans are those individuals who identify with these corresponding parties (in Q1) but whose identification is not strong (in Q2). Weak Democrats and Republicans are those individuals who choose to identify as an independent (in Q1) but are willing to acknowledge a partisan bent (in Q3). Other versions of this same seven-category scale refer to weak partisans as Democratic or Republican leaners, with the term "pure independents" reserved to those individuals who identify as an independent (in Q1) and reject any partisan inclinations (in Q3). Despite some debate over the proper scaling of party identification, in almost every such version, independents are placed squarely in the middle.

The linear scale of party identification is perhaps the most widely adopted measure in studies of American politics and political behavior in particular. John Petrocik's observation that "the index of party identification is so universally accepted as the variable around which to organize a discussion of political behavior in the United States that it is difficult to find a monograph or research article which does not introduce party identification as a consideration in the analysis" (1974, 31) remains true today (Keith 1992, 196). Although the measure has its critics (Miller and Wattenberg 1983; Dennis 1992), the linear measurement scale remains essentially unchanged (Green 1988). But it remains unclear whether this measure is appropriate for understanding the party identification of Asian Americans.

DESCRIPTIVE PATTERNS OF PARTISANSHIP

What, then, do we know about the party attachments of Asian Americans? As we discussed earlier in this book, speaking with any precision about how Asian Americans are likely to vote come November is an elusive task. This is so for many reasons, starting with the limited, often unsystematic, unrepresentative, or unreliable data on the political beliefs and behaviors of Asian Americans. A notorious example of the variability and suspect quality of data here is the striking difference between two California exit polls following the 1996 general elections. The Voter News Services found Asian Americans to be more Republican than Democratic (48 percent to 32 percent), but the *Los Angeles Times* found the opposite— more Democratic than Republican (44 percent to 33 percent). Despite these seemingly intractable data challenges—challenges we believe we have addressed with the 2008 NAAS—a clear and emerging pattern is apparent even with less than optimal existing poll data on Asian Americans.

As with Latinos, Asian Americans appear partial to the Democratic Party, a pattern that has developed over the past few decades. In the first major study of Asian American partisanship, Bruce Cain, Roderick Kiewiet, and Carole Uhlaner found a roughly even split in partisanship (1991). Notably, this study, which was based on a 1984 survey of California adults, also found that Asian Americans were far more Republican than were Latinos. The authors explain this difference as a result of the salience of foreign policy concerns among Chinese, Koreans, and Southeast Asians and further suggest that the effect of being a racial-ethnic minority that one might expect to pull Asians toward the Democratic Party among their second and third generation respondents was absent. By the 1990s, according to one review of twelve national, state-level, and metropolitan-level surveys, the approximately even split in Asian American partisanship begins to take a distinctly Democratic turn, especially by the 1998 off-year elections (Lien 2001). This leaning has become solid in recent years. In the postelection 2000–2001 Pilot National Asian American Politics Study—the first multicity, multiethnic, multilingual academic survey of Asian Americans—Democratic identifiers outnumbered their Republican counterparts by more than two-to-one, and across all ethnic subgroups except for Vietnamese Americans, who lean toward the Republican Party (Lien, Conway, and Wong 2004).

This partisan leaning is also evident in how Asians vote when we turn to exit poll data in figure 4.1.[2] Although party identification is not the same as presidential vote choice, the exit poll data offer one of the few clues as to how the party orientations of Asian Americans and, to some extent Latinos, have changed over the past two decades. At least three findings are worth noting from figure 4.1. First, in the 1992 election—featuring the Democrat Bill Clinton, the Republican George H. W. Bush, and the third-party upstart H. Ross Perot—fewer than one in three Asian Americans, according to the Voter News Service, reported voting for Clinton. Second, by the most recent presidential election, the 2008 National Election Pool finds a decisive 63 to 34 percentage points split in favor of

Figure 4.1   Democrat Share of Presidential Vote

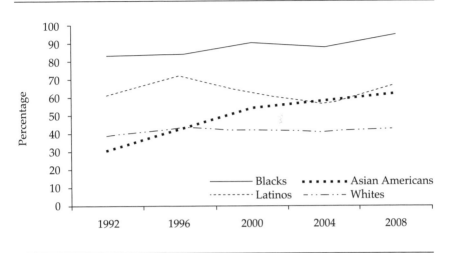

Source: Authors' compilation of data from Voter News Service and National Election Pool
exit polls (*New York Times* 2008).

Barack Obama over John McCain. This emerging pattern of favorability
toward the Democratic Party presidential candidate is also mirrored by
voter registration studies in 2004 and 2006 by the Asian American Legal
Defense and Education Fund in New York and Asian Pacific American
Legal Center (APALC) in southern California, which found marked increases in the number of Asian American registered Democrats. A 2008
AALDEF exit poll—a nonpartisan poll that is admittedly nonrandom in
its sample—found 58 percent of its respondents identified as Democrats,
14 percent as Republicans, and 26 percent as unaffiliated.[3]

The third finding of note in figure 4.1 is that the upward trajectory in
Democratic partisanship is more pronounced for Asian Americans than
for any other group. There is almost no shift in self-reported voting patterns for whites during this period (1992 to 2008) and a more modest upward shift for African Americans. For Latinos, figure 4.1 shows more of a
peak-and-trough pattern, but we note here a considerable degree of controversy over the validity of exit poll data on Latinos, especially in the
2004 presidential election.[4] One important question about this trend is
how the change happens. The literature generally reports three types of
partisan shifts: party conversion, when previously non-Democratic Asian
Americans adopt new attachments (Burnham 1970); mobilization, when
significant numbers of previously unnaturalized, unregistered, or other-

wise unincorporated Asian Americans are brought into politics with a Democratic inflection (Andersen 1979); or generational replacement, when (for example) older Asian Americans who might have been more Republican because of their hawkish foreign policy preferences are replaced by younger counterparts who are more Democratic because of their domestic social policy preferences (Beck and Jennings 1979).

Being able to properly check out and sort between these accounts requires the availability of good quality longitudinal data on Asian American partisanship. The 2008 NAAS, however, does allow us to mostly confirm these general patterns found in exit poll data. Figure 4.2 shows the distribution of party identification for the full sample and for each ethnic subgroup in our sample. Party identification here is defined by answers to the root question on whether, generally speaking, respondents think of themselves as Democrats, Republicans, or independents. Overall, a far greater proportion of respondents think of themselves as Democrats (48 percent) than as Republicans (22 percent) or independents (27 percent). When a more generous definition of a partisan is used—inclusive of those independents who confess a leaning toward one of the two major parties—the favorability of NAAS respondents toward the Democratic Party over the Republican Party remains by a greater than two-to-one margin (61 percent to 29 percent), with 11 percent identifying as pure independents (results not shown in figure 4.2).

Figure 4.2 also shows interesting and important ethnic subgroup differences in party identification. Most groups show a strong partiality with the Democratic Party. This is perhaps not surprising for Asian Indians, for whom racial discrimination and profiling became a more significant issue after the September 11 attacks. However, we also find strong levels of Democratic identification among Japanese and Koreans and, to a lesser extent, Filipinos. These results largely hold true even when taking into account independent leaners. Figure 4.2 also shows that Vietnamese Americans are the one Asian national-origin group that identifies more closely with the Republican Party than the Democrats. As with Cuban Americans, the persistence of Republican attachment can likely be explained by the combination of anticommunist sentiment and assigning blame on past Democratic presidents for failure in anticommunist military actions, as well as the electoral success of ethnic elected officials who are Republican. A third distinctive finding in figure 4.2 is the extraordinary proportion of Chinese Americans who self-identify as independents (46 percent). Even when partisan leaners are taken into account (20 percent Democratic and 7 percent Republican), 18 percent of the Chinese sample in the NAAS are pure independents. Thus, for most Asian American groups, the days of Republican leaning or a roughly third split between Democrats, Republi-

Figure 4.2   Party Identification Among Asian Americans

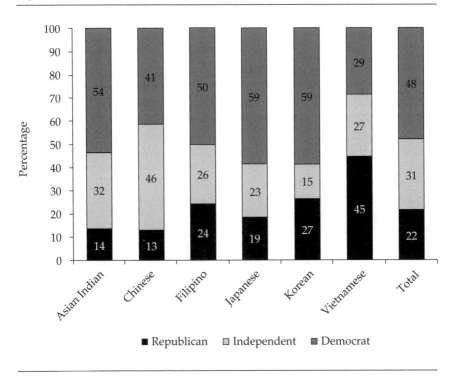

Source: Authors' compilation of data from the 2008 National Asian American Survey (Ramakrishnan et al. 2011).
Note: "Don't know" and "Do not think in these terms" are excluded from the analysis.

cans, and independents are gone. Given the paucity of time-series data on Asian American partisanship by ethnic group, it is unclear whether the increasing shift in identification toward the Democratic Party is due to economic prosperity under the Clinton era, having a greater sense of racialization and discrimination over time, living in states and counties dominated by Democrat voters, or being represented by Asian American officials who are Democrats. In fact, preliminary analysis of the NAAS data does suggest that those who naturalized under Clinton are more likely to be Democrats. In contrast, experience with discrimination, having an Asian American representative who is a Democrat and living in a predominantly Democratic state are not associated positively with Democratic party identification. However, our data do not allow us to capture over time changes in the population. The incorporation of new cohorts of

Asian American voters with characteristics that differ from earlier cohorts may be influencing the overall partisan trend. Unfortunately, we cannot capture this dynamic with survey data collected at a single point in time.

IDENTIFIERS AND NON-IDENTIFIERS

We have thus far highlighted two defining features of Asian American partisanship: its contingency across time and data sources and its growing Democratic flavor. But these features, important as they are, mask what we think is an even more central one—the tendency to remain outside the partisan scale. As we noted earlier, in most studies of party identification, the ability of survey respondents to place themselves on a conventional scale of partisanship is taken as a given. No lesser source than *The American Voter* proclaims that "the partisan self-image of all but the few individuals who disclaim any involvement in politics permits us to place each person in these samples on a continuum of partisanship extending from strongly Republican to strongly Democratic" (Campbell et al. 1960). For well-established groups in the United States such as whites and African Americans, this assumption is reasonable. In the American National Election Study cumulative file from 1948 to 2004, fewer than 7 percent of the black and white sample chose one of the following nonpartisan responses: no preference, none, neither, other, don't know, or otherwise refused to answer question. It comes as no surprise, then, that most studies of partisanship simply dismiss this group of non-identifiers as an anomaly, code them as missing, and drop them from analysis altogether.[5]

Yet for more heavily immigrant groups such as Latinos and Asian Americans, there is a critical prior question that affects whether and how the standard party identification is viewed. As predominantly immigrant or second-generation Americans, many Latino and Asian American survey respondents must first grapple with what it means to be a partisan, as Zoltan Hajnal and Taeku Lee contend (2011). In other words, the willingness to think in partisan terms—by which we mean the willingness to place oneself on a party identification spectrum at all—is often a step that is separate from, and prior to, the specific self-placement on a continuum of partisanship assumed in most research on party identification. With Latinos, for instance, the 2006 Latino National Survey shows that fully 38 percent of respondents are uncommitted to a partisan category and nonpartisans (non-identifiers and independents, together) make up 55 percent of all responses.

These numbers are closely mirrored in the 2008 National Asian American Survey. Thus, perhaps the most pronounced finding on partisanship in the 2008 NAAS is that the modal respondent in our survey simply does not make heads or tails out of the conventional party identification question. As table 4.1 shows, fully 35 percent of NAAS respondents are what we call non-identifiers, meaning that they either indicate that they "do not think in these [partisan] terms," where the terms of partisanship are self-identifying as a Republican, Democrat, or independent, or that they do not know how to answer the question, or simply refuse to answer the question. When non-identifiers are combined with those Asian Americans who identify as independents, 55 percent of NAAS respondents do not identify as either a Democrat or a Republican.

Unlike many other findings from the 2008 NAAS, this tendency to not identify with a major party is pervasive across ethnic subgroups. The incidence of non-identifiers ranges between 31 percent and 39 percent in table 4.1. Chinese Americans, who we earlier saw to be the most likely to identify as independents, are also the most likely to be non-identifiers: fully two out of three Chinese Americans identify as an independent or are partisan non-identifiers.

This prevailing nonpartisanship among Asian Americans, moreover, is politically consequential. One of the eye-popping general findings from the NAAS with respect to the 2008 presidential horse-race is the high proportion of respondents—for a survey fielded just weeks before Election Day—who reported being undecided between John McCain and Barack Obama. Even among likely voters, we found roughly one in three respondents uncertain of how they were going to vote. For partisans, this uncertainty diminishes considerably (19 percent of self-identified Democrats and 23 percent of self-identified Republicans); among nonpartisans, 45 percent of independents and 57 percent of non-identifiers who were likely voters reported being uncertain of their vote choice in the weeks ahead. Of the 46 percent of our sample who were identified as likely voters, however, the proportion of non-identifiers shrinks from 35 percent to 21 percent.

EXPLAINING THE PARTISAN CHOICES OF ASIAN AMERICANS

As we see later in this chapter, whether and how Asian Americans identify with the choice between the two major parties in American politics is a potential key to understanding who is politically active and who remains disengaged. As a prelude to this analysis, we first examine the distribution of Asian American partisanship we find. To do so, we first briefly revisit explanations that emerge from the traditional party identification literature. We then move on to consider the relevance of immigrant incorporation as a core process structuring Asian American partisanship. In

Table 4.1   Party Identification

	Asian Indian	Chinese	Filipino	Japanese	Korean	Vietnamese	Total
Republican	9	8	16	13	17	31	14
Democrat	35	25	34	40	38	20	31
Independent	21	28	17	16	10	18	20
Non-identifier	35	39	32	31	35	31	35

Source: Authors' compilation of data from the 2008 National Asian American Survey (Ramakrishnan et al. 2011).
Note: Rates are in percentages.

particular, we focus on how patterns of party identification vary across the primary demographic and socioeconomic background factors that describe the diversity of the Asian American population. Once we have brought together the literatures on party identification and political incorporation, we return to our interest in partisanship as a potentially key determinant of the political engagement of Asian Americans.

Because traditional accounts of partisanship either overlook nonpartisans and non-identifiers altogether or dismiss partisanship as irrelevant to the political arena, it is not surprising to find that these traditional theories offer little in the way of a direct explanation of the phenomenon. Nevertheless, one can extrapolate a story from these theories. A Downsian might infer that Americans with decidedly moderate views would be the most likely to remain nonpartisan. For these middle-of-the-road Americans, with few strong policy positions, the motivation may be too scant to drive a partisan choice in the first place. This explanation does not take us very far, because the view that non-identifiers are ideological moderates is easily rebutted. In the 2008 NAAS, the parallel between the high proportion of Asian Americans who do not identify as a Democrat, independent, or Republican and the proportion that do not identify as a liberal, moderate, or conservative is striking. The basic distribution of ideological views is 15 percent conservative, 21 percent liberal, 33 percent moderate, and 31 percent who do not identify with any of these categories. Only 27 percent of partisan non-identifiers self-identify as moderates, 12 percent as liberal, and 10 percent as conservative. Fully 51 percent do not identify with a conventional ideological category.

A missing element in the information and market-based approach to explaining party identification is a previous account of how newcomers form preferences over partisan goods. Here the reliance on political socialization in the Michigan school of party identification would seem felicitous. From the standpoint of *The American Voter*, one might think of non-identifiers as those who fail to identify with a party by virtue of their having been raised by parents who were also uncommitted and apolitical, or in social and institutional settings that fostered inattention to or disdain for party politics. This raises an interesting question about whether non-identification is a habit that is passed on from generation to generation—a question not explicitly raised by advocates of the Michigan school.

To gain some insight into the extent of intergenerational transmission of partisanship (and nonpartisanship) among Asian Americans, the 2008 NAAS asked native-born respondents about the partisanship of their parents when they were young. This is admittedly a noisy measure, because the parents may well have been born outside the United States and arrived as immigrants. Thus categories like Democrat, Republican, and

Table 4.2   Distribution of Respondent's Partisanship by Respondent's Parents' Partisanship

	Mother Republican	Mother Democrat	Mother Independent or Other	Mother Non-Identifier
Republican	38	9	13	11
Democrat	23	64	40	39
Independent	23	18	22	18
Non-identifier	16	10	25	32

	Father Republican	Father Democrat	Father Independent or Other	Father Non-Identifier
Republican	33	8	12	11
Democrat	27	66	42	37
Independent	25	16	21	19
Non-identifier	15	10	26	34

Source: Authors' compilation of data from the 2008 National Asian American Survey (Ramakrishnan et al. 2011).
Note: Rates are in percentages.

independent may be meaningless, may have meanings that do not parallel the U.S. meanings, or may force a translation of other partisan labels in non-U.S. contexts into one of these three partisan categories.

Table 4.2 shows the distribution of respondents' partisanship by the reported partisanship of their parents. The NAAS findings show that intergenerational transmission of partisanship is strongest when parents are identified as having been Democrats during respondents' formative years: when the mother is identified as a Democrat, 64 percent of respondents self-identify as a Democrat (71 percent if self-identified; independents who lean to the Democratic Party are included). In the father's case, 66 percent of respondents also self-identify as a Democrat (72 percent including leaners). The transmission of partisanship is weakest when parents are identified as independents (3 percent) or affiliated with some other party (22 percent). Here only about one in five respondents (20 percent) self-identify as an independent or a member of a third party, an unsurprising outcome in light of the fact that the other party category is quite prevalent when applied to respondents' parents and the reasonable surmise that in most of these cases, the other party refers to a political party that is not U.S.-based.

The final observation is the modest degree of intergenerational transmission of non-identification. When respondents reported that their parents did not think in partisan terms (roughly 22 percent of the time), or did not know how to identify their parents' partisanship (roughly 7 percent), or refused to identify their parents thus (less than 1 percent), they too were more likely to view their own partisanship in one of these terms. As table 4.2 shows, the incidence of non-identifiers is highest when respondents' parents are also non-identifiers.

We remind readers here that these parental partisanship items were only asked of U.S.-born respondents of the NAAS.[6] Most respondents are foreign-born, and nonpartisanship is more prevalent among this segment of the Asian American population. Here, we further note that socialization-based theories of partisanship offer an incomplete account for immigrants. If the population in question is not politically socialized (especially in the pre-adult years, as in *The American Voter*) in the United States, then socialization per se cannot explain the remarkably high proportion of non-identifiers.

What is obviously absent from these traditional models is a consideration of the immigrant experience and its aftermath. This is not the result of explicit omission on the part of Michigan and Downsian schools of thought, because these theories originated during a period of far lower rates of immigrant stocks and flows. If one's immigrant experience does have a bearing on one's status as uncommitted and unattached to either of the two parties, then we need to integrate key elements of this immigrant experience into any discussion of the party identification of Asian Americans.

IMMIGRANT SOCIALIZATION AND PARTY IDENTIFICATION

We first describe the general distribution of party identification across different subsets of the Asian American population. Our aim here is see how well our expectations stand up to a rough cut at the data. Cross-tabulations, when carefully matched to sound reasoning and coherent theorizing, are often remarkably robust to fancier statistical modeling. We therefore check here to see whether our data pushes us past this important first post. Specifically, we compare indicators of straight-line assimilation, which assumes a linear relationship between length of residence and generation and political incorporation, to alternative dimensions of political incorporation.

As before, our four categories of party identification are self-identification as a Democrat, a Republican, an independent, or remaining uncommitted to one of these conventional forms of identification. We start with the role that lived experience in the United States plays in structuring par-

Figure 4.3   Party Identification by Nativity and U.S. Residency

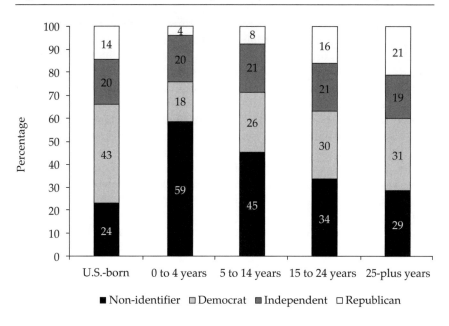

Source: Authors' compilation of data from the 2008 National Asian American Survey (Ramakrishnan et al. 2011).

tisan attachments (Cho 1999; Pantoja, Ramirez, and Segura 2001; Wong 2000). Specifically, in figure 4.3, we compare the U.S.-born to the foreign-born, the latter group disaggregated by the number of years they have lived in the United States. The cut-points distinguish respondents who have lived in the United States for less than five years, for between five and fourteen years, between fifteen and twenty-four years, and twenty-five years and beyond.

This figure broadly supports a straight-line assimilation account of partisanship acquisition. Time in the United States translates into greater likelihood of holding partisan attachments. Asian immigrants who have lived here for less than five years, for example, are more than twice as likely to be uncommitted about their partisanship than their counterparts who have lived here for more than twenty-five years (59 percent versus 29 percent). Almost all of this decrease in one's likelihood of being uncommitted between partisan categories over time is absorbed by the greater likelihood of identifying as a Democrat (from 18 percent to 31 percent over the same cohort comparisons) or a Republican (from 4 percent to 21 percent). The likelihood of identifying as an independent remains remarkably constant over time: the range is from 19 percent to 21 percent, across all categories in figure 4.3.

To the extent that developing attachments to a political party is a key mode of immigrant political incorporation, our findings affirm that length of residence increases prospects of political incorporation. As we saw in chapter 2, there are similar expectations of a straight-line pathway to assimilation with respect to other dimensions of immigrant incorporation. For example, as one becomes more assimilated, one's socioeconomic resources are expected to rise and lead to a concomitant increase in political participation.

The findings in figure 4.3 also hint at a story behind the over-time trend in Asian American partisanship shown earlier. Specifically, figure 4.1 showed a clear increase over time in Democratic partisanship (in the proportion of the three-way split between Democrat, Republican, and independent). Although longitudinal data on Asian American voting behavior is too limited to produce a reliable trend analysis of whether the increasing affiliation as Democrats is due to conversion, mobilization, or generational replacement, figure 4.3 suggests that a significant part of the growing Democratic partisanship of Asian Americans over time is due to non-identifiers who become more partisan. Thus, although only 18 percent of those Asian immigrants who have been a resident in the United States for less than five years self-identify as Democrats, fully 31 percent of those who have for twenty-five years or longer do so, and 42 percent of U.S.-born Asians identify as Democrats.[7]

We next examine whether this relationship holds across various income and educational levels. These results suggest a tangible connection between class and partisanship, perhaps more powerfully so for education than income. With income, the likelihood is discernably higher of identifying as an Independent or a Democrat and correspondingly lower of being a non-identifier among the richest Asian Americans (compared with their poorest counterparts), and less discernible in identifying as a Republican across income categories. These differences are modest.

With education, the effects are more pronounced. As figure 4.4 makes clear, 51 percent of Asian Americans with only some high school education are non-identifiers, whereas only between 27 percent and 32 percent of those with at least some college education are. As with income, the largest share of this change is captured by independents: only 10 percent of those with the least education are independents, while 27 percent of those with a college degree are.

Taken together, these results on education and family income illustrate the potential pitfalls of focusing on party affiliation with the two major

Figure 4.4   Party Identification by Educational Attainment

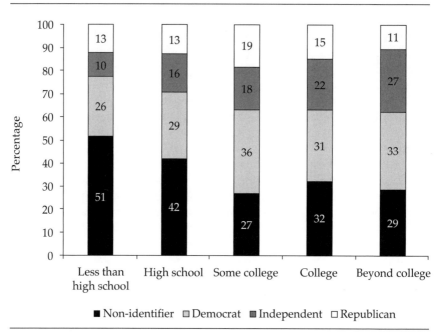

Source: Authors' compilation of data from the 2008 National Asian American Survey (Ramakrishnan et al. 2011).

parties alone. There is only a modest association—especially with min-max comparisons of those in the lowest and highest levels of family income and education—between socioeconomic status and major party affiliation. This does not, however, mean that there is no relationship between these indicators of SES and partisanship, more broadly conceived. Specifically, with both income and education, the NAAS suggests a possible substitution of non-identification for identification as an independent as SES rises. As Zoltan Hajnal and Taeku Lee argue, this substitution underscores two important aspects of nonpartisanship (2011). First is that non-identifiers are distinct from independents and cannot be lumped together. Second is that, to the extent that high SES indirectly measures political interest and sophistication, independents are not all nonpartisan by virtue of being ignorant, unsophisticated, or otherwise disinvested from politics.

Beyond socioeconomic status, several other relevant associations must be considered. First are age and gender effects, shown in table 4.3. Age

Table 4.3   Distribution of Partisanship by Age and Gender

	Republican	Democrat	Independent	Non-Identifier
Age				
Eighteen to twenty-four	14	36	22	29
Thirty-five to forty-nine	12	29	22	37
Fifty to sixty-four	15	31	19	35
Sixty-five and older	19	33	15	33
Male	16	30	24	30
Female	12	32	16	39

Source: Authors' compilation of data from the 2008 National Asian American Survey (Ramakrishnan et al. 2011).
Note: Rates are in percentages.

appears to shape partisanship in some expected ways: respondents sixty-five or older are more likely to identify as Republicans than younger adults; similarly, the highest proportion of Democratic identifiers are among eighteen- to thirty-four-year-olds. Perhaps more unexpectedly, young adults (eighteen- to thirty-four-year-olds) are the least likely to be a non-identifier. With gender, table 4.3 shows—consistent with relationships in the general (non–Asian American) population—that men are more likely to identify as Republicans and independents and women more likely to identify as Democrats. The surprise here may be the gender gap among non-identifiers: 39 percent of women reject the traditional tripartite partisan categorization, and only 30 percent of men do so.

As we noted in chapter 2, a key factor in characterizing the politics of Asian Americans is the experience of immigrant socialization. In table 4.4, we consider five key indicators of that socialization experience: whether respondents were educated in the United States or elsewhere; their self-reported English speaking ability; the language in which the survey interview was conducted; whether respondents live in a traditional, small, or new destination for Asian immigrants (see chapter 3); and whether respondents are U.S. citizens.

The results in table 4.4, for the most part, follow in a straightforward way from expectations of a linear assimilation process, at least in terms of whether one can identify with the traditional three-category rendition of partisanship. Asian Americans educated outside the United States, who

Table 4.4   Partisanship by Immigrant Socialization

	Republican	Democrat	Independent	Non-Identifier
Education history				
Educated in the United States	16	37	22	25
Educated outside the United States	13	28	19	40
Spoken English ability				
Not at all	9	29	15	47
Just a little	15	24	16	44
Pretty well	19	27	17	36
Very well	20	33	26	20
Language of interview				
English interview	13	33	21	33
Asian language interview	16	28	19	37
Settlement context				
Small Asian American settlements	19	26	23	32
Traditional settlements	14	34	18	34
New settlements	14	26	24	37
Citizenship				
Citizen	18	35	20	27
Not a citizen	7	24	19	50

Source: Authors' compilation of data from the 2008 National Asian American Survey (Ramakrishnan et al. 2011).
Note: Rates are in percentages.

report little or no spoken English ability, who choose an Asian language of interview, who live in new Asian immigrant destinations, and who are not citizens are all more likely to be non-identifiers. In the cases of language-of-interview and new Asian settlements, the effects are very modest, but in other cases are far more pronounced. Fully half of noncitizens in our sample are non-identifiers versus 27 percent of citizens; 40 percent of those educated outside the United States are non-identifiers versus 25 percent of those educated within its boundaries; 47 percent of those with no spoken English ability are non-identifiers versus 20 percent of those who report speaking English very well.

Table 4.4 also shows some associations between our measures of socialization and the three-way choice between Democrat, Republican, and independent. Education in the United States seems to increase the incidence of identifying as a Democrat and independent but not Republican; greater language skills appear to increase the likelihood of identifying as a Republican or independent but not Democrat; citizens are more likely to identify as a Republican or Democrat but not independent. Note the intransitivities across these measures of socialization. What this pattern of findings reiterates, echoing an earlier point, is that expectations from a straight-line assimilation account help us understand whether someone identifies with the traditional party categories (Democrat, Republican, or independent), but do little to help us predict which of these choices Asian Americans will make.

One other relevant aspect of the socialization contexts in which Asian Americans are likely to form their partisan attachments is political geography—that is, one reasonable expectation might be that Asian immigrants who live in red states are more inclined to be Republican than their counterparts in blue states. Such spatially defined influences on partisanship acquisition might also scale down to smaller geographic areas. Another potentially relevant dimension of political geography is the presence and type of partisan competition in electoral district of residence. A reasonable expectation here would be that Asian Americans in battleground states or in marginal districts would be less likely to be non-identifiers than those in safe districts and clearly partisan states. Similarly, we might expect that those in states that allowed direct democracy might be more politicized and those in counties and municipalities with local nonpartisan elections might be less partisan. Although each of these relationships might be reasonable to expect, the NAAS data show a general absence of any significant effects between political geography and patterns of partisanship. The one notable exception is that respondents who live in jurisdictions with local nonpartisan elections and in states with direct democracy ballot initiatives are somewhat more likely to be Republican.

PRELIMINARY ANALYSIS OF DETERMINANTS OF PARTY IDENTIFICATION

In this section we investigate in a more statistically precise way how each of these different elements affects the party identification of Asian Americans. Our goal is to take some initial steps toward explaining how key social, demographic, and immigration markers differentiate who identifies with a political party and which political party they identify with. The analytic strategy here is similar to that taken in the previous chapters—namely, to clarify which of the relationships we have described thus far remain salient once we control for each of the other relationships, and which fade into insignificance. Unlike previous chapters, however, the estimation is complicated by the specific argument we have advanced about the dependent variable, party identification. As we noted, the modal response among Asian Americans to the standard party identification question is non-identification, with a large majority among them opting for nonpartisanship (non-identification or identifying as an independent). The distinctiveness of residual categories of nonpartisanship that we find suggests, following Hajnal and Lee (2011), that partisanship acquisition follows two steps: first, the individual comes to see the three-way categorization of Democrat-independent-Republican as a meaningful choice; second, that person actively chooses one of these categories.

This sequence is ignored in most studies of party identification. More often than not, categories are scaled on a continuum from strong identification with the Democratic Party at one end, independents in the middle, and strong identification with the Republican Party at the other end. Non-identifiers—the large proportion of Asian Americans who indicate that they do not think in partisan terms, are unsure of or do not know what party they identify with, or otherwise refuse to answer the question—would be treated as missing values and excluded from the statistical analyses. The dependent variable (measuring party identification as Democrat or independent or Republican) is then estimated using a least squares regression or an ordered, polychotomous choice (probit or logit) regression.

This approach predominates, but it suffers from two limitations. First, a primary theme of this chapter has been that the choices Democrat, Republican, and independent are unordered (Petrocik 1974; Weisberg 1980, 1983; Hajnal and Lee 2011). Do all those who claim to be independent really sit squarely in between Democrats and Republicans? One consequence of thinking of partisanship as an unordered choice is to employ a multinomial estimator (Alvarez and Bedolla 2003; Uhlaner and Garcia 2002; Lien, Conway, and Wong 2004). Rather than modeling party identification as a continuum, multinomial logit allows us to estimate the relative probability of identifying between each pair of choices—independent or Democrat, Republican or independent, Democrat or Republican.

A second problem—one common to both ordered and unordered approaches to estimating party identification—is that non-identifiers are treated as missing values and excluded from the statistical analyses. That these omitted cases represent the plurality (35 percent of our weighted sample) of Asian American responses to the party identification question threatens to greatly misinform our understanding of Asian Americans' relationship to political parties in the United States. To account for these limitations and better reflect our views on the sequential nature of partisan choice, we present our statistical analysis here in two stages.

The first results analyze which Asian Americans identify with one of the three traditional partisan choices (Democrat, Republican, or independent) and which are non-identifiers. We examine this binary choice using logit regression models. The second results compare the unordered choice between Democrat, Republican, and independent using multinomial logit regression models. The set of explanatory factors we test for in our statistical model are limited to those factors we have considered in this chapter: education, family income, age, gender, length of time in the United States (if immigrant generation), national origin, educational history (U.S. or non-U.S.), English skills, language of interview, settlement destinations, citizenship, and (for U.S.-born respondents) the partisanship of parents during the respondents' childhood.

When these factors are combined, the results show a strong role of several key factors and a lesser role for others. In the first stage, we find several pronounced and significant effects. Specifically, more education, longer time in the United States, greater spoken English skills, citizenship, and parents who identify with a major party all have an especially strong effect on decreasing respondents' likelihood of being a non-identifier. Using post-estimation predicted effects, we estimate the following:

- Non-identification is higher among the less educated—37 percent of those with some high school or less versus 26 percent of those with a college degree and 21 percent of those with a professional degree or a doctorate.

- Non-identification is higher among the recently arrived—33 percent of those who have been in the United States for a year or less versus 27 percent of those here for twenty years and 22 percent of those here for forty years.

- Non-identification is higher among non-English speakers—31 percent of those with no spoken English ability versus 19 percent of those with fluency.

- Non-identification is higher among noncitizens—40 percent of noncitizens versus 25 percent of citizens.

The upshot of this multivariate statistical analysis may not be surprising, but is important to emphasize nonetheless. Asian Americans become familiar with and are able to choose between the traditional partisan categories in U.S. politics when they are better educated, more skilled in English, acquire citizenship, and have parents who identify with a major party. These effects, though significant, do not crowd out the lingering particularities of some ethnic-national origins. Chinese and Koreans are both more likely to be non-identifiers (33 percent) than the baseline comparison group in our statistical analyses, Japanese Americans (27 percent).

When we turn to the second stage of partisanship acquisition—the three-way choice between identifying as a Democrat, Republican, or independent—the story is more complicated, if for no other reason than three pairwise choices are simultaneously being estimated. For expository simplicity, we highlight the main findings here by pairwise choices:

Democrat or Republican. We find that Republican identifiers are likelier to be older, male, and, to lesser degrees of statistical significance (p < .10), also likelier to have higher family income, to have lived in the United States for a longer time (if foreign-born), and to be citizens. Parents' partisanship has a clear effect here: 65 percent of respondents who identify both parents as Democrats also identify as Democrats (against a baseline of 47 percent); 57 percent of those who identify both parents as Republicans also identify as Republicans (against a baseline of 20 percent). There are also some residual national-origin differences: Asian Indians are less likely than the reference group (Japanese) to identify as Republicans, but Filipinos and Vietnamese more likely to do so. The effects for Vietnamese here are especially large: an estimated 38 percent of Vietnamese identify as Republicans, but only 17 percent of the rest of the sample do so.

Democrat or independent. We find that Asian Americans with higher family incomes, men, citizens, those living in traditional Asian immigrant destinations, and U.S.-born respondents who do not identify their parents as Democrats are all likelier to identify as independents than as Democrats. Less statistically significant, Asian Americans with less education, those educated in the United States, and those who identify their parents as Republicans are also likelier to identify as independents. We also find that Chinese and Vietnamese are more likely to identify as independents than the reference group, and Koreans less likely.

Republican or independent. Finally, we find that Asian Americans who are older, less educated, citizens, and who identify their parents as Republicans are more likely to identify as Republicans than as independents. Here too are several large residual ethnic group differences: Asian Indians and Chinese are both more likely to identify as independents than Japanese; Koreans and Vietnamese, by contrast, are less likely to identify as independents. In both Democrat-independent and Republican-independent choices, the effects for Chinese Americans here are especially large: we estimate 51 percent to identify as independents compared to 26 percent of Japanese Americans.

POLITICAL FACTORS AND PARTY IDENTIFICATION

We reiterate again that our aim here is not to propose a full or correct model of party identification. Rather, it is to test for the relative salience of a set of factors we consider important in describing the structural contexts shaping Asian American politics. With any statistical model, the worry is misspecification: had other salient predictors of partisanship been included in our estimates, the factors identified as important in explaining the party identification of Asian Americans might prove insignificant. But it is beyond the scope of this chapter to consider an exhaustive roster of candidates excluded from our analysis.

In this final section, we do however briefly consider an important rejoinder. Namely, partisanship is fundamentally political, and we have (except for citizenship status and parents' reported partisanship) neglected to consider potentially critical political factors. This is without question an important caveat to our analyses. Yet we tread lightly in taking this rejoinder to heart for at least two reasons. First, it is difficult to consider a broader range of political variables without potentially running afoul of the caution against using politics to predict politics. We are reminded here of the core insight from the authors of *The American Voter* that remains, by and large, valid even today: partisanship, when it matters, is at the portal end of a funnel of causality—that is, it is much more likely that partisanship predicts a host of political outcomes of interest than the other way around. The second and related reason for treading lightly is that a full consideration of possible political variables and their antecedent, intervening, or posterior relationships to party identification is beyond the scope of this chapter.

Tiptoeing into a consideration of other potentially salient correlates of party identification, then, we first focus on two important aspects of politics. First, at individual, institutional, and discursive levels, much of politics in America is organized around and framed in terms of a liberal-to-conservative ideological continuum. Second, at the individual level, some people have a natural interest in politics and others do not. We then examine, in a very preliminary way, the first-order relationship between party identification and our key measures of political engagement that are the focus throughout this book.

Figure 4.5   Party Identification by Ideology

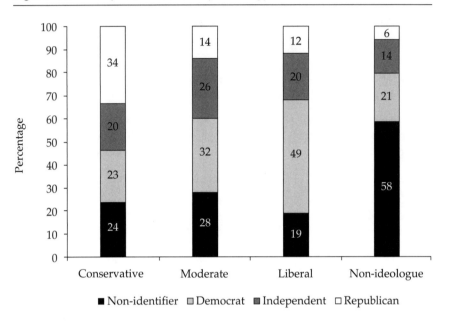

Source: Authors' compilation of data from the 2008 National Asian American Survey (Ramakrishnan et al. 2011).

For many scholars of American politics, partisan choices are, at their heart, about issue positions and ideology. As noted earlier, the Downsian account of partisanship implies that we choose the party closest to our views along the main liberal-conservative divide that separates the two parties. Thus, liberals should identify as Democrats, Republicans should end up with ties to the Republican Party, and moderates should identify as independent or perhaps remain uncommitted between conventional partisan categories. Is this account of American politics true for Asian Americans?

Figure 4.5 examines this question by dividing Asian Americans into four groups: those who self-identify as liberal, moderates, or conservatives and those who reject these conventional categories. The table shows decidedly mixed support for the claim that partisanship is anchored by ideology. Roughly one of every two self-identified liberals also self-identify as Democrats. At the same time, only 34 percent of self-identified conservatives identify as Republicans. In fact, the strongest evidence of a cor-

Figure 4.6   Partisanship by Political Interest

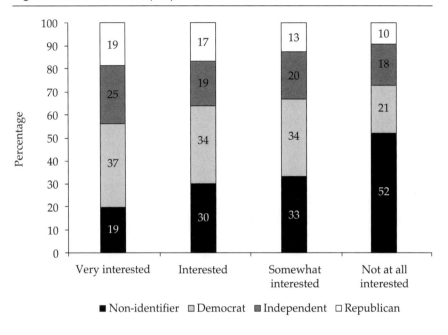

Source: Authors' compilation of data from the 2008 National Asian American Survey (Ramakrishnan et al. 2011).

respondence between partisanship and ideology is among non-identifiers: 58 percent of respondents who reject the three-way categorization of ideology between liberals, conservatives, and moderates also reject the three-way partisanship between Democrats, Republicans, and independents.[8]

Beyond ideology, another other key political factor that appears unambiguously to sharpen the partisan focus of Asian Americans is information. As argued earlier, because Asian Americans are predominantly immigrants or the second generation, a common base of knowledge about and attentiveness to politics cannot be assumed. In the absence of familiarity with what parties have to offer, it is entirely reasonable for these groups to remain skeptical about partisanship and withhold judgment. The NAAS includes at least two ways of distinguishing "low information" Asian Americans from their "high information" counterparts. The first is a measure of general political interest, shown in figure 4.6. Political interest is admittedly not a direct measure of how informed one is per se, and it surely also measures other factors, such as the desire to be politically involved or perceived as being politically involved (regardless of actual levels of information and engagement).

Nonetheless, the results here are unambiguous. Respondents' likelihood of identifying as Democrat or Republican increases and their likelihood of being a non-identifier decreases sharply with their levels of political interest. More than half of Asian Americans who report being not at all interested in politics are non-identifiers, whereas among those who are very interested, fewer than one in five are non-identifiers. The proportion of self-identified Republicans increases from 10 percent of those who are not at all interested to 19 percent among those who are very interested, whereas for self-identified Democrats the equivalent percentages are 21 percent and 37 percent, and for independents 18 percent and 25 percent.

A second measure of information and attentiveness is whether respondents are able to differentiate between the Democratic and Republican parties. In the NAAS, perceived partisan differences are measured through a somewhat complex series of branched questions: respondents are first asked to identify up to three issues they consider the most important for government to address, then which among these issues is most important to them personally, next whether they see important differences between the Democratic and Republican parties on this one issue, and finally, if important differences are seen, which party is closer to their views on the issue.

Here again, the inference is indirect that Asian Americans able to note differences between the Democratic and Republican parties on an issue that matters to them personally are better informed than those unable to discern any differences between the major parties even on an issue that is important to them. Yet the effect on partisanship is marked. Among respondents who do not see any partisan differences, 46 percent are non-identifiers whereas only 21 percent of those who do see differences are. The likelihood of identifying as a Republican, Democrat, or independent increases among those who perceive party differences. Moreover, fully 61 percent of respondents who view the Democratic Party as closer to their views on the issue that they identify as personally salient self-identify as Democrat; 53 percent of those who see the Republican Party as more proximate self-identify as Republican.

Finally, we consider the initial association between party identification and political engagement. As with previous chapters, we limit our purview on modes of political participation to five: voting, contributing money, contacting officials, protesting, and community activism. Table 4.5 shows the basic distribution of partisanship across these five measures.

Several results from this initial cut at the data are interesting. First, the relationships between the four categories of partisanship we have focused

Table 4.5   Partisanship and Political Participation

	Likely Voter	Political Contributor	Contact Government Officials	Protester	Community Activist
Republican	53	16	14	7	23
Democratic	51	19	10	6	23
Independent	42	11	12	4	27
Non-identifier	36	7	5	2	16

Source: Authors' compilation of data from the 2008 National Asian American Survey (Ramakrishnan et al. 2011).
Note: Rates are in percentages.

on vary across the five measures. In each case, non-identifiers are the least participatory group of Asian Americans when categorized in partisan terms. Only 36 percent of non-identifiers are likely voters versus 53 percent of Republicans, 51 percent of Democrats, and even 42 percent of independents. Second, independents clearly have a different relationship to political engagement than non-identifiers. With some modes of engagement (of those we examine in table 4.5, contacting and solving community problems), independents are just as active as Asian Americans who identify with a major political party. Third, political parties do not attach themselves uniquely to particular modes of participation—across the five kinds of engagement presented in table 4.5, Republican identifiers are more similar to their Democratic counterparts than they are different. Republicans are every bit as likely to engage in protest politics and community activism as Democrats and the differences in political contributions are modest at best.

Party identification is important for another reason: political parties may be reluctant to mobilize voters that do not show a clear preference for their party. The NAAS data suggest that party mobilization is somewhat rare, even for groups that exhibit relatively high rates of party identification. Vietnamese are the most likely to be strong partisans, but are the least likely to be mobilized or contacted by a political party (see chapter 8).

CONCLUSION

It is difficult to understand political behavior in the United States without attention to party identification. Yet as the demographics of the United States change, so must our understanding of this important set of attitudes (Hajnal and Lee 2011). The findings in this chapter look closely at how Asian Americans adopt and express their preference for political parties. A reluctance to identify with traditional partisan labels is an important commonality within the Asian American population. Asian Americans, like their Latino counterparts, include a large proportion of individuals who do not identify in conventional party terms. A plurality of Asian Americans claim that they don't know which party they prefer or that they do not think in these terms when it comes to identifying as Democrat, Republican, or independent. In this respect, Asian Americans are distinct from their African American and white counterparts. Lack of partisanship, then, distinguishes Asian Americans as a whole. Our analysis also shows, however, that internal group cleavages having to do with socioeconomic resources, national origin, English-language proficiency, and other demographic and political traits play a critical role in determining whether an individual identifies in conventional party terms or not. The acquisition of partisanship is an area in which group differences within the Asian American community matter a great deal. Several other key themes emerge.

One important theme is that traditional models of party identification, either the Michigan school, which emphasizes socialization and social identity as key determinants of one's party identification, or the Downsian model, which emphasizes rational calculation based upon one's political ideology, fail to fully explain how Asian Americans make their partisan choices. The Michigan school, with parental socialization at its core, does not take the immigrant experience into account. Hence, it falls short when considering first- and second-generation immigrants who may not experience early childhood socialization into the U.S. party system. Although we identify some correspondence between political ideology and party identification, the association between the two is not particularly strong among Asian Americans. Instead, we find that markers of social, economic, and political incorporation tend to exhibit a strong association with the acquisition of party identification.

A second key result from this chapter is that independents are not the same as non-identifiers. The process of coming to terms with America's political system of two-party competition—transforming from a non-identifier to a political subject who can infer meaningful distinctions between the categories of Democrat, Republicans, and Independent—is much like coming to terms with the Asian immigrant experience in America more generally. Once the traditional three-way categorization of party identification is rendered meaningful, however, correlates of greater political incorporation (for example, higher education, years lived in the United States) often predict a greater likelihood of identifying as an independent.

Finally, we hope to have made our case that understanding how Asian

Americans come to terms with two-party competition in the United States has implications for their political engagement and participation. An especially decisive distinction we find is between non-identifiers who tend to be less politically engaged than those who think in more conventional terms (as Democrats, Republicans, and independents). In chapter 7, we conduct additional analyses to test whether party identification remains an important influence on political participation once we account for the full range of other factors that are likely to matter, each discussed in other chapters of this book.

Chapter 5 | National Origin, Pan-Ethnicity, and Racial Identity

IDENTITIES ARE AT once paradoxically personal and collective. My identity is what defines me personally and uniquely. Yet if my identity is Asian American, it is a fingerprint of individuality shared by roughly 15 million others. Consider for a moment any other trait or aspect you give as an answer to the defining identitarian question, "Who am I?" That answer will surely be shared.

The mystery that wraps this riddle is that the juxtaposition of Asian and American together does not lend itself to obvious interpretation, especially under the rubric of a unitary, coherent collective identity. Lisa Lowe writes, "The American of Asian descent remains the symbolic 'alien,' the *metonym* for Asia who by definition cannot be imagined as sharing in America" (1996, 6). In some versions of Asian American, one identity dominates the other; in other versions, they coexist somewhere between détente and pluralist heaven, each retaining a willful integrity with respect to the other, and yet elsewhere they reconstitute in a hybrid identity—uniquely Asian American and neither Asian nor American.

Asian American is uncommonly diverse: Bengali, Chinese, Filipino, Indian, Indonesian, Japanese, Korean, Lao, Malay, Pakistani, Thai, Vietnamese, to mention just a few of the national origin groupings lumped together under this pan-ethnic rubric. An Asian American is Buddhist, Catholic, Confucian, Hindu, Muslim, Protestant, or one who eschews religious affiliation altogether. An Asian American may be a brand-new immigrant, just minutes through customs at Seattle-Tacoma International Airport, or the great-great-grandchild of immigrants from distant shores.

Sometimes an ethnic or racial label may emerge or crystallize as a result of identity-making work of doing politics together, like the Asian American (Yellow Power) movement of the 1960s or Philip Vera Cruz's multiracial labor activism. At other times, it is wrought by malice and fear by external agents like Ronald Ebens and Michael Nitz, who clubbed Vincent Chin to death, mistaking his Chinese ancestry for a Japanese one. At other times, the crystallization may occur in the hands of state actors, such as when U.S. citizens of Japanese descent were forcibly resettled into internment camps or, in the current post-9/11 climate of fear, citizens of Muslim faith or Middle Eastern phenotype are subject to surveillance, scrutiny, and extraordinary rendition.

One key to thinking clearly and researching carefully about Asian American identity is to be explicit and purposeful about our aims and limits. Our analysis in this chapter is mainly descriptive in its focus on identity and its expected consequences for the politics of Asian Americans. Our focus is on identity at the individual level. We begin with a brief overview of what has been written before on the topic of Asian American identity and a brief consideration of how Asian Americans have been classified in racial-ethnic terms.

BACKGROUND

A reasonable starting point in considering Asian American identity is to examine where the label Asian American comes from and whether the population it is intended to categorize sees it as relevant. Classifying who is Asian in the United States has never been a simple exercise. Using a geographic land mass definition, agencies of the federal government overseeing the granting of legal entry into the United States today include new entrants from Turkey and Iran as immigrants from Asia. At the same time, the Census Bureau adopts a different classification system, defining six specific Asian categories (Asian Indian, Chinese, Filipino, Japanese, Korean, Vietnamese) and three Pacific Islander categories (Native Hawaiian, Guamanian, Samoan), and allowing write-in areas for "Other Asian" and "Other Pacific Islander" race. The two Asian groupings are distinct from the other government-defined racial categories of "White," "Black, African Am., or Negro," and "American Indian or Alaska Native." People are also asked whether they identify as "Spanish / Hispanic / Latino" in a question in the 2010 census enumeration.

For Asian Americans, inconsistencies in the contemporary classification of race pale in comparison to earlier systems set forth by agencies of the U.S. federal government. The Census Bureau began to enumerate Asians as a separate racial category in 1860 when Chinese in California were first counted. In the next census, the category was expanded to include Japanese, and starting with the 1910 census, additional categories including Filipino and Korean were added. Over time, the federal government has changed the way it counted Asian Americans. For example, Asian Indians classified as Asian in the 1980, 1990, and 2000 censuses would have been counted as Hindu between 1920 and 1940, as Other Race between 1950 and 1960, and as white in 1970 (Gibson and Jung 2006, 5).

In addition to the Census Bureau, federal courts issued judgments on racial classification throughout the nineteenth and twentieth centuries, with the status of white hotly contested during the nearly hundred-year period of Asian exclusion from the United States. Discrimination against Asian Americans during this time was codified by federal legislation barring migration from Asian nations as well as naturalization to citizenship for people classified as Asian. A pair of U.S. Supreme Court cases—Ozawa v. U.S. (1922) and U.S. v. Thind (1923)—made it clear that Asians, in these cases a Japanese American and an Asian Indian, would be marked as non-white regardless of the color of their skin and even if their native homeland was not included in a geographic land mass defined as part of Asia. In an abrupt diversion from the land mass definition used to justify the decision in Ozawa less than a year earlier, the court in Thind invoked a common man standard that Asian Indians were, at face value, not white (Haney-López 2006).

The dynamism in the meaning of Asian and Asian American in the United States is a function not only of the rapid rise in new immigrants from Asia, but also of the fluidity of racial categories. The notion that there are clear divisions even between the big five racial categories is tenuous at best.[1] Nevertheless, government agencies, social scientists, political parties, and other mobilizing organizations continue to think about people in racial categories while honoring national origin distinctions and ethnic identities. Among political scientists, the concept of identity, whether based in party affiliation, racial grouping, or gender assignment, is most often treated as an individual-level resource for political behavior in the United States. People who are more strongly identified with the Democratic or Republican parties, for example, are much more likely to be active in a variety of political and civic activities than those who claim either a weaker affiliation or who do not identify with a party. Similarly, racial and ethnic identities and antipathies play an important role in individual and group political activism within the United States and beyond (Horowitz 1985; Laitin 1998; Brady and Kaplan forthcoming; Espiritu 1992; Petersen 2002).

Although there is good evidence of a politicized racial identity and a sense of linked fate among African Americans (Dawson 1994, 2001; Tate 1993), the extent to which pan-ethnic racial group membership is both embraced and then used to form political bonds among nonblack minority Americans is unclear. Complicating matters for Asian Americans are particular geographic dispersion and immigrant settlement patterns that produce distinctive manifestations of the pan-ethnic racial category. Studies of Asian American ethnic and racial identity have shown that such identities vary in their experiences and expressions in different regions of the United States (Lien, Conway, and Wong 2003, 2004). The contours and depth of identities of people classified as Asians in the United States—as Asian Americans—is thus very much an open question.

The previous research here fully supports grounds for skepticism about whether group identity constitutes the sturdiest base from which Asian Americans may organize politically. Most prior work on the identities of Asian Americans starts with two interrelated questions. What is the evidence for the presence of an Asian American pan-ethnic identity? Are Asian Americans more likely to identify in ethnic or pan-ethnic terms? To the first question, the preponderance of the research indicates that a relatively small minority of Asians in the United States thinks of themselves first and foremost in pan-ethnic terms under ordinary circumstances (Lien, Conway, and Wong 2003). In the 2001 Pilot National Asian American Survey, for instance, only 15 percent of respondents chose to identify as Asian American over alternatives. Yet a much larger proportion of respondents saw Asian American as a relevant, if not chief, category of identification. Of those in the PNAAPS who did not opt to identify as Asian American in the first instance, roughly one in two replied yes to the question, "Have you *ever* thought of yourself as an Asian American?" [emphasis added].[2]

To the second question, previous research makes another clear point: Asians in the United States tend to identify first in ethnic terms, whether solely by their ethnic-national origin identifier or conjoined with a hyphen to American. Turning again to the PNAAPS, 30 percent of respondents opted for a sole national-origin identifier (for example, Japanese, Filipino) and 34 percent chose a modified ethnic identifier (for example, Japanese American, Filipino American). Much of the existing research on Asian American identity that do not rely on social surveys, in fact, focus almost exclusively on the trade-off between ethnic and modified ethnic identifiers using ethnographic or qualitative interview methods (Gibson 1988; Kibria 1997, 2000; Zhou and Bankston 1998; Min and Kim 1999; Hong and Min 1999).

The important exceptions to this general description are key studies of Asian American pan-ethnicity by Yen Le Espiritu (1992) and Dina Okamoto (2003, 2006). Espiritu looks back in time to uncover historical moments when Asian Americans organized on a pan-ethnic basis. She argues that these pan-ethnic moments occur in response to perceived external threats and in response to salient policy debates and take the form of ethnic, national-origin groups organizing instrumentally in the contexts of social service provision, protest activity, and electoral politics. A further site for the construction of Asian American identities is found in bureaucracies themselves—namely, that the census not only defines the categories, but that the state's role in reinforcing these categories constitutes racial projects with implications for the formation of racial groupings (Omi 1997). Here, too, Asian groups may themselves play a role in choosing the terms used to define them, such as the mobilization of Pacific Islander advocates to report out statistics for Native Hawaiians and Pacific Islanders (NHPI) separately from Asian Americans after 2000, and the more everyday choices of Asian Americans between ethnic and pan-ethnic identifiers (Rim 2009).

Instances of pan-ethnicity can also be found in quantitative studies of social movement events and community organizations. Okamoto (2003) constructs a database of collective action events involving Asian Americans (ethnic and pan-ethnic) based upon content analysis of print media sources. Interestingly, Okamoto also finds that only a small fraction (16 percent) of all collective action events code as pan-ethnic. Cueing us to our focus on context in chapter 3, Okamoto further finds that the likelihood that events will be pan-ethnic vary in response to occupational segregation and to instances of anti-Asian prejudice and discrimination. In a second study, Okamoto (2006) constructs a database of organizations serving the Asian American population and finds that an organization is more likely to code as pan-ethnic when political opportunities are present (specifically, whether the federal administration in the previous year is Democratic); when there are other pan-ethnic organizations present in that group's metropolitan area; when the Asian population in the metro area is diverse; when there is a high rate of anti-Asian attacks; and when boundary formation factors are in place (when the occupations of Asian Americans are segregated and stratified; when there is a high rate of in-migration of non-Asians to the metropolitan area).

This review suggests an important revision to our starting observation that for many, the idea of Asian American identity is no simple matter. The reasonability of this sentiment is apparent on reflection on the diverse histories of the ethnic groups that make up the Asian American community discussed in chapter 2 and on reflection on the messy process of ethnoracial classification. Yet several clear patterns are beginning to surface on the key questions of how Asians in the United States identify themselves and whether this ethnic or racial identity is politically meaningful. In the sections that follow, we update and build on this emerging body of work by describing what the 2008 NAAS has to say on these questions. We first set out how we conceptualize identity.

ASIAN AMERICAN AS A SOCIAL IDENTITY

A growing body of scholarship in recent years has focused on the concept of identity in the social sciences (see Turner 1987; Olzak 1992; Dawson 1994; Somers 1994; Nagel 1995; Bobo and Hutchings 1996; Stryker et al. 2000). One review, using Social Science Citation Index counts, finds a dramatic increase in the number of articles on identity from nearly zero mentions in 1988 to more than 12,000 mentions by 1999 (Abdelal et al. 2009). Another review focuses on doctoral dissertations alone and finds an almost three-fold increase in the presence of identity as a key variable between 1981 and 1991 (Fearon 1999). This tendency to examine social science phenomena through the lens of group identity has been especially prominent in the area of race relations and racial-ethnic politics. The post-1965 emergence of large Latino and Asian American populations, the creation of a newly enumerated category of multiracial identity, and the rising salience of multiple, cross-cutting identity claims are just three contemporary instantiations that make identity issues especially prominent in the social sciences (see, for example, Lopez and Espiritu 1990; Lowe 1996; Portes and Rumbaut 1996; Cohen 1999; Espiritu and Omi 2000; Nobles 2000; Brewer 1991; Strolovitch 2007).

As with any trends and transformations in social inquiry, there are some who are quick to jump on the bandwagon (for fear of missing out on something big) and others who find such shifts to be suspect. Advocates point to the rich body of empirical research that demonstrably shows the explanatory power of our identities. As we explore in chapter 4, nowhere is this more resoundingly true, at least for most Americans, than with political party identification (Campbell 1960; Green, Palmquist, and Schickler 2002). In studies of race and ethnicity, group identities appear to play a key role as a collective resource that can be mobilized (Miller et al. 1981; Shingles 1981; Leighley and Vedlitz 1999; Stokes 2003; Wong, Lien, and Conway 2005) and to serve as a powerful heuristic in one's general political calculus (Allen, Dawson, and Brown 1989; Dawson 1994).

Others, by contrast, find many grounds for skepticism. The authors of one review declare that studies of identity face "a crisis of overproduction and consequent devaluation of meaning" (Brubaker and Cooper 2000, 3). Another group of collaborators, though more hopeful, find that "there is not much consensus on how to define identity; nor is there consistency in the procedures used for determining the content and scope of identity; nor is there agreement on where to look for evidence that identity indeed affects knowledge, interpretations, beliefs, preferences, and strategies; nor is there agreement on how identity affects these components of action" (Abdelal et al. 2009, 1).

At the heart of these doubts are important issues to ask of any theoretical construct. How different is identity, as a proposed concept, from others that have been used before? How consistently is identity theorized across the range of works and scholars who use the construct? How reliably and validly is identity measured across the range of works and scholars who use it? These questions—on conceptual clarity and differentiation, theoretical utility, and measurement validity—redound especially heavily on a group that exhibits the remarkable degree of diversity and heterogeneity that Asian Americans do. Simply put, the greater the variation and complexity within an identity category, the lesser the likely explanatory usefulness of that identity category.

We aim to cut through some of the potential confusion and clarify the range of potential effects of identity as a variable by leaning on the primary framework for studying identity among scholars of political behavior: social identity theory. Social identity theory is an account developed in the 1970s and 1980s by Henri Tajfel and his successors (Tajfel 1978; Tajfel and Turner 2004; J.C. Turner 1987). Identity here is thought of as "that part of an individual's self concept which derives from his knowledge of his membership of a group (or groups) together with the value and emotional significance attached to the membership" (Tajfel 1978, 63). Identity is thus the collective dimension of one's sense of self and is both meaningful and cherished. Humans are wired to strive for a positive sense of their social self by endeavoring to optimize the distinctiveness between an in-group and relevant out-groups. As Tajfel famously shows, this striving is so ubiquitous that groupness can be defined and defended over boundaries as seemingly inconsequential and arbitrary as preferring the art of Kandinsky over Klee.[3]

In general, scholars tend to reduce the processes of social identity formation into the following three levels. First, individuals classify themselves (or are classified by others) into distinct groups, separate worlds of us and them (social categorization). Second, individuals attach their sense of self to one of these distinct groups (social identity). Third, comparisons are made between the group one identifies with (in-group) and other groups (out-groups), with a defining need for positive distinctiveness attached to one's in-group (social comparison). Observationally, the upshot of these processes is that where social identity is present, one should see evidence of in-group solidarity, out-group differentiation, and intergroup competition (Huddy 2001).

Our choice to examine Asian American identity using survey data and a social identity framework comes with some important theoretical priors.

- First, we see ethnic and racial identity as historically contingent in terms of migration history and time in the United States. Thus, the extent to which individuals identify with a national origin or a pan-ethnic racial category will depend on where they came from and how long ago they or their families arrived (Kibria 2002; Lee and Zhou 2004; Kim 2008; Segura and Rodrigues 2006).

- Second, ethnic and racial identity is complex, and individuals classified as Asian in the United States can hold identities that might variously be perceived to have origins in cultural similarities, political imperatives, or economic interests (Bobo et al. 2000; Lien, Conway, and Wong 2004; Junn and Masuoka 2008).

- Third, racial and ethnic identity is dynamic and contextually dependent. Given the diverse Asian American population in terms of national origin, migration history, language, religion, and social and economic resources, the interaction between individuals and the political, labor market, and social environment will have unique influence on not only dimensions of identity, but on the relationship of group consciousness to political engagement (Dawson 1994; García Bedolla 2005).

- Fourth, ethnic and racial identity has a relationship to politics inasmuch as a stronger sense of group membership and belonging should produce higher levels of political and social engagement in the United States (Shingles 1981; Lien 1994; Chong and Rogers 2005; Sanchez 2006).

- Finally, ethnicity and race should be thought of as discrete markers within a constellation of heterogeneous, hybrid, and multiple identity markers that are often cross-cutting and intersectional (Lowe 1996; Cohen 1999; Roccas and Brewer 2002).

In this chapter, we begin to explore some of these key aspects of Asian American identity and its putative relationship to political engagement at the individual level. Our focus is mainly descriptive and keys in on available measures of self-categorization, in-group solidarity, out-group differentiation, and intergroup competition in our survey (figure 5.1). Specifically, we examine the following items in the 2008 National Asian American Survey. We begin with four measures of in-group identification:

- How respondents think of themselves vis-à-vis a range of ethnic, hyphenated ethnic, and pan-ethnic identity markers (a direct measure of self-categorization).

- Whether respondents view their personal lot in life as linked to that of others in their in-group, whether defined ethnically or pan-ethnically (a cognitive measure of in-group solidarity).

- Whether respondents believe that Asians in the United States have a commonality, whether rooted in race, culture, economic interests, or political interests (context-specific measures of in-group solidarity).

- Whether respondents would, holding other candidate qualities constant, prefer to vote for an in-group candidate rather than an outgroup candidate for political office.

We then move to three measures of out-group differentiation and intergroup competition. The first of these is our most direct measure of differentiation and competition and the second two examine narrower and more indirect facets of intergroup competition and hostility:

- In the realms of politics, whether Asian Americans have a commonality with African Americans, Latinos, and whites.

- Whether respondents have experienced unfair treatment or discrimination across multiple contexts of intergroup relations.

- Whether respondents have been the victim of a hate crime.

Finally, the willingness to vote for a co-ethnic candidate for political office can be interpreted as both an expression of in-group solidarity as well as a reflection of inter-group competition.

BASIC CONTOURS OF ETHNIC AND RACIAL IDENTITY

We examine this broad range of survey measures on the NAAS intended to capture various aspects of ethnic and racial identity. This section details the distribution of these measures for all survey respondents as well as for individuals grouped by self-described national origin. Subsequent analyses will focus on the questions on self-identification as measures of in-group solidarity, we also present data on out-group differentiation as well as intergroup competition.

Table 5.1 shows the distribution across the six major national origin groups in response to the following question: "People of Asian descent in

Figure 5.1   Systematic Assessments of Racial and Ethnic Identification

Racial and Ethnic Identification

In-Group Identification
Self-categorization; linked fate; in-group commonality; vote for in-group candidate

Out-Group Differentiation
Commonality with out-groups; experiences with discrimination and hate crimes

Source: Authors' compilation.

the U.S. use different terms to describe themselves. In general do you think of yourself as . . . i) An Asian American, ii) A [Ethnic Group] (i.e., Korean), iii) A [Ethnic Group American] (i.e., Korean American), and iv) An Asian." The options were rotated so that respondents had an equal chance of getting one of these four group labels that relate to social identity. We gave respondents the option of saying yes or no to more than one of these categories, and we also recorded other answers that the respondent gave, including American and Other responses that were more open-ended. To avoid any confusion between the labels as offered in the survey and the terms we use throughout this book (such as Asian American, Vietnamese, and so on) we mark survey responses to the social identity question in italics. For example, in the case of a Filipino respondent, the four identity labels are *Filipino, Filipino American, Asian,* and *Asian American.*

As we can see in table 5.1, nearly half of all survey respondents said they think of themselves as *Ethnic American,* with 47 percent saying yes to this descriptor. A slightly smaller proportion (40 percent) say they think of themselves as part of their *Ethnic Group,* while 21 percent identifies as *Asian American,* and 19 percent as *Asian.* Because respondents could select more than one label, the proportions total more than 100 percent for the overall survey sample as well as for the various national-origin groups.

Looking across national-origin groups, we find some important differences. Those of Vietnamese and Korean descent are the ones most likely to identify as *Ethnic American* (that is, for example, Vietnamese American) (69 percent and 64 percent respectively). A similarly large proportion of those with Korean ancestry (70 percent) say they identify as *Korean* alone. On identification with *Ethnic Group,* the other notable finding is that Indians stand out as the ones least likely to adopt this descriptor (28 percent). Indians are also more likely to identify as *Asian American* than Filipinos

Table 5.1   Racial-Ethnic Self-Categorization (All Mentions)

	India	China	Philippines	Japan	Korea	Vietnam	Total
Ethnic American	36	40	46	44	64	69	47
Ethnic group	28	38	40	36	70	37	40
Asian American	21	20	15	13	43	20	21
Asian	12	17	15	12	48	16	19
American	6	4	3	5	2	1	4
Other	3	2	5	4	0	2	3

Source: Authors' compilation of data from the 2008 National Asian American Survey (Ramakrishnan et al. 2011).
Survey question: "People of Asian descent in the U.S. use different terms to describe themselves. In general, do you think of yourself as . . . ?" [check all that apply; do not read "American" or "Other"]

and Japanese Americans (21 percent versus 15 percent and 13 percent, respectively), and just as likely to identify with this pan-ethnic label as Chinese and Vietnamese Americans. This finding is important because it runs counter to the bias that many scholars have pointed out in the scholarship and politics surrounding Asian American activism and identity, with Indians and other immigrants from South Asia seen as wholly distinctive from other Asian American groups, and relatively marginal to Asian American identity and politics (Shankar and Srikanth 1998; Kibria 1998; Dave et al. 2000). What we find here is that Indian Americans are not at all distinctive with respect to adopting the *Asian American* label. Indeed, they are just as likely to adopt the pan-ethnic label as Chinese Americans, and are much more likely to do so than Japanese Americans, the group who arguably is most central to the historical development of an Asian American identity.

Finally, another important aspect of self-categorization that emerges from a comparison across national origins is that Koreans are much more likely to identify with multiple categories than members of other national origin groups. On average, Koreans in our survey identified with 2.2 categories. The next closest frequency is among Vietnamese, who on average identify with 1.4 categories. For the remaining groups, the average number of categories identified with ranges from 1.1 to 1.2. This discrepancy has important consequences because Koreans have the highest levels of identification in all four categories, with levels often twice as high as those found for other groups.[4] Depending on the research question, it may make sense to standardize the four categories by the total number of mentions within each group before making comparisons across groups. Such a comparison would reveal, for instance, that the gap between *Ethnic Group* identification and *Asian American* identification is greatest for Filipinos and Japanese Americans, and least for Indian Americans. Regardless of the measure used, however, the data in table 5.1 present a fairly clear storyline on self-categorization: a relatively small proportion of Asians in the United States self-identify as *Asian American*, a larger proportion as *Ethnic Group*, and the largest proportion as *Ethnic American*, which combines their national origin and American identities.

Self-identifying with a label itself, however, provides a limited view of identity and its link to politics. Take the example of the potential political significance of the pan-ethnic label *Asian American*. Perhaps during the height of the Asian American movement of the late 1960s and 1970s, the label carried clear political meaning (Wei 1993). Even in its height, this movement originated from elite educational institutions (Takagi 1998) and several decades of dramatic demographic change have occurred since then. Its current use more likely simply reflects popular usage of the label as a social convention. Rather than being a measure of a politicized pan-ethnicity, individuals who identify with the label *Asian American* may instead be acquiescing with and assimilating into dominant norms and conventions.

Several findings are worth noting, however, with respect to the relationship between the categories of self-identification and a sense of linked fate. The concept of linked fate has a distinguished pedigree in research on racial politics. The belief that one's personal lot in life is intimately intertwined with the lot of others in one's ethnic group has been shown to be an important feature of African American public opinion. Several studies have shown that it is this sense of linked fate that helps African Americans (and, to a large extent, Latinos) to overcome some of the political divisions that one might anticipate based on education and income within each of the groups (Dawson 1994; Tate 1993).

The National Asian American Survey includes two measures of linked fate. We asked respondents, "Do you think what happens generally to other groups of Asians in this country affects what happens in your life?" This measure is nearly identical to the measure that has been used in prior studies of African Americans. At the same time, given the high level of *Ethnic Group* and *Ethnic American* identification among Asian Americans, we also included a question on linked fate that has the respondent's ethnic group as the reference category.

Interestingly, those who say they think of themselves as Asian Americans are the most likely to say that their fate in politics is somewhat or very linked to other Asians in the United States. Among the four identity categories we measure, 54 percent of those who classify themselves as *Asian American* feel a sense of linked fate. This proportion is larger than among those who call themselves *Asian* (47 percent), *Ethnic American* (45 percent), or *Ethnic Group* (44 percent). Similarly, when asked the same question about a sense of linked fate but this time with respect to their ethnic group (rather than to the pan-ethnic *Asian American* group), the findings by identity self-category follow a similar but slightly less dramatic pattern. Fifty-seven percent of those who call themselves Asian Americans agree that they have some or very strong linked fate with those in their ethnic group, followed by 54 percent of those who categorize themselves as Asian, 53 percent of those who say they are *Ethnic American*, and 52 percent who select the *Ethnic Group* term. However, in contrast to the findings above about the relatively strong sense of linked fate among those who choose the identity label of Asian American, we find that those who chose the *Ethnic Group* identity are the ones most likely to say they would vote for a co-ethnic candidate (66 percent) for political office. *Ethnic Americans* were next at 64 percent, *Asian Americans* at 62 percent and *Asians* at 61 percent. These differences are modest, of course.

In addition to asking the higher-order question, of how racial self-identification may relate to a sense of linked fate among Asian Americans, we also need to examine the more basic question of how linked fate varies across national origin groups. Table 5.2 displays the differences by national origin group on the two linked fate measures in the NAAS.

To the first question asking whether respondents think what happens generally to other groups of Asians in the United States affects what happens in their lives, 44 percent agree to a sense of linked fate, but fewer than 10 percent feel that their fate is very linked to other Asians in this country. The variation among national origin groups is most substantial among Korean Americans: 57 percent agree with the concept of linked fate with other Asians in the United States; 13 percent of Koreans feel their fate is very closely linked. Filipinos and Vietnamese, by contrast, are the least likely to exhibit a linked fate orientation.

When the referent for the linked fate question is given as people who share the same ethnic or national-origin group, the overall sense of linked fate is somewhat stronger: half of the NAAS respondents agree that what happens to others in their national-origin group affects what happens in their life, and one in eight believe that this link is strong. Again, Korean Americans are the strongest supporters of a sense of ethnic-group linked fate, nearly two-thirds agreeing and almost one in five agreeing strongly. On ethnic-group linked fate, Filipinos and Vietnamese no longer look so different from Asian Indians, Chinese, and Japanese Americans.

One final observation on table 5.2 is the degree of similarity in the distribution of responses to our two linked fate measures. Despite differences in emphasis, the rank-order of responses is identical: the modal response is that fates (ethnic or pan-ethnic) are unlinked, followed in frequency by

Table 5.2 Pan-Ethnic and Ethnic Linked Fate

	India	China	Philippines	Japan	Korea	Vietnam	Total
Pan-ethnic linked fate							
Fate very linked	7	9	8	7	13	7	9
Fate somewhat linked	32	32	16	26	40	27	28
Fate not very linked	4	7	13	7	4	6	7
Fate not linked	49	43	60	50	35	47	48
Don't know	8	10	3	10	7	13	8
Ethnic linked fate							
Fate very linked	10	11	10	12	19	17	12
Fate somewhat linked	33	31	19	27	43	30	30
Fate not very linked	7	8	16	9	4	3	8
Fate not linked	42	40	50	43	28	42	42
Don't know	8	10	5	9	7	10	8

Source: Authors' compilation of data from the 2008 National Asian American Survey (Ramakrishnan et al. 2011).
Note: Rates are in percentages.
Survey questions: "Do you think what happens generally to other groups of Asians in this country affects what happens in your life?" "Do you think what happens generally to other [R ETHNIC GROUP] Americans affects what happens in your life?"

Figure 5.2   Sense of Commonality with Other Asians in the
              United States

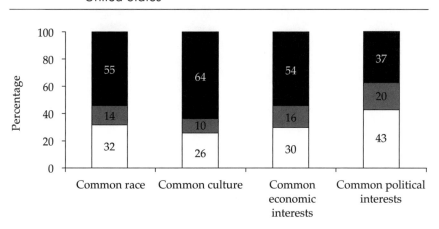

Source: Authors' compilation of data from the 2008 National Asian American Survey (Ramakrishnan et al. 2011).
Survey question: "What, if anything, do Asians in the United States share with one another? Would you say they share . . . a race? . . . a culture? . . . economic interests? . . . political interests?"

the view that fates are somewhat linked. Far less common are the views that fates are very linked or not very linked, or that the respondent simply does not know how to answer the question.

In addition to linked fate, we also asked respondents whether they felt a sense of in-group solidarity in specific contexts of commonality. Specifically, we asked whether respondents thought that Asians in the United States shared a common race, a common culture, common economic interests and common political interests. The results for the overall population, as well as by national-origin group, are shown in figure 5.2. In addition to marginal distribution indicating the proportion who agree that Asians in the United States have commonalities, we also provide the percentage who said they did not know. In some instances, substantial proportions of people chose a "don't know" response.

Of the four types of commonalities among Asians in the United States—race, culture, economic, and political interests—Asian Americans overall were most likely to say that they have a common culture (64 percent), despite distinctive linguistic, religious, and country-of-origin differences.

More than half (55 percent) said Asian Americans were of the same race and had common economic interests (54 percent). A much smaller proportion, 37 percent, said Asian Americans have common political interests, though this question yielded many more "don't know" responses.

Among the various national-origin groups, Asian Indians have the strongest sense of a shared culture and shared economic interests, and Korean Americans are the strongest supporters of the notion of a common race. Vietnamese are more likely than any other group to indicate that they did not know how to answer these commonality questions. Japanese are notable for being the least likely to feel some basis for pan-Asian commonality.

With the likely exception of perceived cultural commonality as the basis for a pan-Asian formation, each of the remaining contexts—race, economic interests, and political interests—represent potential links between a racial identity category to a collective politics based on that category. Our final measure of in-group solidarity is the most explicitly political, situated in the real-world context of electoral competition. NAAS respondents, specifically, were asked whether—given a hypothetical election in which two candidates for political office are otherwise equal in experience and qualifications, but one candidate had the same national origin as the respondent—the respondent would vote for the co-ethnic candidate.

We examined whether NAAS respondents look to ethnic cues to break a tie between two candidates on the basis of experience and qualifications. More than half (58 percent) responded they would be more likely to vote for the co-ethnic candidate. Again, Korean Americans were the most enthusiastic supporters (83 percent). Vietnamese Americans were next (68 percent), followed by Filipino Americans (63 percent). Chinese (53 percent) and Asian Indians (41 percent) were the least likely to say they would support a co-ethnic candidate. Bear in mind that the identity marker is ethnic (the reference is to national origin) rather than pan-ethnic. We also note the moderate proportion of people who responded with "don't know" to this question: 15 percent of the sample and about 20 percent of Chinese and Vietnamese respondents responded this way.

We turn next to several measures of out-group differentiation and intergroup competition. Our most directly political measure here is one that asks NAAS respondents about the extent to which they felt Asian Americans had a commonality with African Americans, Latinos, and whites in terms of government services, political power, and representation. Figure 5.3 shows the results of this analysis for all groups and for the survey population overall.

By a small margin, Asian Americans say they have the most in common with whites, less with Latinos, and still less with African Americans.

Figure 5.3   Commonality with Other Groups

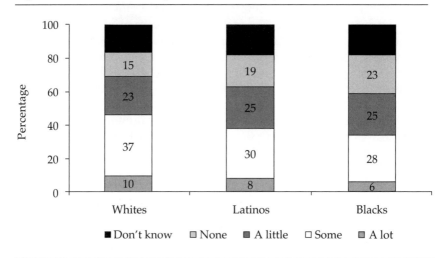

Source: Authors' compilation of data from the 2008 National Asian American Survey (Ramakrishnan et al. 2011).
Survey question: "Thinking about government services, political power and representation, would you say Asian Americans have a lot in common, some, little in common, or nothing at all in common with . . . African Americans? . . . Latinos? . . . whites?"

When the categories of "a lot" and "some" commonality are combined, 47 percent of NAAS respondents feel at least some political commonality with whites, compared to 38 percent with Latinos and 34 percent with African Americans. Roughly one in six respondents (16.5 percent) answered "don't know" to this question. Overall, we do not consider these small differences in feelings of commonality with various groups dramatic, but we do believe that they can play a limited role in important decisions such as vote choice (see Ramakrishnan et al. 2009).

When the responses are broken down by national-origin groups (shown in table 5.3), Koreans are the most likely to indicate some or a lot of commonality with African Americans (43 percent) and Latinos (51 percent). Filipinos are also quite apt to note political commonality with Latinos (48 percent), but less with African Americans (34 percent). By contrast, the greatest distance with other minority communities is found among Vietnamese Americans. Only about one in four Vietnamese NAAS respondents indicate some or a lot of commonality with African Americans (26 percent) or Latinos (27 percent). Vietnamese, for that matter, are also least likely to feel politically connected to whites (35 percent). Interestingly, for every national-origin group, the perception of political commonality with whites is more prevalent than for African Americans or Latinos.

Finally, in addition to the more typically examined measures of identity discussed, we asked survey respondents about their experiences with racial discrimination and hate crimes in the United States as indirect indicators of intergroup competition. We asked slightly different questions of the native-born and the foreign-born to account for the possibility that the latter may experience discrimination related to their immigrant status or Asian language accent in addition to race or ancestry. The referent was the same for both groups in terms of the types of discrimination one might face. These included unfairly being denied a job or being fired because of race, being unfairly denied a promotion at work, unfairly treated by police, unfairly prevented from renting or buying a house or apartment, and being treated unfairly or badly at restaurants or stores. Experiences with discrimination based on racial and ethnic group membership is important to Asian American political engagement because the collective experience could motivate political action. Although these experiences are less likely to influence voting, racial discrimination is most likely to spur local activity, such as community work or protest, and might also compel individuals to contact officials or make political contributions in an effort to obtain redress discriminatory practices. Unlike the electoral arena where messages sent through voting are more diffuse, contacting can provide precise and directed information to elected officials about political grievances.

The proportions we report are distinctive for foreign-born respondents, who make up nearly 80 percent of the survey sample, and for native-born Asian Americans, who make up 20 percent of the interviews. Among the foreign-born, people are most likely to report discrimination in terms of being treated badly in retail stores and restaurants, nearly one in five (20 percent) saying they have experienced this type of treatment. Almost double that proportion of native-born Asian Americans report experiencing this type of discrimination, 36 percent saying they have been treated unfairly or badly in a restaurant or store. This is the only measure of racial discrimination that is higher for native-born than foreign-born Asian Americans. The latter are slightly more likely to report experiencing discrimination in the workplace, by police, and in the housing market, the last being the least frequent for both groups.

In terms of hate crimes incidence, one in ten Asian Americans reported experience with verbal or physical abuse, or damage of their property specifically because of their race or ethnicity. Among national-origin groups, Asian Indians (12 percent) and Japanese (11 percent) are the most likely to report being a victim of a hate crime. Koreans are least likely (4 percent). Hate crimes are a strong form of racial and ethnic discrimina-

Table 5.3 Commonality by National Origin

	India	China	Philippines	Japan	Korea	Vietnam	Total
Whites							
Some or a lot in common	47	47	49	43	52	35	47
Nothing in common	19	14	16	9	13	22	15
Latinos							
Some or a lot in common	32	36	48	29	51	27	38
Nothing in common	28	16	16	22	12	25	19
Blacks							
Some or a lot in common	38	33	34	26	43	26	34
Nothing in common	24	21	26	24	18	26	23

Source: Authors' compilation of data from the 2008 National Asian American Survey (Ramakrishnan et al. 2011).
Note: Rates are in percentages.

tion, and we would expect this experience to have a similar affect on political engagement, influencing most strongly activities such as protest,
community work, and contacting officials.

Experiences with discrimination and hate crimes are related in predict-
able and interesting ways to one another and to a sense of commonality
with Asian Americans and with other racial and ethnic groups. While the
hate crime and discrimination measures are correlated at .29 (1.0 indicating perfect correlation) their relationship to commonality with other racial
and ethnic groups is more modest (.10) and even lower for common Asian
American characteristics (.05). The two commonality measures—culture,
politics, economic interests, and race shared with Asian Americans and
shared political interests with whites, blacks, and Latinos—are correlated
at .25. It does not seem to be the case that feelings of commonality with
Asian Americans comes at the expense of feelings of commonalities with
other groups, as the two are only modestly related to one another. Respondents who reported being the victim of a hate crime had a much
stronger sense of political commonality with other racial and ethnic
groups, but only a moderately stronger sense with other Asian Americans. The same pattern holds for those who have experienced discrimination on the basis of their ethnicity or race.

ETHNIC AND RACIAL IDENTIFICATION
AND ITS ANTECEDENTS

Thus far we have presented basic contours of the multiple measures of
racial and ethnic identity available to us in the 2008 NAAS. The portrait
we have drawn confirms the multidimensionality and complexity of
Asian American identity. In this section, we examine factors related to the
dimensions of ethnic and racial identification, beginning with the first-
order relationships between demographic and assimilation factors and
the extent to which respondents in the NAAS identify with racial and ethnic labels. Table 5.4 summarizes the association between foreign-born status, citizenship status, age, gender, education, and residence in a new immigrant destination and each of the measures of racial and ethnic identity.
Breakdowns of the data used to construct this summary table are included
in appendix C.

In terms of nativity and citizenship, we can look separately at noncitizens, foreign-born respondents who have naturalized as citizens, and native-born Asian Americans in the second generation and beyond. The results are clear. Noncitizen Asian Americans are by far most likely to
self-identify with *Ethnic Group* (62 percent), a substantially larger proportion than found among both naturalized and native-born Asian Ameri-

Table 5.4   Factors Related to Ethnic and Racial Identification

	Foreign-Born*	Citizen-ship**	Age	Female	Higher Education	New Destination
Ethnic Group	+					
Ethnic American		+	+			
Asian American				+		
Asian				+		
Pan-ethnic linked fate		+	−		+	
Ethnic linked fate			−	+	+	
Commonality with Asians						
Political commonality with others		+	−		+	
Discriminated against		+	−	−	+	
Victim of hate crime		+				
Vote for co-ethnic candidate	+		+		−	

Source: Authors' compilation of data from the 2008 National Asian American Survey (Ramakrishnan et al. 2011).
Note: A + or − sign signifies that the association is positive or negative, respectively, and statistically significant at the 0.10 level or greater.
*Native-born is the comparison group. **Among foreign-born only.

cans. This group's second most frequent choice of identity is an *Ethnic American* identity and they are the group that is least likely to self-identify as *Asian American* compared with naturalized and native-born citizens. By contrast, both naturalized and native-born Asian Americans show a clear preference to self-identify by their *Ethnic American* identity (57 percent and 61 percent, respectively). The proportion in these groups who self-identify as *Asian American* is roughly equivalent to self-identification by national-origin group, with native-born respondents being more likely to self-identify in pan-ethnic terms than *Ethnic Group* terms. The proportion of NAAS respondents who self-identify as *Asian* is highest among non-citizens, followed by naturalized citizens and then with only a small pro-portion (10 percent) of native-born Asian Americans who adopt the iden-tity label of *Asian*.[5]

How does identification compare by nativity beyond these identity la-bels? Several additional measures of racial and ethnic identity are mea-sured in the 2008 NAAS, including linked fate with both an ethnic and pan-ethnic referent, commonality with Asians across culture, race, and political and economic interests, a sense of commonality in political inter-ests with whites, blacks, and Latinos, the experience of being discrimi-nated against across a range of situations, being the victim of a hate crime, and voting for a co-ethnic candidate. In this analysis, we truncate the linked fate measures by aggregating the response categories somewhat and very linked. In terms of commonality with Asians, responses were counted as affirmative across culture, politics, economic interests, and race, yielding a high proportion of respondents who said they felt com-monality with Asians on one or more of these domains. Similarly, we summed the questions on commonality with other racial and ethnic groups, and the vast majority of Asian Americans report feeling a shared sense of political interests. For this analysis, the discrimination measure includes those who indicated that they had experienced discrimination in at least one realm of social or economic interaction (workplace, housing, stores or restaurants, police). The measures for hate crime and co-ethnic voting remain the same as reported earlier in the chapter.

In terms of nativity and citizenship, there is little variation in a sense of ethnic linked fate, but a modestly greater tendency for native-born Asian Americans to agree that their fates are linked to that of other Asian Amer-icans than for their foreign-born counterparts. A similar pattern can be seen in the extent to which NAAS respondents feel there is political com-monality with non-Asian groups: native-born Asians and naturalized citi-zens are likelier to agree that there is some or a lot of politically shared interests with African Americans, Latinos, and whites than with foreign-born Asians. Native-born Asian Americans are also much more likely to report experiences of discrimination and slightly more likely to say they have been the victim of a hate crime than noncitizens. In contrast, they are much less likely to say they would vote for a co-ethnic candidate.

In terms of differences by gender, differences between men and women in their choice of racial and ethnic identity labels are minor. Overall, women and men say they identify with their ethnic group (41 percent versus 39 percent) and think of themselves as Asian (21 percent versus 17 percent) at about the same rate. There is almost no difference between men and women in terms of the pan-ethnic linked fate measures or a sense of linked fate with others in their national-origin group. Men and women are equally likely to have a sense of commonality with other Asians and people of other races and ethnicities. In contrast, men are slightly more likely to say they have been discriminated against (39 percent versus 34 percent) than women, but a similar proportion of men than women say they have been the victim of a hate crime (10 percent versus 8 percent).

In terms of differences by age, the data were analyzed by four age groupings: eighteen to thirty-four, thirty-five to forty-nine, fifty to sixty-four, and sixty-five and older. Differences by age show some modest variation with older Asian Americans demonstrating the most distinctive responses. Interestingly, age is inversely related to adopting a label that captures *Ethnic Group*, but positively related to calling oneself an *Ethnic American*. Age, generation of migration, and years in the United States are associated in distinctive ways, particularly by national origin group. The measures of identity encompassing linked fate and discrimination show interesting patterns. The young are much more likely than older respondents to report a sense of linked fate both with their national-origin group and with Asian Americans more generally. Older respondents were also somewhat less likely to say they had a sense of political commonality with other racial and ethnic groups. Likewise, older Asian Americans were less likely to say they had experienced discrimination. Interestingly, however, older Asian Americans were much more supportive of co-ethnic candidates for political office than their younger counterparts.

In terms of educational attainment, there were few strong differences in the identity labels between those with higher or lower levels of formal education. One category—those with a high school education or less—showed a number of outlier findings. For this group, *Ethnic American* and *Ethnic Group* were the most common labels chosen, followed by *Asian American* and *Asian*. Although the pattern is similar across increasing educational levels, what is interesting is that those with some college were much less likely to identify as *Ethnic Group* as other groups were. Respondents at the highest educational levels are most likely to call themselves *Asian American* (26 percent among college graduates and 21 percent among respondents with advanced postgraduate degrees). This may be due to the potential of higher-education experiences to provide a unique socializing environment through Asian American studies courses and Asian American clubs.

Beyond these identity labels, there are also distinct patterns between higher educational attainment and the sense of linked fate. Higher levels of education are associated with a stronger sense of linked fate, both to one's national-origin group and to Asian Americans more generally. Equally interesting is the nonlinear pattern of perceptions of in-group and out-group commonality: those respondents with some college—our middle category—and the highest levels of education are most likely to perceive political commonality with other Asians and non-Asians. The monotonic decline from this educational level is asymmetric, however: those with advanced degrees are substantially more likely than those with less than a high school equivalency to see Asian Americans as having common interests with each other and with whites, Latinos, and African Americans. In addition, the well-educated are almost twice as likely to report experiencing discrimination. Again, those with some college are also more likely to report being a victim of a hate crime than those with less education. Well-educated respondents are, however, less likely to say they would vote for a co-ethnic candidate for political office.

In terms of the place where higher education took place, the NAAS data indicate that those educated in the United States are less likely than those who completed their education elsewhere to call themselves *Asian* (15 percent versus 21 percent), but similarly likely to self-identify as *Asian American* (23 percent versus 20 percent). For those educated outside the United States, the incidence of self-identification with *Ethnic Group* (48 percent) and with *Ethnic American* (43 percent) are roughly the same. Among the U.S.-educated, by contrast, there is a much greater likelihood of identifying with an ethnic group label (24 percent *Ethnic Group* versus 55 percent *Ethnic American*). Among the other identity items, those educated in the United States are slightly more likely to report a sense of pan-ethnic linked fate (45 percent versus 37 percent) compared with those who completed their formal education outside the United States. Rates of ethnic linked fate are about the same. There are no differences on commonality with Asians, but those educated in America are much more likely to say they share a lot or some common political interests with whites (55 percent versus 42 percent), Latinos (47 percent versus 33 percent), and African Americans (43 percent versus 29 percent). At the same time, 43 percent of those educated in the United States report being dis-criminated against in some form, ten points more than those educated outside the United States. Similarly, a slightly higher proportion of those educated in the United States report being the victim of a hate crime (11 percent versus 8 percent). At the same time, those educated in the United States are less likely to say they would vote for a co-ethnic candidate for office (53 percent versus 61 percent), if the two candidates possessed equal experience and qualifications.

We examine how people with varying English-language skills identify in racial and ethnic terms, as well as on the other measures of identity, in-cluding linked fate, commonality with Asians, experiences with discrimi-nation, being the victim of a hate crime, preference for a co-ethnic candi-date in political office, and feeling that one has nothing in common with non-Asians. Regardless of whether the NAAS interviews were conducted in English or an Asian language, the pattern of covariance by self-reported spoken English skills is quite consistent. The stronger one's English skills, the greater the likelihood of identifying as Asian American and Ethnic American. The opposite is also true—the weaker the English skills, the greater the likelihood of identifying with the *Ethnic Group* label.

In terms of the other measures of identity, the stronger the spoken Eng-lish-language skills, the greater the sense of both linked fate and common-ality with Asians. Similarly, the stronger one's ability to speak English, the more unlikely people are to say they have nothing in common with Afri-can Americans, Latinos, and whites. English-language ability also has a positive relationship with experiences with discrimination for both those interviewed in English as well as an Asian language, and the same rela-tionship is true in terms of reporting being the victim of a hate crime. Vot-ing for a co-ethnic candidate has an inconsistent relationship with Eng-lish-language skills, and those who report speaking English very well were least likely to support a candidate on the basis of his or her ethnic background, all else being equal.

Finally, there are virtually no differences in ethnic and racial identity choice in terms of the locations in which Asian Americans live. Figure 5.4 shows the proportion of people in places that have had new, rapid in-creases in their Asian American populations (new settlements) and their choice of ethnic and racial identity labels (see chapter 2). We find that the results are not that different from traditional destinations or places that have remained small in terms of their Asian American populations. [6] There are also almost no marked differences when one turns to other mea-sures of identity: linked fate, political in-group and out-group commonal-ity, and experiences of discrimination.

Figure 5.4   Ethnic and Racial Identification by Destination

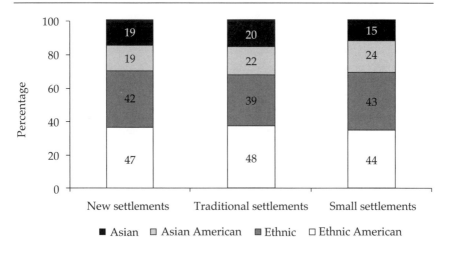

Source: Authors' compilation of data from the 2008 National Asian American Survey (Ramakrishnan et al. 2011).

ETHNIC AND RACIAL IDENTITY
AND POLITICAL ACTIVISM

In this final section, we invert the explanatory lens and begin to consider the relationship between ethnic and racial identity and political participation. Our analysis of the determinants of Asian American political engagement receives its full treatment in chapter 7, and this analysis lays out the basic relationship between measures of racial identification in terms of identity labels and forms of political participation. Although the NAAS measures numerous acts of participation, as detailed in the introductory chapter, we focus on several dimensions of political activity, including an overall voting index, a standard measure of protest activity, and three measures of political participation beyond voting.

The results of this initial analysis are suggestive (table 5.5). For the two measures of identity that connote some degree of integration or incorporation—*Asian American* and *Ethnic American* identity—the association between identity and four of our five key measures of participation appears to be positive. At the bivariate level, those who self-identify as *Asian American* or *Ethnic American* appear to vote, contribute money, contact government officials, and work with others in their community at higher

Table 5.5   Ethnic and Self-Identified Categories by Political Participation

	Likely Voter	Political Contributor	Contact Government Officials	Protester	Community Activist
Asian American	49	15	10	4	24
Ethnic American	48	15	11	5	21
Ethnic group	42	9	6	4	17
Asian	44	9	7	4	16

Source: Authors' compilation of data from the 2008 National Asian American Survey (Ramakrishnan et al. 2011).
Note: Rates are in percentages.

levels than those who self-identify with their *Ethnic Group* or as *Asian*. Those who self-identify as *Asian American* or *Ethnic American* engage in these activities at more or less comparable rates vis-à-vis each other; similarly, those who identify as *Asian* or with their *Ethnic Group* appear to engage in these four activities at comparable rates. The relationship between racial or ethnic identification and protest activity appears to be minimal.

Although only a modest relationship (if any) is apparent between identity choices and the five forms of political engagement we analyze here, differences in participation by some other indicators of racial and ethnic identity are important. Table 5.6 summarizes the differences in level of participation in voting, contributing, contacting, protesting, and working with others in the community to solve problems by the two measures of linked fate, commonality with Asians and other racial groups, and experiences with discrimination and hate crimes.

In terms of voting, evidence of differences between respondents with varying levels of racial and political identity beyond the identity labels is scant. Only a sense of political commonality with other racial and ethnic groups has a positive relationship. In contrast, both of the commonality items—with Asians in this country and with other racial groups—is important with respect to contributions, with those holding a sense of commonality much more active in this form of engagement. Likewise, experiences with discrimination and hate crimes are also positively associated with making political contributions. Contacting officials shows a similar pattern to contributing, with strong relationships for the commonality and bias measures. This is also the case for activity with others in the community to solve problems. The same patterns are apparent, but to a lesser degree, for protest activity.

Table 5.6   Rates of Political Participation by Ethnic Identification

	Likely Voter	Political Contributor	Contact Government Officials	Protester	Community Activist
Pan-ethnic linked fate					
Yes	46	15	11	6	24
No	45	11	8	4	20
Ethnic linked fate					
Yes	46	15	11	6	23
No	45	11	8	3	20
Commonality with Asians					
Yes	45	14	10	5	23
No	47	8	5	3	15
Political commonality with others					
Yes	46	14	10	5	23
No	39	6	3	2	12
Discriminated against					
Yes	44	17	13	6	27
No	46	10	7	4	18
Victim of hate crime					
Yes	42	16	17	8	29
No	46	12	9	4	21
All	43	13	9	4	21

Source: Authors' compilation of data from the 2008 National Asian American Survey (Ramakrishnan et al. 2011).
Note: Rates are in percentages, representing the proportion of those with a specific score on the identity measure (linked fate, commonality with other Asians, and so forth) who also took part in the political activity.

CONCLUSION

As social identity theory would predict, Asian American identity is dynamic, complex, and linked to immigration history and social context. We find that among Asian Americans, the most common identity is *Ethnic American*. That is, nearly half of all Asian Americans identify with both their national-origin group and as American (for example, as Vietnamese American or Chinese American). A smaller, but still significant, proportion identify with the pan-ethnic label, *Asian American*. We also observe a sense of linked fate, or the belief that one's personal lot in life is intimately intertwined with that of others in one's in-group, but that sentiment is not deeply held and national-origin group variation is considerable. Asian Americans do feel a sense of commonality, especially in terms of a common culture. Only one-third, however, claim to have a common political interest with other Asian Americans. Korean Americans share the strongest sense of in-group solidarity. We speculate that multiple contextual forces likely feed into this result, such as Korean migrants' group history, geographic concentration, a solidarity wrought out of the 1992 Los Angeles riots, and, perhaps most important, ties to community organizations such as ethnic churches and business associations. Asian Americans in our study were also asked about their attitudes toward non–Asian American groups. Overall, Asian Americans tend to express more commonality with whites, then Latinos, and then blacks. However, no dramatic distinctions were made between feelings of commonality with each of these groups. Although prominent instances of black-Korean conflict appear in U.S. history, Koreans claim to feel more in common with blacks and Latinos than any other Asian American national origin group do. Asian Americans do report experiencing both hate crimes and discrimination. We observe similar rates of reporting among the foreign-born and native-born, with one exception—the U.S.-born are twice as likely (36 percent) as their foreign-born counterparts (18 percent) to report being treated unfairly in restaurants and stores. Hate crime reporting is most prevalent among Japanese and Indian Americans. Both groups are characterized by relatively high socioeconomic status, as well as stark historical experiences of racial discrimination, including the internment of Japanese Americans during World War II and the violent targeting of South Asians in the wake of the terrorist attacks of 9/11.

If Asian Americans themselves do not consistently or strongly identify as *Asian American* across national-origin groups, and if only a small proportion express sharing political interests in common, is there any justification for treating them as a meaningful political category? Group identity is an evolving phenomenon. We see that Asian Americans are more likely to adopt the *Ethnic American* label if they are citizens and native-born. Thus, consistent with social identity theory, we observe that identity varies across contexts. The analysis in this chapter reveals that although Asian Americans may not currently identify as a coherent group, the development of a common identity and racialized experiences that reinforce that identity would likely exert a strong and positive influence on political participation. Consistent with our hypotheses, we also find that those who identify as *Asian American* or *Ethnic American* are more likely to engage with politics than those who identity as *Asian* or as *Ethnic Group*. Without studying the group as a whole, the potential political power of mobilizing individuals around the pan-ethnic *Asian American* identity label would not be recognized. We take a closer look at these associations in chapter 7 and attempt in that chapter to connect these findings to the question of whether Asian Americans represent a case of immigrant assimilation or immigrant racialization when it comes to the political sphere.

Chapter 6 | Civic Engagement: Secular and Religious Organizations

SCHOLARS HAVE LONG debated the effects of ethnic and racial heterogeneity on democratic stability, citizenship, and civil society (Lijphart 1968; Easterly and Levine 1997; Dahl 1971). Some scholars of comparative politics argue that racial and ethnic diversity weaken civil society as the result of ethnic conflict and competition over scarce resources (Alesina and La Ferrara 2000). For example, Dora Costa and Matthew Kahn's research suggests that citizens in racially diverse places tend to be less civically engaged, undermining civil society (2003). Others, such as Christopher Anderson and Aida Paskeviciute, find that ethnic heterogeneity can exert a positive effect on civil society, depending on the context and aspect of civil society examined (2006). Asian Americans increasingly add to the demographic diversity of the American landscape—but to what extent do they reinforce or undermine American civil society?

In this chapter, we examine Asian Americans and their civic engagement, a key aspect of civil society (Coleman 1990; Putnam 1993, 2000). Scholars of civic engagement assert that involvement in social, civic, and political groups and activities benefits individuals and the larger society. According to proponents, civic engagement contributes to economic mobility, greater citizen input in government decision-making, and perhaps at an even more fundamental level of self-interest, greater health and happiness (Putnam 2000; Verba, Schlozman, and Brady 1995). Theda Skocpol and Morris Fiorina (1999) connect civic engagement to the vitality of the American democratic system, and Robert Putnam (2000) sees it as the social glue necessary to hold an increasingly diverse American society together. Finally, some have argued that diverse racial and ethnic communities represent sources of new and more politicized forms of civic engagement, something that was especially evident in the massive immigrant rights marches of spring 2006 (Voss and Bloemraad 2010).

The term civic engagement is a relatively broad concept in the social sciences, some scholars referring not only to the involvement of individuals in community organizations and informal associations, but also "social activities and political activities of all kinds" (Skocpol and Fiorina 1999, 8; Verba, Schlozman, and Brady 1995). Thus, for instance, participating in protests and making campaign contributions can be seen as civic activities on the same plane as volunteering in a health center or serving on the board of a homeless shelter. Others, however, have argued for a clearer distinction between civic engagement and political engagement, the former excluding activities that involve direct contacts between an individual and the state. Karthick Ramakrishnan and Irene Bloemraad note that civic engagement should refer expansively to "involvement in communal activities that have some purpose or benefit beyond a single individual or family's self-interest," including particular community organizations, social groups, or the general public (2008, 16). They contend, however, that the term should not extend to activities related to formal political institutions and process, whether these are conventional forms of participation such as voting or unconventional forms such as protests.

Here, we focus on a particular type of civic engagement—involvement in community groups and organizations, both religious and secular. We concur with the findings of previous studies that immigrants' involvement in community organizations may represent a critical source of political socialization and mobilization, especially given the relative absence of other mobilizing institutions in their everyday lives (Jones-Correa 1998; Ramakrishnan 2005; Wong 2006). Scholars of immigration and minority politics emphasize the important role of community organizations in facilitating political participation absent explicit policies of multiculturalism. For instance, Kristi Andersen notes that:

> because political parties no longer invest time and energy to link new groups to elected and appointed officials and because most local and state governments in the United States do not have explicit policies fostering political incorporation, the voluntary sector becomes critical, a site where individuals and families are able to acquire the knowledge and skills to navigate and interact with the larger society and particularly with political and governmental systems. (2008, 91)

At the same time, research on the civic and political engagement of immigrants has acknowledged the limits of community organizations in bringing excluded groups into the political system (Wong 2006; Ramakrishnan and Bloemraad 2008, 32). We adopt the perspective that civic engagement, as involvement in community organizations, can be treated as conceptually distinct from political participation. Thus, although participation in community organizations may lead to greater interest and involvement in politics for some, it may play no role in the decisions of others. Indeed, for some individuals, participation in community organizations may lead to an avoidance of political activities, either because of a greater sense of efficacy through civic involvement or from a desire to avoid mixing political activities with the work of nonprofit organizations (Berry 2003).

Finally, we pay close attention to a specific type of community organization here—religious organizations. Religion and religious institutions have long been considered an important resource for political organizing for minority groups, such as African Americans and Latinos (Harris 1999; Jones-Correa and Leal 2001). Religious institutions serve a critical role in bringing immigrants into the political system because they help endow members with important civic skills that can be transferred into the political sphere (Verba, Schlozman, and Brady 1995). Further, for immigrant communities in particular, religious institutions often serve as civic associations, places of intergenerational cultural transmission and ethnic reproduction, social service providers, advocates for immigrant rights, and as mediators between the immigrant community and American society (Jones-Correa and Leal 2001; Miller, Miller, and Dyrness 2001; Ebaugh and Chafetz 2000; Warner and Wittner 1998). For these reasons, recent scholarship views religion as a positive force for immigrants' political engagement and adjustment to American life.

As we shall see, participation in community organizations, secular or religious, is neither a necessary nor sufficient condition for political participation among Asian Americans. Still, few dispute the idea that community organizations have the potential to do important work in terms of driving political inclusion. To better understand the role and influence of secular and religious community organizations in the political lives of Asian Americans, we seek answers to the following questions: To what extent do Asian Americans join community groups and organizations? What are the characteristics of those who are involved in community organizations versus those who are not? Finally, to what extent do community organizations mobilize Asian Americans to get involved in politics, and do these linkages vary between religious and secular organizations?

RACE AND CIVIC ENGAGEMENT

The literature on race and civic engagement is not large, but does point to some important patterns. Past studies mainly focus on levels of civic engagement among different racial and ethnic groups—particularly whites, blacks, and Latinos—and how key variables, such as socioeconomic status, religiosity, political orientations, and migration, relate to civic participation (Verba, Schlozman, and Brady 1995; Ramakrishnan 2005; Wong 2006). More recent data suggests that, after taking into account individual resources and demographic characteristics, blacks participate in community groups and organizations at the same rate as whites. Moreover, after one accounts for neighborhood poverty, blacks participate in more organizations than whites (Stoll 2001). Further, demographic factors alone do not explain the participation gap between whites and Latinos or whites and Asian Americans. However, when one includes migration-related variables, racially integrated social networks, and neighborhood poverty, one no longer observes gaps in participation between whites and other groups (Stoll and Wong 2007).

More germane to the current study is an examination of the motivations that drive different racial and ethnic groups to join groups and organizations. Most studies find that resources and demographic factors matter for all groups when it comes to engaging in civic life. Many decades of research show that those individuals who have access to more income and education are more likely to take part in civic activities and groups (Verba, Schlozman, and Brady 1995; Brady et al. 2002; Galston 2007). Furthermore, those who are middle-aged tend to participate more than those who are young or very old. Finally, there is a consistent relationship between attendance at religious services and secular civic engagement, particularly among mainline Protestants, and the association is weaker among Catholics and evangelical Protestants (Wuthnow 1999).

But in addition to those traditional variables, Fredrick Harris (1994) suggests that being involved in church activities, outside attending Sunday services, is especially important for black Americans' engagement in secular organizations. He finds that "the more [African Americans] are active in church groups, the more they are active in secular groups, which, in turn, supports their interests in political affairs" (126). Harris's emphasis on religion as a resource for social and political activism builds on Verba, Schlozman, and Brady's (1995) assertion that churches constitute a more potent source of civic engagement for African Americans than for whites and Latinos. Not only do black churches provide a civic training ground, they are also a source of psychological inspiration and provide a language of resistance that encourages group-based civic engagement.

In terms of predicting civic engagement across groups, Gary Segura, Harry Pachon, and Nathan Woods (2001) argue that it is increasingly important to take citizenship into account, especially given contemporary immigration flows to the United States from around the world. They find that for Latinos in their study sample, "being a noncitizen is likely to be a substantial impediment to civic engagement, and noncitizen status does indeed reduce the likelihood of participating even in those activities that are unconnected to government. Noncitizens uniformly had less experience volunteering, working on community problems, giving money, and contacting officials."[1] Yet noncitizens had more positive attitudes toward their local communities and seemed to have a greater sense of efficacy than citizens. Beyond citizenship, other studies of civic voluntarism that rely on the Current Population Survey find that first-generation immigrants, even those who are naturalized citizens, are less likely to participate in civic organizations than those in subsequent generations. Indeed, many of the racial disparities in participation can be explained by the varying mix of immigrant generations among whites, blacks, Latinos, and Asian Americans (Ramakrishnan 2006).

In addition to nativity and immigrant generation, Louis DeSipio identifies several other migration-related influences that affect Latinos' involvement in U.S. organizations and which might, then, also affect Asian Americans (2006). Perhaps not surprisingly, those with more established ties to the United States in terms of length of residence and the location of their family members (half or most in the United States versus mostly in the home country) also tend to be more involved in U.S. organizations. As one might expect of the "organizationally engaged," those who take part in organizations focused on the country of origin may also channel their energy into U.S. organizations.

Because the Asian American community includes an even larger proportion of immigrants than found among Latinos, one might expect similar migration-related factors, such as nativity, citizenship status, and length of residence, to have an impact on their involvement in groups and organizations. In fact, studies suggest that migration-related characteristics and behaviors play important roles in Asian American involvement in civic and political activities, such as working with others in their communities to solve a problem or attending a public meeting, rally, or fundraiser. Using the Pilot National Asian American Political Survey, Lien and her colleagues (2004, table 5.4) report that citizenship is unrelated to taking part in these activities, but that being foreign-born or having been educated mostly outside of the United States depresses this type of civic engagement. In contrast to the role that religion plays among African Americans, Lien and her colleagues find that attendance at religious services is not a predictor of civic engagement beyond voting. This is not surprising given that a significant proportion of Asian Americans affiliate with non–Judeo Christian religions that do not emphasize regular services. Their study, and more than a decade of research on Asian American religious groups, highlights the fact that attendance at religious services only captures one aspect of religiosity and attachment to religious institutions for many Asian Americans (Yoo 1999; Iwamura and Spickard 2003; Carnes and Yang 2004). Using the Social Capitol Benchmark Study, however, Elaine Ecklund and Jerry Park (2005) find a strong positive association between both participation in religious services and religious voluntarism and involvement in civic organizations.

National origin and racial identity stand out as two potentially powerful drivers of Asian Americans' civic engagement. Lien and her colleagues write that "experiences that may heighten one's racial or panethnic group consciousness" may enhance certain types of civic engagement (2004, 171). Yet Eric Uslaner and Richard Conley provide a more critical assessment of the role that ethnic identity plays in civic engagement (2003). Based on analysis of a 1997 *Los Angeles Times* sample of Chinese in southern California, they conclude that "different types of social networks and different sets of values lead to dissimilar types of civic engagement.... People who are not well integrated with the larger culture and who feel more comfortable in exclusively Chinese settings will either join only ethnic civic associations or might simply opt out of civic life altogether" (Uslaner and Conley 2003, 355). We investigate the role of ethnic identity and participation in civic organizations made up exclusively of Asian Americans later in this chapter.

PATTERNS OF CIVIC ENGAGEMENT AMONG ASIAN AMERICANS

What proportion of Asian Americans are involved in civic life? The results from the NAAS indicate that nearly 40 percent say they are involved in community organizations, whether secular or religious. This figure is almost identical to the proportion of all Americans in the 2008 American National Election Study who claim to be a "member of an organization."[2] Importantly, however, our question on civic involvement in the National Asian American Survey asks about involvement in organizations, not just membership. Furthermore, it questions respondents about involvement in religious as well as secular organizations, asking them about civic activities in their place of worship first (among those who say they attend religious services), and then asks all respondents about involvement in other types of organizations. Thus we are able to differentiate among those involved exclusively in religious organizations (21 percent), those exclusively involved in secular organizations (7 percent), and those involved in both (11 percent). The ANES does not differentiate between religious and secular organizations.

Using the NAAS, we find a higher level of organizational involvement among Asian Americans compared to estimates of Asian American organizational involvement in the Current Population Survey (Ramakrishnan 2006; Sundeen, Garcia, and Wang 2007). As we noted in chapter 1, the CPS is limited in its coverage of Asian Americans because it conducts interviews only in English and Spanish. With greater coverage of limited-English proficient individuals in the NAAS, and with separate questions about involvement in religious institutions and secular institutions, we find that participation in organizations among Asian Americans is nearly double that found in the Current Population Survey (40 percent versus estimates ranging from to 23 percent). This gap may be explained by the fact that the CPS does not ask a similar, two-part question about religious attendance followed by other types of involvement at the place of worship. Whatever the reason, it is important to keep some of these differences in baseline rates of organizational involvement as we examine differences in participation along particular dimensions within the Asian American community.

In this section, we examine the ways in which patterns of civic engagement among Asian Americans vary along lines of internal differentiation. These include factors related to immigrant socialization that we discussed in chapter 2, as well as particular contexts of settlement and a host of demographic factors that studies have shown to be important predictors of involvement in civic organizations (such as age, gender, and education).

FACTORS RELATED TO IMMIGRANT SOCIALIZATION

Table 6.1 presents Asian American involvement in secular and religious community organizations. Although rates of involvement among Asian Americans in secular organizations are lower than those in religious organizations, they are not dramatically low with respect to that of Americans more generally. Consistent with findings in previous chapters, we detect differences in civic engagement across national origin. Filipino-origin respondents report higher rates of involvement in secular organizations (26 percent) than Chinese (14 percent) and Vietnamese (10 percent), and their involvement at religious places of worship is relatively high as well. However, high rates of participation in one realm of civic life (working with others in one's community) do not necessarily translate into high rates of participation in another realm (involvement with a religious organization). For example, those of Korean origin report relatively high levels of involvement in religious organizations (45 percent), but relatively low rates in secular organizations (17 percent). On average, Filipinos (54 percent), Koreans (49 percent), and Asian Indians (43 percent) report the highest levels in any type of organization.

Although national origin may be a starting point for understanding patterns of civic involvement among Asian Americans, one must be cautious about assuming that these differences emerge from essential cultural differences. It is critical to take into account a group's history, internal cohesion, resources, and opportunities for organizing when attempting to explain differences in involvement across national origin. For example, we note that Filipinos, Koreans, and Asian Indians tend to have the highest rates of civic engagement, especially when we examine secular and religious involvement together. In fact, participation in religious organizations is a large component of these groups' civic engagement. Involvement in Protestant Christian organizations is likely the most important factor driving Korean American civic engagement. Korean migrants arrive from one of the most heavily Protestant nations in Asia (Kim 2000), and the proportion of Protestant Koreans in the United States is higher than in Korea (Hurh and Kim 1990). Some scholars make the case that Korean Protestant churches in the United States not only provide a religious home, but also constitute important community organizations with social service functions (Min 1992). In light of this observation, we argue that the demarcation between secular and religious organizations may not be as stark as it might appear at first glance. This is likely the case for participation in religious organizations among groups such as Asian Indians and Filipinos as well (Kurien 2001; Brettell 2005). Religious organizations provide important institutional avenues for civic engagement within these communities. Group resources matter also. Pooled data from the 2005 and 2006 American Community Surveys show that among the six groups included in the NAAS survey, Filipinos, Asian Indians, and Koreans also have the highest rates of educational attainment (Sakamoto, Goyette, and Kim 2009). Thus, educational resources may also be part of the explanation for group differences in civic engagement. Regardless of the origins of national-origin group differences, we highlight them here because they may translate into differences in group representation in the civic sphere and in civil society (Ramakrishnan and Bloemraad 2008).

Involvement with a community organization also varies by length of residence in the United States (figure 6.1). Asian Americans who have lived in the United States for thirty years or more are more than twice as likely (24 percent) to be involved with a secular organization as those who have been in the country for less than ten years (12 percent). This pattern holds for the most part across all the national-origin groups. Furthermore, the power of length of residence is underscored by the fact that, among Asian Indians, Japanese, and Korean respondents, involvement with a secular organization is higher among those in the United States thirty years or more than among the U.S.-born. In terms of involvement in reli-

Table 6.1   Civic Engagement

	Secular	Religious	Any
Asian Indian	20	35	43
Chinese	14	18	26
Filipino	26	47	54
Japanese	21	26	37
Korean	17	45	49
Vietnamese	10	28	32
Total	18	32	39

Source: Authors' compilation of data from the 2008 National Asian American Survey (Ramakrishnan et al. 2011).
Survey questions: "Other than a religious group or place of worship, is there any other group or organization in your community that you are involved with?" (Atheist, agnostic, nonreligious coded as 0); "Other than attending services or prayer, do you take part in any activity with people at your place of worship?"

gious organizations, the association between length of residence and involvement is less systematic, but still demonstrates a positive trend. Note that the native-born tend to be active in religious organizations at a slightly lower rate than long-term resident immigrants.

In addition to length of stay, studies of immigrant civic participation also indicate that citizens tend to be more active in the civic realm than noncitizens (Segura, Pachon, and Woods 2001; DeSipio 2006). At first, this may seem surprising, in that involvement in community organizations does not require U.S. citizenship, or even the intention of becoming a citizen. Indeed, studies of transnational organizations among Mexican immigrants suggest that there are civic spaces even for undocumented residents (Bada, Fox, and Selee 2006; Ramakrishnan and Viramontes 2010). Despite various opportunities for noncitizen participation, however, studies based on the Current Population Survey have consistently found that citizens are much more likely than noncitizens to participate (Ramakrishnan 2006; Sundeen, Garcia, and Wang 2007). Our analysis of the NAAS also shows significant gaps between the civic engagement of citizens and noncitizens (33 percent versus 43 percent), although the gaps are nowhere near those found in the CPS, where citizens are more than twice as likely as noncitizens to participate (Ramakrishnan 2006). We also find that the gap between citizens and noncitizens is smaller for involvement in religious organizations, where noncitizens are about 20 percent less likely to participate, than in secular organizations, where they are 40 percent less likely to participate.

As to why citizenship may still matter for civic engagement, although it is not a formal requirement for participation, using cross-sectional sur-

Figure 6.1   Involvement in Civic Organizations

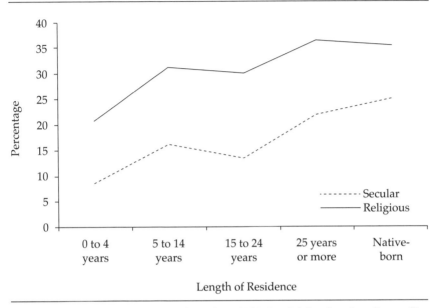

Source: Authors' compilation of data from the 2008 National Asian American Survey (Ramakrishnan et al. 2011).

vey data to find adequate answers has a few limitations. Thus, for instance, we can note that citizens tend to be pay more attention to English-language news sources, and thus may be more informed about volunteering opportunities. Or, perhaps the longer duration of stay among citizens than noncitizens may account for greater exposure to opportunities for civic engagement, and perhaps even greater receptivity to requests for involvement. Our survey is unable to provide answers in this regard. For now, however, we lean on findings from qualitative studies of civic engagement, which suggest that greater residential mobility, language barriers, gender discrimination, and lack of information about civic opportunities among noncitizens often lead to lower levels of involvement (Jones-Correa 1998; Ramakrishnan and Viramontes 2006).

What role do other factors related to immigrant socialization play in the civic engagement of Asian Americans? We find that rates of involvement in community groups or organizations tend to be higher among those educated in the United States (table 6.2). It may be that U.S. educational institutions play an important socializing role when it comes to civic involvement, but it is also likely that education in the United States is a more general proxy for length of residence, citizenship, and social in-

Table 6.2   Civic Engagement and Immigrant Socialization

	Secular	Religious
Educated in United States	21	33
Educated outside United States	16	32
English-speaking ability (Asian-language interviews only)		
Not at all	2	16
Just a little	10	31
Pretty well	16	27
Very well	23	36
English-language interview	20	34
Asian-language interview	14	30
Small Asian American settlements	21	34
Traditional Asian American settlements	17	31
New Asian American settlements	19	36

Source: Authors' compilation of data from the 2008 National Asian American Survey (Ramakrishnan et al. 2011).
Note: Rates are in percentages.

tegration, all of which encourage organizational involvement. We find a different pattern when it comes to participation in religious organizations. Those educated outside the United States are no more likely than those educated inside it to be involved in a religious organization.

English-speaking skills are another important measure of socialization. Involvement in secular community organizations appears to be closely associated with how well respondents speak English. That is, involvement in secular organizations increases steadily with English-speaking skills among those who took the survey in an Asian language. However, for the same individuals, involvement in a religious organization does not appear to be closely tied to English-speaking skills once respondents acquire even minimal English-speaking proficiency (table 6.2). Note that civic engagement varies by language of interview in ways one might expect given the previous analysis. Those who opted to take the survey in English are much more likely to be involved in a secular organization and slightly more likely to be involved in a religious organization than those who opted for the Asian-language interview.

Despite tremendous scholarly and popular interest in immigrants' settlement in nontraditional places in the United States, we observe little difference in rates of civic engagement among those living in new immigrant destinations and those who have settled in more traditional locations (table 6.2). This finding is somewhat surprising. Because new immigrant destinations are home to a much more limited set of immigrant-serving and ethnic organizations and worship sites than those places with a long history of Asian American settlement, one would suspect that, based on the opportunity structure alone, civic engagement would be lower in new destinations. However, this is not the case. The greater importance of individual-level factors may account for this finding. Asian Americans in new destinations exhibit similar rates of citizenship, educational attainment, and nativity as the those in traditional destinations.

DEMOGRAPHIC FACTORS

More than half a century of research identifies formal education as a consistent and powerful predictor of civic engagement and other aspects of democratic citizenship in the United States. Thus, it is perhaps no surprise that, as with the general population, the association between educational attainment and civic engagement among Asian Americans is strong (Verba, Schlozman, and Brady 1995; Nie, Junn, and Stehlik-Barry 1996). Looking at figure 6.2, we see that just 5 percent of those with less than a high school degree, versus nearly 30 percent of those with an advanced degree, take part in secular community groups and organizations. It is clear, however, that the association between education and civic engagement varies by type of organization. For example, the association between educational attainment and involvement in religious organizations is curvilinear. Just over 20 percent of Asian Americans with less than a high school degree report involvement in a religious organization, versus about 35 percent with a college degree. Involvement in religious organizations then dips slightly among the most highly educated. Further, the association between income and involvement in civic organizations (secular or religious) is not linear. The association seems to increase as one moves from the very lowest income levels to the comfortably middle class, then remain relatively steady as income levels increase.

One might draw a number of conclusions from these findings. When it comes to secular organizations, education is likely to endow individuals with specific cognitive and organizational skills that help to facilitate participation in civic groups. But the story is more complicated than that. For example, when it comes to religious organizations, these skills may matter, but may not be as critical. Instead, other characteristics, especially those related to religiosity, may come into play. The observation that religiosity declines among the very highly educated is fairly well established (Uecker, Regnerus, and Vaaler 2007; Ecklund and Scheitle 2007). Such a

Figure 6.2   Civic Engagement and Education

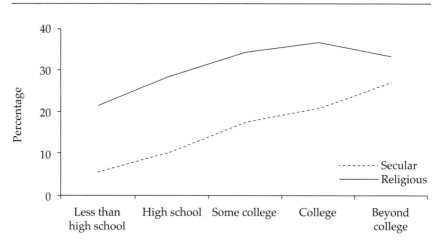

Source: Authors' compilation of data from the 2008 National Asian American Survey (Ramakrishnan et al. 2011).

trend would lead to the kind of decline in participation in religious organizations that we observe among the most educated individuals in the NAAS sample.

The NAAS data also suggest that education and income play different roles in facilitating civic engagement. Education likely provides individuals with civic skills and a central place in social networks (Nie, Junn, and Stehlik-Barry 1996), both of which exert a positive impact on civic engagement. Income is a material resource, however. Thus, it makes sense that once individuals have reached a level of economic security that allows them the extra time and resources necessary to participate in an organization, increasing levels security do not necessarily correspond to involvement. After all, there are only so many extra hours in a day that might be devoted to civic engagement and the dues or monetary costs associated with a typical community organization tend to be standardized, not sliding, to encourage membership.

Age may also be significantly related to civic participation. The findings from the NAAS suggest that participation in secular community groups or organizations increases considerably between younger cohorts (ages eighteen through thirty-four) and those in older age groups, from 12 percent to about 20 percent. Secular involvement among the elderly declines slightly, but the differences are not statistically significant. A similar pattern can be found for involvement in religious organizations, but the increases are smaller in proportional terms, from 27 percent to about 35 percent. These trends are likely tied to the lifecycle and life stages. As one moves from a young adult to middle age, one is likely to become more established in a particular community and invest in that community through civic engagement. It is interesting to note, however, that a recent study finds that Asian American youth age eighteen to twenty-five are civically engaged (they work on community problems and volunteer more than their white, Latino, and African American counterparts), but their engagement is not necessarily tied to formal membership in an organization (Lopez et al. 2006).

Finally, we find some important differences in participation by gender. Studies of Asian American civic engagement report conflicting findings on the role of gender in civic engagement. Ecklund and Park (2005) find no overall differences in organizational participation among Asian American men and women using the 2000 Community Benchmark Survey. In a study of participation in voluntary organizations using the 2004 Current Population Survey on volunteering, however, Richard Sundeen, Cristina Garcia, and Lili Wang (2007) report that women tend to volunteer more than men. Neither of these studies, however, offered interviews in Asian languages. These studies also do not distinguish between secular and religious organizations. Our analysis of the NAAS data indicates that Asian American men and women participate in secular organizations at about the same rates (19 percent for men and 17 percent for women), but when it comes to religious organizations, women are more likely to be involved (35 percent to 30 percent).[3]

RESULTS FROM MULTIVARIATE ANALYSIS

As in each of the last several chapters, we home in on the main effects associated with civic engagement by using multivariate analysis on the demographic and immigrant socialization factors we have considered, focusing on secular organizations. Specifically, we regress involvement in a secular organization on sex, education, age, whether the respondent lives in a traditional or new destination, national origin, and a range of migration-related variables.

Among the U.S.-born, once sex, age, and national origin are taken into account, education is the only variable that appears to be associated with involvement in a community group or organization. The native-born sample size is relatively small (under five hundred) when compared to the foreign-born sample (over 4,000). Among the foreign-born, involvement in secular organizations is positively tied to higher education and longer stay in the United States.

These findings reveal that at the individual level, education plays a powerful role in civic engagement for Asian Americans, consistent with trends in the general population. The strong association between education and civic engagement is attributed in part to the congnitive and organizational skills that education imparts, but also to the social values and networks individuals are exposed to at institutions of higher education (Nie, Junn, and Stehlik-Barry 1996; Egerton 2002). In this regard, a socioeconomic model explains Asian American civic engagement well. However, at the aggregate level, we see that Asian American civic engagement tends to lag behind that of other racial groups, especially among higher-educated groups (Stoll and Wong 2007). This may be related to social sorting within institutions of higher education. The kinds of social networks and associated socialization experiences they provide vary across racial groups within the same educational setting (Mayer and Puller 2008). It follows that racially segmented social networks in institutions of higher education would lead to different civic engagement opportunities.

In addition, our analysis of the foreign-born sample in the NAAS suggests that Asian American civic engagement is not driven by educational achievement alone. Length of U.S. residence must also be taken into consideration; it most likely serves as a proxy for greater familiarity and experience with U.S. civic institutions (Wong 2006) and also for entrance into a greater variety of social networks. We would expect that those most familiar with civic institutions would also be the most comfortable getting involved in those institutions. Complicating this conclusion, however, is that we observe after controlling for years of education, national origin, and foreign-born status a negative association between having had more education in the United States (versus abroad) and involvement in a secular organization. Our data suggest, then, that education is a consistent and powerful resource when it comes to secular organizational involvement, but where that education takes place is less important. For the foreign-born, socialization in U.S. educational institutions (versus home country institutions) does not seem to be critical to promoting organizational involvement. This is a puzzling finding given the emphasis that researchers of civic engagement and education place on socialization processes and social networks in institutions of higher education. Perhaps for the foreign-born, the most important social networks for civic engagement develop over time in the United States and is not necessarily tied to educational settings.

Even after controlling for socioeconomic status and length of residence, the analysis reveals that national origin continues to differentiate propensity to belong to secular civic organizations. Recall from table 6.1 that at the bivariate level, Filipinos (26 percent), Japanese (21 percent), and Asian Indians (20 percent) exhibited the highest rates of participation in secular organizations. The findings from the multivariate analysis suggest that some of the national-origin differences in participation we observed in table 6.1 are due to group differences in demographic characteristics. For example, once demographic factors are taken into account, Filipino and Chinese immigrants exhibit lower rates of organizational involvement than their Japanese counterparts. This result underscores the importance of considering national-origin differences from a broad perspective that encompasses demographic features and group histories, rather than essential group characteristics alone.

Finally, the analysis shows that after taking into consideration key demographic factors, living in a new immigrant destination is positively associated with involvement in a community organization. That is, once demographic characteristics are accounted for, those living in newer immigrant destinations participate more than those in more established destinations. These results are somewhat consistent with the findings from the earlier cross-tabulations between place of settlement and civic engagement. Although one might assume that traditional immigrant destinations would house a more established organizational infrastructure (and therefore provide more opportunities to take part in civic life), we do not find evidence of this scenario playing out at the level of individual involvement in secular community organizations.

ORGANIZATIONAL HOMOGENEITY

As Eric Uslaner and Richard Conley point out, whether people join groups matters for social capital, but we might also be concerned about the people with whom joiners associate (2003, 333). To what extent do individuals join groups composed of people like themselves? Uslaner and Conley argue that "if we only socialize with people like ourselves and only join organizations composed of people like ourselves, we will not have the opportunity to get to know folks from different backgrounds. If knowing people leads to trusting them, we will not develop faith in people unlike ourselves. This confidence in others is an essential part of social capital, leading to widespread cooperation" (333). A popular stereotype associated with Asian Americans is that they tend to be insular and unwilling to associate with those who do not share their racial or ethnic backgrounds. For example, Mary Danico and Franklin Ng observe that "instead of viewing the Asian American population as one that helps to support the local

Table 6.3   Civic Engagement: Background by National Origin

	All Members of Ethnic Group	All College-Educated
Asian Indian	41	36
Chinese	23	26
Filipino	20	29
Japanese	20	24
Korean	61	39
Vietnamese	39	17
Total	31%	30%

Source: Authors' compilation of data from the 2008 National Asian American Survey (Ramakrishnan et al. 2011).
Note: Row percentages are calculated using weighted data.
Survey question: "Other than a religious group or place of worship, is there any other group or organization in your community that you are involved with?" [Please tell me the name of the organization or group that is most important to you.] "And how many members of this group would you say are [Rs group from A1] – all of them, most, about half, some of them, or none?"

economy, a perception of Asian Americans as being exclusive, insular, and cliquish emerges. Instead of gaining support from the larger society, they are often criticized for supporting only Asian issues, and their loyalty to American society and its culture is questioned" (2004, 57). Similarly, the writer Helen Zia claims that the Chinese Exclusion Acts had a "a two-pronged impact: for Asian Americans, it verified that their voices were neither expected nor desired; for others it confirmed that Asians are a silent, insular minority with nothing to say" (2001, 236).

The focus of the following analysis, as mentioned, is on secular organizations only. Table 6.3 presents the degree to which Asian Americans join organizations composed exclusively of co-ethnics. About 30 percent of those involved in a secular community organization report that the group is made up entirely of co-ethnics (that is, those of the same national origin group). The extent to which Asian Americans join ethnically homogenous groups and organizations depends on national origin. Some 23 percent of Chinese, fewer than 20 percent of Japanese and Filipinos, but about 40 percent of Asian Indians and Vietnamese in a community group or organization claim that all of the members are co-ethnics. By contrast, fully 61 percent of Koreans say that every member of the organization shares their national origin. Of course these differences likely stem from factors beyond national origin, such as a group's average length of residence, the proportion of foreign-born in a particular group, and specific histories of migration and settlement.

Are these organizations educationally homogenous? Again, there is a great deal of variation in terms of the degree to which the organizations in which Asian Americans participate tend to be integrated along class lines (table 6.3). Among Koreans who take part in secular community organizations, close to 40 percent report that all of the other members are college-educated, versus 17 percent of Vietnamese. These national-origin differences may be due in large part to differences in average education among Koreans and Vietnamese. However, average education among each national-origin group does not appear to provide a full explanation. Note that only 24 percent of Japanese (the group with the highest levels of average education) who are involved secular organizations report that all of the members of their organization are college educated.

Is class or ethnic homogeneity more the norm among the organizations that Asian Americans join? We see from the results reported in table 6.3 that no clear pattern exists. Overall, about one in every three Asian Americans involved in a secular community organization report that all the members of their group share their ethnic or educational background. The organizations Koreans and Vietnamese join tend to be more ethnically than educationally homogenous, whereas those Filipinos join tend to be the reverse.

Uslaner and Conley assert in their study of civic engagement among Chinese in southern California that those who join ethnically homogenous organizations will exhibit lower levels of generalized trust and withdraw from civic life that does not involve co-ethnics. According to this line of reasoning, such ethnic-centered joining diminishes the benefits of social capital, especially the bridging variety that Putnam theorizes provides the social glue that holds Americans together: "The 'social' part of social capital depends upon trust in people who are different from yourself. It is far from clear that any social ties can produce social trust. But if people associate mainly with people like themselves, any possibility that social ties could help to resolve larger collective-action problems will be minimal" (Uslaner and Conley 2003, 355).

Do Asian Americans who join ethnic organizations participate in American politics less than those who don't belong to such organizations? Do they tend to be less trusting or believe it is better to avoid contact with the government in Washington? We do not replicate Uslaner and Conley's study here, but do explore some of their general hypotheses using basic analyses. We compare those who are not involved in any community group or organization with those who are involved in an organization composed completely of other people with the same national origin, and those involved in more ethnically or racially integrated organizations.

Table 6.4 shows that those in integrated community organizations or

Table 6.4   Participation Organization

	Not Involved	Ethnic Organization	Integrated Organization
Participated in political activity beyond voting	29	50	70
Agrees somewhat or strongly can trust government in Washington to do what is right	43	52	44
Strongly or somewhat disagrees that it is better to avoid contact with government	56	59	72

Source: Authors' compilation of data from the 2008 National Asian American Survey (Ramakrishnan et al. 2011).
Note: Rates are in percentages.

groups participate in nonvoting political activities (70 percent) more than those in ethnically homogenous organizations (50 percent). However, both groups are much more likely to take part in political activities than those who do not belong to any community group or organization. We also examine the association between belonging to an ethnically homogenous organization and trust by focusing on trust in the government. The results suggest that at the bivariate level the association between membership in an ethnic organization and trust in the federal government is only slight—and not in the expected direction. Those involved in ethnic organizations are slightly more likely to trust the government in Washington compared with those in more integrated organizations. Note that those involved in a secular organization, ethnically homogenous or not, hardly vary from those not involved in any organization on this question.

Probed with a slightly different question about their attitudes toward American government, Asian Americans involved in ethnically integrated organizations tend to strongly disagree that "it is better to avoid contact with the government" at slightly higher rates (72 percent) than either those involved in ethnic organizations (59 percent) or those not involved in community groups or organizations (56 percent). In their earlier study, Uslaner and Conley found that those who joined ethnic organizations were less trusting and less likely to participate in civic life even compared to those who were not involved at all in any community group or organization (2003). Data from the NAAS suggest that involvement in either group is associated with deeper involvement in civic life and sometimes results in more positive attitudes toward contact with the government compared with those who remain unattached to any community group or organization.

Multivariate analyses (not shown) confirm that after taking account of socioeconomic status, demographic factors, nativity, and national origin, those in both integrated and ethnically homogenous organizations demonstrate higher rates of participation in political activities than those who do not belong to any community organization at all. Once potential intervening variables are taken into consideration, those who take part in ethnically integrated organizations are less likely to say that they believe that "it is better to avoid contact with the government" than those who do not belong to any community group or organization. In contrast, those belonging to ethnically homogenous organizations show no distinction on this measure. Finally, multivariate analyses reveal that those in ethnically homogenous organizations tend to be more trusting of the government in Washington than those who do not belong to any organization, though no statistically significant differences in trust exist among those who belong to more integrated organizations and those not involved in any organization.

Thus, ethnic organizations may attract distinct groups of people, and may provide different types of opportunities for civic involvement, but do not seem to drive down democratic participation or trust in the government as research might predict.

RELIGIOUS AFFILIATION, ATTENDANCE, AND CIVIC ENGAGEMENT

Until the 1990s, studies of Asian American religions were rare. For most of its history, U.S.-based religious studies failed to consider the religious experiences of post-1965 immigrants, particularly nonwhite immigrants such as Asian Americans (Yang 2000). At the same time, Asian American studies tended to elide the subject of religion, in part because of the secular and anticolonialist orientation of early scholars in the field (Yoo 1999). Finally, social science studies fared poorly in attempts to measure and analyze Asian American religiosity. For example, most such studies focused on church attendance and ignored the ways in which religiosity might be expressed in noncongregational settings, such as temples and home shrines (Min 2005b). Together, these factors marginalized the study of Asian American religiosity across fields. Since the 1990s, the study of Asian American religiosity has gained prominence as evidenced by several important edited volumes on the topic (Yoo 1999; Iwamura and Spickard 2003; Carnes and Yang 2004). Quantitative studies of religion and civic life remain rare, however, leading scholars to observe that "the next step [in Asian American religious studies] . . . may include quantitative survey research comparing various Asian American ethnic groups of one religion and various religions of one ethnic group" (Yang 2000; Lien and Carnes 2004). We take heed of this call and bring the NAAS data to bear on the topic of Asian American religious affiliation and religiosity, especially as it relates to civic engagement. In fact, one of the most prevalent modes of civic engagement among Asian Americans is involvement in a religious institution. We discuss specific findings related to religious affiliation and attendance from the NAAS study here and elaborate on their implications at the end of this section.

Of our full sample, roughly 40 percent indicate that they attend a place of worship at least once a week, versus about 54 percent of Americans more generally (Pew Research Center 2008). Variation in attendance across national-origin groups is substantial, however: Koreans (69 percent) and Filipinos (65 percent) are most likely to attend almost weekly or more frequently; Vietnamese (37 percent) and Asian Indians (32 percent) fall in the middle of the pack; Chinese and Japanese (each 20 percent) are least likely. This variation, to a significant extent, reflects group differences in propensity to hold any religious faith. Fully 22 percent of the full NAAS sample either identify as atheist or agnostic or do not claim any religious affiliation. These secular respondents are disproportionately Chinese (70 percent). Within groups, there is an especially high proportion of nonbelievers among Chinese (56 percent) and Japanese respondents (30 percent). By contrast, almost none of the Filipino (1 percent) and Asian Indian (3 percent) profess no religious faith or affiliation.

In terms of taking part in activities beyond regular services or prayer, we observe similar patterns (see table 6.1). Although the proportion of respondents who attend services and prayer tends to be higher than the proportion taking part in other kinds of activities for most national origin groups, there are no similar differences among Japanese and Indian Americans. These patterns reflect religious background to some extent (table 6.5). Korean and Vietnamese communities include large proportions of Christian and Catholic adherents. The vast majority (99 percent) of Filipinos and more than 80 percent of all Koreans claim to be Christian or Catholic. Those groups that affiliate primarily with non-Judeo-Christian religions, including Buddhism and Hinduism—Vietnamese, Asian Indian, and Japanese—have lower rates of regular attendance at religious worship sites.

Finally, we find that across all groups, women attend a place of worship more often than men. This relationship is statistically significant among the Asian American sample as whole.[4]

To what extent does religious attendance translate into participation in other realms of civic life? One observes substantial overlap between those who attend religious services and those involved with secular community

Table 6.5   Religious Affiliation By National Origin

	India	China	Philippines	Japan	Korea	Vietnam	Total
Christian	5	27	21	28	65	4	24
Catholic	4	2	78	3	17	34	24
Buddhist	1	14		38	4	51	14
Hindu	77						14
Sikh	6						1
Muslim[1]	1						<1
Other non-Christian	3	1					1
Agnostic, atheist, or no religion	3	56	1	30	14	11	22

Source: Authors' compilation of data from the 2008 National Asian American Survey (Ramakrishnan et al. 2011).
Note: Proportions less than 1 percent are left blank; percentages may not add up to 100 due to rounding.
[1] As we detail in appendix D, one limitation of our sample method is the limited ability to draw in Asian Muslims, many of whom do not have distinctively Asian names.

organizations. A small proportion of people (10 percent) never attend religious services but are involved in secular organizations; by contrast nearly 25 percent of those who attend religious services regularly are also involved in secular organizations. Of those involved in secular community organizations, just 13 percent are either secular or identify with a religion but never attend services; in other words, the vast majority attend religious services at least sometimes.

Although 24 percent of Asian Americans affiliated with a Western religious tradition (Christians or Catholics) and a similar proportion of those who attend a place of worship almost weekly or more are involved with a secular group, a nearly equal 22 percent of their counterparts who attend worship less frequently also belong to such groups. By contrast, the association between attendance at religious services and involvement in a secular organization among those who practice a non-Western religious tradition is stronger: 25 percent of those who attend their place of worship almost weekly or more are also involved with a secular group, whereas only 15 percent of Asian Americans of non-Western faiths who attend their place of worship less often report active involvement in a secular organization.

Similar to findings reported from studies of the general American population, among Asian American Christians, a positive association exists between frequent attendance at a place of worship and higher rates of voter registration and higher general election voting rates. In contrast, when one examines other types of civic participation, such as contributing to a political campaign or taking part in a demonstration or protest, the association is weak.

Which Asian Americans attend a place of worship frequently? Again, multivariate analysis provides an answer. When we regress attendance at religious services on sex, age, national origin, and other variables of interest, we observe that education is a strong predictor of attendance at a place of worship (table not shown). This is true for both the U.S.-born and foreign-born. Among the U.S.-born, even after controlling for other demographic factors, some national origin distinctions remain. Compared with U.S.-born Japanese respondents, attendance at a place of worship is more frequent among both Chinese and Korean respondents.

Multivariate analysis of the foreign-born sample (again, not shown) shows a strong association between attendance at a place of worship and a number of demographic factors. When attendance at a place of worship is regressed on demographic and migration-related variables, we see a positive association between attending a place of worship frequently and being female and being more educated. Further, citizenship is a strong predictor of attending a place of worship, even after taking into account length of residence and other demographic factors. Although U.S.-born Chinese are more likely attend a place of worship than their Japanese counterparts, among the foreign-born, Chinese are less likely to attend a place of worship. Koreans and Filipinos attend more than Japanese, even after other demographic and migration-related factors have been taken into account. Finally, once we control for these other factors, living in a new immigrant destination, versus living in a more traditional gateway, is positively associated with attending a place of worship. This may be explained by the fact that religious sites tend to function as a valuable social service and cultural resource for immigrants, especially when few other culturally specific resources exist (Min 1992; Bankston and Zhou 1995; Hurh and Kim 1990).

Analysis of the NAAS data highlights the importance of considering religion when studying Asian American communities and their involvement in civic life. Several key findings deserve more discussion. First, religious diversity within the Asian American community is marked. As Jane Iwamura observes, "the sheer diversity of ethnic communities and religious traditions that fall under the rubric of Asian and Pacific America can make things appear quite chaotic" (2003, 1). And yet attention to this diversity may force one to reconsider assumptions about the Asian American community. For example, the national-origin differences in civic engagement may be traced in large part to religious affiliation and attendant institutional support for civic participation, rather than to the cultural norms associated with particular Asian American groups. Second, we find quite a bit of religious diversity within particular national origin groups, especially in terms of the practice of Western and non-Western religions. Among the Chinese, for example, 27 percent identify as Christian, 14 percent as Buddhist, and more than 50 percent with no religious tradition. This internal religious diversity has implications for civic engagement: frequent attendance at one's place of worship is associated with greater involvement in secular organizations among Asian Americans who affiliate with a non-Western religious tradition, but not among those affiliated with a Western religious tradition.

Finally, the data presented suggest that religious organizations may be potentially important avenues of political socialization and involvement for Asian Americans, especially if their role extends beyond the spiritual, as seems to be the case for many immigrant-dominant groups (Min 2005b, 1992; Bankston and Zhou 1995; Hurh and Kim 1990). One important question for the future, then, has to do with the substantive nature of the civic and political orientations fostered in places of worship and in religious settings. Karen Yonemoto's research on Asian American pan-ethnic churches, for example, suggests that the civic engagement they encourage tends to be moderate, rather than radical or system-challenging (2009). For example, church leaders are more likely to provide opportunities for members to volunteer at a homeless shelter than to join a political protest challenging state or national welfare policies. Still, Yonemoto argues that because they are some of the largest civic organizations in the Asian American community, evangelical churches are among the most powerful in terms of bringing a large number of Asian American Christians into the civic sphere (Wong and Iwamura 2007; Wong, Rim, and Perez 2008).

MOBILIZATION BY COMMUNITY GROUPS AND ORGANIZATIONS

Untangling the causal relationship between contact by a community organization or group and political participation is difficult. Do community organizations actively mobilize those who would not ordinarily take part in politics, or are the most active members of society also the most attractive targets for community organizations' mobilizing efforts?

About 15 percent of all Asian Americans in our sample report being contacted by a group other than a political party to participate in the November 2008 election. Overall, Filipinos, Japanese, and Koreans were the most likely to report being contacted and Asian Indians, Chinese, and Vietnamese the least likely. These results are somewhat surprising given that significant proportions of the latter groups live in presidential battleground states where mobilization would be expected to be highest (see chapter 3). Chinese and Vietnamese, but not Asian Indians, also tend to live in places with at least moderate opportunities to be represented by an Asian American elected official.

Bivariate analysis reveals that one's likelihood of being contacted by a community organization did not vary much by whether one intended to vote for Obama or McCain in that election. About equal proportions (25 percent) of Obama and McCain supporters reported contact by a community group or other nonparty organization. However, those who were planning to vote for a third-party candidate or who were undecided were less likely to be contacted than those supporting one of the two major party candidates. This provides some limited evidence that even community-based organizations were deeply invested in mainstream partisans among the Asian American population and less interested in mobilizing the undecided. Further, our analysis suggests that in the context of a presidential election season, most of those contacted were citizens (85 percent of the total). Put another way, 20 percent of all Asian American citizens in the sample—but only 6 percent of noncitizens—report being contacted.

Table 6.6   Civic Engagement and Political Participation

	Likely Voter	Political Contributor	Contact Government Officials	Protester	Community Activist
Involved in secular organization	53	25	19	9	41
Not involved	44	10	7	3	17
Involved in religious organization	49	18	14	6	31
Not involved	44	10	7	3	17

Source: Authors' compilation of data from the 2008 National Asian American Survey (Ramakrishnan et al. 2011).
Note: Rates are in percentages.

CIVIC ENGAGEMENT AND POLITICAL PARTICIPATION

Our final inquiry has to do with the association between civic engagement and political participation, which we present in table 6.6. We find that those involved with secular or religious organizations tend to be the most active in politics—for example, to be voters. When it comes to participation beyond voting, those involved with a secular organization are more than twice as likely to protest, make a political contribution, contact a government official or work with others in the community to solve a problem than those who are not involved with a secular organization. Involvement in religious organizations, particularly taking part in activities other than services and prayer at one's place of worship, is also associated with higher rates of political activity. The association between frequency of attendance at religious services and political participation is less clear (not shown in tables). Differences based on frequency of attendance at one's place of worship in terms of protest activity or making political contributions are not statistically significant. However, those who attend religious services frequently do have higher rates of community activism and contact with officials than those who do not attend services frequently.

CONCLUSION

To what extent does racial and ethnic diversity reinforce or undermine American civil society? We contend that because Asian Americans are one of the fastest growing racial-ethnic groups in the United States, the answer may depend in part on civic engagement. Understanding Asian American civic engagement is thus a first step to answering this question. This chapter began with a set of inquiries about Asian American involvement in community organizations. We focus on civic and religious organizations in part because they constitute some of the most important institutional engines of pan-ethnic group formation (Espiritu 1993). The question of whether Asian Americans are a coherent and meaningful political category rests in large part on the degree to which they join organizations that foster a sense of pan-ethnicity. The most prominent Asian American secular organizations in the United States tend to be pan-ethnic. Asian American religious organizations have moved in this direction as well (Yonemoto 2009). Further, even when organizations explicitly serve or represent a particular group, there is communication and community-building among organizational leaders.

We ask whether some Asian Americans are more likely to join groups than others, whether different community organizations encourage distinct types of participation and attitudes toward politics, and which Asian Americans are most likely to be the targets of mobilization by community groups. Overall, about one in five Asian Americans report involvement in secular organizations (similar proportions claim to work with others in their community to solve a problem). About one out of every three Asian Americans claim to be involved with a religious organization. About 40 percent of Asian Americans are involved in at least one of these types of organizations. Further, about the same proportion of Asian Americans attend a place of worship frequently.

We find that involvement in community organizations depends on the type of organization, resources, and other demographic factors, such as national origin, citizenship status, and nativity. For all Asian Americans, education is associated with more involvement in secular organizations. Multivariate analysis (not shown) reveals that among the foreign-born, length of residence in the United States—but not citizenship status—predicts involvement in secular community organizations. In addition, national-origin differences in organizational involvement persist, even after taking into account demographic and migration-related factors.

We compared involvement in ethnically homogenous community organizations (secular) to that in their more ethnically integrated counterparts. Does involvement in ethnic organizations lead Asian Americans to withdraw from other aspects of civic life or to be less trusting of other types of civic institutions? At the bivariate level, we find that those who take part in more integrated organizations participate in American politics at higher rates than those involved in ethnic organizations. Still, we find that those who join either type of organization tend to participate more than those who are uninvolved, even after taking into account length of residence, citizenship, and educational resources. For the most part, belonging to an ethnic organization is not associated with less trusting attitudes toward the government. Thus, we do not see evidence that ethnic organizations foster civic balkanization or encourage withdrawal from American civic life more generally.

Religious variation is a hallmark of the Asian American community: 24 percent of NAAS respondents identify as Christian, 24 percent as Catholic, 14 percent as Buddhist, and 14 percent as Hindu. Nearly 10 percent, however, do not affiliate with any tradition or identify as agnostic or atheist. Frequency of attendance at a place of worship depends in part on whether Asian Americans are part of a Western religious tradition such as Christianity or Catholicism. This is not surprising, because many non-Western religious traditions fall outside a congregational Sunday-service model. Frequency of attendance at places of worship is associated with involvement with a secular organization among adherents of non-Western religions, but not among Christians and Catholics.

Community organizations do appear to be sources of political mobilization for some Asian Americans. About 15 percent of our sample reported being contacted about a campaign by community groups and similar organizations. These organizations appeared to target citizens and supporters of one of the two main party candidates. Thus it could be argued that those who already tied most closely to mainstream politics were also the most easily reached and open to contact by community organizations.

Finally, based on the simple analysis presented in this chapter, we anticipate that involvement with secular and religious civic organizations will be strongly associated with voting, even when taking into consideration demographic diversity in terms of national origin and socioeconomic status. In fact, it is likely, based on the bivariate analysis presented, that involvement in secular and religious civic organizations will be a strong predictor of all types of political participation, including protest and campaign activity. We also expect frequency of religious attendance to be most strongly associated with voting, but perhaps also with other types of political activity. Finally, we argue in the next chapter that the results of this analysis, particularly the findings related to religious organizations and Asian Americans' political participation, fits in nicely with a larger concern around Asian American religions and their place in U.S. religious studies.

Chapter 7 | Making Sense of the Whole

So FAR, WE have laid out a careful descriptive account of Asian American political participation as seen through five broad sets of factors: immigrant socialization, residential contexts, party socialization, racial identification, and civic association. We have treated each of these sets of factors as a series of lenses through which to see Asian American political participation. Some of these lenses have been much more sharply grounded in political science, and our task has been to refashion them to consider the experiences and trajectories of groups that are overwhelmingly foreign-born. Other lenses, such as those relating to immigrant socialization and racial identification, have been much more strongly developed in disciplines such as sociology and history, and our task has been to train their attention toward political behavior.

As we have argued, such a foundational descriptive approach is necessary, because of both the blind spots in each of these disciplinary traditions and the lack of satisfactory national survey data to provide a definitive account of Asian American political attitudes and behavior. Thus, whereas much social science scholarship rushes toward findings based on multivariate statistical analysis, we argue that it is essential to provide a definitive account of Asian American political attitudes and behavior—using a large, nationally representative sample of the Asian American population—that relies primarily on descriptive findings and bivariate relationships that can be widely understood, not only in academic circles but also among wider audiences such as news reporters and community-based organizations.

At the same time, a descriptive approach to understanding patterns in political participation can only go so far. For instance, it can tell us that those Asian Americans who are still trying to figure out their party identification are less likely to vote or write to their elected officials. However, it cannot tell us the relative importance of this lack of party identification

210

when compared to other factors such as being born in the United States, having a college degree, or experiencing racial or ethnic discrimination. Thus, in addition to analyzing how each of these groups of factors may relate to political participation, it is also important to consider ways in which these factors jointly account for variations in political participation among Asian Americans.

Typically, this kind of analysis is done using a multivariate regression that controls for all relevant variables, with simulated effects on each variable while holding all others constant. We conducted such an analysis, with variables grouped by the various pathways articulated throughout this book and a set of important demographic factors that have consistently been shown to be important predictors of political participation (including age, gender, education, homeownership, and income). For the sake of simplicity and clarity, we present the model results in the appendix and take the time here to discuss the findings less susceptible to variations in model specification (see appendix D). After reviewing the major findings, we focus on three narratives that emerge from the multivariate results and are particularly relevant to the experiences of Asian Americans. These include the extent to which civic and political resources may help compensate for group advantages or disadvantages in socioeconomic status, the extent to which political behavior among Asian Americans seems to conform to standard models of immigrant assimilation or newer models of group racialization, and how the high proportion of non-Christians and secular identifiers reshapes our understanding of religion and politics in America.

BRINGING THE PATHWAYS TOGETHER

One way to make sense of the whole when it comes to the various sets of predictors of political participation is to put them all in a standardized multivariate model. The detailed results of such an analysis can be found in appendix D. Looking across five key measures of political participation—voting, contributing money, contacting government officials, protesting, and community activity—we see a set of consistently important indicators, as well as unique patterns of effects associated with these explanatory factors. We base the following discussion on results from multivariate analyses that take into account demographic background and other key control variables, such as age and gender.

Immigrant socialization.   Because the Asian American population is an immigrant-dominant community, we expect to see several important associations between indicators of immigrant socialization and political participation. In fact, we do see lower rates of political participation among those who have been socialized outside the United States. For example, the foreign-born participate at lower rates for most political activities. Similarly, those who are more recent residents, are educated abroad, or more closely follow ethnic news tend to participate less than their more acculturated counterparts. But, we also see that the effects of immigrant socialization vary across types of political participation. This is most clear when it comes to protest activity. Those who appear more connected to the community of origin, through following ethnic news and taking part in homeland politics, are also more likely to take part in protests in the United States.

Party identification.   Party identification, or lack thereof, is critical to understanding political participation among Asian Americans. Affiliation and interaction with political parties are strongly associated with political participation, suggesting that party identification provides a key pathway to political participation for this group. Asian Americans who do not identify with one of the two major parties are less likely to vote, make a political contribution, contact a public official, and even work with others in their community to solve a problem than those who identify as Democrats or Republicans. Further, mobilization by a political party is a very important predictor of almost all types of political activities. Of course, it may be that political parties target the most active Asian Americans.

Racial identification.   Perhaps surprisingly—given what we know about black and Latino Americans—group solidarity does not appear to motivate political participation among Asian Americans. Rather, experience with racial discrimination or being the victim of a hate crime is the aspect of racial identification that most clearly influences (more) political participation in the United States. To some extent, believing that Asian Americans have much in common with other groups seems to encourage political participation, especially when it comes to voting and working with others in one's community.

Religious and civic organizations.   Multivariate analysis suggests that involvement in civic and religious organizations is an important pathway toward political participation for Asian Americans. Mobilization by a group other than a political party is positively associated with most types of political participation. Similarly, Asian Americans who belong to a religious organization or a secular organization tend to make political contributions, contact elected officials, protest, and work with others in their communities to solve a common problem more often than other Asian Americans.

Residential contexts.   Finally, we find very little association between residential contexts (for example, a new immigrant destination, a place with an Asian American elected representative) and participating in politics. This is quite surprising, but suggests that geographic context is not the most important path toward Asian American political incorporation in the United States.

As we can see from the summary, having a standard model for multivariate analyses across types of participation has many benefits, chief among which is to ascertain which variables remain significant predictors when controlling for potentially intervening factors. Such models, however, do not tell a good story, especially when several outcomes and dozens of variables are involved. A causal story with a smaller set of factors is possible using structure equation model (SEM). An illustration of such a model by Andrew Flores and Karthick Ramakrishnan can be found in the online appendix, available at http://www.russellsage.org/Wong_et_al _onlineappendix.pdf.

Here, we revisit the question raised most explicitly in the introductory chapter of this book—how do we best understand Asian Americans— a population that is exceptional in its internal cultural, linguistic, religious, socioeconomic, and phenotypic diversity, a population that is heavily foreign-born and second-generation immigrant, a population with high rates of exogamy and multiracial identification—as a meaningful group in American politics? We highlight national origin and socioeconomic standing as the most prominent points of potential internal divergence within the Asian American community. The empirical findings from our study help us make sense of how these variations within the community are likely to matter for the group's political presence in U.S. politics. Thus, we dig deeper into our survey data but also rely on other primary and secondary sources of evidence to provide more flesh to the findings.

Does internal economic, national origin, or religious diversity preclude a coherent or cohesive Asian American politics? Recognition among scholars is widespread that the image of Asians as highly educated and prosperous masks significant variations in socioeconomic status within the racial category, and Southeast Asian refugees are particularly disadvantaged. We explore the extent to which civic and political resources may help compensate for relative group advantages or disadvantages in socioeconomic status, perhaps yielding a different ranking of national-origin groups based on political participation. In a related vein, we also consider the extent to which immigrant assimilation or immigrant racialization may relate to political participation. Finally, we also pay attention to the importance of secular versus religious affiliation when it comes to civic associations, and advance the literature on religion and politics to include the experiences of significant non-Christian groups.

SOCIOECONOMIC STANDING AND POLITICAL PARTICIPATION

The standard narrative that has emerged since the liberalization of U.S. immigration policy in 1965 has been one of Asian Americans as being highly educated, ambitious, and prosperous, serving as a model for other groups, such as Latinos and African Americans, to follow. Just a year after passage of the 1965 Immigration Act, the mainstream U.S. media began to pay attention to the socioeconomic status of the Asian population in the United States. Reports in the *New York Times Magazine* and *U.S. News and World Report* highlighted the achievements of Japanese and Chinese Americans (Pettersen 1966; U.S. News and World Report 1966). The two groups were praised as examples of academic and economic success, especially after decades of racial discrimination. The authors of these articles emphasized the role of Asian cultural values to explain the economic and educational achievements of Chinese and Japanese Americans, including respect for education, filial piety, and a commitment to hard work. The groups were also characterized as peaceful and morally upright, in contrast to African Americans, who were following a model of protest politics in the 1960s to make socioeconomic and political gains.

Even though the model minority stereotype was born from comparisons between blacks and native-born Chinese Americans and Japanese Americans, it gained strength with the arrival of thousands of Asian immigrants during the decade following the Immigration Act of 1965. Because most of these immigrants came under the professional preference categories of the law—in occupations ranging from doctors and nurses to engineers and scientists—they tended to have levels of education far exceeding those among Latinos and African Americans and rivaling those of native-born whites. Despite the fact that much of this group advantage in educational attainment and economic standing was the product of U.S. immigration policy and not any distinctive Asian values, the model minority stereotype remains strong even today (Junn 2008).

Since the influx of Southeast Asian refugees in the 1970s, however, a more nuanced and differentiated picture of Asian American group standing has emerged. Faced with a massive humanitarian crisis of boat people fleeing Vietnam in the years following the fall of Saigon and Cambodians escaping after the fall of the Khmer Rouge, the United States had to reach beyond its existing provisions of professional visas and family-based unifications. The U.S. government instituted the Orderly Departure Program in 1979 that helped nearly five-hundred thousand Vietnamese refugees settle in the United States, and eventually provided assistance to more than 1 million refugees from Vietnam, Cambodia, and Laos. Unlike the majority of other Asian immigrants who had come to the United States, many of these refugees came from rural areas and most had not completed a high school education. Although many were able to make a living after some initial assistance from the U.S. government and civic organizations, gaps in educational attainment and household income remain between Southeast Asians and immigrants from other parts of Asia. Indeed, recent studies have shown that these group disparities persist even among those born in the United States, with second-generation Southeast Asian Americans less likely to have college degrees than other Asian groups or black, Hispanic, and Native Americans (Lee and Kumashiro 2005). Thus, though the notion of Asian Americans as a model minority on socioeconomic outcomes remains prevalent in media coverage and public opinion (Ghosh 2010; Kinder and Kam 2009), scholarship indicates refugees from Vietnam and other Southeast Asian countries have generally fared much worse than immigrants from India and China (Uba 1992; Yang 2004; Ngo and Lee 2007; Rumbaut 2008; Takaki 1995).

What has been unexamined, however, is whether these group differences in socioeconomic status translate into similar inequalities when it comes to political participation. One would suspect that, consistent with the standard socioeconomic model of political participation, groups with the least access to resources would also have the lowest rates of political participation. Analysis of the NAAS data reveals some surprising patterns and suggests that the story of political participation is more complex (table 7.1). For instance, even though Vietnamese Americans have the lowest educational attainment and household incomes among Asian Americans, they are also among the most likely to vote and to engage in protest politics. Similarly, Japanese Americans have lower levels of educational attainment than Chinese Americans, but are much more likely to vote and make political contributions. Finally, Asian Indians have the highest levels of household income and educational attainment, but are in the middle when it comes to activities like making political contributions and voting in elections. These findings thus challenge the expectation that relative group advantage (or disadvantage) based on socioeconomic resources will automatically translate into similar positions based on political participation.

What, then, accounts for the divergence in relative group standing based on socioeconomic resources versus political participation? Part of

Table 7.1   Rankings by Socioeconomic and Political Participation Outcomes

Group Ranking	Income: Median Household	Educational Attainment: Over Age Twenty-Five, with Bachelor's Degree or Higher	Likely Voter	Protester	Political Contributor
1	Asian Indian 86,615	Asian Indian 69	Japanese* 65	Vietnamese* 8	Japanese* 18
2	Filipino 78,918	Chinese 52	Vietnamese* 48	Asian Indian 4	Filipino 17
3	Chinese 67,893	Korean 52	Asian Indian** 47	Chinese 4	Asian Indian** 12
4	Japanese 65,201	Filipino 48	Filipino 47	Filipino 4	Chinese** 11
5	Vietnamese 55,746	Japanese 46	Korean 40	Japanese 3	Korean 11
6	Korean 54,210	Vietnamese 27	Chinese** 39	Korean 3	Vietnamese 7

Sources: Authors' compilation of data from the 2008 American Community Survey (U.S. Census Bureau 2008a) and the 2008 National Asian American Survey (Ramakrishnan et al. 2011).
Note: * Political participation higher than SES expectations.
** Political participation lower than SES expectations.

the answer lies in the distribution of these six major groups on other factors that are relevant to political behavior, and that may either reinforce or counteract class biases in participation. In table 7.2, we present the rankings and distributions of the six major Asian national origin groups on various explanatory factors we found to be relevant in our multivariate analysis. For instance, our regressions indicate that a longer stay in the United States is associated with higher participation for most major political activities. Thus, that Filipinos and Japanese Americans have been in the United States the longest helps boost their political participation higher than what we would expect based on their socioeconomic resources alone.

Taken together, the various group rankings in table 7.2 help craft a composite story for each group, indicating what might account for greater- or lower-than-expected levels of participation. For Japanese Americans, the pathway to greater participation is built on a longer stay in the United States, high levels of civic organization, and high levels of political mobilization. This is in line with scholarship on Asian American politics, which has shown that Japanese American civic organization has a long-standing basis in the United States. In particular, the creation of the Japanese Amer-

Table 7.2 Group Rankings and Distributions on Select Explanatory Factors

Group Ranking	Foreign-Born (−)		Years in the United States (+)		Educated Abroad (−)		Political News Index (+)		Discrimination Index (+)	
1	Asian Indian	93	Filipino	23.1	Asian Indian	77	Chinese	0.12	Chinese	0.78
2	Vietnamese	89	Japanese	21.4	Korean	76	Vietnamese	0.03	Filipino	0.70
3	Korean	86	Korean	21.4	Filipino	70	Korean	0	Asian Indian	0.69
4	Chinese	82	Vietnamese	19.2	Vietnamese	65	Japanese	-0.18	Korean	0.65
5	Filipino	78	Chinese	18.6	Chinese	60	Asian Indian	-0.25	Japanese	0.63
6	Japanese	40	Asian Indian	17.1	Japanese	41	Filipino	-0.27	Vietnamese	0.51
Average		81%		19.7		66%		-0.08		0.69

Group Ranking	Strong Party Identifier (+)		Mobilized by Party (+)		Religious Organization (+)		Civic Organization (+)		Mobilized by Civic Organization (+)	
1	Vietnamese	33	Japanese	41	Filipino	47	Filipino	26	Filipino	22
2	Filipino	28	Filipino	32	Korean	45	Japanese	21	Japanese	20
3	Asian Indian	21	Korean	26	Asian Indian	35	Asian Indian	20	Korean	16
4	Japanese	20	Asian Indian	25	Vietnamese	28	Korean	17	Vietnamese	
5	Korean	14	Chinese	22	Japanese	26	Chinese	14	Chinese	12
6	Chinese	12	Vietnamese	17	Chinese	18	Vietnamese	10	Asian Indian	11
Average		20%		26%		32%		18%		15%

Source: Authors' compilation of data from the 2008 National Asian American Survey (Ramakrishnan et al. 2011).
Note: Rates are in percentages.

ican Citizens League (JACL) in 1929 and subsequent efforts of the organization to advocate for the civil rights of Japanese Americans and other Asian Americans has provided Japanese Americans with a relatively strong organizational platform for political mobilization (Takaki 1989; Takezawa 2000; Toji 2003; Lien, Conway, and Wong 2004). This political mobilization was especially active during the redress movement that began in the early 1970s and ended in 1988 with the signing of the Civil Liberties Act, which provided a formal apology and monetary compensation to the victims of internment during the World War II. The work of the JACL continues even today, with advocacy and litigation on behalf of immigrant rights in cases such as Arizona's immigration enforcement legislation in 2010 (SB1070) and political mobilization over gay rights in cases such as the California's Proposition 8, banning gay marriage in 2008 (Ko 2010; Japanese American Citizens League 2010).

The organizational strengths of the JACL, combined with the decades-long presence of Japanese American citizens and party activists in the western United States, has made Japanese Americans important targets for campaign contributions and political mobilization. These, in turn, have helped boost participation rates well above what might be expected based on socioeconomic resources alone. But though Japanese American activism may have emerged in opposition to the Alien Land Law in California and the subsequent internment of Japanese Americans, our survey indicates that contemporary experiences with discrimination play a relatively modest role in prompting greater political participation.

For Vietnamese Americans, the pathway to greater-than-expected political participation is built largely on strong levels of party identification. Group characteristics on factors such as party mobilization, civic organization membership, and nativity actually compound the political disadvantages Vietnamese Americans may face related to their low levels of education and income. How, then, does party identification among Vietnamese Americans remain high and political mobilization and civic organization remain low? Our evidence from the National Asian American Survey, when combined with existing literature on Vietnamese Americans, suggests that the politicization of the group is internally generated rather than externally mobilized (Collet 2005, 2008). By internally generated, we mean that factors internal to the political history, mode of entry, and settlement patterns in the United States have played a greater role in spurring Vietnamese American participation than externally induced factors such as mobilization by political parties.

As was true for Cubans, war and political conflict played a central role in bringing large numbers of Vietnamese to the United States. Many of the early refugees had close ties to the South Vietnamese government or to the American military presence. Even though later refugees had been less centrally involved in the war, fear of persecution and determination to leave their homeland nevertheless played an important role in shaping their political beliefs and behaviors. Clearly, Vietnamese refugees were a politically informed and motivated group even before coming to the United States. Once they arrived, several factors contributed to their high levels of political interest and identification with the Republican Party. Various government assistance programs, often administered through the Catholic Church, played an important role in helping Vietnamese refugees to gain an economic foothold, enter civic life, and prepare for U.S. citizenship (Bloemraad 2006). Many Vietnamese refugees became citizens or first-time voters during the Reagan presidency, which tended to reinforce the perception of Democrats as weak on anticommunism.

Many Vietnamese Americans also decided to re-migrate from their initial areas of refugee settlement to growing areas of ethnic concentration in Orange County, San Diego, San Jose, and Minneapolis. These secondary migration patterns, when combined with high rates of naturalization, created potent constituencies in particular cities and congressional districts. However, state and local Republican organizations did little at first to mobilize Vietnamese Americans—and most of the early efforts can be attributed to Vietnamese American political entrepreneurs who managed to gain seats in city councils before running for state legislative offices (see Collet 2005, 2008).[1]

For groups who participate in politics less than we might expect based on their socioeconomic resources alone (Indian Americans and Chinese Americans), the same two pathways seem to emerge, with shorter time in the United States and lower civic and political mobilization as important limiting factors. In many ways, the Chinese American story that emerges most aptly fits the Asian American puzzle of political participation: a group with relatively high levels of income and education but relatively low levels of reported political interest and political participation. Although their history in the United States extends back for generations, the majority of Chinese Americans today have lived in the United States for a relatively short time. But, the far greater disparity between this group and others seems to be their low levels of party identification, affiliation with religious and civic groups, and mobilization.

What accounts for these patterns? In large part, the group's experience suggests the importance of considering immigrant socialization when evaluating Asian American political participation. Pei-Te Lien's in-depth interviews with foreign-born Chinese about their political attitudes and behavior are informative here (2004b). She finds that low rates of political and civic participation can be traced in part to lack of experience with direct political participation under repressive regimes in the home country. Her interviews also point to the ways in which language barriers, lack of political information, and lack of prior political participation may all interact to depress the likelihood of political participation in the United States. For example, one respondent explained that "a lot of Chinese are timid or indifferent; they have language problems; they are not familiar with the candidates and are afraid to vote for the wrong candidate; some don't have citizenship; some are afraid of jury duty" (Lien 2004b, 101). In line with our evidence from the 2008 NAAS, Lien also finds that many Chinese immigrants are unfamiliar with the major political parties and, even among those who are aware, they are often ambivalent about whom to support. For example, one naturalized citizen noted that "the less tax the better, of course. For children's education, I am in favour of the Republicans. On minority issues though, I am in favour of the Democrats. I just think it is the right thing to take care of the minorities in society. The Republicans tend to take care of the rich few. The government's responsibility is to take care of the middle class majority. That's what politics is about" (Lien 2004b, 98–99). Chinese Americans' reluctance to commit to either of the two political parties does not, in of itself, account for low party mobilization. As we saw in the case of Vietnamese Americans, high levels of party identification are not sufficient to ensure party mobilization. Still, stronger group identification with one or both major parties may be a necessary step for mainstream political organizations to invest in strategies to mobilize Chinese American voters.

Indian Americans might be expected to display the highest levels of political participation, given that they have the highest levels of educational attainment and income among the six major Asian American groups. However, they also have spent the least time in the United States, whether measured as the number of native-born residents or by the years in the country among the foreign-born. In several respects, however, they are unlike Chinese Americans. Low levels of party identification and of civic organization activity are not drains on political participation. Thus, only 41 percent of Indian American citizens are independents or political non-affiliates, versus 63 percent of Chinese Americans. The contrast with Chinese Americans is also strong with respect to religious organizations, as Indian Americans are twice as likely to be part of such groups.[2] We may have also expected the high level of English proficiency among Indian Americans to boost political participation, but as our multivariate analyses indicated, this factor is important only for contacting public officials.

Recency of immigration among Indian Americans is thus the primary reason that high socioeconomic status has not yet translated into active political participation. This factor will likely recede in importance in the coming decades as immigrants stay longer in the United States, gain citizenship, and enter the ranks of voters and political activists. Many first-generation political activists are still concerned about U.S. foreign policy toward India, and political action committees like the U.S. India Political Action Committee (USINPAC) channel political contributions and activities to bolster cooperation between the United States and India on a range of economic and security matters.[3] However, as our survey indicates, transnational involvement in homeland politics is relatively rare: only 5 percent of Indian American residents are involved in homeland politics. Although involvement is higher among those who contribute money to politics, it is still only about 7.5 percent, much lower than what one would expect given the attention accorded to Indian politics and U.S. foreign policy in the Indian ethnic media (Mishra 2009).

The shift toward domestic political concerns is also evident in the rise of second-generation Indian Americans working for political campaigns and, increasingly, running for political office. Indeed, the 2010 midterm elections saw a record number of Indian Americans winning their party nominations for Congress. As Chris Van Hollen (D-MD), chair of the Democratic Congressional Campaign Committee, noted, "They're obviously an enormously entrepreneurial group, and they've also contributed through science and research in the United States and around the world. . . . In terms of domestic politics but also playing a role as a bridge to American investment in India, the Indian-American community plays a very important role" (Talev 2010). Although all the Democratic candidates lost in the midterm election, which was extremely unfavorable to Democrats generally—2010 did produce the election of Nikki Haley (R-SC), who was the second Indian American govenor after Bobby Jindal (R-LA), another successful gubernatorial candidate who had served previously in the U.S. House of Representatives.

The success of Haley and Jindal have prompted some political analysts to speculate that Indian Americans may be ripe for mobilization by both parties. As one source put it, as "Indian Americans amass wealth and become more active in politics, they're being increasingly sought out, especially as donors, by Democrats and Republicans. They're disproportionately wealthy, well educated, and employed at high levels in fields—such as health science, technology, engineering and energy—politicians see as key to the nation's economic future" (Talev 2010). Although such a rosy projection may be warranted, our survey indicates that large-scale political mobilization of Indian Americans has yet to materialize. Furthermore, extant participation in this group is not related solely to socioeconomic success. As we have seen, Indian Americans also report the highest levels of hate crime attacks of any Asian American group, and some of the highest levels of racial and ethnic discrimination in various contexts. Thus, even for a largely "successful" group, racial discrimination continues to play a significant role in shaping political participation.

The empirical data in the preceding chapters suggest that although socioeconomic and national origin differences often loom large within the Asian American community, these internal cleavages alone do not determine the degree to which members of the Asian American community act politically as a group. In fact, factors related to immigrant socialization (length of residence, experience, and familiarity with the U.S. political system) seem to play a major role in explaining why Asian Americans do or don't participate in politics. Despite the group's differences in terms of national origin and socioeconomic status, our findings suggest that the experiences of immigration, past and present, constitute a common and powerful force in shaping the political participation of Asian Americans.

IMMIGRANT ASSIMILATION AND RACIALIZATION

Related to the issue of Asian American socioeconomic standing is the question of immigrant assimilation. The debate about immigrant assimilation in the United States is wide-ranging, and scholars disagree in fundamental ways as to whether the post-1965 wave of immigrants are following the footsteps of earlier waves of European immigrants—from economic marginalization and social exclusion to upward mobility and intermarriage—or are undergoing a fundamentally different process, with economic and social barriers prompting individuals to maintain relatively sharp racial and ethnic identities (Portes and Zhou 1993; Alba and Nee 2003). Contemporary scholars of immigrant assimilation fall in the former camp, and those in the latter can be loosely described as adopting the perspective of immigrant racialization. Assimilationist scholars argue that the occupational and status mobility of immigrants from Asia and Latin America today is similar to that of Irish and Italian immigrants in earlier waves of migration (Alba and Nee 2003; Perlmann 2005). According to this perspective, various changes in American society since the 1960s—including the passage of civil rights laws, enforcement of nondiscrimination in the workplace, and changing American attitudes about race—have minimized barriers to economic and status mobility that would lead to permanent discrimination.

On the other hand, scholars of immigrant racialization point to the persistence of factors such as employment discrimination, residential segregation, ethnic business enclaves, and nativist movements to argue that immigrants today are experiencing economic and sociocultural trajectories that fall well short of convergence with native-born whites. Theories of racialization include those that see ethnicity as a potential resource for socioeconomic mobility (Glazer and Moynihan 1963; Portes and Jensen 1989), as well as those that argue that racial discrimination and structural barriers, such as lacking access to good public schools, result in downward assimilation for some groups (Portes and Zhou 1993). More recently, studies by Frank Bean and colleagues (Bean and Stevens 2003; Lee and Bean 2004; Brown and Bean 2006) have sought to differentiate between these variants of racialization by arguing that reactive identification (maintaining racial and ethnic identities because of persistent discrimination) is more likely among those in lower socioeconomic backgrounds, whereas selective identification (maintaining strong identities for economic advancement) and symbolic identification (maintaining superficial and vestigial identities after economic success) are more likely among those in higher socioeconomic backgrounds.

Our contribution to this debate is to focus on political participation, an outcome that has been relatively neglected in studies of immigrant adaptation in favor of measures such as educational attainment, occupational mobility, health outcomes, and residential integration (but see DeSipio 1996; Ramakrishnan and Espenshade 2001; Lee, Ramakrishnan, and Ramirez 2006). We do not anticipate that focusing on political participation will settle the larger ongoing debates over immigrant assimilation or racialization. Rather, we seek to assess the claims that flow from these contemporary theories, to gauge their relevance in explaining political participation among Asian Americans. One potential problem, however, is that both immigrant assimilation and racialization may be expected to lead to higher participation. Standard assimilation theories would predict that participation is highest among groups and individuals that exhibit the most social and economic integration. At the same time, the political experiences of African Americans since the 1950s have shown that experiences with discrimination may also lead to higher political participation if they are prodded along by feelings of group consciousness and solidarity. Absent such feelings of group solidarity, we may expect discrimination to lead to lower participation.

One way to conduct this analysis is to examine group-level outcomes: are the highest levels of participation among those groups who report the most racial and ethnic discrimination, or are they among those who report the least discrimination? As we saw in table 7.2, the groups reporting the highest levels of discrimination (Chinese and Filipino Americans) have much lower rates of political participation than groups that report relatively low levels of discrimination (Japanese and Vietnamese Americans). However, the problem with this bivariate assessment is that other factors, such as nativity and length of stay in the United States, may account for both high discrimination and low political participation. The multivariate results we discussed earlier (and reported in appendix D) control for these other factors, and the results indicate that discrimination experiences are indeed associated with higher participation, regardless of whether the individual expresses feelings of group solidarity.

Indeed, the multivariate results help make a stronger case for immigrant racialization than for immigrant assimilation leading to higher political participation. Standard theories of assimilation would predict that the greatest differences in political participation will be between those who are acculturated versus those who are not (say, as measured by English proficiency). By contrast, theories of racialization would predict that differences in participation would be greatest between those who experience more versus less racial discrimination. We find that English proficiency has a relatively marginal impact on political participation, whereas experience with discrimination has a consistently positive effect. At the same time, if one considers other factors such as educational attainment and years in the United States as indicators of immigrant assimilation, then the sum of evidence can be seen as supportive of both racialization and immigrant assimilation. Finally, theories that distinguish between reactive and selective ethnicity would look at the interaction of discrimination and socioeconomic status, predicting that racial discrimination will fuel political activism among those in low SES backgrounds, but not among those in high SES backgrounds. We ran an alternative multivariate model to test for this possibility and found no significant difference for the effects of discrimination on participation by socioeconomic background. Regardless of whether they are high earners or low earners, Asian Americans who report experiences with discrimination are more likely to get involved in politics.

BEYOND RELIGIOUS DIVERSITY: CHRISTIANS, NON-CHRISTIANS, AND SECULARS

What does religious diversity within the Asian American community mean for our conceptualization of Asian Americans as a coherent political group? We find little evidence that religious cleavages create deep and consistent differences in political participation. In fact, marginalization has been a common experience across many Asian religious groups. Throughout most of the field's history, American religious studies has neglected to recognize the practice of Asian religions in America, thereby restricting the notion of American religions to a relatively narrow set of experiences and practices. Attending to the diverse religious experiences of Asian Americans reveals an American religious history that is much more varied and complex than one might assume based on traditional scholarship (Yoo 1999, 4). David Yoo, for example, points out that immigrants from all over Asia have carried their religious traditions and belief systems with them to the United States. Over generations, the Asian American community built "new spiritual homes" for themselves, transforming the religious terrain in America (Yoo 1999, 4).

Exploring this terrain from an Asian American perspective forces one to reconsider so-called standard empirical measures and concepts. For instance, because most of the focus of American religious studies has been on Judeo-Christian religions, frequency of church attendance is a common measure of religious participation in the United States. As recently as 2007, the Gallup Poll was using the question "How often do you attend church or synagogue—At least once a week, almost every week, about once a month, seldom, or never?" as a primary question about America's religiosity (Newport 2007). Church or synagogue attendance has long been a popular indicator of religious participation and religiosity (compare Herberg 1960; Warner 1993). Scholars point out that such measures neglect the varieties of Asian American religious practices in the United States because the adherents of many of these religions do not often attend a place of worship regularly as part of their spiritual practice. For example, attendance at regular weekly services, particularly in a congregational setting, is a prominent feature of Judeo-Christian religions, but not Buddhism or Hinduism. Major studies of political participation rely on attendance at religious services as a primary measure of religiosity and find that those who attend religious services most often also tend to participate in politics at a higher rate than those who do not attend such services (Wald and Calhoun-Brown 2010). As shown in chapter 6, nearly one in three Asian Americans affiliate with a non-Judeo-Christian religious tradition. As such, focusing on Asian Americans allows us to see the link between religion and political participation from a vantage point that recognizes a wider array of American religious traditions than conventional studies.

In chapter 6, we also observed that frequency of attendance at religious services is associated with participation in secular civic organizations among those in non-Western religious traditions, but not Western ones. However, multivariate analysis suggests that religious tradition makes little difference to vote turnout, contributing to a campaign, protesting, or working with others in a community when comparing Asian Americans who identify with a Western tradition, a non-Western tradition, and no religion. Thus the experience of Asian Americans suggests that involvement in both Western and non-Western services is associated with deeper involvement in the secular civic sphere as well. In Brooklyn, New York, for example, volunteers from the Tzu Chi Buddhist Foundation helped build homes for Habitat for Humanity in October 2010 (Collins 2010). This is in line with Carolyn Chen's study of evangelical and Buddhist Taiwanese immigrants (2008). She found that though the two groups differed in their rationale and in forms of civic engagement, both valued civic voluntarism. Similarly, leaders at the Temple of the Woodlands, a Hindu temple in Texas, hope to provide social services and education to the larger community, offering yoga, language and SAT courses, as well as tutoring and free health clinics (Stephens 2011).[4]

The literature on ethnic churches is vast, and suggests that one of the most prominent features of the ethnic Christian church in Asian American communities is that it provides not only spiritual sustenance to its members, but also social services and maintenance of ethnic communities across generations (but see Yang 1998). Beginning in the mid-1980s, studies of Korean immigrant Christian churches in particular, but also other ethnic communities, suggested that "immigrant congregations are no longer just sites for religious worship; they are assuming multiple functions, including both religious and secular classes, provision of social services, recreational centers, and social spaces for civic functions such as voting and citizenship classes" (Yang and Ebaugh 2001, 275; see also Kim 1987; Hurh and Kim 1990; Min 1992; Kwon, Ebaugh, and Hagan 1997). Michael Jones-Correa and David Leal's (2001) article on Latino religions and political participation suggests that regardless of religious tradition—in this case Protestant versus Catholic—churches endow their members with critical skills that are transferrable to the civic arena and that facilitate political activity outside of the church environs.

To what extent do Asian American religious spaces constitute training grounds for other types of civic participation? Our data shed some light on this question. In particular, we find that on the whole those who are involved in religious activities also tend to be more involved in politics and secular civic activities, lending some credence to the idea that these spaces do promote skills that facilitate political participation in other contexts. Religious organizations can provide important resources, then, for civic participation. In her study of Korean American Evangelicals, Elaine Howard Ecklund notes that ethnic churches bring people together for secular voluntary activities. One respondent told her that he mainly volunteered in the community through specific activities organized by his Korean American church: "I went to help in the youth shelter. . . . Like that is something I definitely would not have done by myself, because it would have been awkward for me to just show up. Just by myself" (Ecklund

2006, 108). Of course, different religious institutions promote varying degrees and kinds of civic involvement (Ecklund 2006; Chen 2008).

Finally, studies of immigrants in the United States largely challenge the secularization thesis in American religious studies and the idea that religiosity declines along with modernization. In fact, Fenggang Yang (1998) and other studies of Asian American religions show that immigrants often become more religious after migrating to the United States. Yet in contrast to other racial and ethnic groups in the United States, Asian Americans include a large proportion of individuals who do not identify with any religious group (Frasure et al. 2009). Among NAAS respondents, nearly 20 percent do not identify with any religion. This is especially true among particular national origin groups, such as Chinese Americans. More than half of all Chinese in the NAAS claim no religious affiliation. The NAAS data, then, allow us to better understand the political behavior of groups with a long tradition of claiming no religion. It is true that those who take part in activities other than services and prayer at a place of worship are more likely to be members of secular civic organizations than those who do not take part in these religious activities, but we find little evidence of a difference in political participation—voting, contributing to a campaign, protesting, or working with others in their community—between those who identify with a religion and those who do not. Our analysis reveals that, similar to the general population, those who identify with no religious tradition tend to be more liberal on abortion issues. We find, though, that there is no difference between the religious and secular when it comes to immigration or health-care policies.

Religious diversity is a hallmark of the Asian American community. However, religious diversity does not present an enduring or systematic cleavage in the community when it comes to political participation. Rather, religious diversity has been accompanied by shared experiences of marginalization. Further, we find more commonalities than differences across religious traditions in terms of how religion (or lack of religion) affects Asian Americans' participation in U.S. politics.

CONCLUSION

In this chapter we focus on how key factors such as immigrant socialization, geographic context, party identification, racial identification, and civic and religious involvement come together as a whole and their relative influence on Asian Americans' political participation. We find that some of these factors affect the group's participation in a relatively consistent way, and that others diminish in importance once we introduce multiple variables and control for key demographic indicators. We also address the broader question of how internal differences along national origin, socioeconomic, and religious lines matter for thinking about Asian Americans as a meaningful group in American politics. This discussion highlights the ways in which the experiences of Asian Americans move forward critical dialogues about the extent to which civic and political resources may help compensate for group advantages or disadvantages in socioeconomic status, the extent to which political behavior among new immigrants seems to conform to standard models of immigrant assimilation or newer models of group racialization, and how the high proportion of non-Christians and secular identifiers reshapes our understanding of religion and politics in America. These narratives also underscore our larger assertion that despite a high degree of internal diversity, there are compelling reasons to conceptualize Asian Americans as a group. Taken together, Asian Americans play a central role in larger questions of democratic inclusion and immigrant political incorporation in the contemporary moment. What might the future hold? We turn to this question in the next and final chapter.

Chapter 8 | Activists and the Future of Asian American Political Participation

I just don't care to put any time into something that I don't have enough knowledge about, meaning voting, and I think I have just an overall feeling of, my vote doesn't count. Which I know is what everyone's trying to preach to us, that your vote does count, but I think in reality it doesn't really mean too much, so I don't put myself into it.

—Fifty-year-old second-generation Chinese American male[1]

I voted because . . . I feel as a citizen of the U.S., it's one of the freedoms that we're allowed, to make change or state how we feel on the state of the country. It also helps—it also gives us the opportunity to choose who we want to lead our country and govern our country. . . . I was also very interested in immigration policies. . . . And also, I guess the war in Iraq was a very big deal, that was something that also guided how I was gonna vote.

—Twenty-nine-year-old second-generation Filipino American male[2]

THE CENTRAL QUESTION motivating this book is why Asian Americans participate, or do not, in politics. In more concrete terms, how do we explain the different levels of engagement with politics expressed by the two Asian American individuals just quoted? To address this question, we sought throughout this book to better understand the nature and dynamics of Asian American political engagement. In chapters 2 through 6, we suggest that five pathways exist to facilitate political participation among Asian Americans. In chapter 7, we draw out the implications of our findings, focusing on the ways in which the analysis informs larger theoretical debates in the literature on Asian Americans and politics. In this last chapter, we seek to apply our findings to two practical concerns. First, who are

229

the Asian American political activists and what characteristics distinguish them from those who are reluctant to get involved in politics? Second, what do the findings in this book suggest about what the future holds for the participation of Asian Americans in U.S. politics? Related to this second concern, we assess the extent to which Asian Americans are coming together or diverging as a group when it comes to their political trajectories, and shed a light on the enduring gap between Asian American participation and the lack of party mobilization.

COUCH POTATOES AND SUPER-PARTICIPANTS

Why do some Asian Americans choose never to get involved in politics and others take to politics with verve and frequency? The term *Asian American political activist* is an uncommon phrase; some might even consider it an oxymoron given the common impression of Asian Americans as passive observers and compliant political subjects. But as the data from the 2008 NAAS has shown, Asian Americans, particularly native-born citizens, are as likely—and for some activities more likely—than whites to take part in a range of political activities.

Here we introduce the category of the Asian American super-participant. These high-propensity participators engage in at least five of the ten political activities of registering to vote, voting in the last presidential election, voting in the 2008 primaries and caucuses, working on a campaign, donating money, contacting, working with others in the community, engaging in online politics, protesting, and taking part in the 2006 immigration protests.[3] Note that super-participants are somewhat rare in the Asian American population—just under 10 percent of the group (figure 8.1). Looking across the ten measures of political engagement in the available in the National Asian American Survey, we set cut-points to define two participatory archetypes: those Asian Americans in roughly the top tenth percentile and those in the bottom tenth percentile. Although not shown in figure 8.1, the modal level of engagement is three participatory acts, and 20 percent of the unweighted NAAS sample falls into this category.[4] Low-propensity participators (a little over 10 percent of the sample)—our political couch-potatoes—have not engaged in any of the ten activities we consider.[5] In this section, we describe the characteristics of two participatory archetypes of Asian Americans and also for specific forms of political activity.

High-propensity participators are distinguished from low-propensity participators in the following ways (see table 8.1).

Figure 8.1   Levels of Political Engagement

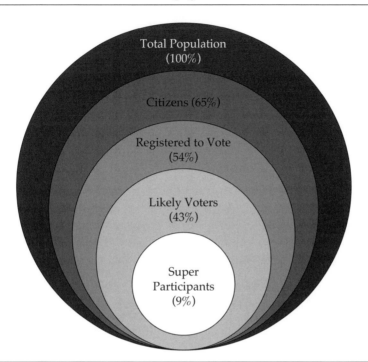

Source: Authors' compilation.

- In terms of background demographic factors, super-participators are more likely to be male, much more likely to own their own homes (89 percent), and more likely to be well educated (39 percent have higher than a college degree).

- In terms of immigrant socialization factors, super-participants are significantly more likely to be born in the United States (43 percent), educated in the United States (61 percent), and interviewed in English (76 percent). The obverse is found for nonparticipants, who are overwhelmingly foreign-born (95 percent), educated outside the United States (88 percent), and less likely to choose to be interviewed in English (56 percent).

- Our various measures of geographic and political context differentiate participation to a very modest extent. There are no statistically significant differences between super-participants and nonparticipants in

Table 8.1   Characteristics of Asian American Political Activists*

	All Asian Americans	Super-Participants	Non-Participants
Male	47	53	41*
Mean age	51	53	51
Own home	69	89	54*
Less than college	42	25	60*
College degree	34	35	26*
Postgraduate degree	24	39	15*
Foreign-born	81	57	95*
Length of U.S. stay (immigrants)	19	28	15*
Educated in U.S.	34	61	12*
English interview	63	76	56*
Immigrant gateway	65	65	64
Direct democracy state	53	61	51
Local nonpartisan ballot	74	81	73
Republican	14	16	5*
Democrat	30	43	15*
Non-identifier	34	14	64*
Mobilized, party	26	73	4*
Civic organization member	18	45	5*
Religious member	32	51	21*
Mobilized, nonparty	15	46	1*
Discrimination or hate crime	39	53	27*
Commonality in-group	37	45	27*
Commonality out-group**	26	36	13*

Source: Authors' compilation of data from the 2008 National Asian American Survey (Ramakrishnan et al. 2011).
Note: All figures except for mean age are row percentages.
* Significantly different from super participant category at $p<.05$. The significance figures for mean age are based on pairwise correlations with the outcomes of interest.
** Compared the top quartile in perceived out-group commonality to everyone else.

settlement patterns (small Asian American settlements, traditional gateways, new destinations). In terms of political context, super-participants are significantly more likely to be found in direct democracy states and in local jurisdictions with nonpartisan ballots.

- Partisanship also differentiates our participatory archetypes in interesting ways. Super-participants are significantly more likely to be Democrats (43 percent) and mobilized by a party or candidate (73 percent); they are less likely to be non-identifiers (14 percent). Nonparticipants, by contrast, are less likely to be Republicans or Democrats and more likely to be non-identifiers (64 percent). Only 4 percent of non-participants report being recruited by a party or candidate.

- Civic participation also differentiates between types of Asian American engagement. Those high propensity participators are more likely to belong to both civic and religious organizations and more likely to report being recruited by a party or candidate, whereas low propensity participators have weaker civic ties. For example, only 1 percent of nonparticipants report being contacted by a nonpartisan organization.

- Finally, we find some significant differences by racial identification variables. High-propensity participators are more likely to report experiencing a hate crime or being discriminated against, more apt to perceive Asian Americans as sharing common political interests, and more likely to perceive a strong degree of political connectedness to non-Asian groups. The obverse again is true of nonparticipants across all three measures.

Asian American political activists can thus be characterized as a highly resourced group in terms of education (both level and being educated within the United States) and home ownership. Furthermore, they are structurally advantaged by nativity (and, by corollary, citizenship), by the political institutions where they live, and by their ties to partisan and civic organizations. Finally, activism can be spurred by one's sense of common political interests (both with other Asian Americans and with non-Asian racial groups) and by one's experience of discriminatory treatment. What is especially notable from table 8.1 are the implications of what it would take to arouse nonparticipants from states of inertia to political action.

The most striking associations here are with civic and partisan organizations. Only a tiny minority of nonparticipants self-identify with a major party or belong to a secular civic organization and, relatedly, a similarly negligible proportion report being contacted and mobilized by a partisan (4 percent) or nonpartisan (1 percent) organization. We can conclude, therefore, that differences in individual Asian American attitudes and resources take us only so far in explaining why some do and some do not participate in politics. External factors, such as institutional outreach and mobilization efforts by parties and community-based organizations, are also likely to spur political engagement among Asian Americans. Indeed, research based on randomized field experiments has shown that community-based organizations do not simply attract those who are already inclined to be politically engaged. Instead, contact with a community-based organization can actually have an independent and positive effect on

Asian American political involvement (Wong 2005). Thus, the recruitment and mobilization of Asian Americans, both by civic organizations and political campaigns, are key steps in growing the ranks of super-participants. (See appendix E for the results of multivariate analysis of the factors that predict super-participation beyond voting).

LOOKING FORWARD: ASIAN AMERICAN VOTERS AND ACTIVISTS IN 2012 AND BEYOND

The 2008 National Asian American Survey provides a contemporary snapshot of Asian Americans and patterns of political participation within that community. Although we are unable to make comparisons to other groups using the same survey instrument, there are enough contemporary examples of public opinion surveys of whites, Latinos, and African Americans to make comparisons on key aspects of political attitudes and behavior. What emerges from some of these comparisons is that they lean Democratic and tend to favor Democratic presidential candidates, which echoes a pattern similar to Latinos, although the shift away from the Republican Party since the early 1990s is much stronger in the case of Asian Americans than for Latinos (see chapter 4, and figure 4.1 in particular). Still, like Latinos, Asian American voters include a large proportion of non-identifiers, and Democrats certainly cannot take their support for granted (Hajnal and Lee 2011). Analysis of the NAAS data also shows that the group as a whole exhibits some of the strongest levels of support for universal health care found in public opinion surveys (more than 80 percent approve of "the government guaranteeing health care for everyone"). These levels are much higher than the national average of 60 percent to 64 percent in 2007 and 2008, respectively (Toner and Elder 2007; Quinnipiac University Polling Institute 2008). Finally, Asian Americans tend to be relatively liberal in their views about whether abortion should be legal in all cases. In 2008, 35 percent of NAAS respondents supported this position, compared to 17 percent of Americans more generally (Smith and Pond 2008).

Because of their rapid population growth and political orientations, Asian Americans have the potential to influence the future direction of the nation in terms of both partisan balance and critical issues such as health-care reform and abortion rights—but only if their numbers translate into political influence through the power of participation. One limitation of the kind of survey data we rely on here is that they are collected over a relatively short period of time and, as a result, do not include multiple data points to measure trends over time. Still, we can do some preliminary projections about what the future holds for Asian Americans and the

U.S. political system—with the standard caveat that past results are no indicators of future trends—based on the relationships uncovered in this analysis and time trends in the settlement, demographic, and voting patterns of Asian Americans.

As noted in the introductory chapter of this book, Asian American involvement in politics is lower than might be expected based upon a resource or socioeconomic model of political participation. Furthermore, there seem to be significant national-origin differences in participation patterns that a casual observer might relegate to deeply held—and perhaps immeasurable—cultural factors. However, as subsequent chapters of this book illustrated, these puzzles of Asian American political participation are solved in part by taking into account other factors, particularly those related to membership in heavily immigrant communities, most notably immigrant generation and length of residence in the United States. Scholars hypothesize that length of residence and generation are so closely tied to immigrants' political participation because they are associated with greater familiarity with the political system, strengthened party attachments, more experience dealing with government agencies, and having a greater stake in local and national politics (Cain, Kiewiet, and Uhlaner 1991; Wong 2000; Jones-Correa 1998; Ramakrishnan and Espenshade 2001). When coupled with aggregate trends in population growth and age, these factors help to inform some cautious predictions about Asian Americans' political participation in the long term.

As discussed in chapter 2 (figure 2.2), political participation tends to increase with each immigrant generation. In fact, in both simple and more complex analyses (bivariate cross tabulations and multivariate analysis), differences in political participation between the foreign-born and native-born appear to be quite prominent. This is especially true of voting, making a political contribution, contacting government officials, and working with others in the community to solve a problem. The exception is protest activity, which is more common among the first than among subsequent generations. Although we cannot predict how future immigration policy will affect Asian migration, it is worth noting that the proportion of second-generation immigrants is expected to increase over time, especially among those groups experiencing a leveling-off in immigration rates in the past few decades. For example, Korean immigration seems to have peaked in the 1980s and has declined significantly since then. Vietnamese and Filipino immigration surged in the 1980s and 1990s, but tapered off considerably into the 2000s. These groups are expected to include a growing number of second-generation children of immigrants who will likely boost political participation rates among the Asian American community as a whole.

Other groups, especially Asian Indians and Chinese, have a large proportion of first-generation immigrants, and their numbers continue to grow due to relatively high rates of migration. This is particularly true for Indians, for whom the H-1B visa program as a pathway to eventual permanent resident status is reshaping the national origin mix of Asian Americans more generally. With Indian and Chinese Americans accounting for more than 40 percent of Asian Americans in the United States, their political involvement is likely to have a greater impact on the future of Asian American political participation than in the past. Steady migration from India and China will mean that transnational connections will remain robust, as both of these heavily foreign-born groups tend to be very active in the transnational sphere. Analysis of the NAAS data suggests that the net effects of these transnational activities on participation will likely be positive—participation in homeland politics exhibits the strongest association (positive) with contacting government officials, protest activity, and working with others to solve a community problem.

Consistent with past research, our study identifies length of residence in the United States and, to a lesser degree, age as important predictors of political participation among Asian Americans. As observed in table 2.6, nearly half of the foreign-born Asian American community (47 percent) might be considered long-term residents (twenty years or more). Even those national-origin groups that include a large proportion of recent arrivals also count among their members a significant proportion of long-term residents. For example, although Asian Indians include the largest proportion of recent migrants, more than one in every three Asian Indian immigrants is a long-term resident. As the proportion of long-term residents grows and ages, we expect a gradual increase in Asian Americans' political participation, especially when it comes to voting and contacting government officials.

Of course, future predictions must recognize that multiple demographic trends come into play at once. Not only must we consider immigrant generation, but also how immigrant generation interacts with age, length of residence, and the size of a particular community. For example, we note that Japanese Americans include the greatest proportion of second and third generation immigrants. About two-thirds of this group consists of native-born Americans. As a result, political participation rates tend to be relatively high among the Japanese in comparison with other groups (see table 2.4). However, because the group is characterized by relatively low rates of new immigration, a large elderly population (22 percent among Japanese versus 8 percent among other Asian groups), and a high level of interracial marriage, the self-identified Japanese population has declined since 2000. Despite their relatively high rates of political involvement, then, the overall impact of Japanese Americans on Asian

American political participation into the future will be mitigated by their smaller (and shrinking) population.

Still, because the Asian American community as a whole is growing at a rapid pace, we expect that Asian American political participation will increase as it becomes more established over time and generations. Further, citizenship rates, already high, continue to increase over time in the Asian American community. With longer stay in the United States, Asian Americans also seem to be gaining stronger party identification, often to the benefit of the Democratic Party. We believe that these factors are important catalysts in moving Asian Americans from being emerging constituents to more active players in American politics in the years and decades to come.

In addition to predicting an overall increase in Asian American political participation, might we also anticipate a greater convergence in political outcomes across the various national origin groups? One fruitful way to answer this question is to look at whether national-origin differences increase, decline, or persist from the first to subsequent immigrant generations. We conducted such an analysis on various measures of political attitudes and behavior, as well as on some of the important predictors of political participation found in our earlier analysis. Given the difficulty in tracking differences across six different groups across a host of outcomes, we calculated a single measure of national group dispersion (a Gini coefficient that ranges from 0, indicating full equality, to 1, indicating complete inequality). In other words, we have tried to capture the degree to which differences between national origin groups persist across generations—and the extent to which they recede—across a range of variables. In figure 8.2, we present the convergence in outcomes across national-origin groups, which is calculated by taking the percent reduction in the Gini coefficient when moving from the foreign-born population to the native-born.[6]

As we can see for most of the measures, there is a significant convergence across groups in political outcomes when shifting from foreign-born to native-born Asian Americans. This change is most pronounced on predictors of political participation, such as educational attainment and English-language use, with increases in convergence of 71 percent and 86 percent, respectively. We also find strong convergence on various aspects of political attitudes and behavior, such as voting for Obama over McCain (73 percent), Democratic Party identification (65 percent), and public opinion on abortion (45 percent). We find similar increases on measures of civic engagement, whether it is involvement in religious organizations (78 percent) or involvement in secular civic organizations (57 percent). We find smaller but still significant instances of national-origin convergence

Figure 8.2   Changes in National-Origin Differences, Foreign-Born to
Native-Born

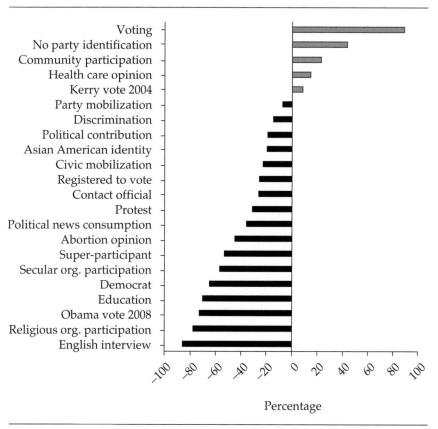

Percentage

Source: Authors' compilation of data from the 2008 National Asian American Survey (Ra-makrishnan et al. 2011).
Note: The figures are changes in the Gini coefficient of inequality across national origin.

on issues of racial identification, including identifying with the pan-ethnic label of Asian American (20 percent) and reporting instances of racial discrimination (15 percent). Finally, we also find a noticeable convergence across groups on most aspects of political participation, including the category of super-participant (53 percent), protest behavior (31 percent), writing public officials (26 percent), and making political contributions (19 percent). In five of the twenty-two measures we consider, however, there is a greater divergence by national origin, most notably on voting and the proportion of those who lack party identification.[7] Still, on most dimensions, the pattern of national-origin differences becoming much less important is clear and unmistakable. Thus, to the extent that the native-born represent the future trajectory of Asian American politics, we find compelling evidence for greater convergence across national-origin groups on various political dimensions in the not-so-distant future. Despite the dramatic internal diversity of the Asian American population, this analysis provides important empirical support for the validity and resonance of the pan-ethnic Asian American category. It remains to be seen, however, whether political and community organizations will capitalize on the patterns and trends that suggest an emerging political constituency—which include increasing length of stay in the United States, growing political participation, and increasing political convergence across immigrant generations.

ASIAN AMERICANS AS EMERGING CONSTITUENTS

We have drawn attention to the ranks of super-participants within the Asian American population, but many comparative studies have shown that Asian Americans are less likely to be mobilized than members of other racial and ethnic groups (Wong 2006; Frasure et al. 2009; Ramakrishnan 2005). Why are candidates and parties less likely to seek out Asian Americans? First, the group is relatively small—not yet even 5 percent of all registered voters despite being the fastest-growing racial-ethnic group in the United States. Hence their immediate clout is not readily apparent in terms of raw numerical influence. Second, as an immigrant-dominant population, they include a fair number of noncitizens and recent immigrants who either cannot vote or who have a weak voting history. It is unlikely that political parties will devote limited resources toward mobilizing ineligible or low-propensity voters. Third, as we saw in chapter 4, Asian Americans lean Democrat in party identification, but the most distinguishing characteristic of the group in this respect is the large proportion who fail to identify with either party. That is, about one in five identifies as independent, and more than one in three doesn't even think in traditional partisan terms. As such, the political parties, with their relentless focus on likely voters, may be reluctant to mobilize a group that does not exhibit clear party preferences because they fear that encouraging its members to vote will not necessarily guarantee a vote for their party. This dynamic is well illustrated by Kathay Feng, former director of the Voting Rights and Anti-Discrimination Unit of the Asian Pacific Legal Center, in a comment to a reporter in 2002, suggesting that "politicians are very savvy and very calculating about how they spend their education or marketing dollars. A politician's greatest fear is . . . to wake up the voters who are going to come out and vote for someone else" (quoted in Somashekhar 2002, 1).

Even among those national-origin groups with relatively high levels of both citizenship and support for one party or another, however, party mobilization is relatively rare. Indians exhibit high levels of Democratic Party identification among citizens (47 percent overall and nearly a 4-to-1 ratio over self-identified Republicans), but are much less likely to have been contacted by party organizations or candidates than Japanese Americans—who display similar patterns of party identification. The gap between high levels of party identification and party mobilization is also remarkable among Vietnamese Americans, who are characterized by the highest levels of strong-party identification (mostly toward the Republican Party), but the lowest levels of mobilization by partisan organizations. It may be that other factors, including geographic concentration in noncompetitive places and the challenge of targeting a population in multiple languages, contribute to these gaps as well.

The geographic concentration of Asian Americans in states and localities where political competition is rare limits some of the incentives for political parties to mobilize Asian Americans. As we point out in chapter 3, Asian Americans are less likely to live in presidential battleground states than their white and black counterparts. Close to half of white Americans live in battleground states, but only one in three Asian Americans. Further, the group is even less likely to live in counties characterized by competitive parties. Lack of competition at either the national or local level may indeed discourage parties and candidates from mobilizing new Asian American voters, who might be seen as potentially disruptive to existing political coalitions (Jones-Correa 1998; Mollenkopf 1992, 79; Wong 2006).

Finally, parties and candidates may find it challenging to conduct an effective campaign targeting Asian Americans in multiple languages. In particular, voter education and Get Out the Vote efforts are most effective when groups contact Asian Americans using bilingual materials and bilingual staff (Wong 2005; Asian Pacific American Legal Center 2008). Yet very few campaigns have developed the expertise to reach out to Asian Americans in English as well as in multiple Asian languages. This point is underscored by Eugene Lee, of the Asian Pacific American Legal Center, who noted in 2008, "They [elected officials] think that Asian Americans voters are hard to reach, they have to outreach to too many different languages, and it's just too difficult for them to do" (Pimentel 2007).

Although nonpartisan civic organizations, including labor organizations, religious institutions, and ethnic advocacy organizations, may be expected to step into the breach left by political parties in order to mobilize Asian American voters, their impact may be limited (Wong 2006, 2007). We show in chapter 6, for instance, that involvement in civic institutions is associated with more political participation. Yet, with the exception of religious organizations, relatively few Asian Americans (or Americans in general) report regular involvement with civic institutions. Further, political mobilization is often one of many goals for civic organizations. It is rare that political mobilization is a primary goal even for those organizations that engage in political mobilization. In addition, civic organizations face serious constraints in terms of mass mobilization because they tend to be nonprofits operating on very tight budgets.

In the immediate future, it may be strategic for political parties to ignore the Asian American population for the many of the reasons stated. Asian Americans remain a relatively small group with weak partisan attachments concentrated in places that are not politically competitive. However, evidence indicates that such an approach may be short-sighted. Not only is the community growing rapidly, but gains in the proportion of long-term U.S. residents is expected to increase the number of active Asian American participants in American politics in the years and decades to come.

Appendix A | Conceptualizing Race and National Origin

THROUGHOUT THIS BOOK, we use the terms *Asian* and *Asian American* interchangeably. This use does not intend to imply an indelible groupness to our sample as defined by essential and shared biological traits or even unique geographic origins. Although it is true that Asian Americans constitute a racial group, or a group shaped by the concept of race, our understanding of race is that it is "a concept that signifies and symbolizes sociopolitical conflicts and interests in reference to different types of human bodies" (Omi and Winant 1994, 55). Thus, the terms represent racial categories, not races per se. These categories have been created through social, historical, and political interactions, including state and institutional—as well as local and individual—efforts to organize and redistribute resources by reference to different types of physical features.[1] That racial categories have come about as the result of processes of social construction and the fact that they are historically and contextually contingent does not mean that they have little consequence (after all, *male*, *foreigner*, and *Republican* are all social categories). As Shilpa Dave, LeiLani Nishime, and Tasha Oren write, "Race, as we all know, is a social construct, a mass fantasy in which we all participate, yet it persists as a constant material force as well as a visceral and lived reality" (2005, 8). In fact, social categorization is a powerful determinant of status, resources, and representation in all aspects of life. Hence we seek to better understand how those categorized as Asian or Asian American participate in politics.

In addition, scholars and advocacy groups have long emphasized that the category actually encompasses "groups of different national origins that continue to be divided along class, linguistic, and generational lines" with "distinctive histories and separate identities" (Espiritu 1993, 2). Many observe that the term Asian American masks important distinctions among distinct national origin groups. Paul Spickard writes, for example, that the "panethnic concepts 'Asian' and 'Pacific Islander' mask profound differences between some of their constituent groups. Punjabis and Koreans share very little history or experience, yet they are in the Asian American coalition" (2001, 596). Several scholars point out that income statistics based on an aggregate of Asian Americans present a picture of overall socioeconomic success and fail to recognize the unique economic challenges faced by particular national origin groups (Kao and Thompson 2003; Kim and Mar 2007; Sakamoto, Goyette, and Kim 2009). For example, although Asian Americans as a whole earned the highest median income of any racial group in the United States in 2004 ($57,518), specific subgroups, such as the Vietnamese, earned less than Asian Americans as a whole or non-Hispanic whites.

National origin is very closely related to the concept of ethnicity, a term described by prominent psychologist Jean Phinney in her seminal 1996 article to refer to "broad groups of [Americans] on the basis of both race and culture of origin" (1996, 919). As such, national origin is most often treated by social scientists as a discrete, categorical variable (925). We use this convention in the current study (that is, we refer to national-origin groups such as Koreans, Vietnamese, and Chinese). However, we are keenly aware of the limitations of this approach. In reality, national origin is notoriously difficult to capture, especially using a survey instrument. Even when respondents self-label their national origin, as in this study, the same labels may be associated with different meanings among different people and individuals are likely to invoke different labels depending on a particular situation (Waters 1990; Oboler 1995; Espiritu and Omi 2000). Further, the meanings attributed to and significant of national origin change over immigrant generation and social, economic, and political contexts. For example, Min Zhou and James Gatewood make the compelling argument that "diversity among the second and third generations associated with homeland cultures is blurred because of these groups' rapid language switch to English and high rates of out-marriages" (2000, 19). Multiracial and multiethnic identities further complicate national-origin categorization. We note several other complications with the notion of national origin. Linguistic differences are often cited as an important reason for the salience of national-origin differences in the scholarship on Asian Americans. Yet language does not always map on neatly to national origin. In some cases, language is thus intimately wedded to a person's socialization and sense of personal identity, even in ways unrelated to national origin. This is especially true in Southeast Asia and South Asia, where many countries are linguistically diverse. The Philippines has at least thirteen indigenous languages with at least a million speakers. India has 22 official languages and 452 overall (Lewis 2006). In several instances too, speakers of the same language may have different national origins. Immigrants speaking Tamil, for example, may primarily be from India, but there are also Tamil speakers who hail from Sri Lanka, Malaysia, Singapore, and elsewhere. The case of the Tamil diaspora or the overseas Chinese diaspora points to another potential problem with the national-origin classification for Asian Americans—namely that country of origin may not coincide with ethnic self-identification. Thus, for instance, someone who identifies as Chinese American may have been born in Malaysia, and subsequently moved to the United Kingdom for college, and then to the United States for work. In such an instance, the relevant ethnic group may be based on language (Chinese) rather than country of birth (Malaysia), or country of origin (United Kingdom).

With these caveats in mind, and with an understanding that national origin is ideally conceptualized as a multidimensional construct (Phinney 1996, 925), we draw attention to national origin throughout the analysis. Though national origin as measured here constitutes a relatively blunt instrument for measuring group differences, we do in fact find enough relevant distinctions to suggest that it is important to disaggregate the sample along these lines.

Appendix B | Survey Instrument

THE 2008 NAAS was a comprehensive interview that included questions about political behavior and attitudes as well as personal experiences in immigration to the United States. Although a relatively long survey, the NAAS is similar to other social and political surveys such as the American National Election Study and the General Social Survey. The overall length of interview was about twenty-nine minutes, English-language interviews taking a little longer than twenty-six minutes and Asian-language interviews taking thirty-two minutes. Our response rates are in line with typical telephone surveys, with cooperation rates (those who agree to take the survey, of those we actually reach) of 47 percent, and an overall incidence rate (those who take the survey, as a percentage of all numbers dialed) of 12 percent.

The interview began with screening questions that allow respondents to interview in the language of their choice and allow us to meet our sampling targets (for example, by ethnic or national-origin group and county of residence). To obtain an adequate representation of multiracial Americans of Asian ancestry, we added two follow-up screening questions to our racial identifier. Following these screener items are questions on nativity and citizenship, and the questionnaire ends with standard demographic measures of individual-level characteristics on education, income, home ownership, length of residence, and other items known to influence voting and other forms of political participation, such as mass media consumption. The main body of the instrument is composed of modules described below that measure our dependent variables and indicators of our hypothesized factors that explain these dependent variables.

Party identification, mobilization, and political orientations. We ask the conventional party identification and party mobilization measures. For a randomly selected quarter of our respondents, we also ask

246

about perceived party differences, the perceived role of parties, Democratic and Republican party likes and dislikes, and parents' party identification. To gauge the diverse political space of Asians in America, we ask a series of policy attitude items that are likely to be electorally consequential (abortion, immigration, health care, Iraq, gay marriage). We also ask about respondents' ideological self-placement, trust, and political efficacy.

Racial identity formation. In addition to our racial screening items, we ask respondents about how they label themselves racially, their sense of linked fate (to other Asian Americans, others in respondents' ethnic group, and to African Americans and Latinos), their in-group candidate preferences, their personal experiences with racial discrimination and hate crimes.

Immigrant socialization. We ask about immigration status, immigrant generation, years in the United States, contact with one's home country, remittances, home country political engagement, transnational civic engagement, and language assimilation.

Social capital and civic engagement. This module begins with a focused series of questions about religious beliefs and activity, a form of civic engagement that we believe to be especially important to Asian Americans. We also ask about organizational participation (and the racial-ethnic composition of these organizations) and about political information sources (including ethnic media). Other sections of the survey further include measures of transnational civic engagement (in the immigrant socialization module) and labor union participation (in the closing demographic battery of questions).

This is an intensive and innovative set of measures in three key respects. First, measures of party identification that were designed in the 1950s—an era that predates the demographic transformation in the United States over the last four decades—may not travel so well when applied to the relationship of an emerging, immigration-based electorate like Asian Americans. Following the Pilot National Asian American Political Survey conducted by Pei-Te Lien, we allow respondents to indicate when they do not think in terms of the conventional U.S. party identification categories. Similarly, most surveys continue to use categorical measures of racial identification that typically force respondents to choose just one among a fixed menu of categories, while most scholars now accept, as a theoretical commitment, that race and ethnicity are heterogeneous, hybrid, and contingent social constructions. We allowed multiple answers to our primary question on racial and ethnic identity. In addition, we included a more intensive battery of questions in the case of party identification, and a wider range of items for racial and ethnic identification.

SURVEY QUESTIONS
SELECTION

R1   Are you comfortable continuing this conversation in English?

Yes [SKIP TO R3a or R3b, depending on RDD or LIST]
No

R2   Would you prefer we talk in another language? [IF NON-ENGLISH, LIST]

Mandarin
Cantonese
Korean
Vietnamese
Hindi
Hmong
Tagalog
Other [TERMINATE]

R3a   [IF LIST] May I please speak to [NAME ON LIST]?

R3b   [IF PHONE NUMBER IS RDD] May I please speak to someone in your household 18 years or older with the most recent birthday? Is that you? May I please speak to that person?
    We are conducting a public opinion survey of people like you, to see what you think about some important issues facing our country. [IF NECESSARY, MENTION] We are not selling anything, and I will not ask you for a contribution or donation.

R4   Just to be sure, are you eighteen years old or older?

Yes
No [END INTERVIEW]

R5   Your participation is voluntary, you can refuse to answer any question, and your answers will remain completely anonymous.

SCREENING

[MARK SEX OF RESPONDENT]

Female
Male
Uncertain

S1   [IF UNCERTAIN OF SEX OF RESPONDENT] Are you male or female?

Female
Male
Refused

S2   What race or ethnicity do you consider yourself? [IF MORE
THAN ONE RESPONSE, ENTER FIRST RESPONSE HERE, AND
OTHER RESPONSES ON NEXT SCREEN. PROBE FOR RE-
SPONSE BY READING FIRST FIVE CATEGORIES IF RESPON-
DENT SAYS DON'T KNOW OR REFUSE; OTHERWISE DO NOT
READ. IF RESPONDENT SAYS "(ETHNIC GROUP) AMERI-
CAN" (i.e., "CHINESE AMERICAN") MARK ETHNIC GROUP]

Black/African American
Asian or Asian American [CODE SAME AS 06-32 BELOW]
Native American/American Indian
Hispanic/Latino
White/Caucasian
Asian ethnicity [CHECK ONE]

Chinese
Indian
South Asian
Filipino
Vietnamese
Korean
Japanese
Hmong
Asiatic
Bangladeshi (Bangladeshi American)
Bhutanese (Bhutanese American)
Burmese (Burmese American)
Cambodian/Kampuchean (Cambodian American)
Indochinese
Indonesian

Iwo Jiman
Laotian
Madagascar
Malaysian
Maldivian
Nepalese
Okinawan
Pakistani
Singaporean
Sri Lankan
Taiwanese
Thai

Other (no Asian group mentioned)
Don't know
Refused

S3   Are there any other racial or ethnic groups that describe you?
[CHECK UP TO TWO MENTIONS]

No, no other racial or ethnic groups describe me
Black/African American
Asian or Asian American
Native American/American Indian
Latino
White
Asian ethnicity [CHECK ONE]

Chinese
Indian
South Asian
Filipino
Vietnamese
Korean
Japanese
Hmong
Asiatic
Bangladeshi (Bangladeshi American)
Bhutanese (Bhutanese American)
Burmese (Burmese American)
Cambodian/Kampuchean (Cambodian American)
Indochinese
Indonesian

Iwo Jiman
Laotian
Madagascar
Malaysian
Maldivian
Nepalese
Okinawan
Pakistani
Singaporean
Sri Lankan
Taiwanese
Thai
Other (no Asian group mentioned)
Don't know
Refused

S4   [IF S2 NOT EQUAL TO "Asian" OR "Asian ethnicity" OR S3
NOT EQUAL TO "Asian" OR "Asian ethnicity"] Do you consider
any part of your family background to be Asian?

Yes
No [END INTERVIEW]
Don't know [END INTERVIEW]
Refused [END INTERVIEW]
[IF S4 = "YES" AND S2 = DK/REF AND S3 = DK/REF]

S5   What part of Asia is that part of your family from? [IF MORE
THAN ONE RESPONSE, ENTER FIRST RESPONSE HERE]

China
India
South Asia
Philippines
Vietnam
North Vietnam
South Vietnam
Korea
Japan
South East Asia
Bangladesh {QUALIFIES FOR INDIAN QUOTA}
Bhutan {QUALIFIES FOR INDIAN QUOTA}
Burma/Myanmar
Cambodia/Kampuchea

Indochina
Indonesia
Iwo Jima
Laos
Malaysia
Maldives {QUALIFIES FOR INDIAN QUOTA}
Nepal {QUALIFIES FOR INDIAN QUOTA}
Okinawa
Pakistan {QUALIFIES FOR INDIAN QUOTA}
Singapore
Sri Lanka {QUALIFIES FOR INDIAN QUOTA}
Taiwan
Thailand
Other
Don't know
Refused

MODULE A: ETHNICITY AND NATIVITY

[ASK A1 ONLY IF S2 NE "ASIAN ETHNICITY" AND S3 NE "ASIAN
ETHNICITY"; ALL OTHERS FILL IN S2, FILL IN S3 IF S2 NE "ASIAN
ETHNICITY" AND S3="ASIAN ETHNICITY"]

A1   What is your ancestry or ethnic origin? [DO NOT READ. IF
      MORE THAN ONE RESPONSE, ASK WHICH IS MORE IMPOR-
      TANT AND CHECK ONE]

      Chinese
      Indian
      South Asian
      Filipino
      Vietnamese
      Korean
      Japanese
      Hmong
      Asiatic
      Bangladeshi
      Bhutanese
      Burmese
      Cambodian (Kampuchean)
      Indochinese
      Indonesian
      Iwo Jiman

Laotian
Madagascar
Malaysian
Maldivian
Nepalese
Okinawan
Pakistani
Singaporean
Sri Lankan
Taiwanese
Thai

Other (SPECIFY) _____
Don't know
Refused

A2   Now I want to ask you about where your parents were born. Was
      your mother born in the United States?

Yes
No
Don't know
Refused

A3   How about your father; was he born in the U.S.?

Yes
No
Don't know
Refused

A4   How about you? Were you born in the United States or some
      other country?

United States
Some other country
Don't know
Refused

A5   [If A4 NE "United States"] What country were you born in? [DO
      NOT READ]

United States
China (PRC)
India
Philippines

Vietnam
South Vietnam
North Vietnam
Korea
South Korea
North Korea
Japan
Bangladesh
Bhutan
Burma / Myanmar
Cambodia / Kampuchea
Indonesia
Laos
Malaysia
Maldives
Nepal
Other
Pakistan
Singapore
Sri Lanka / Ceylon
Taiwan
Thailand / Siam

Don't know
Refused

A6   [If foreign-born] What year did you first come to live in the
United States on a permanent basis?

Specify _____
Respondent taking too much time to recall
Don't know
Refused

A6a   [IF A6="R taking too much time to recall" or "Don't know"]
How old were you when you first came to live in the United
States on a permanent basis?

[RECORD AGE _____]
Don't know
Refused

A7   [IF FOREIGN-BORN] When you first came to the U.S., what city
did you live in?

Anaheim, CA
Anchorage, AK

Arlington, TX
Austin, TX
Bellevue, WA
Berkeley, CA
Boston, MA
Charlotte, NC
Chicago, IL
Chula Vista, CA
Columbus, OH
Dallas, TX
Daly, CA
Denver, CO
El Monte, CA
Fremont, CA
Fresno, CA
Fullerton, CA
Garden Grove, CA
Garland, TX
Glendale, CA
Hayward, CA
Honolulu, HI
Houston, TX
Huntington Beach, CA
Irvine, CA
Irving, TX
Jacksonville, FL
Jersey City, NJ
Las Vegas, NV
Long Beach, CA
Los Angeles, CA
Lowell, MA
Milwaukee, WI
Minneapolis, MN
New York, NY
Oakland, CA
Oklahoma, OK
Philadelphia, PA
Phoenix, AZ
Plano, TX
Portland, OR
Riverside, CA
Sacramento, CA
San Antonio, TX
San Diego, CA

San Francisco, CA
San Jose, CA
Santa Ana, CA
Santa Clara, CA
Seattle, WA
St. Paul, MN
Stockton, CA
Sunnyvale, CA
Tacoma, WA
Torrance, CA
Vallejo, CA
Virginia Beach, VA
Washington, DC
West Covina, CA
Other

A8   [IF FOREIGN-BORN] How many years did you live there?

Less than one year
One to five years
Five years or more
Don't know
Refused

MODULE B: ISSUE SALIENCE

Now I'd like to ask about your views on current issues.

B1   How interested are you in politics – very interested, interested, somewhat interested, or not at all interested?

Very interested
Interested
Somewhat interested
Not at all interested
Don't know
Refused

B2   People rely on different sources for political information. Do you read newspapers for information about politics?

Yes
No
Don't know
Refused

B2a   [If B2=YES] Is that Asian-language, English-language, or both?

Asian-language
English-language
Both
Don't know
Refused

B2aa   Do you listen to the radio for political information?

Yes
No
Don't know
Refused

B2ab   [If B2aa=YES] Is that Asian-language, English-language, or both?

Asian-language
English-language
Both
Don't know
Refused

B3   Do you watch television for political information?

Yes
No
Don't know
Refused

B3a   [If B3=YES] Is that Asian-language, English-language, or both?

Asian-language
English-language
Both
Don't know
Refused

B4   Do you use the Internet for political information?

Yes
No
Don't know
Refused

B4a   [If B4=YES] Is that in an Asian language, in English, or both?

Asian-language
English-language
Both

Don't know
Refused

B5   What do you think is the most important problem facing the
      United States today? [DO NOT READ]

Iraq war
Economy in general
Unemployment / Jobs
Terrorism
Ethics / Morality / Family decline
Education / Educational system
Immigration / Illegal immigration
More services for immigrants / Lack of immigrant rights
Poverty / Homelessness / Hunger
Lack of / cost of healthcare / hospital services
Fuel / Gas / Oil prices
Race/ethnic relations/Ethnic groups getting along
Racial discrimination
Language barriers
Other
Don't know
Refused

B5aa   What other important problem faces the United States today?

Iraq war
Economy in general
Unemployment / Jobs
Terrorism
Ethics / Morality / Family decline
Education / Educational system
Immigration / Illegal immigration
More services for immigrants / Lack of immigrant rights
Poverty / Homelessness / Hunger
Lack of / cost of healthcare / hospital services
Fuel / Gas / Oil prices
Race/ethnic relations/Ethnic groups getting along
Racial discrimination
Language barriers
Other
Don't know [SKIP TO Module C]
Refused [SKIP TO Module C]

B5bb   Any other important problem facing the United States today?

Iraq war
Economy in general
Unemployment / Jobs
Terrorism
Ethics / Morality / Family decline
Education / Educational system
Immigration / Illegal immigration
More services for immigrants / Lack of immigrant rights
Poverty / Homelessness / Hunger
Lack of / cost of healthcare / hospital services
Fuel / Gas / Oil prices
Race/ethnic relations/Ethnic groups getting along
Racial discrimination
Language barriers
Other
Don't know
Refused

B5a   [IF B5aa NE DK, REF] Which one of these issues is the most important to you personally? [READ ONLY IF NECESSARY]

Iraq war
Economy in general
Unemployment / Jobs
Terrorism
Ethics / Morality / Family decline
Education / Educational system
Immigration / Illegal immigration
More services for immigrants / Lack of immigrant rights
Poverty / Homelessness / Hunger
Lack of / cost of healthcare / hospital services
Fuel / Gas / Oil prices
Race/ethnic relations/Ethnic groups getting along
Racial discrimination
Language barriers
Other
Don't know
Refused

MODULE C: POLITICAL PARTICIPATION AND 2008 ELECTION

Next, I would like to ask you about your views on political issues and the U.S. presidential election. I am interested in your views, even if you are not eligible to vote or not registered to vote here.

C1   These days, people are so busy they cannot find time to register to vote or they have moved and their voter registration has lapsed. Are you now registered to vote at your current address?

Yes
No
Not eligible
Don't know
Refused

C1a   [IF C1="Yes"] Which political party are you registered with?

Democratic
Republican
Independent /Decline to state (volunteered)
Other party
Don't know
Refused

C1b   [IF C1 NOT EQUAL TO "Yes"] Are you planning to register to vote before the November 2008 election?

Yes
No
Not eligible
Don't know
Refused

C2   [IF C1="Yes" OR C1b="Yes"] I would like you to rate the chances that you will vote in the presidential election in November. Are you absolutely certain to vote, will you probably vote, or is the chance 50-50, or less than that?

Absolutely certain to vote
Will probably vote
Chance is 50-50
Less than that
Don't know
Refused

C3   [IF C1="Yes" OR C1b="Yes"] Do you plan to vote for [random-ize order for McCain and Obama] John McCain, the Republi-can, or Barack Obama, the Democrat, or another candidate for President of the United States, or are you unsure at this point in time?

John McCain
Barack Obama
Bob Barr
Ralph Nader
Other
Unsure at this time
Don't know
Refused

C3a   [IF C3="Unsure at this time" OR C3="Don't know"] Which can-didate for president are you leaning toward voting for? Are you leaning toward voting for [randomize order for McCain and Obama] John McCain, the Republican, or Barack Obama, the Democrat, or someone else?

John McCain
Barack Obama
Bob Barr
Ralph Nader
Other
Don't know
Refused

C4   [IF C1 NOT EQUAL TO "YES" OR C1B NOT EQUAL TO "YES"] If you could vote, would you vote for [randomize order for Mc-Cain and Obama] John McCain, the Republican, or Barack Obama, the Democrat, or another candidate for President of the United States, or are you unsure at this point in time?

John McCain
Barack Obama
Bob Barr
Ralph Nader
Other
Don't know
Refused

4-WAY SPLIT SAMPLE (one quarter get each variant of C4a-d)]

C4a   Does the fact that Barack Obama grew up in Indonesia make you have a more favorable impression of him, a less favorable impression of him, or does it not change your opinion of him?

C4b   Does John McCain's experience in Vietnam make you have a more favorable impression of him, a less favorable impression of him, or does it not change your opinion of him?

C4c   Does the fact that John McCain has an adopted daughter from the Asian country of Bangladesh make you have a more favorable impression of him, a less favorable impression of him, or does it not change your opinion of him?

C4d   Does the fact that Barack Obama has a sibling sister from Indonesia make you have a more favorable impression of him, a less favorable impression of him, or does it not change your opinion of him?

More favorable impression
Less favorable impression
Does not change opinion
Don't know
Refused

C7   Thinking about past elections, did you vote in the 2004 U.S. presidential election?

Yes
No
Not eligible
Don't know
Refused

C8   [IF C7="Yes"] Who did you vote for president in the 2004 election? Was it [randomize order for Bush and Kerry] George W. Bush, John Kerry, or someone else?

George W. Bush
John Kerry
Ralph Nader
Other candidate
Did not vote
Not eligible to vote
Don't know
Refused

C9   [IF C7="Yes," DO NOT ASK IF C8 = DID NOT VOTE OR NOT
      ELIGIBLE TO VOTE] Did you vote by absentee ballot?

      Yes
      No
      Don't know
      Refused

C10   [IF C1="Yes"] Generally speaking, fewer people vote in primaries
      and caucuses before the November general election. How about
      you? Did you vote in your state's primary or caucus earlier this
      year?

      Yes
      No
      Not eligible
      Don't know
      Refused

C10a [IF C10="Yes"] Which presidential candidate did you vote for in
      your state's primary or caucus? [DO NOT READ] {PROGRAM-
      MER: NOTE CHANGE IN ORDER OF PUNCHES}

      Hillary Clinton
      John Edwards
      Rudy Giuliani
      Mike Huckabee
      Dennis Kucinich
      Barack Obama
      Bill Richardson
      John McCain
      Mitt Romney
      Fred Thompson

      Other candidate
      Don't know
      Refused

C11   [IF NJ RESIDENT AND IF C1="Yes" OR C1b="Yes] If the election
      for senator were held today, for whom would you vote [ROTATE
      CHOICES] Frank Lautenberg the Democrat, or Dick Zimmer the
      Republican?

      Frank Lautenberg
      Dick Zimmer

Don't know
Refused

C12   [IF NJ RESIDENT] Do you approve or disapprove of the way Jon
      Corzine [CORE-ZYNE] is handling his job as governor?

      Approve
      Disapprove
      Don't know
      Refused

C13   [IF NY RESIDENT] Do you approve or disapprove of the way
      David Paterson is handling his job as governor?

      Approve
      Disapprove
      Don't know
      Refused

Now we have some questions about how people spend their time.

C14   If you had one extra hour per day, how would you spend it? For
      example, would you spend [ROTATE CATEGORIES 1 AND 2
      ONLY] more time with family and friends, more time at work, or
      something else?

      Family and friends
      Work
      Something else
      Other
      Don't know
      Refused

C15   People take part in many types of civic and political activities. In
      the last twelve months, have you [RANDOMIZE ORDER] [READ
      EACH CATEGORY AND CHECK ALL THAT APPLY]

      Discussed politics with family and friends
      Worked for a candidate, political party, or some other campaign
      organization
      Contributed money to a candidate, political party, or some other
      campaign organization
      Contacted your representative or a government official in the U.S.
      Worked with others in your community to solve a problem
      Visited an Internet site or on-line community to discuss a candi-
      date or issue

Attended a protest march, demonstration, or rally
Don't know
Refused

C16   In the past twelve months, has a political party or candidate contacted you about a campaign?

Yes
No
Don't know
Refused

C17   Did any other organization contact you about a campaign in the
past twelve months? [IF RESPONDENT ASKS FOR CLARIFICA-
TION] We are talking about groups like unions, community
groups, and other organizations outside of political parties and
campaigns.

Yes
No
Don't know
Refused

C18   Did you take part in any of the mass marches about immigration
during the spring of 2006?

Yes
No
Don't know
Refused

Now I have a few questions about the country where you or your ances-
tors are from.

C19   In the past twelve months have you ...

Sent money to people in that country?
Participated in any activity dealing with the politics of that coun-
try?
Been in contact with family or friends in that country?
None/Have not done any
Don't know
Refused

C20   [IF FOREIGN-BORN] Finally, thinking about before you came
the United States, were you involved in a political party or o'
type of political organization?

Yes
No
Don't know
Refused

C21   Do you think there are important differences between the [RAN-
DOMIZE ORDER OF DEMOCRATIC PARTY AND REPUBLI-
CAN PARTY] Democratic Party and the Republican Party on [R
ANSWER FROM B5 if B5aa = DK, REF, OTHERWISE R ANSWER
FROM B5a]?

Yes
No
Don't know
Refused

C22   [If D2="Yes" or D2="Don't know"] Which party do you think is
closer to your views on this issue?

Republican
Democratic
Neither
Don't know
Refused

MODULE D: POLITICAL ORIENTATIONS

D1   We are interested in how people are getting along financially
these days. Would you say that you (and your family) are better
off, worse off, or just about the same financially as you were a
year ago?

Better off
Worse off
Just about the same
Don't know
ᵊfused

1="Better off"] Much better or somewhat better?

ᵗter
ᵇetter

ᵗo
ᵉr

¹ Much worse or somewhat worse?

Much worse
Somewhat worse
Don't know
Refused

D2 Next, how would you rate your overall physical health—excellent, very good, good, fair, or poor?

Excellent
Very good
Good
Fair
Poor
Don't know
Refused

D3 Now I'm going to read you a list of statements. For each statement, please tell me if you agree strongly, agree somewhat, neither agree nor disagree, disagree somewhat, or disagree strongly? [READ EACH CATEGORY AND RECORD RESPONSE; REPEAT RESPONSE CHOICES AS NEEDED]

A   The U.S. should get our military troops out of Iraq as soon as possible.
B   The federal government should guarantee health care for everyone.
C   Abortion should be legal in all cases.
D   The U.S. should provide a path to citizenship for people in this country illegally.
E   U.S. immigration policy should favor people with professional qualifications over those who already have family in the United States?

Agree strongly
Agree somewhat
Neither agree nor disagree
Disagree somewhat
Disagree strongly
Don't know
Refused

D5 How about [RANDOMLY ROTATE CATEGORIES] [READ EACH CATEGORY AND RECORD RESPONSE; REPEAT RE SPONSE CHOICES AS NEEDED]

A   Sometimes politics and government seem so complicated that a person like me can't really understand what's going on.

B   We can trust our government in Washington to do what is right.

C   Public officials and politicians don't care much what people like me think

D   People are better off avoiding contact with government

Agree strongly
Agree somewhat
Neither agree nor disagree
Disagree somewhat
Disagree strongly
Don't know
Refused

D6   [IF CA RESIDENT] Do you favor or oppose changing the California State Constitution to define marriage as between a man and a woman, thus barring marriage between gay and lesbian couples?

Favor changing the Constitution
Oppose changing the Constitution
Don't know
Refused

D7   Generally speaking, do you think of yourself as a [RANDOMIZE ORDER OF REPUBLICAN AND DEMOCRAT] Republican, Democrat, independent, some other party, or do you not think in these terms?

Republican
Democrat
Independent
Other party [SPECIFY _____]
Do not think in these terms
Don't know
`efused

'7="Republican"] Would you call yourself a strong Republi-
\`ot a strong Republican?

`iblican
`Republican

D7b   [IF D7="Democrat"] Would you call yourself a strong Democrat or not a strong Democrat?

Strong Democrat
Not a strong Democrat
Don't know
Refused

D7c   [IF D7="Independent"] Do you think of yourself as closer to the Republicans or the Democrats?

Closer to Republicans
Closer to Democrats
Don't know
Refused

D8   [IF U.S.-BORN] When you were growing up, did your father think of himself mostly as a Democrat, a Republican, or did he not think in terms of political parties?

Democrat
Republican
Independent (volunteered)
Other
Did not think in terms of parties
Don't know
Refused

D8a   [IF U.S.-BORN] Now thinking about your mother, when you were growing up, did your mother think of herself mostly as a Democrat, a Republican, or did she not think in terms of political parties?

Democrat
Republican
Independent (volunteered)
Other
Did not think in terms of parties
Don't know
Refused

D9   When it comes to politics, do you usually think of yourself as a liberal, a conservative, or a moderate, or haven't you thought much about this?

Liberal
Conservative
Moderate
Haven't thought much about this
Don't know
Refused

D9a   [IF D9="Liberal"] Do you think of yourself as a strong liberal or as a not so strong liberal?

Strong liberal
Not so strong liberal
Don't know
Refused

D9b   [IF D9="Conservative"] Do you think of yourself as a strong conservative or as a not so strong conservative?

Strong conservative
Not so strong conservative
Don't know
Refused

D9c   [IF D9="Moderate" OR "Haven't thought much about this"] Do you think of yourself as more like a liberal or more like a conservative?

More like a liberal
More like a conservative
Don't know
Refused

MODULE E: RACIAL IDENTITY

I now have a few questions about groups in society.

E1   People of Asian descent in the U.S. use different terms to describe themselves. In general do you think of yourself as [RANDOMIZE ORDER OF FOUR CHOICE CATEGORIES] [CHECK ALL THAT APPLY]

An Asian American
A/An [R'S ETHNIC GROUP FROM A1]
A/An [R'S ETHNIC GROUP FROM A1] American

An Asian
Other
American [DO NOT READ]
None of these [Do not read]
Don't know
Refused

E2   Do you think what happens generally to other Asians in this
country affects what happens in your life? [ROTATE ORDER OF
E2 AND E3]

Yes
No
Don't know
Refused

E2a   [IF E2="Yes"] Will it affect you a lot, some, or not very much?

A lot
Some
Not very much
Don't know
Refused

E3   Do you think what happens generally to other [R ETHNIC
GROUP FROM A1] Americans affects what happens in your life?
[MARK "MAYBE," "SOMEWHAT," "A LITTLE," "SORT OF" AS
YES]

Yes
No
Don't know
Refused

E3a   [E3="Yes"] Will it affect you a lot, some, or not very much?

A lot
Some
Not very much
Don't know
Refused

E4   Suppose you have an opportunity to decide on two candidates
for political office, one of whom is [R ETHNIC GROUP FROM
A1] -American. Would you be more likely to vote for the [R ETH-

NIC GROUP FROM A1]-American candidate, if the two candidates are equally experienced and qualified?

Yes
No
Don't know
Refused

E5   [IF FOREIGN-BORN] We are interested in the way you have been
treated in the United States, and whether you have ever been
treated unfairly because of your race, ancestry, being an immigrant, or having an accent. Have you ever been: [READ EACH
CATEGORY AND RECORD RESPONSE]

A   unfairly denied a job or fired?
B   unfairly denied a promotion at work?
C   unfairly treated by the police?
D   unfairly prevented from renting or buying a house or apart-
    ment?
E   treated unfairly or badly at restaurants or stores?
Yes
No
Don't know
Refused

E5a   [IF U.S.-BORN] We are interested in the way you have been
treated in the United States, and whether you have ever been
treated unfairly because of your race or ancestry. Have you ever
been: [READ EACH CATEGORY AND RECORD RESPONSE]

A   unfairly denied a job or fired?
B   unfairly denied a promotion at work?
C   unfairly treated by the police?
D   unfairly prevented from renting or buying a house or apart-
    ment?
E   treated unfairly or badly at restaurants or stores?
Yes
No
Don't know
Refused

E6   Have you ever been a victim of a hate crime? That is, have you
ever had someone verbally or physically abuse you, or damage
your property specifically because of your race or ethnicity?

Yes
No
Don't know
Refused

E7   What, if anything do Asians in the United States share with one another? Would you say they share [RANDOMLY ROTATE CATEGORIES]

A   a common race
B   a common culture
C   common economic interests
D   common political interests
Yes
No
Don't know
Refused

Now I'm going to read you two statements that relate to groups in society. For each statement, please tell me if you agree strongly, agree somewhat, neither agree nor disagree, disagree somewhat, or disagree strongly? [READ EACH CATEGORY AND RECORD RESPONSE; REPEAT RESPONSE CHOICES AS NEEDED]

E8   Thinking about government services, political power, and representation, would you say Asian Americans have a lot in common, some, little in common, or nothing at all in common with [INSERT FIRST CATEGORY, BASED ON CATEGORY ROTATION OF "AFRICAN AMERICANS OR BLACKS," "LATINOS OR HISPANICS," "WHITES"]

A lot in common
Some
Little
Nothing at all in common
Don't know
Refused

E8a   How about [SECOND CATEGORY]? Would you say Asian Americans have a lot in common, some, little in common, or nothing at all in common politically with [CATEGORY 2]?

A lot in common
Some
Little

Nothing at all in common
Don't know
Refused

E8b   How about [THIRD CATEGORY]? [READ IF NECESSARY]
Would you say Asian Americans have a lot in common, some, lit-
tle in common, or nothing at all in common politically with [CAT-
EGORY 2]?

A lot in common
Some
Little
Nothing at all in common
Don't know
Refused
[HALF SAMPLE (only half get E9 and E10)]

E9   We are interested in how you would describe your appearance.
How would you describe your skin color with 1 being very light
and 5 being very dark or some number in between?

1 / Very light
2 / Light
3 / Medium
4 / Dark
5 / Very dark
Don't know
Refused

E10   [IF E9=1,2,3,4,5] Now, thinking about the golfer Tiger Woods' appearance, how would you would you describe his skin color using the same scale, with 1 being very light and 5 being very dark
or some number in between?

1 / Very light
2 / Light
3 / Medium
4 / Dark
5 / Very dark
Don't know
Refused

MODULE H: CIVIC ENGAGEMENT

Next, we have some questions about your community.

H1   What is your religious background? [RECORD CURRENT RELI-
      GION. IF RESPONDENT SAYS I WAS RAISED CATHOLIC, BUT
      AM NOW EPISCOPALIAN, RECORD EPISCOPALIAN. PROBE
      OR READ LIST *AS NEEDED.*]

      7th Day Adventist
      African Methodist Episcopal/ AME
      Agnostic or Atheist [SKIP TO H5]
      Baptist
      Buddhist
      Catholic
      Christian
      Christian Scientists
      Church of the Nazarene
      Congregationalist (includes United Church of Christ)
      Disciples of Christ, Churches of Christ
      Episcopalian, Anglican
      Hindu
      Jehovah's Witnesses
      Jewish
      Lutheran
      Methodist
      Mormon, Church of the Latter Day Saints
      Muslim, Mohammedan, Islam
      Orthodox, Eastern Orthodox
      Pentecostal (includes Church of God in Christ)
      Presbyterian
      Protestant (no denomination given)
      Reformed, Dutch Reformed, Christian Reformed
      Unitarian, Universalist
      Jain
      Sikh
      Falun Gong
      Other Non-Christian [SPECIFY] _____
      No religion [SKIP TO H5]
      Don't know [SKIP TO H5]
      Refused [SKIP TO H5]

H3   [IF H1 IS NOT = 2, 4, 12, 14, 18, 20, 25, 30, 31, 32] Would you de-
      scribe yourself as any of the following [READ: "A fundamentalist
      or evangelical Christian, a born-again Christian, Pentecostal or
      Charismatic"]?

Yes
No
Don't know
Refused

H4   [IF H1 IS NOT = 2, 4, 12, 14, 18, 25, 30, 31, 32] Have you always
       been a Christian, or did you convert at some point in time?

       Always Christian
       Converted
       Don't know
       Refused

H4a   [IF H4="Converted" AND FOREIGN-BORN] Did you convert
       before migrating to the United States?

       Yes
       No
       Don't know
       Refused

H2   How often do you attend your place of worship: at least every
       week, almost every week, a few times a month, only a few times
       during the year, hardly ever or never?

       At least every week
       Almost every week
       A few times a month
       Only a few times a year
       Hardly ever
       Never
       Don't know
       Refused

H2a   Other than attending services or prayer, do you take part in any
       activity with people at your place of worship?

       Yes
       No
       Don't know
       Refused

H5   Other than a religious group or place of worship, is there any
       other group or organization in your community that you are in-
       volved with?

Yes
No
Don't know
Refused

H5a   [IF H5="Yes"] Could you please tell me the name of the group or organization? [IF MORE THAN ONE GROUP] Please tell me the name of the one that is most important to you. [IF R IS UNSURE ABOUT EXACT NAME, ENTER BEST GUESS]

Name [SPECIFY _____]
Don't know
Refused

H5b   [IF H5="Yes"] And how many members of this group would you say are [R'S ETHNIC GROUP FROM A1] – all of them, most, about half, some of them, or none?

All of them
Most
About half
Some of them
None
Don't know
Refused

H5c   [IF H5="Yes"] How many members of this group would you say are college-educated – all of them, most, about half, some of them, or none?

All of them
Most
About half
Some of them
None
Don't know
Refused

MODULE J: DEMOGRAPHICS

J1   What is the highest level of formal education you completed?

Primary or grammar school
Some high school

High school graduate
Some college
College graduate
Masters (all except MBA; e.g., MA, MSc, MPH, MPA, MPP, MArch, MEd)
Business Degree (MBA)
Law Degree (JD)
Medical Degree (M.D., D.O.; Dentistry, Optometry, Pharmacy)
Doctorate (all other Doctorates; Ph.D., Ed.D., Psych D.)
Other
Don't know
Refused

J2   Did you complete all of your formal education in the United States?

Yes
No
Don't know
Refused

J3   Are you currently married or living as married with someone – or are you widowed, divorced, separated, or have you never been married?

Married / living as married
Widowed
Divorced
Separated
Never married
Don't know
Refused

J3a   [IF J3 NE "Married / living as married"] Are you currently in a serious relationship?

Yes
No
Don't know
Refused

J3b   [IF J3="Married / living as married" OR J3a="Yes"] What is the race or ethnicity of your wife, husband, or partner? [CHECK UP TO TWO CATEGORIES]

Black/African American
Asian

Native American/American Indian
Hispanic/Latino
White/Caucasian
Asian ethnicity [CHECK]
Chinese
Indian
South Asian
Filipino
Vietnamese
Korean
Japanese
Laotian
Pakistani
Cambodian (Kampuchean)
Hmong
Thai
Taiwanese
Indonesian
Bangladeshi
Sri Lankan
Malaysian
Bhutanese
Burmese
Indochinese
Iwo Jiman
Madagascar
Maldivian
Nepalese
Okinawan
Singaporean
Asiatic
Other
Don't know
Refused

J3c   [IF J3="Divorced" OR J3="Separated" OR J3="Widowed" AND
J3B NOT ASKED] What is the race or ethnicity of your former
wife, husband, or partner? [CHECK UP TO TWO CATEGORIES]

Black/African American
Asian
Native American/American Indian
Hispanic/Latino
White/Caucasian

Asian ethnicity [CHECK]
Chinese
Indian
South Asian
Filipino
Vietnamese
Korean
Japanese
Laotian
Pakistani
Cambodian (Kampuchean)
Hmong
Thai
Taiwanese
Indonesian
Bangladeshi
Sri Lankan
Malaysian
Bhutanese
Burmese
Indochinese
Iwo Jiman
Madagascar
Maldivian
Nepalese
Okinawan
Singaporean
Asiatic
Other
Don't know
Refused

J4   Including yourself, how many people live at home with you?

1 [SKIP TO J6]
2
3
4
5
6
7
8

9
10 or more
Refused

J5   How many of them are children under 18?

0
1
2
3
4
5
6
7
8
9
10 or more
Refused

J6   Which of the following best describes the total pre-tax income earned by everyone in your household last year? [READ CATE-GORIES]

Up to $20,000
$20,000 to $35,000
$35,000 to $50,000
$50,000 to $75,000
$75,000 to $100,000
$100,000 to $125,000
$125,000 to $150,000
$150,000 and over
Don't know
Refused

J7   What is your employment status? Are you: working full-time, working part-time, laid off, a student, a homemaker, retired, permanently disabled, or something else? [CHECK ONE ONLY]

Working full-time
Working part-time
Laid off
A student
Homemaker
Retired
Permanently disabled

Unemployed
Other
Don't know
Refused

J8   [IF J7="Working full-time" OR "Working part-time"] On average how many hours a week do you work?

[RECORD NUMBER _____]
Don't know
Refused

J9   Do you belong to a union?

Yes
No
Don't know
Refused

J10   What year were you born?

[RECORD YEAR _____ (RANGE 1900-1990)]
Don't know [ASK R TO GUESS OR GIVE DECADE]
Refused

J10a [IF J10= DK OR REF] Could you give the decade when you were born? [Do not read response categories]

1910s
1920s
1930s
1940s
1950s
1960s
1970s
1980s
1990s
Don't know
Refused

J11   How many years have you lived at your current address?

[RECORD NUMBER _____]
Don't know
Refused

J12   Do you own or do you rent the place where you currently live?

Own
Rent
Don't know
Refused

J13   [ASK IF FOREIGN-BORN AND C1 NE YES; FILL IN "CITIZEN"
        IF FOREIGN-BORN AND C1=YES; FILL IN "CITIZEN" IF HID-
        DEN NATIVITY VARIABLE =U.S.-BORN] Many people in the
        U.S. are not citizens. Some are on student or travel visas, or they
        have green cards because they are permanent residents. Are you
        currently on a visa, have a green card, or are you a U.S. citizen?

Visa
Green card
U.S. citizen
Don't know
Refused

J13a   [IF J13="Visa"] Is the visa the H category such as H1b or H4, or
        an F category visa for students, or something else?

H1b visa
H4
F (student visa)
Something else
Don't know
Refused

J14   [IF J13="U.S. Citizen"] What year did you become a U.S. citizen?

[RECORD YEAR _____]
Respondent taking too much time to recall
Don't know
Refused

J14a   [IF J14="R taking too much time to recall" or "Don't know"] How
        old were you when you became a citizen? [IF RESPONDENT IS
        VAGUE ON THE AGE AND SAYS "IN MY 20s" ETC. MARK AS
        DON'T KNOW]

[RECORD AGE _____]
Don't know
Refused

J15   [IF J14 NOT EQUAL TO "U.S. Citizen"] Are you currently applying for U.S. citizenship, planning to apply, or not planning to become a citizen?

Currently applying
Planning to apply
Not planning to apply
Don't know
Refused

J16   [IF LANGUAGE INTERVIEW IS NOT ENGLISH] Now I would like to ask you about your English language skills. How well can you speak English? Very well, pretty well, just a little, or not at all?

Very well
Pretty well
Just a little
Not at all
Don't know
Refused

J16a   [IF LANGUAGE INTERVIEW IS NOT ENGLISH] How well can you read English? Very well, pretty well, just a little, or not at all?

Very well
Pretty well
Just a little
Not at all
Don't know
Refused

J17   [IF LANGUAGE INTERVIEW IS ENGLISH] Now I would like to ask you about your [LANGUAGE OF R'S ETHNIC GROUP AT A1] language skills. How well can you speak [LANGUAGE OF R'S ETHNIC GROUP AT A1]? Very well, pretty well, just a little, or not at all?

Very well
Pretty well
Just a little
Not at all
Don't know
Refused

J17a [IF LANGUAGE OF INTERVIEW IS NOT ENGLISH AND R IS A CITIZEN] If election materials were available to you in your language, would you make use of them?

    Yes
    No
    Don't know
    Refused

J18   I have just two more questions to ask. Sometimes, people can tell a lot just from listening to a person's voice over the telephone. During the interview did you think I was white, African American, Latino, Asian, or someone of another race?

    White
    African American
    Latino
    Asian
    Another race
    Don't know
    Refused

J19   Finally, the researchers for this study wish to explore some of these issues after the November elections. Would it be okay if another interviewer contacted you to discuss some of the things we talked about?

    Yes
    No
    Don't know
    Refused

Thank you for participating in our survey today, your answers have been very helpful.

Appendix C | Additional Bivariate Tables

Table C.1   Identification by Nativity

	Noncitizen	Naturalized	Native-Born
Ethnic group	64	29	16
Ethnic American	26	58	71
Asian American	13	29	18
Asian	20	19	9
Pan-ethnic linked fate	36	35	46
Ethnic linked fate	41	44	46
Commonality with Asians	81	84	80
Political commonality with others	85	90	96
Discriminated against	34	37	48
Victim of hate crime	8	9	17
Vote for co-ethnic candidate	57	58	47

Source: Authors' compilation of data from the 2008 National Asian American Survey (Ramakrishnan et al. 2011).

Note: Rates are in percentages, representing the proportion in each category (by column) who rank positively in each outcome (by row); respondents were allowed to choose more than one identity label.

Table C.2   Ethnic and Racial Identification by Age

	18 to 34	35 to 49	50 to 64	65 and Older
Ethnic group	50	44	42	36
Ethnic group-American	44	41	52	54
Asian American	20	16	27	20
Asian	14	19	16	19
Pan-ethnic linked fate	45	41	38	24
Ethnic linked fate	48	49	41	37
Commonality with Asians	84	88	79	80
Political commonality with others	89	93	85	85
Discriminated against	40	36	41	31
Victim of hate crime	10	10	11	6
Vote for co-ethnic candidate	58	56	53	66

Source: Authors' compilation of data from the 2008 National Asian American Survey (Ramakrishnan et al. 2011).
Note: Rates are in percentages, representing the proportion in each category (by column) who rank positively in each outcome (by row); respondents were allowed to choose more than one identity label.

Table C.3   Ethnic and Racial Identification by Educational Attainment

	High School or Less	High School Grad	Some College	College Grad	Advanced Degree
Ethnic group	47	47	29	43	42
Ethnic group-American	46	46	61	45	42
Asian American	28	21	18	30	20
Asian	23	19	11	21	15
Pan-ethnic linked fate	24	32	40	40	41
Ethnic linked fate	39	38	49	41	48
Commonality with Asians	62	83	87	78	90
Political commonality with others	73	82	92	90	94
Discriminated against	17	36	36	42	41
Victim of hate crime	6	9	16	10	10
Vote for co-ethnic candidate	61	64	53	58	51

Source: Authors' compilation of data from the 2008 National Asian American Survey (Ramakrishnan et al. 2011).
Note: Rates are in percentages, representing the proportion in each category (by column) who rank positively in each outcome (by row); respondents were allowed to choose more than one identity label.

Table C.4   Identification by Gender

	Male	Female
Ethnic group	40	44
Ethnic group-American	47	46
Asian American	17	23
Asian	13	23
Pan-ethnic linked fate	36	39
Ethnic linked fate	40	47
Commonality with Asians	82	82
Political commonality with others	91	90
Discriminated against	42	33
Victim of hate crime	11	9
Vote for co-ethnic candidate	57	56

Source: Authors' compilation of data from the 2008 National Asian American Survey (Ramakrishnan et al. 2011).
Note: Rates are in percentages, representing the proportion in each category (by column) who rank positively in each outcome (by row); respondents were allowed to choose more than one identity label.

Table C.5   Identification by Location

	Small Asian American Settlement	New Destination	Traditional Gateway
Ethnic group	43	42	42
Ethnic group-American	45	47	46
Asian American	24	19	21
Asian	15	19	18
Pan-ethnic linked fate	33	39	37
Ethnic linked fate	40	45	44
Commonality with Asians	81	82	82
Political commonality with others	88	89	89
Discriminated against	36	38	37
Victim of hate crime	8	11	10
Vote for co-ethnic candidate	57	56	56

Source: Authors' compilation of data from the 2008 National Asian American Survey (Ramakrishnan et al. 2011).
Note: Rates are in percentages, representing the proportion in each category (by column) who rank positively in each outcome (by row); respondents were allowed to choose more than one identity label.

Appendix D | Multivariate Models of Participation

IN SPECIFYING OUR models of political participation, we are confronted with several choices that entail trade-offs between telling a simpler story with basic statistical techniques and few assumptions, or a more complicated story where the pathways to participation vary by activity and perhaps even the type of group being considered. Here, we opt for the former strategy rather than the latter. Thus, for instance, even though our discussion of pathways might suggest a causal ordering of factors—where some are placed before others in a structural equation model (say, from residential contexts and immigrant socialization to racial identification, civic organization, and party identification)—we have no strong theoretical priors to assume that there is any clean causal ordering of these pathways.[1]

In table D.1 we present the relationship of various factors to our five basic outcomes of interest. Because our voting measure is an index based on four components (turnout in 2004, voting in the 2008 primaries, registration status, and likely turnout in November 2008), we use OLS regressions for the first model, and logit regressions for the rest of the models since the outcomes are either 0 (did not participate) or 1 (participated). Also, because the variables often have different ranges in values, we present the results as standardized regression coefficients, with a uniform variance of 1 across all factors. Finally, we have a slightly reduced set of factors in our multivariate model when compared to all of the factors we explored in chapters 2 through 6. This is because of problems of multicollinearity between the excluded factors and some others included in this analysis, particularly in the case of racial identification and political context. Rather than opting for index measures that make for difficult interpretation, we have chosen to include a subset of factors that our previous analysis would suggest as having the strongest impact.

To help organize our findings and discussion, we group these thirty-eight variables by the various pathways articulated throughout this book and add a set of important demographic factors that have consistently been shown to be important to political participation. As a reminder, our variables are operationalized as follows:

Our *immigrant socialization* factors are respondent national origin; nativity, either foreign-born or U.S.-born; and longevity in the United States if foreign-born; second-generation status if U.S.-born. We also consider several indirect measures of immigrant socialization: the language used to conduct the interview; whether respondents were primarily educated in the United States or abroad; whether respondents actively engage in the political affairs of their country; their reliance on various mass media outputs for their information about politics; the extent to which these outputs are Asian-language media.

Our *geographic and political context* factors are respondent settlement contexts: residence in a small Asian American population community or a new destination; representation by an Asian American politician; residence in a direct democracy state, a municipality with nonpartisan ballots, or a presidential battleground county.

The institutional role of *political parties* is assessed by comparing self-identified Democrats, self-identified Republicans, and nonidentifiers to independents; we also consider those who had been contacted by a political party or candidate to test for the effects of mobilization.

We limit our measures of *racial group identity* to respondent perceptions of political commonality with other Asians; perceptions of political commonality with non-Asians (whites, African Americans, and Latinos); and self-reported experiences of being discriminated against or being a victim of a hate crime.

Our measures of *civic engagement* are respondent's frequency of attendance at a place of worship; participation in activities other than services or prayer with people at their place of worship; membership in secular civic organizations; and mobibilization by nonpartisan groups.

Finally, we also examine the effects of various demographic factors: age (measured in linear years and in a nonlinear squared value of respondents' age), sex, educational attainment, family income, and home ownership. The effects of these demographic factors on our dependent variables are not simply in their typical residual function as controls. Here, they serve the more analytically important function of testing for the effects of the baseline SES model of participation.

Table D.1 Determinants of Political Participation

	Voting	Contribute	Contact	Protest	Community
Indian	0.123***	0.221	0.422	-0.186	0.490***
Filipino	0.036*	-0.055	0.389*	-0.346	-0.03
Japanese	0.032	-0.384**	0.238	-0.358	-0.216
Korean	0.011	-0.054	-0.341	-1.189**	-0.294**
Vietnamese	0.113***	0.008	-0.227	1.110***	0.052
Other Asian	0.023	-0.069	0.167	-0.047	0.027
Foreign-born	-0.165***	-0.523**	-0.519*	-0.838	-0.471***
Second generation	-0.054**	-0.012	0.077	-0.357	-0.126
Years in United States	0.104***	0.631***	0.523**	-0.24	0.229*
Interview in English	-0.007	0.21	1.939***	0.155	0.043
English-speaking skills	0.027	-0.056	1.747***	0.195	0.253
Ethnic news index	-0.064***	-0.29	0.213	1.427***	0.088
General news index	0.166***	0.999***	0.977***	0.499	0.505***
Educated abroad	-0.089***	-0.398**	-0.556***	-0.359	-0.014
Homeland political participant	-0.031**	0.123	0.539***	1.168***	0.231***
Small Asian American settlement	-0.016	0.196	0.044	0.072	0.091
New destination	-0.026	0.121	0.184	0.534	-0.024
Any Asian elected official	0.025	0.148	0.026	-0.003	-0.179*
Local nonpartisan election	-0.031	-0.006	0.089	-0.006	0.304**
Direct democracy	0.046**	-0.032	-0.339	0.257	-0.159
County battleground	-0.015	0.02	0.009	0.035	-0.123
Democrat	0.085***	0.664***	-0.22	0.599	-0.289**
Republican	0.082***	0.476***	-0.001	0.39	-0.259**
Non-party-identified	-0.085***	-0.226	-0.695***	-0.472	-0.326***

(Table continues on p. 292.)

Table D.1 *Continued*

	Voting	Contribute	Contact	Protest	Community
Mobilized by party	0.121***	1.236***	1.284***	1.397***	0.335***
Common with Asians	0.005	0.006	0.007	0.046	0.05
Common with other races	0.034**	0.156	0.081	0.596	0.259**
Discrimination and hate crime	-0.016	0.318**	0.423***	0.527*	0.282***
Frequency of religious attendance	0.006	-0.099	0.383*	0.423	0.196
Member of religious organization	0.016	0.489***	0.474**	0.728*	0.617***
Member of civic organization	0.007	0.422***	0.342**	1.203***	0.779***
Mobilized by other organization	0.049***	0.636***	0.491***	0.996***	0.266***
Age	0.401***	1.332	2.215*	-1.111	0.376
Age squared	-0.192*	-0.362	-2.372*	1.695	-0.788
Female	0.026*	-0.112	-0.262	-0.188	-0.247**
Education	0.053***	0.740***	1.186***	-0.287	0.664***
Family income	0.004	0.326*	0.001	-0.409	-0.16
Own home	0.003	0.11	-0.158	-1.274***	0.131
N in model	3606	4498	4505	4502	4503
N for DV	4080	5145	5155	5152	5154

Source: Authors' compilation of data from the 2008 National Asian American Survey (Ramakrishnan et al. 2011).
Notes: Multiple imputation of income, age, and in-group/outgroup variables (based on citizenship, employment status, education, nativity, years in the United States, English ability, marital status, household size, and ethnic origin) and MIM analysis using STATA.
Standardized betas; * $p < .10$; ** $p < .05$; *** $p < .01$.

Appendix E | Stages of Participation

Past studies of voter participation often distinguish multivariate results at different stages such as citizenship, registration, and voting (Wolfinger and Rosenstone 1980; DeSipio 1996; Lien 2001). We advance this analysis one step by looking at participation beyond voting to systematically assess the factors that lead some to go beyond voting to become super-participants and others to refrain from doing so (see chapter 8 for our definition of super-participant). We should note from the outset that we are not making a strong claim that only voters can be super-participants; indeed, in our survey, 6 percent of those who are classified as unlikely voters, and 2 percent of noncitizens are classified as super-participants, when compared with 18 percent of likely voters.

Of each stage in this sequence of participation, we ask the same question as we did in chapter 7: which among the various factors from each pathway are most significant to inducing participation? The corollary interest to specifying the factors that are most salient at each step along the way to becoming participatory is to disentangle structural barriers to participation from more situational factors that could potentially serve as the basis for further mobilizing and activating Asian Americans politically. A stylized summary of these regression results is shown in table E.1.

FROM IMMIGRANTS TO CITIZENS

In the first stage of becoming an emerging constituent, a range of factors related to background demographics, immigrant socialization, context, partisanship, and organizational mobilization are significant predictors of immigrants who naturalize as citizens. More specifically, the following demographic types of respondents are most likely to become a citizen: the very oldest respondents, women, and those who own their own home.[1] The magnitudes of these demographic effects are, for the most part, rela-

Table E.1   From Immigrants to Voters: Determinants of Participation

	Immigrants to Citizens	Citizens to Registered Voters	Registered to Likely Voters	Likely Voters to Super-Participants
Immigrant socialization				
Indian	0.338*	1.012***		0.647**
Filipino	−0.382**			
Japanese	−1.790***			−0.724**
Korean	−0.569***			
Vietnamese	0.575***	0.608***	0.360***	
Other Asian		0.338**		
Foreign-born		−1.388***	−0.670***	−1.244***
Second generation		−0.993***		
Years in United States	2.648***	0.352*	0.554***	0.685**
Interview in English	0.644**			
English-speaking skills	0.839***			
Ethnic news index	−0.363**	−0.404*	−0.332***	
General news index	0.327**	1.048***	0.397***	1.285***
Educated abroad	−0.761***	−0.504***	−0.327***	
Homeland political part			−0.226***	
Residential contexts				
Small Asian American settlement	−0.290**		−0.229***	
New destination	−0.591***		−0.161*	
Any Asian elected official		0.251*		
Local nonpartisan election			−0.212**	
Direct democracy	0.422**			
County battleground			−0.169**	
Party identification				
Democrat		0.374**	0.439***	
Republican	0.285*	0.512***	0.410***	
Non-party-identified	−0.557***	−0.385**		
Mobilized by party	0.976***	0.950***	0.261***	0.968***
Racial identification				
Common with Asians				
Common with other races		0.305**		0.357*
Discrimination and hate crime			−0.138*	0.541***
Religion and civic organization				
Frequency of religious attendance				

Table E.1   (Continued)

	Immigrants to Citizens	Citizens to Registered Voters	Registered to Likely Voters	Likely Voters to Super-Participants
Member of religious organization		0.482***	−0.238**	0.659***
Member of civic organization				0.693***
Mobilized by other organization	0.372**	0.617***		0.878***
Resources, demographic factors				
Age		1.458*	2.883***	
Age squared	1.917**		−2.016***	
Female	0.368***	0.332**		
Education		0.476***		0.959***
Family income	−0.247*			
Own home	0.494***			
N in model	3999	3627	2992	1625
N for DV	5158	4113	3399	1868

Source: Authors' compilation of data from the 2008 National Asian American Survey (Ramakrishnan et al. 2011).
Note: Standardized betas; $^*p < .10$; $^{**}p < .05$; $^{***}p < .01$.

tively modest. Notably, educational attainment appears to have no bearing on the likelihood of becoming a citizen.

When we turn to socialization factors, ethnic, national-origin groups differentiate naturalization rates. Of the groups we surveyed, Vietnamese and Asian Indians appear the most likely to naturalize, net of all the other factors we simultaneously consider; compared with Chinese Americans, Asian Indians are 3 percent more likely and Vietnamese nearly 7 percent more likely to report being citizens if foreign-born. Japanese respondents, by contrast, are by far the least likely: 65 percent less likely, by our predicted probability estimates, than Chinese Americans.[2]

Among the strongest effects we find is the number of years lived in the United States. The effect is nonlinear: predicted probability of being naturalized for someone who has lived in the United States for ten years, according to our calculations, is 72 percent; at about twenty years, it jumps up to 87 percent; by around thirty years, it is close to 94 percent, with ever rapidly diminishing marginal returns of each additional year of having lived in the country to one's likelihood of being naturalized.[3] That naturalization should correspond so strongly with time in the United States as an immigrant or that so much of the naturalization should occur within the first decades of residence is hardly surprising. More surprising is the relationship between differential rates of naturalization and longevity in the United States across groups. In particular, the effect of time on naturalization is conspicuously less strong for Japanese Americans. Among Japanese NAAS residents, only 11 percent naturalize within their first ten years and 23 percent by the first twenty years, but only 43 percent after thirty years .

A third key aspect of immigrant socialization that appears key to naturalization rates is the role of language and information. NAAS respondents who chose to interview in English and who reported high proficiency in English were significantly more likely to naturalize than those for whom English is unfamiliar or unpracticed. Similarly, those who kept politically informed across multiple media venues (television, radio, print media, or Internet) are much more likely to naturalize than those who remain uninformed about politics. Of those who rely on multiple media venues for the political information, those who choose Asian in-language ethnic media are significantly less likely to become a citizen.

Our results on this first stage into participation also highlight the relatively small yet statistically significant effects of residential context. Three contextual factors appear to add to our story of who naturalizes and who does not. Respondents who live in either small Asian American settlements or new immigrant destinations for Asian Americans were less likely to be citizens, but by relatively small margins (3 percent and 4 percent, respectively). Residing in a state with an initiative or direct democracy process were also 2 percent less likely to be naturalized.

Another chief finding is that political parties are an important component, even today, that determines whether Asians naturalize. Those Asian Americans in the NAAS who identify with a major party are more likely to be citizens than their counterparts who identify as independents, but only the effect for self-identified Republicans is significant (they are 4 percent more likely to naturalize). The stronger effect is among nonidentifiers, who are about 6 percent less likely to naturalize than independents and fully 10 percent less likely than Republicans. The effect of institutional mobilization here is also clear, and the role of parties continues to weigh more heavily than that of nonpartisan organizations: respondents who reported being mobilized by a party or party candidate were 8 percent more likely to be citizens than those who were not; those who reported being mobilized by a civic, religious, or other nonpartisan organization were about 4 percent more likely to also report being naturalized than those who were not.

The relationships we discuss are merely statistical associations, very carefully measured and considered. In some cases, the relationship underlying an association is clearly structural and linear: longevity matters to naturalization if for no other reason than the residency requirement before a legal immigrant can apply for citizenship. In other cases, the directionality of the relationship is far from clear: political parties and their candidates that contact immigrants may motivate naturalization, but it is perhaps more likely that being a citizen increases the likelihood that parties and their candidates will contact someone.

FROM CITIZENS TO REGISTERED VOTERS

The next stage we examine—registering to vote—is often cited as the weakest link in the chain of immigrant incorporation for Asian Americans. In our sample, the baseline (unweighted) proportion of citizens who report being registered to vote was 83 percent. Of the demographic factors examined, we find that older, female, and more well-educated respondents are more likely to have registered. Of these effects, age is the strongest. A twenty-five-year-old has a predicted 71 percent likelihood of being vote registered, a fifty-year-old 86 percent, and a seventy-five-year-old 94 percent.

Several aspects of immigrant socialization also drive Asian American voter registration. Asian Indians are about 8 percent and Vietnamese nearly 6 percent more likely to be registered to vote than Chinese Americans; there are no statistically significant national-origin differences between Chinese, Filipinos, Japanese, and Koreans. Foreign-born and second-generation Asian Americans are, unsurprisingly, less likely to be registered than those who are third generation; the effects of longevity and education in the United States are both positive, but relatively weak. Finally, of the socialization factors we examine, those who are politically informed using multiple media sources are much more likely to be registered to vote than those who do not. When the media sources are in an Asian language, however, respondents are less likely to be registered.

Institutional factors play perhaps the most consistent role in whether Asian Americans register to vote. Predictably, parties make a difference. Those who identify with a major party are more likely to be registered than independents (3 percent for Democrats and 5 percent for Republicans); independents are more likely to be registered than nonidentifiers (by 4 percent); and those who report being recruited by a party or candidate are 7 percent more likely to be registered than those who have not been mobilized. The combined effects of mobilization and partisanship are also illustrative. Roughly 87 percent of self-identified Democrats, if citizens but not contacted by parties or a candidate, are registered; when self-identified Democrats are mobilized, this proportion increases to about 93 percent. The effect is slightly weaker for self-identified Republicans: more than 89 percent of those not contacted are registered; of those who have been contacted, more than 94 percent are registered. The strongest effect here is among nonidentifiers: fewer than 82 percent of Asian American citizens who reject party labels and have not been contacted by parties are registered; when that contact is made, 90 percent are.

Several other institutional keys also have an impact on voter registration. Those who belong to a church or place of worship are significantly more likely to register, but the effect is somewhat modest. Those contacted by a nonpartisan organization are also more likely to be registered. The effect here is decidedly stronger than the effect of civic mobilization on naturalization (those who were mobilized are 5 percent more likely than those who were not), but still weaker than the effect of partisan mobilization. The final result worth noting here is that those respondents who perceive a great deal of political commonality with non-Asian racial groups are about 4 percent more likely to be registered than those who see no political commonality there at all.

FROM REGISTERED TO LIKELY VOTERS

The penultimate stage we examine is those registered voters who turn out on Election Day. As we noted earlier, the first thorn on the side of our analysis here is that we do not directly observe voting behavior (the NAAS is a preelection poll, not an exit poll), and the reliability of self-reported voting is suspect. As a result, we use as our outcome variable the likely voter measure that we have used throughout the book, derived from a bare-bones estimate of who is likely to vote and who is not.[4] The results are interesting in several respects.

Among the strongest relationships we find is between age and one's likelihood of voting. The effects here are dual: there is a direct positive relationship between age in years and voting and a nonlinear negative relationship between the squared value of age and voting. In effect, older respondents are more likely to vote up to a point, beyond which they are less likely to do so. Although the baseline (unweighted) probability of voting among those registered to vote in the NAAS is almost 79 percent, we find that only 9 percent of those twenty-five years old are likely voters; among thirty-five-year-olds, the turnout rate inches up to 20 percent; one does not approach the mean probability of voting for the sample (55 percent) until one is about fifty-three years old.

To the extent that age is an indirect measure of socioeconomic status, this result is to be expected. When we turn to more direct measures of the putative SES-participation link, however, the most conspicuous finding in table E.1 is that none of our three more direct measures of SES—home ownership, family income, and educational attainment—appear to have a statistically significant influence on voting among those already registered to vote.

Among immigrant socialization and national-origin factors, several results are salient. Even when we limit our analysis to registered voters, nativity sharply differentiates voters from nonvoters: U.S.-born respondents are an estimated 22 percent more likely to vote than their foreign-born counterparts. Two related factors are time in the United States among the foreign-born and education abroad. For longevity, the marginal effect of each additional year lived in the United States is a .6 percent higher likelihood of voting: to put this in more commonsensical terms, an immigrant in their twentieth year in the United States is 6 percent more likely to turn out to vote than their neighbor who immigrated just ten years ago, even when both are registered. For educational context, those U.S.-educated respondents are 8 percent more likely to vote. Our two measures of political information also show up as significant factors here: general media consumption for political information induces voting, whereas reliance on ethnic, Asian-language media for that information impedes it. Perhaps the most surprising and potentially controversial finding from our analysis is that—net of all other factors we consider—there is a statistically significant difference between those active in the politics of their country of origin and those who are not. Transnationalism, at least for NAAS respondents, appears to have a depressing effect on turnout in the United States, and with a relatively sizeable 13 percent marginal effect. Finally, one national-origin group difference is prominent: Vietnamese are 13 percent more likely to vote than the reference group in our estimates, Chinese Americans.

We also find from our analyses several notable findings with respect to settlement and political contexts. Those living in small settlement areas and in new immigrant destinations are significantly less likely to vote, by moderate levels of 10 and 8 percent, respectively. Furthermore, those living in areas that conduct local nonpartisan elections are 6 percent less likely to vote. That those living in battleground counties are significantly less likely to vote than their counterparts in traditional gateways is somewhat counterintuitive. Thus, though residents in battleground regions are usually highly coveted electoral resources, the effect seems absent among

Asian Americans. Interestingly, among NAAS respondents, those living in county battlegrounds are no more likely to report being mobilized by a party or candidate than those living elssewhere.

The voting behavior of Asian Americans, unsurprisingly, also emerges from an institutional context. Self-identified partisans are much more likely to vote (by an 11 percent margin for Democrats and 13 percent for Republicans) than independents. Being contacted by a party or a candidate also has a mobilizing effect on turnout (8 percent). Interestingly, among this group of registered voters, contact by nonpartisan organizations has no significant bearing on voting behavior. In fact, the only measure of civic engagement that appears to encourage voting is nonreligious engagement in a religious place of worship (by a measured 5 percent). We also find two additional, information-related institutional influences on voting. Respondents who got political information from multiple media sources were significantly more likely to participate than those who did not (those who reported receiving information from all sources—television, radio, print media, and the Internet—were 20 percent more likely to vote than those who did not). Respondents who reported relying exclusively on ethnic, in-language media sources were significantly (11 percent) less likely to report voting than those who never used such sources.

FROM VOTERS TO HIGH PROPENSITY PARTICIPATORS

The final stage of political engagement we examine is the step from being a voter (measured as a probability along a factor scale of voting propensity) to being a super-participant (measured as participating in five or more of the ten measures of political activity in the NAAS). As we saw in figure 8.1, only 9 percent of our sample report participating at these super levels. Among those identified as voters by our likely voter models, however, this proportion increases to 18 percent. Which of the various factors in our pathways foretell being a high-propensity participant?

The results point to the significance of a smaller but more focused set of factors vis-à-vis our previous stages of political engagement. There are some passing influences of demographic background (those who are more well educated are more likely to be high-propensity participants) and national origin (Asian Indians and, to a lesser degree, Vietnamese are more likely to be super-participants), but the most consistent effects are found among our measures of immigrant socialization and civic engagement. Quite unsurprising here is that foreign-born Asians, those who have not lived in the United States for very long, and those not educated in the United States are less participatory at these high levels than their native-born, longer tenured, and U.S.-educated counterparts. Perhaps more surprising, however, is that—among likely voters—those who engage in transnational politics are 9 percent more likely to be a super-participant than those who do not. Taking a step back, however, it is not hard to imagine that those who are politically active in their country of origin might be politically active in the United States as well, especially when we expand our notion of high participation beyond casting a ballot. Certainly, this finding runs contrary to worries that homeland political participation is a drain on U.S. participation.

With respect to civic engagement, three of our measures hold a statistically significant and positive relationship to high propensity participation. The effects of membership in a church or other house of worship and membership in a secular organization are both sizeable, 10 and 11 percent, respectively. Mobilization by a nonpartisan organization also has a moderately strong effect on being a super-participant, 8 percent. Related to these effects are the influence of reliance on various media sources for political information, which we view as both a measure of immigrant socialization and civic ties. The general effect of relying on various media sources for political information is moderately strong: those who rely on all four sources are 14 percent more likely to be a super-participant than those who rely on none. The effect of reliance on ethnic language sources, though significant, is much more modest.

Finally, being a super-participant does have certain racial tones. Those who see Asian Americans as sharing a great deal in common politically with non-Asians are about 5 percent more likely to be a super-participant, although this is a relationship that could easily be bidirectional (or flow from high levels of participation to greater sense of shared political interests with racial out-groups). More sharply defined and stronger is the effect of having been a victim of a hate crime or being discriminated against, which leads to a 11 percent greater likelihood of being a super-participant. Again, this association might run in both directions. Partisanship effects are conspicuously absent in explaining high propensity participation compared to being a likely voter alone, with the exception of being mobilized by a political party.

Appendix F | Survey Design

THIS TECHNICAL APPENDIX provides details about survey methods, including the design of the sampling frame, the interview method and questionnaire, and the weighting technique used to relate our final interview sample to the characteristics of the Asian American population as found from U.S. Census Bureau data sources.

OVERALL DESIGN OF THE NATIONAL ASIAN AMERICAN SURVEY

The National Asian American Survey (NAAS) gathered information about the social and political attitudes and behavior of 5,159 Asian American adults between August 12 and October 29, 2008. These telephone interviews were conducted by Interview Services of America (ISA) of Van Nuys, California. Seventy-two percent of interviewers were bilingual in English and an Asian language, and the remaining were English-only interviewers. Overall, 40 percent of respondents proceeded with the interview in English. There were significant variations in Asian-language interviews across ethnic groups: 83 percent of Vietnamese interviews were conducted in Vietnamese; 74 percent of the Korean interviews were conducted in Korean; 57 percent of the Chinese interviews were conducted in either Mandarin (44 percent) or Cantonese (13 percent); 16 percent of the Filipino interviews were in Tagalog; 10 percent of the Japanese interviews were in Japanese; and 2 percent of the Asian Indian interviews were in Hindi. [1] For those who began the interview in an Asian language, interviewers asked respondents first whether they were "comfortable continuing the conversation in English" in order to reduce the incidence of Asian-language interviews based on the accent of the interviewer and social desirability expectations on the part of the respondent.

Interview length was approximately twenty-six minutes for the English-language interviews and thirty-two minutes for the Asian-language interviews. ISA managers and the principal investigators conducted extensive interviewer training on subject matter and language. Asian-language translations were done from English to Cantonese, Mandarin, Vietnamese, Korean, Tagalog, Japanese, and Hindi. We conducted this process with two vendors and made cross-comparisons for precision and accuracy.

LISTED SAMPLES

For the general U.S. population, a random probability sample of residents is the simplest theoretically and the easiest to justify methodologically with respect to providing a representative snapshot of public opinion and behavior. For Asian Americans, however, a simple random sample of all residential telephones would not have been desirable because of the low population of Asian Americans in many parts of the United States. Currently, Asian Americans account for just over 5 percent of the U.S. population, which means that about 95 percent of contacts with a household would terminate after the first minute of the screener after determining that the respondent is not Asian American. In addition, we would not have many clues a priori about what language the respondent spoke. Not only would random digit dialing (RDD) selection been prohibitively expensive, it would also have been difficult on interviewers to have such a low contact rate for potential Asian American subjects. Nevertheless, we attempted a test of RDD case selection with residential telephones and dialed through 2,410 numbers. This test yielded eight completed interviews at a cost per interview (CPI) of $281, more than five times our average CPI of $59. Finally, given the short window of time during which we wanted to complete the NAAS—during the heat of the 2008 general election campaign—doing straight RDD for more than 5,000 cases would have taken much longer.

Given these constraints, we opted for a list sample of Asian Americans based on records from commercial vendors and state registrars, and stratified by Asian ethnicity. We obtained our listed samples from Catalist, and supplemented the list for Filipinos from Scientific Telephone Samples (STS). We utilized STS for the Filipino sample because of systematic undercoverage of Filipinos in the Catalist samples obtained in the summer of 2008.[2] The listed sample from Catalist is the most comprehensive and up-to-date sample of registered voters, regardless of their party affiliation, but also includes those not registered to vote. The primary source for records in the Catalist databases are from the registered voter rolls provided by county registrars and secretaries of state. Catalist acquires the files directly from the states or counties as appropriate, and these files usually contain names, addresses, some history of elections the voter participated in, and often birthdate. Although Catalist has some limitations, which we address shortly, it is a rich dataset for appending administrative information on voter registration and turnout.

After initial acquisition of these raw data, Catalist standardizes the files, matches them, and eliminates any duplication before using an outside vendor (InfoUSA) to further clean the data, using techniques such as address standardization, application of national change of address (NCOA), geocoding, and application of select census data. Catalist also uses data from InfoUSA to append additional records of non-registered residents in the United States based on more than three hundred fields of marketing data including product warranty registration, automobile registration, magazine subscriptions, and other mailing lists that can be matched to residential telephone numbers.

To identify respondents' race and ethnic group background, Catalist classifies names as either *likely Asian* or *very likely Asian* based on an analysis of first names, last names, and census block concentration of Asians. We used the lower threshold of likely Asian in order to capture as many Asians as possible who may not have distinctively Asian names. Most of the Asian names were assigned to particular ethnic groups, but about 11 percent could not be so assigned, and we included these in our sampling frame. Daniel Ichinose of the Asian Pacific American Legal Center also ran a cross-check of the sample against the organization's own well-established Asian name database to help ensure proper classification by national origin group.

Relying on a list strategy of identifying Asian Americans has two limitations. First, we are not able to meaningfully include Asian American Muslims in our sample because many of them have nondistinctive Asian names. Thus, though national estimates of the Muslim population in the United States (numbers which themselves vary by one or two orders of magnitude) would peg Muslims as anywhere between 5 to 10 percent of the Asian American population, we were only able to have 1 percent of our sample as Muslim. Improvements in the classification of Asian Muslim names (especially for distinctively South Asian Muslim names) would help ameliorate this situation in the future. Another limitation is that multiracial Asians and others who do not have distinctively Asian first names or surnames are less likely to be picked up in our sample. Given the overwhelming predominance of first-generation immigrants in the adult citizen population, this issue of multiracial Asians is less of a problem today than it will likely be in the future. However, proposed solutions to this problem would either be cost-prohibitive (such as relying on a national random sample of adult residents, only to interview Asian Americans) or would introduce new types biases that are more serious to the study of

Asian Americans (such as a random sample of only those living in areas of high Asian American concentration or known areas of high multiracial concentration).

SAMPLE CHARACTERISTICS

The sampling design of the NAAS does not follow typical U.S. population surveys. Instead, and to account for the spatial dispersion of the Asian American population and the geographic concentration of particular national origin groups in various parts of the United States, we began by sampling at the county level. This selection strategy is consistent with our core interest in demographic, organizational, and political contexts of incorporation. As noted by many studies in economic geography, counties are important units in the analysis of labor markets, consumer markets, and industries (Carlino and Mills 1987; Hoynes 2000; Hanson 2005). Also, county boundaries have not changed in recent U.S. censuses and there is a wealth of demographic information provided by the U.S. Census Bureau at the county level. Data on presidential vote totals are also available at the county level, giving us a useful measure of local political competition that cannot be matched at any lower level of aggregation. Counties are also important political units of analysis because of variations in the strength of party organizations and in tax policies and the public provision of health care and welfare.

Given our interest in producing nationally representative estimates for Asian Americans as well as estimates for new Asian destinations (see chapter 3), we created a random probability national sample, and added a sample of counties that are part of Audrey Singer's pioneering framework on new immigrant destinations (Singer et al. 2008). Overall, these new Asian destinations accounted for 22 percent of the overall sample frame. As noted in chapter 3, there are some slight differences in how one might construct future samples of Asian American destinations based on whether one is interested in examining their integration into contexts of new immigration more generally, of Asian immigrants only, or of Asian Americans more generally. In table F.1, we outline how our survey respondents fall into the new category of Asian American destinations that we proposed in chapter 3, which stratifies all U.S. counties into two characteristics: the number of Asian Americans in the county, and the rate of increase in the population. The time horizon for population growth is the 1990 census and the 2007 ACS, and the cutoff for defining low and high growth rates is the median county-level growth rate for Asian Americans between 1990 and 2007 (197 percent).

In the data, 1,173 interviews (23 percent of our total sample) were con-

Table F.1   Respondents in Different Types of Asian American
            Destinations

	Small (1990 Population Less Than 1,000)	Large (1900 Population Greater Than 1,000)
Low rate of increase	Small settlements N=542	Traditional destinations– Low growth N=2,367
(Growth 1990 to 2007 < median growth rate)	Ex: Riverside County, Cal.; Denver County, Col.; Clark County, Wa.	Ex: Los Angeles County, Cal.; Queens County, N.Y.; King County, Wa.
High rate of increase	New destinations N=1,173	Traditional destinations– High Growth N=1,077
(Growth 1990 to 2007 > median growth rate)	Ex: Lake County, Ill.; Robeson County, N.C.; Atlantic County, N.J.	Ex: Fairfax County, Va.; Middlesex County, N.J.; Santa Clara County, Cal.

Source: Authors' compilation.

ducted with Asian Americans residing in new destinations (defined as U.S. counties with high growth rate in the Asian American population and relatively small absolute numbers in 1990). An additional 542 interviews were completed among respondents residing in *small settlement* counties with small Asian American populations in 1990 and low rates of Asian American population growth. The bulk of the 2008 NAAS sample—3,444 interviews (or 67 percent of the total sample) – resides in traditional destinations. Of these, 2,367 were in "low growth" traditional destinations and 1,077 were in "high growth" traditional destinations.

Regardless of whether future studies of Asian Americans use more general categories of immigrant gateways or our proposed categories of Asian American destinations, one common feature is choosing counties as the most basic geographic unit of sampling. There are several advantages in choosing a nationally representative sample and a new destination oversample based on counties. First, we avoid the limited generalizability that would inevitably arise if we chose only a handful of states or counties. This is especially true for new immigrant gateways, which include hundreds of counties across many states, but is also true for traditional destination counties. For example, there are more than 200 counties that are traditional destinations with high Asian American growth. There are theoretical advantages as well, as we are able to apply the same typology to different levels of analysis (from states to census blocks), and are able to make systematic comparisons to other county-based factors such as party competition (which is slightly lower, on average, in new destination areas than in traditional areas). Thus, with a sample of more than 5,000 respondents, we are able to have a nationally representative sample after appropriate weights, while at the same time being able to systematically analyze the role of social, political, and economic contexts.

One important upshot of our sampling design is that researchers are able to conduct disaggregated analysis not just at the level of ethnic or national-origin groups, but also at the county level and state level. Our final NAAS sample included more than one hundred respondents in twelve counties (Alameda, California; Bergen, New Jersey; Fairfax, Virginia; Honolulu, Hawaii; King, Washington; Kings, New York; Los Angeles, California; Middlesex, New Jersey; Orange, California; Queens, New York; San Francisco, California; Santa Clara, California). When we aggregate counties up to the state level, the final NAAS sample contains more than one hundred respondents in nine states (California, New Jersey, New York, Texas, Virginia, Washington, Hawaii, Maryland, and Georgia), and more than fifty respondents in an additional nine states (Florida, Illinois, North Carolina, Pennsylvania, Colorado, Massachusetts, Oregon, Nevada, and Michigan). In chapter 3, we take a closer look at some of the political consequences of the geographic settlement patterns of Asian Americans.

In addition to following a sampling design that followed these geographic contours and aimed for sufficiently large numbers of Asian Americans from the six largest national-origin groups, budget constraints also weighed heavily into how our sample frame was defined. The sheer cost of defining our sample relative to a random probability sample of all Asian residents in the United States—and using a random digit dialing approach to obtaining sample—required that we opt for a more efficient alternative means of identifying Asians for our survey. In the 2008 NAAS, we opted to use a list sample based on records from commercial sample vendors and state registrars as described. This strategy, as we shall see, leads to modest distortions in our sample composition vis-à-vis general population parameters for Asian Americans.

Figure F.1 displays the distribution of the NAAS 2008 survey population in terms of national origin, comparing the sample to the proportions in the Asian American population according to the 2006–2008 American Community Survey. As the figure shows, some groups are relatively underrepresented compared with their overall population composition, others are relatively overrepresented, and still others fall relatively close. Specifically, compared to U.S. population parameters as estimated in the ACS, the NAAS contains relatively fewer Filipinos and other Asians and relatively greater proportions of Asian Indians, Japanese, and Vietnamese respondents.[3]

Figure F.1 Asian American Population

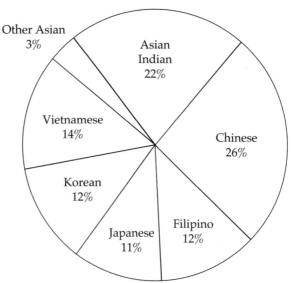

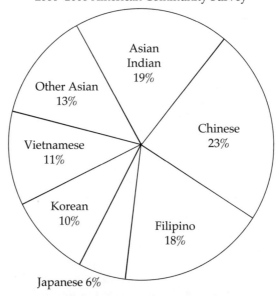

Source: Authors' compilation of data from the 2008 National Asian American Survey (Ramakrishnan et al. 2011) and the 2006–2008 American Community Survey (U.S. Census Bureau 2008c).

Table F.2   Select Demographic Characteristics of Asian American
Adults

	2008 NAAS	2006–2008 ACS
Female	46.2%	51.5%
Foreign-born	88%	76%
Mean age	53	43
Less than high school degree	9%	14%
High school degree	17%	18%
Beyond high school	74%	68%
Immigrant arrived since 1990	52%	55%
More than one race	5%	7%

Source: Authors' compilation of data from the 2008 National Asian American Survey (Ramakrishnan et al. 2011) and the 2006–2008 American Community Survey (U.S. Census Bureau 2008c).

Beyond ethnic and national-origin groups, a sample's representativeness of an underlying population can be compared using other key benchmarks. Table F.2 provides a breakdown of the sample by several other relevant demographic characteristics. Here, too, the NAAS sample approximates general Asian American population parameters on some dimensions, but not all. The NAAS sample has a higher proportion of male, foreign-born, older, and highly educated Asian Americans. These disparities largely reflect our decision to sample by national origin and geographic region, and to use a list sample instead of a random-digit dial sample of all residents, disqualifying anyone who does not identify as Asian American or report any Asian ancestry.

SAMPLE WEIGHTS

Karthick Ramakrishnan and David Crow at the University of California, Riverside, Survey Research Center (SRC) developed and calculated survey weights for the National Asian American Survey. This technical note enumerates the variables and data sources used in the weighting adjustments, offers a general description of the Iterative Proportional Fitting algorithm developed by W. Edwards Deming and Frederick F. Stephan (1940)—known as *raking*—and details its application to the NAAS data set.

NAAS Weighting Adjustment Variables

The NAAS comprises 5,159 observations drawn from a national U.S. sample. We adjusted sample proportions to population proportions estimated from the 2006–2008 three-year average of the Current Population Survey (CPS) and the 2007 American Community Survey (ACS), both conducted by the U.S. Census Bureau. In designing our weights, we defined four categorical weighting adjustment variables:

- Ethnicity, with seven (7) categories: Indian, Chinese, Filipino, Japanese, Korean, Vietnamese, and Other;
- Gender, with two (2) categories: male and female;
- Education, with three (3) categories: less than high school, high school graduate, and at least some college; and
- Nativity-citizenship-years in the United States, with five (5) categories: foreign-born noncitizen recently arrived, foreign-born citizen recently arrived, foreign-born noncitizen long-term resident, foreign-born citizen long-term resident, and native-born citizen.

Weighting adjustments were carried out at the national level, taking into account the size of each group in each state.

Because the number of adjustment cells was very large ($7 \times 2 \times 3 \times 5 = 210$), we estimated survey weights using a technique known as sample balancing or raking, described in the following section.[4] In essence, raking corrects an imbalanced sample by adjusting sample totals (and proportions) to known totals in the population using the marginal distributions of weighting variables when a full cross-classification of these variables is unobtainable or impractical.

Poststratification and Raking Weights

The proportion of respondents in a sample with a given set of characteristics may differ from the proportion of their counterparts in the population for many reasons. These include sampling error, noncoverage error (when the sampling frame omits some members of the population), nonresponse error (when members of some subpopulations respond to a survey proportionally more than members of other subpopulations), and the sample design itself (as in the cases of oversampling and stratified samples with unequal sampling fractions). When for any of these reasons (or others) the proportion survey respondents differ from their known population proportion on one or more characteristics, weighting is often used to adjust sample-to-population proportions. Auxiliary population information is typically obtained from census data or from other studies.

Poststratification (PS) is a weighting technique that matches sample proportions to population proportions on characteristics chosen after data have been collected (see, for example, Gelman and Carlin 2002; Kalton 1983, 74–75; and Lohr 1999, 114–15). First, the sample is divided into H mutually exclusive categories, or strata, on the basis of observable characteristics such as gender, ethnicity, and age, where H is the number of cells resulting from a complete cross-classification of the poststratification variables. Then the proportion of sample members falling in cell h ($p_h = n_h / n$) is multiplied by a weighting factor that makes the sample proportion equal to the proportion in the corresponding population adjustment cell ($\pi_h = N_h / N$). The PS weight for all sample units in cell h is given by:

$$w_h = \frac{N_h / N}{n_h / n} = \frac{\pi_h}{p_h},$$

where N_h is the population size in cell h, N is the total population size, n_h is the number of sample units in cell h, and n is the total number of sample units. The weights average to 1 ($\bar{w}_h = \Sigma_{h=1}^{H} w_h n_h / n = 1$). A cell weight over 1 indicates that the sample units in cell h are upweighted to compensate for underrepresention (with respect to the population); conversely, a cell weight under 1 means the sample units in the cell are being downweighted to compensate for overrepresentation.

But full poststratification is unfeasible in many instances. The number of PS cells is often very large and can even exceed the sample size. Sparse data and zero cell counts make estimation of PS weights highly unstable or impossible.[5] Also, complete cross-classifications of the population are often unobtainable, and only marginal totals are known. A common solution to this problem is to poststratify on the margins, or rake the sample to marginal adjustment totals (Gelman 2007, 155; see also Deville, Sarndal, and Sautory 1993).

Deming and Stephan (1940) proposed the "iterative proportional fitting" algorithm for estimating raking weights. The algorithm sets initial weighting factors for each cross-classification term to 1 and adjusts the weight factors for the first cross-classification term so that the weighted sample becomes representative with respect to the population (that is, it matches the marginal population distribution) for that term. The resulting weight factors are similarly adjusted for the next cross-classification term. Because this disturbs the representativeness of the other cross-classification terms, the process is repeated sequentially until the weighting factors converge (for a description of the algorithm, see Bethlehem 2002, 281).

So, for a two-way table with row variable I and column variable J, each cell proportion in sample row i is multiplied by a factor that makes the marginal proportion for that row ($p_{i+} = \Sigma_{j=1}^{J} p_{ij}$) equal to the row marginal proportion in the population ($\pi_{i+} = \Sigma_{j=1}^{J} \pi_{ij}$).[6] The resulting sample cell proportions in each column j are then multiplied by a factor that makes the sample column proportions $(p_{+j} = \Sigma_{i=1}^{I} p_{ij})$ equal to the population column proportions $(\pi_{+j} = \Sigma_{i=1}^{I} \pi_{ij})$. The sample cell proportions are adjusted to the row marginals again, then the column marginals iteratively until they no longer change appreciably. The repeated lateral and vertical adjustments evoke a "raking" motion that gives its name to the algorithm.

Formally, Deming and Stephan proposed least squares minimization of a sum of residuals:

$$\varsigma = \Sigma(m_h - n_h)^2 / n_h,$$

where n_h is the observed cell frequency in cell h, and m_h is the calculated or adjusted cell frequency. Adjusted cell frequencies are constrained such that when summed across rows or columns, the sum is equal to known population marginal totals. For the two-way case, the marginal constraints are:

$$\Sigma_{j=1}^{I} m_{ij} = N_{i+} \text{ for } i = (1,...,I)$$

and

$$\Sigma_{i=1}^{I} m_{ij} = N_{+j} \text{ for } j = (1,...,J),$$

where N_{i+} and N_{+j} are the population marginals. Deming and Stephan derived normal equations that allow for analytic solutions for two- and three-way contingency tables when some or all of the marginal totals are known. However, they proposed the iterative proportions algorithm just described, which allowed for much more rapid estimation of m_i—often converging after just two or three iterations.

Little and Wu (1991) showed that the raking weights can be estimated in the Generalized Linear Model (GLM) framework. For a two-way contingency table, the model is as follows:

$$f(\hat{\pi}_{ij} / p_{ij}) = \mu + \mu_i + \mu_j$$

where p_{ij} is the observed sample cell proportion, $\hat{\pi}_{ij}$ is the adjusted cell proportion (corresponding to m_h in Deming and Stephan's notation), μ is the intercept, the μ_i's are row effects (with ANOVA-type contrasts or dummy variable identifying constraints), and the μ_j's are column effects (also with identifying constraints). Two possible link functions are the identity link, leading to a least squares estimator, and the natural logarithm, leading to a log-linear model. The raking weights are given by $(\hat{\pi}_{ij} / p_{ij})$, and $\hat{\pi}_{ij}$ is estimated such that it is as close to 1 as possible and conforms to the marginal constraints given by Deming and Stephan (re-formulated here in Little and Wu's notation):

$$\Sigma_{i=1}^{I}\hat{\pi}_{ij} = \pi_{i+} \text{ for } i = (1,\ldots,I)$$

$$\Sigma_{j=1}^{J}\hat{\pi}_{ij} = \pi_{+j} \text{ for } j = (1,\ldots,J) \quad,$$

where π_{i+} and π_{+j} are population marginal proportions.

Adjusting cell proportions to simple marginal totals—that is, of single variables taken one at a time—is the equivalent of the log-linear independence model (subject to the marginal constraints noted above). Estimating raking weights as additive row and column effects "will not work well when interactions exist" (Little and Wu 1991, 88). For its part, full post-stratification can be formulated as the saturated model in log-linear framework. In the two-way case,

$$ln(\hat{\pi}_{ij} / p_{ij}) = \mu + \mu_i + \mu_j + \mu_{ij},$$

where the last term denotes the interaction effects of row i and column j. Extensions to multiway tables are straightforward.

As noted, however, full poststratification is often unfeasible. A compromise solution is to poststratify to joint marginals—that is, the joint probability that two variables will assume given values, independently of the values other variables assume. Poststratification to joint marginals accommodates interaction effects among the raking variables while obviating the necessity for cell probabilities obtained by full poststratification, difficult or impossible under conditions of sparse data.

So, for example, in a three-way contingency table with variables I, J, and K, the joint marginal probabilities for I and J sum the joint distribution of all three variables over the values of K:

$$\Sigma_{k=1}^{K}\pi_{ijk} = \pi_{ij+}$$

If we wanted to rake to the joint marginals for each two-way interaction between I, J, and K (π_{ij+}, π_{+jk}, and π_{i+k}, respectively), the log-linear model π_{ij+} is:

$$ln(\hat{\pi}_{ijk} / p_{ijk}) = \mu + \mu_i + \mu_j + \mu_k + \mu_{ij} + \mu_{jk} + \mu_{ik}$$

Note that this is equivalent to the saturated model with the parameter for the highest-order, three-way interaction set to 0. This formulation of log-linear raking models (and GLM raking models using other link functions) is highly flexible, because any combination of lower-order interactions may be specified to calculate the raking adjustment weights.

NAAS Weights

In estimating raking weights for the NAAS, we used the procedure for poststratifying to joint marginals described in the preceding paragraphs. Recapitulating, there were four raking variables:

I = ethnicity (seven levels)

J = gender (two levels)

K = education (three levels)

L = nativity/citizenship (five levels)

An additional variable, state (M), was used to estimate national-level raking weights based on state ethnic populations.

Theory and prior empirical knowledge led the NAAS principal investigators to believe that the gender, education, and nativity composition of the sample would differ across ethnic groups. This belief implies three bivariate interactions: ethnicity × gender (IJ), ethnicity × education (IK), and ethnicity × nativity (IL). In addition, at the national level, the ethnic composition of the sample varies by state, resulting in the bivariate interaction ethnicity × state (IL).

The national-level raking weights to four sets of joint marginals: IJ, IK, IL, and IM. The log-linear formulation of the raking model is:

$$ln(\hat{\pi}_{ijklm} / p_{ijklm}) = \mu + \mu_i + \mu_j + \mu_k + \mu_l + \mu_m + \mu_{ij} + \mu_{ik} + \mu_{il} + \mu_{im}$$

Note that the model includes no three-way or higher-order interactions, and omits many two-way interactions.

CONCLUSION

Raking is a well-established technique to adjust sample proportions (and frequencies) to known proportions (and totals) in the population when the full cross-classification of the sample is unknown or results in low cell counts. In these cases, poststratification is impossible or unstable. However, raking to single marginal totals doesn't allow survey researchers to account for interactions that may exist between the raking variables. A suitable compromise is raking or poststratifying to joint marginals, the technique described in this note and used to estimate sample weights for the NAAS.

Notes |

CHAPTER 1

1. The census figures on the Asian American population are based on the more inclusive "alone or in combination" identification with Asian or Pacific Islander categories.

2. As Steven Erie (1988) and Gerald Gamm (1989) have noted, however, this mobilization was often selective in many cities before the New Deal, as urban machines often excluded Italian and Jewish immigrants, while at the same time mobilizing Irish immigrants.

3. Note that this distinction includes any family background from countries in East Asia, Southeast Asia, the Philippines, and South Asia.

4. The registered voters in our sample include 784 of Indian origin, 748 Chinese, 521 Vietnamese, 406 Filipinos, 388 Korean, and 340 Japanese. Another 120 are categorized as Other Asian American, which includes multiracial respondents as well as those outside the six largest ethnic origin groups.

5. Our inclusion of community activism and protest politics, jointly, is also informative as a check on the political incorporation of Asian Americans. From the standpoint of pluralism or polyarchy, the generalized underparticipation of Asian Americans could reflect either a widespread sense of apathy (or consent and contentedness), or structural or subjective exclusion from what are formally open and freely competitive modes of political engagement like voting, contributing money, and contacting officials. To the extent that the latter is true, it is useful to look for the expression of residual, unmet political demands through unconventional political acts (Muller 1979).

6. To provide data comparable to our other participation measures, we transform the index into a 0/1 binary scale, with a cutoff point that reflects actual participation rates as reported in the Current Population Survey Voter Supplement in 2008.

7. One inference that is tempting to draw here is that for whites, the street between donations and access runs in both directions, whereas for Asian Amer-

icans, the relationship is more asymmetric. However, it is also possible to read the same data to surmise that Asian Americans are less comprehensive in their approach to gaining political access than whites, and that this may change with greater time in the United States for Asian immigrants.

8. Further, agreement is general that older Americans are more likely to participate due to both cohort effects—those who came of political age in eras of greater participation—and life cycle effects—those who are old enough to own homes and have children are more likely to participate than the young, and participation declines among the very old or infirm (Miller and Shanks 1996). Gender has also been shown to be important for certain types of political activities, such as political contributions, more so than others, such as voting and protest activity (Burns, Schlozman, and Verba 2001)

9. This strategy applies primarily to chapters 4 (party identification), 5 (racial identification), and 6 (religious and civic engagement). The chapters on immigrant socialization and contexts of settlement include, we would submit, factors that are primarily a first-order causal priority, and thus a similar analysis of the outcomes as intermediary dependent variables is not warranted.

CHAPTER 2

1. Elizabeth Grieco (2010) reports that most of those who identify as foreign born in the American Indian and Alaskan Native population were born in Central America, and in Mexico in particular.

2. For more on the scholarly debates over ethnic, racial, and ethnoracial classifications, see appendix A.

3. This includes only those who chose "Asian alone" in the race category. Using the more expansive "Asian alone or in combination with one or more groups," this figure is 82 percent.

4. This figure is based on our analysis of the American Community Survey 2006–2008 micro data file. Population counts in the United States by ethnoracial classification since 2000 are presented in one of two formats as a result of the "mark one or more" format of the race question introduced in the 2000 census. Introduced in recognition of the multiple ethnic lineage of many Americans, the racial self-identification item in the census and other data collections allows people to identify with as many racial categories as they see fit. The only officially recognized marker of ethnicity—Hispanic or Latino—is not an available option under this multiracial identification scheme. For a given group, say Korean, categorized in the racial self-identification question (where Korean is listed as a separate race), the group's population can be counted either by limiting group boundaries only to those who identify that group and no other group (alone) or by adding those who identify with that group and one or more other groups (alone or in combination).

5. This large gender gap, along with the passage of the 1913 Alien Land Law in California, prompted many of these Sikh immigrants to marry Mexican American women, whose citizenship rights enabled the preservation of property claims.

6. The figure is 2.8 million if one considers Filipino in combination with other racial and ethnic categories in the American Community Survey.

7. Also, the Perry expedition itself contained a handful of formerly shipwrecked sailors from Japan who had settled in California.

8. This is based on our analysis of the 2006–2008 American Community Survey microdata file.

9. Details on our weighting method are included in appendix F.

10. Indeed, in the cases of contacting and making political contributions, being a registered voter probably carries even more weight that just being a citizen because elected officials can verify the registration status and voting records of individuals in the databases they collect on constituent registration and voting.

11. Our estimate for the overall Asian American population is 71 percent, which is lower than the 76 percent estimate reported through FactFinder (http://factfinder.census.gov) because we examine "Asian alone or in combination with other races," whereas FactFinder reports on language-use among respondents who are "Asian alone."

12. Tagalog represented the only language of the Philippines and Hindi the only Indian language made available to respondents.

13. It is tempting to suggest that this finding indicates that the returns to participation in going from high to very high levels of English proficiency are minimal. However, we cannot rule out the possibility that those taking English-language interviews had similar levels of proficiency as those who reported speaking English very well because we asked the English proficiency question only of those taking non-English interviews. Still, our finding of a nonsignificant difference between speaking English very well and taking an English-language interview should help build confidence in our self-reported measure of language proficiency as far as the distinction between low and high levels of self-reported proficiency.

14. We asked English-language interview respondents about their proficiency in an Asian language.

15. In the NAAS, newspapers account for 26 percent of the total for all sources, and the comparable figure for the Pew survey is 19 percent. Similar standardized figures for radio are 18 percent in the NAAS and 9 percent in the Pew survey.

16. These include overreporting of civic and political behavior due to social desirability in a survey that is clearly about politics, and overestimating political interest based on limiting the kinds of choices available (for instance, not

including options like individual recreation, team sports, hobbies, and the like).

CHAPTER 3

1. Contemporary scholars have returned to field experimental studies, mostly of get-out-the-vote voter mobilization campaigns and with the benefit of the tremendous methodological strides since Gosnell's original studies of voting in Chicago (Gerber and Green 2000; Green and Gerber 2008; Ramirez and Wong 2006; Garcia Bedolla and Michelson 2009).

2. "The apportionment population base always has included those persons who have established a residence in the United States. The first Census Act of 1790 established the concept of 'usual residence' which has been applied in that and each subsequent census" (U.S. Census Bureau 2004). Although the U.S. Constitution initially excluded untaxed Native Americans and counted slaves as three-fifths of a person for the purposes of apportionment, the 14th Amendment in 1868 established the count for all whole persons, and a federal court decision in New Mexico in 1948 (Trujillo v. Garley) determined that connecting apportionment to taxation was in violation of other provisions in the 14th and 15th Amendments.

3. As before, we use the more expansive category of Asian American and Pacific Islander when discussing population counts of census and ACS data.

4. In 2003, the Office of Management and Budget issued new standards for defining the metropolitan contexts in which Americans live. These new standards redefined single-core and multicore metropolitan areas and established federal definitions for two new statistical areas: micropolitan statistical areas and combined statistical areas. Combined statistical areas (the geographic units shown in table 3.6) add metropolitan and micropolitan statistical areas that have economic and social ties.

5. To determine the average size of a county's Asian American population in 1990, we used a population-weighted average.

6. See appendix F for more details on the areas and number of observations that fit into this new framework.

7. Even if the poststratification weighting scheme we use may not adequately account for our inability to reach native-born Asians in former gateways, we find very similar results using Census 2000 data and the Singer framework.

8. The relatively high proportion of Indians living in small Asian American settlements is likely due to the prevalence of Indians who own or operate motels and convenience stores in many rural areas and small cities (Varadarajan 1999).

9. We find that these factors are insignificant in a multivariate context and oper-

ate in a bivariate context as expected with respect to absentee ballots, but against theoretical expectations in the case of rules on voter registration.

10. Only five states, less than 3 percent of our sample—Arkansas, Illinois, Louisiana, Mississippi, and Ohio—are classified in the intermediate cases where between 25 percent and 75 percent of local jurisdictions in the 2006 ICMA survey are nonpartisan.

11. The figures are the same for any language coverage if we use weighted or unweighted data, and vary by less than 2 percentage points for the number of languages supported.

CHAPTER 4

1. Wilson was not excoriated for these views until 1912, when William Randolph Hearst, who opposed his presidential candidacy, brought them to light. Wilson eventually recanted his views on southern and eastern European immigrants.

2. As with Latinos, there are strong reasons to use exit poll data on Asian Americans with caution. The data are biased by reliance on sampling selective precincts, sampling based on past voting behavior and interviewing only in English with a predominance of particular ethnic, national-origin groups. In more local, multilingual, multiethnic polls in Los Angeles, San Francisco, and New York City, the results show even more decisive margins for Democratic candidates.

3. The 2008 AALDEF exit poll reports a 76 percent to 22 percent split between support for Obama and McCain, substantially greater than that found in National Election Pool results. These polls were taken mostly in precincts with relatively high concentrations of Asian American voters. To the extent that Asian Americans living in less-densely populated areas or in less concentrated areas are more likely to vote for Republicans, such exit polls likely underestimate Republican support among Asian American voters. Of course, the National Election Pool data is biased in the opposite direction—undersampling non-English speakers and Asian Americans as a whole. Furthermore, gleaning party identification from exit polls reveals only information about voters, and not about nonvoters, those not registered to vote, or noncitizens.

4. The National Election Pool (NEP), the successor to the Voter News Service, exit polls initially reported that this 27-percentage point gap had been narrowed to nine, with a 53 to 44 split in the Latino vote share between the Democratic challenger John Kerry and the Republican incumbent George W. Bush. This seemingly sizeable shift in Latino voter preferences led to criticisms of the NEP's exit poll methodology from the National Council of La Raza, the

William C. Velasquez Institute, the Southwest Voter Registration Education Project, and a number of scholars (Fears 2004; Leal et al. 2005; Suro, Fry, and Passel 2005). In response, the NEP re-weighted and revised the 2004 vote share results to show a more modest 39 percent Latino vote share for President Bush. Two primary issues were at play. First, the NEP Election Day exit polls differed quite a bit from the expectations of pre-election polls, which suggested something closer to a 60-30 split in vote share (Leal et al. 2005). Second, the sampling of precincts appeared to produce an unrepresentative sample of Latino voters, including a disproportionate number of Cuban voters in the Miami area, fewer young voters, fewer urban voters, fewer self-identified Democrats, fewer women, and fewer opponents of the war in Iraq, all correlates of a vote preference for Kerry over Bush (Suro, Fry, and Passel 2005).

5. For expository purposes, we refer interchangeably to those who opt for these noncompliant response categories—"no preference," "none," "neither," "other," "don't know," or some other mode of refusal to self-identify as Democrat, Republican, or independent—as uncommitteds and non-identifiers. We further refer to nonpartisans as the larger set of individuals who are either non-identifiers or self-identify as independents.

6. The decision to exclude this question from foreign-born respondents was intentional, because of the insurmountable difficulty of mapping home country party affiliations (or other political orientations, in the case of nondemocracies) with those relating to the two-party system in the United States.

7. Interestingly, the two-way split between Democrat and Republican among those who self-identify with one of these two major parties also changes with longevity in the United States as an immigrant. Of this group of partisans, however, the proportion of Democratic identification decreases over time. Thus although 82 percent of those partisans who have lived in the United States for four years or less self-identify as Democrats rather than Republicans (18 percent to 4 percent), only 60 percent of those in the United States for twenty-five years or longer do so (31 percent to 21 percent)

8. One final way to illustrate the relatively weak relationship between partisanship and ideology is to test the association between both items treated as 7-point scales in the conventional way, where non-identifiers as invalid responses. Even in this case, the pairwise correlation is positive, but relatively small (.26). By comparison, the correlation of partisanship and ideology in the ANES is typically around .50 or higher.

CHAPTER 5

1. The 2000 census introduced a sixth category of Native Hawaiian and Pacific Islander (NHPI), although a significant proportion of those who check off

NHPI also check off Asian in the race category (Humes, Jones, and Ramirez 2011).

2. In the 1995–1996 second wave of the Children of Immigrants Longitudinal Study (CILS), a far more modest 4.5 percent of Asian middle- and high-school age students opted to identify as *Asian American* over alternatives (Portes and Rumbaut 2001). This survey, however, does not cover the racial and ethnic identification of second-generation adults, many of whom grapple with issues of Asian American identity and pan-ethnicity in college and the workplace (Wei 1993).

3. Our discussion here necessarily glosses over some important distinctions between varieties of social identity theory. For instance, in John Turner's self-categorization variant, the group category becomes totalizing and the unique personal identity becomes reduced to one's group identification (J. C. Turner 1987); in Marilynn Brewer and Rupert Brown (1998), the processes of in-group valorization, out-group derogation, and intergroup competition are described as independent components of one's social group identity.

4. Based on our review of our survey instruments, we do not find that this Korean exception with respect to identity choices is a result of variation in survey translation. We can surmise, however, that the much higher rate of identity choice among Korean Americans is due to some combination of the cues given by survey interviewers and the distinctive attitudes of Korean respondents.

5. Another cut at this data is to further disaggregate noncitizens and naturalized respondents by length of stay in the United States. If foreign-born respondents who are recent migrants to the United States are differentiated from those who are more established, the basic pattern continues to hold. The results (not shown) differentiate the following five groups: noncitizen recent migrants; noncitizen established residents; naturalized recent migrants; naturalized established residents; native-born citizens.

6. Using a more expansive, six-category classification scheme pioneered by Audrey Singer and colleagues for immigrant destinations leaves the basic constancy in the distribution of ethnic-racial identification unchanged (Singer, Hardwick, and Brettell 2008).

CHAPTER 6

1. These findings are echoed in Louis DeSipio's (2006) analysis of a subsequent survey of Latinos.

2. Reports of organizational involvement in the Current Population Survey Volunteer Supplement typically show lower rates of participation for respondents, including Asian Americans, than the American National Election Studies (Ramakrishnan 2006).

3. This pattern remains true for most national origin groups, though for Korean and Vietnamese Americans, men are significantly more likely to be involved in secular organizations.
4. For individual national-origin groups, women tend to attend worship services more frequently than men, but the association is not statistically significant.

CHAPTER 7

1. For example, Republican Van Tran became the first Vietnamese American elected to a state legislature when he won a seat representing North Orange County in the California State Assembly in 2004. His political resume up to that point included internships and a stint on the Garden Grove City Council.
2. As we show in the next section, much of this disparity can be attributed to the comparatively low levels of religious affiliation among Chinese Americans.
3. USINPAC is a bipartisan political action committee that models itself after the highly successful American Israeli Political Action Committee and was heavily involved in winning ratification of the 2008 U.S.-India nuclear agreement.
4. Our results differ from those of Elaine Howard Ecklund and Jerry Park (2007), who present one of the most detailed studies of religion and Asian American civic involvement to date. Using the 2000 Social Capital Community Benchmark Study, they find that Buddhists and Hindus were less likely to participate in secular civic institutions than Protestants or the religiously unaffiliated. The difference in findings may be due to contrasting sampling methods—that study was limited to English and Chinese, whereas the NAAS was conducted in eight languages.

CHAPTER 8

1. Interview conducted by Janelle Wong, January 10, 2007.
2. Interview conducted by Janelle Wong, December 1, 2006.
3. Those who engage in five or more of these acts, more specifically, represent 9.6 percent of the unweighted sample of the NAAS and 15.7 percent of the weighted sample.
4. The weighted proportion is 17 percent.
5. Low propensity participants make up 10.7 percent of the unweighted NAAS sample and 15.4 percent of the weighted sample.
6. We present the results from a set of bivariate analyses, using the multiple-imputation data used in the multivariate analysis (chapter 7 and appendix D). We also analyzed national-origin differences in a multivariate analysis, and the change in Gini coefficients do not change much, except for party non-

identification and party mobilization, where the inequality grows even more from the foreign-born to the native-born population).

7. In party identification, this is driven primarily by the considerably higher levels of nonidentification among native-born Chinese. In voting, this is driven primarily by the low levels of voter participation among Vietnamese Americans. Controlling for age and socioeconomic status does not diminish the gap in national origins; indeed, it widens them. Still, the relative paucity of older adults among many of the native-born Vietnamese, Indians, and Koreans suggest the limits on relying too heavily on using cross-sectional data to project future trends.

APPENDIX A

1. Although the creation of a particular racial category (Asian American) relies on reference to physical characteristics, physical characteristics in and of themselves do not define a racial group. What does define the group is instead the social process by which particular physical features are selected for purposes of categorization and the social meanings attached to these features. In fact, it is impossible to categorize a person into a racial group based on one physical feature or even a set. In addition, racial categories, including those of Asian and Asian American, shift over time and according to social and political context.

APPENDIX D

1. Another simplification we make to our models is to refrain from using hierarchical modeling or other multilevel modeling techniques to estimate any independent relationships between contextual factors and participation. As we shall see, our models are already complicated by our use of multiple imputation techniques to fill gaps in the data on factors such as income and age, and hierarchical models add another layer of sophistication and complexity. Furthermore, given the relatively weak relationships between context and our various measures of participation, it is unlikely that we will see any increase in the importance of these contextual factors when using HLM or other similar multilevel modeling techniques.

APPENDIX E

1. The relationships between income (either as given or imputed), wealth (measured as homeownership), and participation tend to shift based on the model specification, but the general finding is that higher socioeconomic resources mean greater participation. The age effect here is nonlinear, measured as the

squared value of age, and can be interpreted as the accelerating effect of age, controlling for the linear effects of age measured in years.

2. To get some calibration on this seemingly huge predicted effect, the raw (unweighted) proportion of foreign-born Japanese in our sample who are U.S. citizens is 44 percent, versus 80 percent among foreign-born non-Japanese.

3. These predicted probabilities are calculated using the "prchange" command in Stata v10. The calculations require assuming the mean value of each of the remaining variables in the equation.

4. An alternative approach here would have been to use self-reporting from voting from a single previous election. Given the drop-off in voter participation in the primaries and caucuses and in off-year congressional elections, the most natural candidate here in the NAAS is self-reported voting in the 2004 presidential contest between George Bush and John Kerry. For the most part, when we run our analysis on this alternate dependent variable, the results remain robust with four notable exceptions that reveal some of the differences between the 2004 and 2008 presidential elections: national origin differences were much more salient in 2004; self-identified Democrats were not more likely to vote in 2004 (they are in our likely voter model); nonpartisan organizational mobilization plays a significant role in the 2004 vote (it does not in the likely voter model); perceived in-group (as Asian American) political commonality appears to drive down voter turnout in 2008, but has no effect in 2004.

APPENDIX F

1. We also translated our survey into Hmong with the goal of obtaining a statistically meaningful sample of Hmong Americans. The incidence and cooperation rates were extremely low, however, and we discontinued our efforts after completing just three interviews with Hmong respondents, only one in the Hmong language.

2. More recently, Catalist has upgraded its ability to classify Filipino names, although this population is still the most difficult to classify as Asian, given the significant overlap with Hispanic names.

3. As we shall discuss, our decision to draw samples both from ethnic enclaves as well as more dispersed areas made it difficult to uniquely identify Filipino names as distinct from Hispanic names. This is a problem common to many surveys of Filipinos. A similar limitation exists with respect to identifying uniquely Asian Muslim names.

4. Estimation of raking weights was performed using Stata's user-contributed "survwgt" routine, developed by Nicholas Winter, Economics, University of Virginia. The routine is available online http://ideas.repec.org/c/boc/bocode/s427503.html (accessed March 18, 2010).

5. Joseph Lang and Alan Agresti (1994) proposed a class of parsimonious models for maximum likelihood (ML) simultaneous estimation of marginal and joint probabilities where some expected cell frequencies are subject to linear constraints. These models are capable of handling large tables and "smoothing" zero cell counts. However, they have yet to be applied to estimation of raking weights.

6. The raking procedure can be performed on cell frequency counts as well as proportions, substituting sample row ($fi+$) and column ($f+i$) marginal totals for sample marginal proportions, and population row ($Fi+$) and column ($F+j$) marginal totals for sample marginal proportions. In this case, the resulting cell weights are equivalent to expansion factors. The Stata "survwgt" routine, in fact, rakes to marginal totals.

References

Abdelal, Rawi, Yoshiko Herrera, Alastair Iain Johnston, and Rose McDermott. 2009. *Measuring Identity: A Guide for Social Scientists.* New York: Cambridge University Press.

Abdulrahim, Raja. 2009. "Students Push UC to Expand Terms of Ethnic Identification." *Los Angeles Times,* March 31.

Abrajano, Marisa A. 2005. "Who Evaluates a Presidential Candidate by Using Non-Policy Campaign Messages?" *Political Research Quarterly* 58(1): 55–67.

Abramowitz, Alan I. 1988. "Explaining Senate Election Outcomes." *The American Political Science Review* 82(2): 385–403.

Achen, Christopher. 2002. "Toward a New Political Methodology: Microfoundations and ART." *Annual Review of Political Science* 5(1): 423–50.

Alba, Richard D., and Victor Nee. 1997. "Rethinking Assimilation Theory for a New Era of Immigration." *International Migration Review* 31(4): 826–74.

———. 2003. *Remaking the American Mainstream: Assimilation and Contemporary Immigration.* Cambridge, Mass.: Harvard University Press.

Alesina, Alberto, and Eliana La Ferrara. 2000. "Participation in Heterogeneous Communities." *The Quarterly Journal of Economics* 115(3): 847–904.

Alex-Assensoh, Yvette, and A. B. Assensoh. 2001. "Inner-City Contexts, Church Attendance, and African-American Political Participation." *The Journal of Politics* 63(3): 886–901.

Allen, James P., and Eugene Turner. 1996. "Spatial Patterns of Immigrant Assimilation." *Professional Geographer* 48(2): 140–55.

Allen, Richard, Michael Dawson, and Ronald Brown. 1989. "A Schema-Based Approach to Modeling an African-American Racial Belief System." *American Political Science Review* 83(2): 421–41.

Allswang, John M. 1977. *Bosses, Machines, and Urban Voters: An American Symbiosis.* Washington, N.Y.: Kennikat Press.

Almond, Gabriel A. 1963. *The Civic Culture; Political Attitudes and Democracy in Five Nations.* Princeton, N.J.: Princeton University Press.

327

Alvarez, R. Michael, and Lisa Garcia Bedolla. 2003. "The Foundations of Latino Voter Partisanship: Evidence from the 2000 Election." *The Journal of Politics* 65(1): 31–49.

Andersen, Kristi. 1979. *The Creation of a Democratic Majority, 1928–1936.* Chicago: University of Chicago Press.

———. 2008. "Parties, Organizations, and Political Incorporation: Immigrants in Six U.S. Cities." In *Civic Hopes and Political Realities: Immigrants, Community Organizations, and Political Engagement*, edited by Karthick Ramakrishnan and Irene Bloemraad. New York: Russell Sage Foundation.

Anderson, Christopher, and Aida Paskeviciute. 2006. "How Ethnic and Linguistic Heterogeneity Influence the Prospects for Civil Society: A Comparative Case Study of Citizenship Behavior." *Journal of Politics* 68(4): 783–802.

Aoki, Andrew, and Don T. Nakanishi. 2001. "Asian Pacific Americans and the New Minority Politics." *PS Political Science and Politics* 34(3): 605–10.

Aoki, Andrew, and Okiyoshi Takeda. 2008. *Asian American Politics.* Malden, Mass.: Polity Press.

Archdeacon, Thomas J. 1983. *Becoming American: An Ethnic History.* New York: Free Press.

Asian Pacific American Legal Center. 2008. *Asian Americans at the Ballot Box: The 2008 General Election in Los Angeles County.* Los Angeles, Calif.: Asian Pacific American Legal Center. Available at: http://www.apalc.org/pressreleases/2009/APALC_Ballot_2008_v3.pdf (accessed August 15, 2011).

Bada, Xóchitl, Jonathan Fox, and Andrew D. Selee. 2006. *Invisible No More: Mexican Migrant Civic Participation in the United States.* Washington, D.C.: Mexico Institute.

Baker, Reginald P., and David S. North. 1984. *The 1975 Refugees: Their First Five Years in America.* Washington, D.C.: New TransCentury Foundation.

Bankston III, Carl L., and Min Zhou. 1995. "Religious Participation, Ethnic Identification, and Adaptation of Vietnamese Adolescents in an Immigrant Community." *Sociological Quarterly* 36(3): 523–34.

Barone, Michael. 2001. *The New Americans: How the Melting Pot Can Work Again.* Washington, D.C.: Regnery Pub.

Barreto, Matt, Gary Segura, and Nathan Woods. 2004. "The Mobilizing Effect of Majority–Minority Districts on Latino Turnout." *American Political Science Review* 98(1): 65–75.

Bartels, Larry M. 2008. *Unequal Democracy: The Political Economy of the New Gilded Age.* New York: Russell Sage Foundation.

Beam, Christopher. 2008. "Chinese Democracy: Why Don't We Ever Hear About the Asian-American Vote?" *Slate.com.* Available at: http://www.slate.com/id/2201246 (accessed March 29, 2011).

Bean, Frank D., and Gillian Stevens. 2003. *America's Newcomers and the Dynamics of Diversity.* New York: Russell Sage Foundation.

Beck, Paul Allen, and M. Kent Jennings. 1979. "Political Periods and Political Participation." *The American Political Science Review* 73(3): 737–50.

———. 1991. "Family Traditions, Political Periods, and the Development of Partisan Orientations." *Journal of Politics* 53(3): 742–63.

Berelson, Bernard, Paul Felix Lazarsfeld, and William N. McPhee. 1954. *Voting: A Study of Opinion Formation in a Presidential Campaign*. Chicago: University of Chicago Press.

Berry, Jeffrey. 2003. "Nonprofit Groups Shouldn't Be Afraid to Lobby." *Chronicle of Philanthropy* 27(November): 33–35.

Bethlehem, Jelke G. 2002. "Weighting Non-Response Adjustments Based on Auxiliary Information." In *Survey Nonresponse*, edited by Robert M. Groves, Don A. Dillman, John L. Eltinge, and Roderick J. A. Little. New York: John Wiley and Sons.

Bhagwati, Jagdish, and Koichi Hamada. 1974. "The Brain Drain, International Integration of Markets for Professionals and Unemployment: A Theoretical Analysis." *Journal of Development Economics* 1(1): 19–42.

Bloemraad, Irene. 2006. *Becoming a Citizen: Incorporating Immigrants and Refugees in the United States and Canada*. Berkeley: University of California Press.

Bobo, Lawrence, and Franklin D. Gilliam. 1990. "Race, Sociopolitical Participation, and Black Empowerment." *American Political Science Review* 84(2): 377–93.

Bobo, Lawrence, and Vincent L. Hutchings. 1996. "Perceptions of Racial Group Competition: Extending Blumer's Theory of Group Position to a Multiracial Social Context." *American Sociological Review* 61(6): 951–72.

Bobo, Lawrence, Melvin L. Oliver, James H. Johnson Jr., and Abel Valenzuela Jr., eds. 2000. "Racial Attitudes in a Prismatic Metropolis: Mapping Identity, Stereotypes, Competition, and Views on Affirmative Action." In *Prismatic Metropolis: Inequality in Los Angeles*. New York: Russell Sage Foundation.

Borjas, George J. 1987. "Self-Selection and the Earnings of Immigrants." *American Economic Review* 77(4): 531–53.

———. 1999. *Heaven's Door: Immigration Policy and the American Economy*. Princeton, N.J.: Princeton University Press.

Bosniak, Linda. 1999. "Citizenship Denationalized." *Indiana Journal of Global Legal Studies* 7: 447–508.

Bowler, Shaun, and Todd Donovan. 2004. "Initiative Politics." In *Politics in the American States: A Comparative Analysis*, edited by Virginia Gray and Russell L. Hanson. Washington, D.C: CQ Press.

Brackman, Harold, and Steven P. Erie. 1995. "Beyond 'Politics by Other Means'?: Empowerment Strategies for Los Angeles Asian Pacific Community." In *The Bubbling Cauldron: Race, Ethnicity, and the Urban Crisis*, edited by Michael Smith and Joe R. Feagin. Minneapolis: University of Minnesota Press.

Brady, Henry, and Cynthia Kaplan. Forthcoming. *Gathering Voices: Political Mobilization and the Collapse of the Soviet Union*. New York: Cambridge University Press.

Brady, Henry, Kay Lehman Schlozman, Sidney Verba, and Laurel Elms. 2002. "Who Bowls? The (Un)changing Stratification of Participation." In *Understanding Public Opinion*, edited by Clyde Wilcox and Barbara Narrande. Washington, D.C.: CQ Press.

Branton, Regina P., and Bradford S. Jones. 2005. "Reexamining Racial Attitudes: The Conditional Relationship Between Diversity and Socioeconomic Environment." *American Journal of Political Science* 49(2): 359–72.

Brettell, Caroline B. 2005. "Voluntary Organizations, Social Capital, and the Social Incorporation of Asian Indian Immigrants in the Dallas-Fort Worth Metroplex." *Anthropological Quarterly* 78(4): 853–83.

Brewer, Marilynn. 1991. "The Social Self: On Being the Same and Different at the Same Time." *Personality and Social Psychology Bulletin* 17(5): 475–82.

Brewer, Marilynn, and Rupert Brown. 1998. "Intergroup Relations." In *Handbook of Social Psychology*, edited by Daniel Gilbert, Susan Fiske, and Gardner Lindzey. Boston: McGraw-Hill.

Brown, Susan, and Frank Bean. 2006. *Assimilation Models, Old and New: Explaining a Long-Term Process*. Migration Policy Institute. Available at: http://www.migrationinformation.com/USfocus/print.cfm?ID=442 (accessed March 29, 2011).

Brubaker, Rogers, and Frederick Cooper. 2000. "Beyond 'Identity'." *Theory and Society* 29(1): 1–47.

Burnham, Walter Dean. 1970. *Critical Elections and the Mainspring of American Politics*. 1st ed. New York: Norton.

Burns, Nancy, Kay Lehman Schlozman, and Sidney Verba. 2001. *The Private Roots of Public Action: Gender, Equality, and Political Participation*. Cambridge, Mass.: Harvard University Press.

Cain, Bruce E., Roderick D. Kiewiet, and Carole J. Uhlaner. 1991. "The Acquisition of Partisanship by Latinos and Asian Americans." *American Journal of Political Science* 35(2): 390–422.

Campbell, Angus. 1960. "Surge and Decline: A Study of Electoral Change." *Public Opinion Quarterly* 24(3): 397–418.

Campbell, Angus, Philip Converse, Warren Miller, and Donald Stokes. 1960. *The American Voter*. Chicago: The University of Chicago Press.

Carlino, Gerald A., and Edwin S. Mills. 1987. "The Determinants of County Growth." *Journal of Regional Science* 27(1): 39–54.

Carnes, Tony, and Fenggang Yang, eds. 2004. *Asian American Religions: The Making and Remaking of Borders and Boundaries*. New York: New York University Press.

Chan, Sucheng. 1991. *Asian Americans: An Interpretive History*. Boston: Twayne.

Chávez, Lydia. 1998. *The Color Bind: California's Battle to End Affirmative Action*. Berkeley: University of California Press.

Chen, Carolyn. 2008. *Getting Saved in America: Taiwanese Immigration and Religious Experience*. Princeton, N.J.: Princeton University Press.

Cheng, Lucie, and Phillip Q. Yang. 1996. "The 'Model Minority' Deconstructed."

In *Ethnic Los Angeles*, edited by Roger Waldinger and Mehdi Bozorgmehr. New York: Russell Sage Foundation.

Chiswick, Barry R. 1977. "Sons of Immigrants: Are They at an Earnings Disadvantage?" *American Economic Review* 67(1): 376–80.

Cho, Hye-na. 2008. "Towards Place-Peer Community and Civic Bandwidth: A Case Study in Community Wireless Networking." *Journal of Community Informatics* 4(1). Available at: http://ci-journal.net/index.php/ciej/article/view/428/396 (accessed June 21, 2011)

Cho, Wendy K. Tam. 1995. "Asians, a Monolithic Voting Bloc?" *Political Behavior* 17(2): 223–49.

———. 1999. "Naturalization, Socialization, Participation: Immigrants and (Non-) Voting." *Journal of Politics* 61(4): 1140–55.

———. 2001. "Latent Groups and Cross-Level Inferences." *Electoral Studies* 20(2): 243–63.

———. 2002. "Tapping Motives and Dynamics behind Campaign Contributions: Insights from the Asian American Case." *American Politics Research* 30(4): 347–83.

———. 2003. "Contagion Effects and Ethnic Contribution Networks." *American Journal of Political Science* 47(2): 368–87.

Chong, Dennis, and Reuel Rogers. 2005. "Reviving Group Consciousness." In *The Poltics of Democratic Inclusion*, edited by Christina Wolbrecht and Rodney E. Hero. Philadelphia: Temple University Press.

Chuong, Chung Hoan, and Minh Hoa Ta. 2003. "Vietnamese." In *The New Face of Asian Pacific America: Numbers, Diversity & Change in the 21st Century*, edited by Eric Yo Ping Lai and Dennis Arguelles. San Francisco: AsianWeek and UCLA Asian American Studies Center Press.

Citrin, Jack, Eric Schickler, and John Sides. 2003. "What If Everyone Voted? Simulating the Impact of Increased Turnout in Senate Elections." *American Journal of Political Science* 47(1): 75–90.

Cohen, Cathy J. 1999. *The Boundaries of Blackness: Aids and the Breakdown of Black Politics*. Chicago: University of Chicago Press.

Cohen, Cathy J., and Michael C. Dawson. 1993. "Neighborhood Poverty and African-American Politics." *American Political Science Review* 87(2): 672–85.

Coleman, James S. 1990. *Foundations of Social Theory*. Cambridge, Mass.: Belknap Press.

Coleman, John J., and Paul F. Manna. 2000. "Congressional Campaign Spending and the Quality of Democracy." *Journal of Politics* 62(3): 757–89.

Collet, Christian. 2005. "Bloc Voting, Polarization, and the Panethnic Hypothesis: The Case of Little Saigon." *The Journal of Politics* 67(3): 907–33.

———. 2008. "Minority Candidates, Alternative Media, and Multiethnic America: Deracialization or Toggling?" *Perspectives on Politics* 6(4): 707–28.

Collet, Christian, and Nadine Seldon. 2003. "Separate Ways…Worlds Apart? The

'Generation Gap' in Vietnamese America as Seen Through the Mercury News Poll." *Amerasia Journal* 29(1): 199–217.

Collier, David, and James E. Mahon. 1993. "Conceptual 'Stretching' Revisited: Adapting Categories in Comparative Analysis." *American Political Science Review* 87(4): 845–55.

Collins, Linda. 2010. "19 Religious Groups Help Build Homes in Bed-Stuy for Habitat for Humanity-NYC." *Brooklyn Eagle*, October 29.

Conway, M. Margaret. 2000. *Political Participation in the United States*, 3d ed. Washington, D.C: CQ Press.

Cornwell, Elmer., Jr. 1960. "Party Absorption of Ethnic Groups: The Case of Providence, Rhode Island." *Social Forces* 38(3): 205–10.

Costa, Dora L., and Matthew E. Kahn. 2003. "Civic Engagement and Community Heterogeneity: An Economist's Perspective." *Perspectives on Politics* 1(1): 103–11.

Cullen, Lisa Takeuchi. 2008. "Does Obama Have an Asian Problem?" *Time*, February 18.

Dahl, Robert A. 1961. *Who Governs? Democracy and Power in an American City*. New Haven, Conn.: Yale University Press.

———. 1971. *Polyarchy: Participation and Opposition*. New Haven, Conn.: Yale University Press.

Danico, Mary Yu, and Franklin Ng. 2004. *Asian American Issues*. Westport, Conn.: Greenwood Press.

Dave, Shilpa, Pawan Dhingra, Sunaina Maira, Partha Mazumdar, Lavina Dhingra Shankar, Jaideep Singh, and Rajini Srikanth. 2000. "De-Privileging Positions: Indian Americans, South Asian Americans, and the Politics of Asian American Studies." *Journal of Asian American Studies* 3(1): 67–100.

Dave, Shilpa, LeiLani Nishime, and Tasha Oren, eds. 2005. *East Main Street: Asian American Popular Culture*. New York: New York University Press.

Davidson, Chandler, and Luis Ricardo Fraga. 1988. "Slating Groups as Parties in a 'Nonpartisan' Setting." *Western Political Quarterly* 41(2): 373–90.

Dawson, Michael C. 1994. *Behind the Mule: Race and Class in African-American Politics*. Princeton, N.J.: Princeton University Press.

———. 2001. *Black Visions: The Roots of Contemporary African-American Political Ideologies*. University of Chicago Press.

DeFrancesco Soto, Victoria, and Jennifer Merolla. 2006. "Vota Por Tu Futuro: Partisan Mobilization of Latino Voters in the 2000 Presidential Election." *Political Behavior* 28(4): 285–304.

De la Cruz, Melany, and Pauline Agbayani-Siewert. 2003. "Filipinos: Swimming With and Against the Tide." In *The New Face of Asian Pacific America: Numbers, Diversity & Change in the 21st Century*, edited by Eric Yo Ping Lai and Dennis Arguelles. San Francisco: AsianWeek and UCLA Asian American Studies Center Press.

Deming, W. Edwards, and Frederick F. Stephan. 1940. "On a Least Squares Adjustment of a Sampled Frequency Table When the Expected Marginal Totals are Known." *Annals of Mathematical Statistics* 11(4): 427–44.

Dennis, Jack. 1992. "Political Independence in America: In Search of Closet Partisan." *Political Behavior* 14(3): 261–93.

DeSipio, Louis. 1996. *Counting on the Latino Vote: Latinos as a New Electorate.* Charlottesville: University Press of Virginia.

————. 2006. "Do Home-Country Political Ties Limit Latino Immigrant Pursuit of U.S. Civic Engagement and Citizenship?" In *Transforming Politics, Transforming America: The Political and Civic Incorporation of Immigrants in the United States,* edited by Taeku Lee, Karthick Ramakrishnan, and Ricardo Ramírez. Charlottesville: University of Virginia Press.

de Sousa Briggs, Xavier. 2008. "What's Happening to My Neighborhood? Lessons Learned About Civic Engagement from Case Studies of Community Development Initiatives." Master's thesis, Massachusetts Institute of Technology.

Deville, Jean-Claude, Carl-Erik Sarndal, and Olivier Sautory. 1993. "Generalized Raking Procedures in Survey Sampling." *Journal of the American Statistical Association* 88(423): 1013–20.

Dignan, Don K. 1971. "The Hindu Conspiracy in Anglo-American Relations During World War I." *Pacific Historical Review* 40(1): 57–76.

Downs, Anthony. 1957. *An Economic Theory of Democracy.* New York: Harper.

Easterly, William, and Ross Levine. 1997. "Africa's Growth Tragedy: Policies and Ethnic Divisions." *Quarterly Journal of Economics* 112(4): 1203–250.

Easton, David. 1965. *A Systems Analysis of Political Life.* New York: Wiley.

Ebaugh, Helen Rose Fuchs, and Janet Saltzman Chafetz, eds. 2000. *Religion and the New Immigrants: Continuities and Adaptations in Immigrant Congregations.* Walnut Creek, Calif.: AltaMira Press.

Ecklund, Elaine Howard. 2006. *Korean American Evangelicals: New Models for Civic Life.* Oxford: Oxford University Press.

Ecklund, Elaine Howard, and Jerry Z. Park. 2005. "Asian American community participation and religion: Civic 'Model Minorities?'" *Journal of Asian American Studies* 8(1): 1–21.

Ecklund, Elaine Howard, and Christopher P. Scheitle. 2007. "Religion among Academic Scientists: Distinctions, Disciplines, and Demographics." *Social Problems* 54(2): 289–307.

Egerton, Muriel. 2002. "Higher Education and Civic Engagement." *British Journal of Sociology* 53(4): 603–20.

Erie, Steven P. 1988. *Rainbow's End: Irish-Americans and the Dilemmas of Urban Machine Politics, 1840–1985.* Berkeley: University of California Press.

Erikson, Robert, Michael MacKuen, and James Stimson. 2002. *The Macro Polity.* New York: Cambridge University Press.

Erikson, Robert, Gerald Wright, and John McIver. 1993. *Statehouse Democracy: Pub-*

lic Opinion and Policy in the American States. New York: Cambridge University Press.

Espiritu, Yen Le. 1993. *Asian American Panethnicity: Bridging Institutions and Identities.* Philadelphia: Temple University Press.

Espiritu, Yen Le, and Michael Omi. 2000. "'Who Are You Calling Asian?': Shifting Identity Claims, Racial Classification, and the Census." In *The State of Asian Pacific America: Transforming Race Relations,* edited by Paul M. Ong. Los Angeles: LEAP Asian Pacific American Public Policy Institute and UCLA Asian American Studies Center.

Evans, Peter. 1997. *State-Society Synergy: Government and Social Capital in Development* Location: Global, Area, and International Archive. Available at: http://escholarship.org/uc/item/8mp05335 (accessed June 21, 2011).

Eveland, William P., and Dietram A. Scheufele. 2000. "Connecting News Media Use with Gaps in Knowledge and Participation." *Political Communication* 17(3): 215–37.

Fearon, James D. 1999. "What Is Identity (as We Now Use the Word)?" Unpublished manuscript. Stanford University.

Fears, Darry. 2004. "Pollsters Debate Hispanics' Presidential Voting." *Washington Post,* November 26, 2004: A4.

Feather, Peter, and W. Douglass Shaw. 1999. "Estimating the Cost of Leisure Time for Recreation Demand Models." *Journal of Environmental Economics and Management* 38(1): 49–65.

Felix, Adrian, Carmen Gonzalez, and Ricardo Ramirez. 2008. "Political Protest, Ethnic Media, and Latino Naturalization." *American Behavioral Scientist* 52(4): 618–34.

Feng, Kathay. 2005. "Statement of Kathay Feng to the National Commission on the Voting Rights Act." Hearing of the National Commission on the Voting Rights Act, Western Regional Hearing (September 27).

Fiorina, Morris P. 1981. *Retrospective Voting in American National Elections.* New Haven, Conn.: Yale University Press.

Franklin, Charles H., and John E. Jackson. 1983. "The Dynamics of Party Identification." *American Political Science Review* 77(4): 957–73.

Frasure, Lorrie, Matt Baretto, Ange-Marie Hancock, Sylvia Manzano, S. Karthick Ramakrishnan, Ricardo Ramirez, Gabriel Sanchez, and Janelle S. Wong. 2009. *Collaborative Mutiracial Post-Election Study.* Unpublished data set. Available at: http://cmpstudy.com (accessed March 29, 2011).

Frasure, Lorrie A., and Michael Jones-Correa. 2010. "The Logic of Institutional Interdependency: The Case of Day Laborer Policy in Suburbia." *Urban Affairs Review* 45(4): 451–82.

Frey, Bruno S. 1971. "Why Do High Income People Participate More in Politics?" *Public Choice* 11(1): 101–5.

Galston, William A. 2007. "Civic Knowledge, Civic Education, and Civic Engagement: A Summary of Recent Research." *International Journal of Public Administration* 30(6): 623–42.

Gamm, Gerald H. 1989. *The Making of New Deal Democrats: Voting Behavior and Realignment in Boston, 1920–1940*. Chicago: University of Chicago Press.

Gans, Herbert J. 1992. "Second-Generation Decline: Scenarios for the Economic and Ethnic Futures of the Post-1965 American Immigrants." *Ethnic and Racial Studies* 15(2): 173–92.

García Bedolla, Lisa. 2005. *Fluid Borders: Latino Power, Identity, and Politics in Los Angeles*. Berkeley: University of California Press.

García Bedolla, Lisa, and Melissa R. Michelson. 2009. "What Do Voters Need to Know?: Testing the Role of Cognitive Information in Asian American Voter Mobilization." *American Politics Research* 37(2): 254–74.

Gay, Claudine. 2001. "The Effect of Black Congressional Representation on Political Participation." *American Political Science Review* 95(3): 589–602.

———. 2004. "Putting Race in Context: Identifying the Environmental Determinants of Black Racial Attitudes." *American Political Science Review* 98(4): 547–62.

———. 2006a. "Diversity in Democracy: Minority Representation in the United States and Freedom Is Not Enough: Black Voters, Black Candidates, and American Presidential Politics." *Perspectives on Politics* 4(2): 398–401.

———. 2006b. "Seeing Difference: The Effect of Economic Disparity on Black Attitudes Toward Latinos." *American Journal of Political Science* 50(4): 982–97.

Geer, John Gray. 2006. *In Defense of Negativity: Attack Ads in Presidential Campaigns*. Chicago: University of Chicago Press.

Gelman, Andrew, 2007. "Struggles with Survey Weighting and Regression Modeling." *Statistical Science* 22(2): 153–64.

———. 2008. *Red State, Blue State, Rich State, Poor State: Why Americans Vote the Way They Do*. Princeton, N.J.: Princeton University Press.

Gelman, Andrew, and John B. Carlin. 2002. "Post-Stratification and Weighting Adjustments." In *Survey Nonresponse*. edited by Robert M. Groves, Don A. Dillman, John L,. Eltinge, and Roderick J. A. Little. New York: John Wiley and Sons.

Gerber, Alan S., and Donald P. Green. 1998. "Rational Learning and Partisan Attitudes." *American Journal of Political Science* 42(3): 794–818.

———. 2000. "The Effects of Canvassing, Telephone Calls, and Direct Mail on Voter Turnout: A Field Experiment." *American Political Science Review* 94(3): 653–63.

Geron, Kim, and James S. Lai. 2002. "Beyond Symbolic Representation: A Comparison of the Electoral Pathways and Policy Priorities of Asian American and Latino Elected Officials." *Asian Law Journal* 9: 41–81.

Gerstle, Gary, and John H. Mollenkopf. 2001. *E Pluribus Unum? Contemporary and Historical Perspectives on Immigrant Political Incorporation*. New York: Russell Sage Foundation.

Ghosh, Palash. 2010. "Asian-Americans Endure Well During Recession, but

'Model Minority' Theory Has Some Holes in It." *International Business Times.* Available at: http://www.ibtimes.com/articles/39534/20100729/asian-americans-unemployment-model-minority.htm (accessed June 21, 2011).

Gibson, Campbell, and Kay Jung. 2006. *Historical Census Statistics on the Foreign Born Population of the United States, 1850 to 2000.* Population Division Working Paper No. 81. Washington: U.S. Census Bureau.

Gibson, Margaret. 1988. *Accommodation Without Assimilation: Sikh Immigrants in an American High School.* Ithaca, N.Y.: Cornell University Press.

Gimpel, James G., Frances E. Lee, and Joshua Kaminski. 2006. "The Political Geography of Campaign Contributions in American Politics." *Journal of Politics* 68(03): 626–39.

Gimpel, James G., Daron Shaw, and Wendy K. Tam Cho. 2006. "Message and Mobilization among Asian Americans: A 2004 Texas Field Experiment." Unpublished manuscript. Institution for Social and Policy Studies, Yale University.

Glazer, Nathan, and Daniel P. Moynihan. 1963. *Beyond the Melting Pot: The Negroes, Puerto Ricans, Jews, Italians, and Irish of New York City.* Cambridge, Mass.: M.I.T. Press.

Goldstein, Kenneth M. 1999. *Interest Groups, Lobbying, and Participation in America.* Cambridge: Cambridge University Press.

Gordon, Milton Myron. 1964. *Assimilation in American Life: The Role of Race, Religion, and National Origins.* New York: Oxford University Press.

Gosnell, Harold Foote. 1927. *Getting Out the Vote: An Experiment in the Stimulation of Voting.* Chicago: University of Chicago Press.

———. 1935. *Negro Politicians.* Chicago: University of Chicago Press.

———. 1937. *Machine Politics: Chicago Model.* The University of Chicago Press.

Green, Donald P. 1988. "On the Dimensionality of Public Sentiment Toward Partisan and Ideological Groups." *American Journal of Political Science* 32(3): 758–80.

Green, Donald P., and Alan S. Gerber. 2008. *Get Out the Vote: How to Increase Voter Turnout.* Washington, D.C.: Brookings Institution Press.

Green, Donald P., Bradley Palmquist, and Eric Schickler. 2002. *Partisan Hearts and Minds: Political Parties and the Social Identities of Voters.* New Haven, Conn.: Yale University Press.

Green, Donald P., Dara Strolovich, and Janelle Wong. 1998. "Defended Neighborhoods, Integration, and Racially Motivated Crime." *American Journal of Sociology* 104(2): 372–402.

Greenstein, Fred I. 1970. "A Note on the Ambiguity of 'Political Socialization': Definitions, Criticisms, and Strategies of Inquiry." *Journal of Politics* 32(4): 969–78.

Grieco, Elizabeth M. 2010. *Race and Hispanic Origin of the Foreign-Born Population in the United States: 2007.* Washington: U.S. Census Bureau.

Griffin, John D. 2006. "Electoral Competition and Democratic Responsiveness: A Defense of the Marginality Hypothesis." *Journal of Politics* 68(4): 911–21.

Griffin, John D., and Brian Newman. 2005. "Are Voters Better Represented?" *Journal of Politics* 67(4): 1206–27.

———. 2008. *Minority Report: Evaluating Political Equality in America*. Chicago: University of Chicago Press.

Guendelman, Sylvia, Jeffrey B. Gould, Mark Hudes, and Brenda Eskenazi. 1990. "Generational Differences in Perinatal Health Among the Mexican American Population: Findings from Hhanes 1982–84." *American Journal of Public Health* 80(supplement): 61–65.

Hacker, Jacob S. 2006. *Off Center: The Republican Revolution and the Erosion of American Democracy*. New Haven, Conn.: Yale University Press.

Hajnal, Zoltan L. 2001. "White Residents, Black Incumbents, and a Declining Racial Divide." *American Political Science Review* 95(3): 603–17.

Hajnal, Zoltan L., Elisabeth R. Gerber, and Hugh Louch. 2002. "Minorities and Direct Legislation: Evidence from California Ballot Proposition Elections." *Journal of Politics* 64(1): 154–77.

Hajnal, Zoltan L., and Taeku Lee. 2006. "Out of Line: Immigration and Party Identification among Latinos and Asian Americans." In *Transforming Politics, Transforming America: The Political and Civic Incorporation of Immigrants in the United States*, edited by Taeku Lee, Karthick Ramakrishnan, and Ricardo Ramirez. Charlottesville: University of Virginia Press.

———. 2011. *Why Americans Don't Join the Party: Race, Immigration, and the Failure (of Political Parties) to Engage the Electorate*. Princeton, N.J.: Princeton University Press.

Hajnal, Zoltan L., and Jessica Trounstine. 2005. "Where Turnout Matters: The Consequences of Uneven Turnout in City Politics." *Journal of Politics* 67(2): 515–35.

Han, Jean. 2008. "The Value of Asian Voters." *AsianWeek*, March 1.

Handlin, Oscar. 1951. *The Uprooted: The Epic Story of the Great Migrations That Made the American People*. Boston: Little, Brown.

Haney-López, Ian. 2006. *White by Law: The Legal Construction of Race*, 10th ed. New York: New York University Press.

Hanson, H. Gordon. 2005. "Market Potential, Increasing Returns and Geographic Concentration." *Journal of International Economics* 67(1): 1–24.

Harris, Fredrick C. 1994. "Something Within: Religion as a Mobilizer of African-American Political Activism." *Journal of Politics* 56(1): 42–68.

———. 1999. *Something Within: Religion in African-American Political Activism*. New York: Oxford University Press.

Hayduk, Ronald. 2006. *Democracy for All: Restoring Immigrant Voting Rights in the United States*. New York: Routledge.

Herberg, Will. 1960. *Protestant, Catholic, Jew: An Essay on American Religious Sociology*, revised ed. Garden City, N.J.: Anchor Books.

Hero, Rodney. 1998. *Faces of Inequality: Social Diversity in American Politics*. New York: Oxford University Press.

———. 2007. *Racial Diversity and Social Capital: Equality and Community in America.* New York: Cambridge University Press.

Hershey, Marjorie Randon. 2009. "What We Know About Voter-ID Laws, Registration, and Turnout." *PS: Political Science & Politics* 42(1): 87–91.

Hong, Joann, and Pyong Gap Min. 1999. "Ethnic Attachment Among Second Generation Korean Adolescents." *Amerasia Journal* 25(1): 165–78.

Horowitz, Donald L. 1985. *Ethnic Groups in Conflict.* Berkeley: University of California Press.

Horton, John, and Jose Calderon. 1995. *The Politics of Diversity: Immigration, Resistance, and Change in Monterey Park, California.* Philadelphia: Temple University Press.

Hoynes, Hilary Williamson. 2000. "Local Labor Markets and Welfare Spells: Do Demand Conditions Matter?" *Review of Economics and Statistics* 82(3): 351–68.

Hsu, Madeline Yuan-yin. 2000. *Dreaming of Gold, Dreaming of Home: Transnationalism and Migration Between the United States and South China, 1882–1943.* Palo Alto, Calif.: Stanford University Press.

Huang, Carol. 2007. "In Some U.S. Cities, a Revived Push to Let Immigrants Vote." *The Christian Science Monitor,* June 18: 3.

Huckfeldt, Robert. 1979. "Political Participation and the Neighborhood Social Context." *American Journal of Political Science* 23(3): 579–92.

———. 1986. *Politics in Context: Assimilation and Conflict in Urban Neighborhoods.* New York: Agathon.

Huckfeldt, Robert, and John D. Sprague. 1987. "Networks in Context: The Social Flow of Political Information." *American Political Science Review* 81(4): 1197–216.

———. 1992. "Political Parties and Electoral Mobilization: Political Structure, Social Structure, and the Party Canvass." *American Political Science Review* 86(1): 70–86.

———. 1995. *Citizens, Politics, and Social Communication: Information and Influence in an Election Campaign.* New York: Cambridge University Press.

Huddy, Leonie. 2001. "From Social to Political Identity: A Critical Examination of Social Identity Theory." *Political Psychology* 22(1): 127–56.

Humes, Karen R., Nicholas A. Jones, and Roberto R. Ramirez. 2011. "Overview of Race and Hispanic Origin: 2010." Washington: U.S. Census Bureau.

Huntington, Samuel P. 1968. *Political Order in Changing Societies.* New Haven, Conn.: Yale University Press.

Hurh, Won Moo, and Kwang Chung Kim. 1990. "Religious Participation of Korean Immigrants in the United States." *Journal for the Scientific Study of Religion* 29(1): 19–34.

Hyman, Herbert H. 1959. *Political Socialization: A Study in the Psychology of Political Behavior.* Glencoe: Free Press.

Ignatiev, Noel. 1995. *How the Irish Became White*. New York. Routledge.

International City/County Management Association. 2006. *Municipal Form of Government Survey, 2006*. Washington, D.C.: International City/County Management Association.

Iwamura, Jane Naomi. 2003. "Envisioning Asian and Pacific American Religions." In *Revealing the sacred in Asian and Pacific America*, edited by Jane Naomi Iwamura and Paul R. Spickard. New York: Routledge.

Iwamura, Jane Naomi, and Paul R. Spickard, eds. 2003. *Revealing the Sacred in Asian and Pacific America*. New York: Routledge.

Jacobs, Lawrence R., and Theda Skocpol. 2005. *Inequality and American Democracy: What We Know and What We Need to Learn*. New York: Russell Sage Foundation.

Jacobson, Matthew Frye. 1998. *Whiteness of a Different Color: European Immigrants and the Alchemy of Race*. Cambridge, Mass.: Harvard University Press.

Japanese American Citizens League. 2010. "JACL Praises Ruling Overturning California's Proposition 8." Press release (August 5).

Jennings, M. Kent, and Richard G. Niemi. 1968. "The Transmission of Political Values from Parent to Child." *American Political Science Review* 62(1): 169–83.

———. 1981. *Generations and Politics: A Panel Study of Young Adults and Their Parents*. Princeton, N.J.: Princeton University Press.

———. 1991. "Issues and Inheritance in the Formation of Party Identification." *American Journal of Political Science* 35(4): 970–88.

Jennings, M. Kent, Laura Stoker, and Jake Bowers. 2009. "Politics Across Generations: Family Transmission Reexamined." *Journal of Politics* 71(3): 782–99.

Jiménez, Tomás R. 2010. *Replenished Ethnicity: Mexican Americans, Immigration, and Identity*. Berkeley: University of California Press.

Jones-Correa, Michael. 1998. *Between Two Nations: The Political Predicament of Latinos in New York City*. Ithaca, N.Y.: Cornell University Press.

———. 2001. "Under Two Flags: Dual Nationality in Latin America and Its Consequences for the United States." *International Migration Review* 35(4): 997–1029.

———. 2005. "Language Provisions Under the Voting Rights Act: How Effective Are They?" *Social Science Quarterly* 86(3): 549–64.

———. 2008. "Race to the Top? The Politics of Immigrant Education in Suburbia." In *New Faces in New Places: The Changing Geography of American Immigration*, edited by Douglas S. Massey. New York: Russell Sage Foundation.

Jones-Correa, Michael A., and David L. Leal. 2001. "Political Participation: Does Religion Matter?" *Political Research Quarterly* 54(4): 751–70.

Junn, Jane. 1999. "Participation in Liberal Democracy: The Political Assimilation of Immigrants and Ethnic Minorities in the United States." *American Behavioral Scientist* 42(9): 1417–38.

———. 2008. "From Coolie to Model Minority: U.S. Immigration Policy and the Construction of Racial Identity." *DuBois Review* 4(2): 355–73.

Junn, Jane, and Natalie Masuoka. 2008. "Asian American Identity: Shared Racial Status and Political Context." *Perspectives on Politics* 6(04): 729–40.

Kahn, Joan R. 1994. "Immigrant and Native Fertility During the 1980s: Adaptation and Expectations for the Future." *International Migration Review* 28(3): 501–19.

Kalton, Graham. 1983. *Introduction to Survey Sampling*. Beverly Hills, Calif.: Sage Publications.

Kao, Grace, and Jennifer Thompson. 2003. "Racial and Ethnic Stratification in Educational Achievement and Attainment." *Annual Review of Sociology* 29: 417–42.

Karp, Jeffrey A., and Susan A. Banducci. 2000. "Going Postal: How All-Mail Elections Influence Turnout." *Political Behavior* 22(3): 223–39.

Kasinitz, Philip, John H. Mollenkopf, Mary C. Waters, and Jennifer Holdaway. 2008. *Inheriting the City: The Children of Immigrants Come of Age*. New York: Russell Sage Foundation.

Katz, Elihu, and Paul Lazarsfeld. 1955. *Personal Influence: The Part Played by People in the Flow of Mass Communications*. New York: Free Press.

Keith, Bruce E. 1992. *The Myth of the Independent Voter*. Berkeley: University of California Press.

Kennedy, Edward M. 1966. "The Immigration Act of 1965." *Annals of the American Academy of Political and Social Science* 367(1): 137–49.

Kernell, Georgia. 2009. "Giving Order to Districts: Estimating Voter Distributions with National Election Returns." *Political Analysis* 17(3): 215–35.

Key, V. O., Jr. 1949. *Southern Politics in State and Nation*. New York: Vintage Books.

Khadria, Binod. 1999. *The Migration of Knowledge Workers: Second-Generation Effects of India's Brain Drain*. New Delhi: Sage Publications.

Kibria, Nazli. 1997. "The Construction of 'Asian American': Reflections on Intermarriage and Ethnic Identity Among Second-Generation Chinese and Korean Americans." *Ethnic and Racial Studies* 20(3): 523–44.

———. 1998. "The Racial Gap: South Asian American Racial Identity and the Asian American Movement." In *A Part, Yet Apart: South Asians in Asian America, Asian American History and Culture*, edited by Lavina Dhingra Shankar and Rajini Srikanth. Philadelphia: Temple University Press.

———. 2000. "Race, Ethnic Options, and Ethnic Binds: Identity Negotiations of Second-Generation Chinese and Korean Americans." *Sociological Perspectives* 43(1): 77–95.

———. 2002. *Becoming Asian American: Second-Generation Chinese and Korean American Identities*. Baltimore, Md.: Johns Hopkins University Press.

Kim, Andrew E. 2000. "Korean Religious Culture and Its Affinity to Christianity: The Rise of Protestant Christianity in South Korea." *Sociology of Religion* 61(2): 117–33.

Kim, Claire Jean. 1999. "The Racial Triangulation of Asian Americans." *Politics and Society* 27(1): 105–38.

Kim, Ilsoo. 1987. "The Nature and Destiny of Korean Churches in the United

States." In *Koreans in North Americas: New Perspectives*, edited by Seong Hyong Lee and Tae-Hwan Kwak. Seoul, Korea: Kyungnam University Press.

Kim, Marlene, and Don Mar. 2007. "The Economic Status of Asian Americans." In *Race and Economic Opportunity in the 21st Century*. London: Routledge.

Kim, Nadia Y. 2008. *Imperial Citizens: Koreans and Race from Seoul to LA*. Palo Alto, Calif: Stanford University Press.

Kim, Thomas P. 2007. *The Racial Logic of Politics: Asian Americans and Party Competition*. Philadelphia: Temple University Press.

Kinder, Donald R., and Cindy D. Kam. 2009. *Us Against Them: Ethnocentric Foundations of American Opinion*. Chicago: University of Chicago Press.

Kinder, Donald R, and Lynn M. Sanders. 1985. "Public Opinion and Political Action." In *The Handbook of Social Psychology*, edited by Gardner Lindzey and Elliot Aronson. New York: Random House.

Kitano, Harry H. L., and Roger Daniels. 1995. *Asian Americans: Emerging Minorities*, 2d ed. Englewood Cliffs, N.J.: Prentice Hall.

Ko, Nalea J. 2010. "JAs Stand Against Arizona's Immigration Law." *Pacific Citizen*, July 16.

Kousser, Thad, and Megan Mullin. 2007. "Does Voting by Mail Increase Participation? Using Matching to Analyze a Natural Experiment." *Political Analysis* 15(4): 428–45.

Kurien, Prema. 2001. "Religion, Ethnicity and Politics: Hindu and Muslim Indian Immigrants in the United States." *Ethnic and Racial Studies* 24(2): 263–93.

Kwon, Victoria Hyonchu, Helen Rose Ebaugh, and Jacqueline Hagan. 1997. "The Structure and Functions of Cell Group Ministry in a Korean Christian Church." *Journal for the Scientific Study of Religion* 36(2): 247–56.

Kwong, Peter. 1996. *The New Chinatown*, rev. ed. New York: Hill and Wang.

Kymlicka, Will, and Wayne Norman. 1994. "Return of the Citizen: A Survey of Recent Work on Citizenship Theory." *Ethics* 104(2): 352–81.

Lai, James, and Don T. Nakanishi. 2007. *National Asian Pacific American Political Almanac, 2007–2008*. 13th ed. Los Angeles: UCLA Asian American Studies Center Press.

Laitin, David D. 1998. *Identity in Formation: The Russian-Speaking Populations in the Near Abroad*. Ithaca, N.Y.: Cornell University Press.

Lang, Joseph B., and Alan Agresti. 1994. "Simultaneously Modeling Joint and Marginal Distributions of Multivariate Categorical Responses." *Journal of the American Statistical Association* 89(426): 625–32.

Lazarsfeld, Paul Felix, Bernard Berelson, and Hazel Gaudet. 1948. *The People's Choice; How the Voter Makes up His Mind in a Presidential Campaign*, 2d ed. New York: Columbia University Press.

Leal, David, Matt Barreto, Jongh Lee, and Rodolfo O. De la Garza. 2005. "The Latino Vote in the 2004 Election." *PS: Political Science and Politics* 38(1): 41–49.

Lee, Eugene, with Tanzila Ahmed. 2009. *Getting Out the Asian American Vote: Achiev-*

ing Double-Digit Increases During the 2006 and 2008 Elections. Asian Pacific American Legal Center and Orange County Asian and Pacific Islander Community Alliance. Press release. Available at: http://www.apalc.org/pressreleases/2009/APALC_OCAPICA_VoMo_FINAL.pdf (accessed March 29, 2011).

Lee, Jennifer, and Frank D. Bean. 2004. "America's Changing Color Lines: Immigration, Race/Ethnicity, and Multiracial Identification." *Annual Review of Sociology* 30: 221–42.

Lee, Jennifer, and Min Zhou, eds. 2004. *Asian American Youth: Culture, Identity, and Ethnicity.* New York: Routledge.

Lee, Joann H. 2006. "Inside the Immigration Debate: A Korean Perspective." *New America Media.* Available at: http://news.newamericamedia.org/news/view_article.html?article_id=a0bb3c2bff3cd2a2fa2fabed4aa156e5 (accessed June 21, 2011).

Lee, Stacey J. 2009. *Unraveling the Model-Minority Stereotype: Voices of High and Low Achieving Asian American Students.* New York: Teachers College Press.

Lee, Stacey J., and Kevin K. Kumashiro. 2005. *Asian Americans and Pacific Islanders in Education: Beyond the "Model Minority" Stereotype.* Washington, D.C.: National Education Association.

Lee, Taeku. 2000. "The Backdoor and the Backlash: Campaign Finance and the Politicization of Chinese Americans." *Asian American Policy Review* 9: 30–55.

———. 2002. *Mobilizing Public Opinion: Black Insurgency and Racial Attitudes in the Civil Rights Era.* Chicago: University of Chicago Press.

Lee, Taeku, S. Karthick Ramakrishnan, and Ricardo Ramírez. 2006. *Transforming Politics, Transforming America: The Political and Civic Incorporation of Immigrants in the United States.* Charlottesville: University of Virginia Press.

Leighley, Jan E., and Jonathan Nagler. 1992. "Socioeconomic Class Bias in Turnout, 1964–1988: The Voters Remain the Same." *American Politics Research* 86(3): 725–36.

Leighley, Jan E., and Arnold Vedlitz. 1999. "Race, Ethnicity, and Political Participation: Competing Models and Contrasting Explanations." *The Journal of Politics* 61(4): 1092–114.

Levitt, Peggy, and Mary C. Waters. 2002. *The Changing Face of Home: The Transnational Lives of the Second Generation.* New York: Russell Sage Foundation.

Lewis, M. Paul. 2006. *Ethnologue: Languages of the World,* 16th ed. Dallas: SIL International.

Lewis, Paul G., and S. Karthick Ramakrishnan. 2007. "Police Practices in Immigrant-Destination Cities: Political Control or Bureaucratic Professionalism?" *Urban Affairs Review* 42(6): 874–900.

Lien, Pei-Te. 1994. "Ethnicity and Political Participation: A Comparison Between Asian and Mexican Americans." *Political Behavior* 16(2): 237–64.

———. 1997. *The Political Participation of Asian Americans: Voting Behavior in Southern California.* New York: Routledge.

———. 2001. *The Making of Asian America Through Political Participation.* Philadelphia: Temple University Press.

———. 2004a. "Asian Americans and Voting Participation: Comparing Racial and Ethnic Differences in Recent U.S. Elections." *International Migration Review* 38(2): 493–517.

———. 2004b. "Behind the Numbers: Talking Politics with Foreign-Born Chinese Americans." *International Migration* 42(2): 87–112.

Lien, Pei-Te, and Tony Carnes. 2004. "The Religious Demography of Asian American Boundary Crossing." In *Asian American Religions: The Making and Remaking of Borders and Boundaries,* edited by Tony Carnes and Fenggang Yang. New York: New York University Press.

Lien, Pei-Te, M. Margaret Conway, and Janelle S. Wong. 2003. "The Contours and Sources of Ethnic Identity Choices Among Asian Americans." *Social Science Quarterly* 84(2): 461–81.

———. 2004. *The Politics of Asian Americans: Diversity and Community.* New York: Routledge.

Lien, Pei-Te, Christian Collet, Janelle Wong, and Karthick Ramakrishnan. 2001. "Asian Pacific American Public Opinion and Political Participation." *P.S.: Political Science & Politics* 34(3): 625–30.

Lijphart, Arend d'Angremond. 1968. *The Politics of Accommodation: Pluralism and Democracy in the Netherlands.* Berkeley: University of California Press.

Lin, Ann Chih. 2010. "Group Inclusion or Group Rights? Ethnic Advocacy Groups and the Political Incorporation of Immigrants." In *Framing Equality: Inclusion, Exclusion, and American Political Institutions,* edited by Kerry L. Haynie and Daniel J. Tichenor (Manuscript under review).

Lipset, Seymour Martin, Paul Lazarsfeld, Allan Barton, and Juan Linz. 1954. "The Psychology of Voting: An Analysis of Political Behavior." In *Handbook of Social Psychology,* edited by Gardner Lindzey. Cambridge, Mass.: Addison-Wesley.

Little, Roderick J. A., and Mei-Miau Wu. 1991. "Models for Contingency Tables With Known Margins When Target and Sampled Populations Differ." *Journal of the American Statistical Association* 86(413): 87–95.

Lohr, Sharon, 1999. *Sampling: Design and Analysis.* Pacific Grove, Calif.: Duxbury Press.

Lopez, David, and Yen Le Espiritu. 1990. "Panethnicity in the United States: A Theoretical Framework." *Ethnic and Racial Studies* 13(2): 198–224.

Lopez, Mark Hugo, Peter Levine, Deborah Both, Abby Kiesa, Emily Kirby, and Karlo Marcelo. 2006. *The 2006 Civic and Political Health of the Nation: A Detailed Look at How Youth Participate in Politics and Communities.* College Park, Md.: CIRCLE.

Lowe, Lisa. 1996. *Immigrant Acts: On Asian American Cultural Politics.* Durham, N.C.: Duke University Press.

Lublin, David. 1997. *The Paradox of Representation: Racial Gerrymandering and Minority Interests in Congress*. Princeton, N.J.: Princeton University Press.

Macedo, Stephen, ed. 2005. *Democracy at Risk: How Political Choices Undermine Citizen Participation, and What We Can Do About It*. Washington, D.C.: Brookings Institution Press.

MacKuen, Michael, and Courtney Brown. 1987. "Political Context and Attitude Change." *American Political Science Review* 81(2): 471–90.

Magpantay, Glenn D., and Nancy W. Yu. 2005. "Asian Americans and Reauthorization of the Voting Rights Act." *National Black Law Journal* 19: 1–31.

Maier, Charles, ed. 1987. *Changing Boundaries of the Political: Essays on the Evolving Balance Between State and Society, Public and Private in Europe*. Cambridge: Cambridge University Press.

Marrow, Helen B. 2009. "Immigrant Bureaucratic Incorporation: The Dual Roles of Professional Missions and Government Policies." *American Sociological Review* 74(5): 756–76.

Massey, Douglas S., ed. 2008. *New Faces in New Places: The Changing Geography of American Immigration*. New York: Russell Sage Foundation.

Massey, Douglas S., and Nancy A. Denton. 1992. "Racial Identity and the Spatial Assimilation of Mexicans in the United States." *Social Science Research* 21(3): 235–60.

Mayer, Adalbert, and Steven L. Puller. 2008. "The Old Boy (and Girl) Network: Social Network Formation on University Campuses." *Journal of Public Economics* 92(1–2): 329–47.

Mayhew, David R. 1986. *Placing Parties in American Politics: Organization, Electoral Settings, and Government Activity in the Twentieth Century*. Princeton, N.J.: Princeton University Press.

McCarty, Nolan M. 2006. *Polarized America: The Dance of Ideology and Unequal Riches*. Cambridge, Mass.: MIT Press.

McGowan, Miranda Oshige, and James Lindgren. 2006. "Testing the Model Minority Myth." *Northwestern University Law Review* 100: 331–78.

Meyer, David S. 2007. *The Politics of Protest: Social Movements in America*. New York: Oxford University Press.

Miller, Warren E., and J. Merrill Shanks. 1996. *The New American Voter*. Cambridge, Mass.: Harvard University Press.

Miller, Arthur H., and Martin P. Wattenberg. 1983. "Measuring Party Identification: Independent or No Partisan Preference?." *American Journal of Political Science* 27(1): 106–21.

Miller, Arthur H., Patricia Gurin, Gerald Gurin, and Oksana Malanchuk. 1981. "Group Consciousness and Political Participation." *American Journal of Political Science* 25(3): 494–511.

Miller, Donald E., Jon Miller, and Grace R. Dyrness. 2001. *Immigrant Religion in the City of Angels*. Los Angeles: Center for Religion and Civic Culture, University of Southern California.

Min, Pyong Gap. 1992. "The Structure and Social Functions of Korean Immigrant Churches in the United States." *International Migration Review* 26(4): 1370–94.

———. 1995. "Korean Americans." In *Asian Americans: Contemporary Trends and Issues*, edited by Pyong Gap Min. Thousand Oaks, Calif.: Sage Publications.

———, ed. 2005a. *Asian Americans: Contemporary Trends and Issues*, 2d ed. Thousand Oaks, Calif.: Pine Forge Press.

———. 2005b. "Religion and the Maintenance of Ethnicity among Immigrants: A Comparison of Indian Hindus and Korean Protestants." In *Immigrant Faiths: Transforming Religious Life in America*, edited by Karen I. Leonard, Alex Stepick, Manuel A. Vasquez, and Jennifer Holdaway. Lanham, Md.: AltaMira Press.

Min, Pyong Gap, and Rose Kim. 1999. *Struggle for Ethnic Identity*. Lanham, Md.: AltaMira Press.

Minnesota Population Center. 2011. "IPUMS USA: Enumerator Instructions." IPUMS USA. Available at: http://usa.ipums.org/usa/voliii/tEnumInstr.shtml (accessed June 2, 2011).

Mishra, Sangay K. 2009. "Political Incorporation and Transnationalism: A Study of South Asian Immigrants in the United States." Ph.D. diss., University of Southern California.

Mollenkopf, John H. 1992. *A Phoenix in the Ashes: The Rise and Fall of the Koch Coalition in New York City Politics*. Princeton, N.J.: Princeton University Press.

Mollenkopf, John H., David Olson, and Timothy Ross. 2001. "Immigrant Political Participation in New York and Los Angeles." In *Governing American Cities: Interethnic Coalitions, Competition, and Conflict*, edited by Michael Jones-Correa. New York: Russell Sage Foundation.

Morawska, Ewa. 2001. "Immigrants, Transnationalism, and Ethnicization: A Comparison of This Great Wave and the Last." In *E pluribus Unum?: Contemporary and Historical Perspectives on Immigrant Political Incorporation*, edited by Gary Gerstle and John H. Mollenkopf. New York: Russell Sage Foundation.

Muller, Edward N. 1979. *Aggressive Political Participation*. Princeton, N.J.: Princeton University Press

Myers, Dowell. 2007. *Immigrants and Boomers: Forging a New Social Contract for the Future of America*. New York: Russell Sage Foundation.

Nagel, Joane. 1995. "American Indian Ethnic Renewal: Politics and the Resurgence of Identity." *American Sociological Review* 60(6): 947–65.

Nakanishi, Don T. 1986. *The UCLA Asian Pacific American Voter Registration Study*. Los Angeles: Institute for Social Research, UCLA.

———. 1991. "The Next Swing Vote? Asian Pacific Americans and California Politics." In *Racial and Ethnic Politics in California*, edited by Byran O. Jackson and Michael B. Preston. Berkeley: IGS Press, Institute of Governmental Studies, University of California at Berkeley.

National Election Pool. 2008. "Election Center 2008: Primary Exit Polls, California: Democrats." Available at: http://www.CNN.com (accessed February 15, 2010).

Newport, Frank. 2007. "Just Why Do Americans Attend Church?" *Gallup.com.*

Available at: http://www.gallup.com/poll/27124/Just-Why-Americans-Attend-Church.aspx (accessed June 8, 2011).

New York Times. 2008. "Exit Polls: Election Results 2008." Available at: http://elections.nytimes.com/2008/results/president/exit-polls.html (accessed March 29, 2011).

Ngai, Mae M. 2004. *Impossible Subjects: Illegal Aliens and the Making of Modern America*. Princeton, N.J.: Princeton University Press.

Ngo, Bic, and Stacey J. Lee. 2007. "Complicating the Image of Model Minority Success: A Review of Southeast Asian American Education." *Review of Educational Research* 77(4): 415–53.

Nicholas, Peter, and Tom Hamburger. 2007. "Clinton Campaign Taps into an Unlikely Treasure-Trove: New York's Chinese Immigrants Shell Out—But It Doesn't All Add Up." *Los Angeles Times*, October 19.

Nie, Norman H., Jane Junn, and Kenneth Stehlik-Barry. 1996. *Education and Democratic Citizenship in America*. Chicago: University of Chicago Press.

Niemi, Richard G. 1976. "Costs of Voting and Nonvoting." *Public Choice* 27(1): 115–19.

Nobles, Melissa. 2000. *Shades of Citizenship: Race and the Census in Modern Politics*. Palo Alto, Calif.: Stanford University Press.

Oberholzer-Gee, Felix, and Joel Waldfogel. 2006. "Media Markets and Localism: Does Local News en Español Boost Hispanic Voter Turnout?" NBER Working Paper Series No. 12317. Cambridge, Mass.: National Bureau of Economic Research.

Oboler, Suzanne. 1995. *Ethnic Labels, Latino Lives: Identity and the Politics of (Re)presentation in the United States*. Minneapolis: University of Minnesota Press.

O'Connor, Alice, Chris Tilly, and Lawrence Bobo. 2003. *Urban Inequality: Evidence from Four Cities*. New York: Russell Sage Foundation.

Oestreicher, Richard. 1988. "Urban Working-Class Political Behavior and Theories of American Electoral Politics, 1870–1940." *Journal of American History* 74(4): 1257–86.

Okamoto, Dina G. 2003. "Toward a Theory of Panethnicity: Explaining Asian American Collective Action." *American Sociological Review* 68(6): 811–42.

———. 2006. "Institutional Panethnicity: Boundary Formation in Asian American Organizing." *Social Forces* 85(1): 1–27.

Okihiro, Gary Y. 2001. *The Columbia Guide to Asian American History*. New York: Columbia University Press.

Oliver, J. Eric, and Tali Mendelberg. 2000. "Reconsidering the Environmental Determinants of White Racial Attitudes." *American Journal of Political Science* 44(3): 574–89.

Oliver, J. Eric, and Janelle Wong. 2003. "Intergroup Prejudice in Multiethnic Settings." *American Journal of Political Science* 47(4): 567–82.

Olzak, Susan. 1992. *The Dynamics of Ethnic Competition and Conflict*. Palo Alto, Calif.: Stanford University Press.

Omi, Michael. 1997. "Racial Identity and the State: The Dilemmas of Classification." *Law and Inequality: A Journal of Theory and Practice* 15: 7–24.

Omi, Michael, and Howard Winant. 1994. *Racial Formation in the United States: From the 1960s to the 1990s.* New York: Routledge.

Ortiz, Vilma, and Edward Eric Telles. 2008. *Generations of Exclusion: Mexican Americans, Assimilation, and Race.* New York: Russell Sage Foundation.

Pantoja, Adrian D. 2005. "Transnational Ties and Immigrant Political Incorporation: The Case of Dominicans in Washington Heights, New York." *International Migration Review* 43(4): 123–46.

Pantoja, Adrian D., Ricardo Ramirez, and Gary M. Segura. 2001. "Citizens by Choice, Voters by Necessity: Patterns in Political Mobilization in Naturalized Latinos." *Political Research Quarterly* 54(4): 729–50.

Pantoja, Adrian D., and Janelle Wong. 2009. "In Pursuit of Inclusion: Asian American Naturalization and Political Incorporation." In *Bringing Outsiders In: Transatlantic Perspectives on Immigrant Political Incorporation,* edited by Jennifer L. Hochschild and John H. Mollenkopf. Ithaca, N.Y.: Cornell University Press.

Park, Robert Ezra. 1925. *The City.* Chicago: University of Chicago Press.

Pateman, Carole. 1970. *Participation and Democratic Theory.* Cambridge: Cambridge University Press.

Perea, Juan F. 2000. *Race and Races: Cases and Resources for a Diverse America.* St. Paul, Minn.: West Group.

Perlmann, Joel. 2005. *Italians Then, Mexicans Now: Immigrant Origins and Second-Generation Progress, 1890 to 2000.* New York: Russell Sage Foundation.

Petersen, Roger Dale. 2002. *Understanding Ethnic Violence: Fear, Hatred, and Resentment in Twentieth-Century Eastern Europe.* Cambridge: Cambridge University Press.

Pettersen, William. 1966. "Success Story, Japanese-American Style." *New York Times Magazine,* January 9, 180.

Petrocik, John R. 1974. "An Analysis of Intransitivities in the Index of Party Identification." *Political Methodology* 1: 31–47.

Pew Research Center. 2008. *U.S. Religious Landscape Survey.* Washington, D.C.: Pew Research Center.

Phinney, Jean S. 1996. "When We Talk About American Ethnic Groups, What Do We Mean?" *American Psychologist* 51(9): 918–27.

Pimentel, Joseph. 2007. "APA Immigration: Survey Reveals Asian Americans Support Immigration Reform." OCAnational.com. Available at: http://www.ocanational.org/index.php?option=com_content&task=view&id=299&Itemid=94 (accessed July 21, 2011).

Portes, Alejandro, and Robert L Bach. 1985. *Latin Journey: Cuban and Mexican Immigrants in the United States.* Berkeley: University of California Press.

Portes, Alejandro, and Leif Jensen. 1989. "The Enclave and the Entrants: Patterns of Ethnic Enterprise in Miami Before and After Mariel." *American Sociological Review* 54(6): 929–49.

Portes, Alejandro, and Rubén G. Rumbaut. 1996. *Immigrant America: A Portrait.* Berkeley and Los Angeles: University of California Press.

———. 2001. *Legacies: The Story of the Immigrant Second Generation.* Berkeley: University of California Press.

Portes, Alejandro, and Min Zhou. 1993. "The New Second Generation: Segmented Assimilation and Its Variants." *Annals of the American Academy of Political and Social Science* 530: 74–96.

Putnam, Robert D. 1993. *Making Democracy Work: Civic Traditions in Modern Italy.* Princeton, N.J.: Princeton University Press.

———. 2000. *Bowling Alone: The Collapse and Revival of American Community.* New York: Simon and Schuster.

———. 2007. "E Pluribus Unum: Diversity and Community in the Twenty-first Century: The 2006 Johan Skytte Prize Lecture." *Scandinavian Political Studies* 30(2): 137–74.

Quinnipiac University Polling Institute. 2008. "National (US) Poll: Voters Say 'Yes We Can' with High Hopes for Obama, Quinnipiac University National Poll Finds." Hamden, Conn.: Quinnipiac University Polling Institute.

Ramakrishnan, S. Karthick. 2005. *Democracy in Immigrant America.* Palo Alto, Calif.: Stanford University Press.

———. 2006. "But Do They Bowl? Race, Immigrant Incorporation, and Civic Voluntarism in the United States." In *Transforming Politics, Transforming America: The Political and Civic Incorporation of Immigrants in the United States,* edited by Taeku Lee, S. Karthick Ramakrishnan, and Ricardo Ramírez. Charlottesville: University of Virginia Press.

Ramakrishnan, S. Karthick, and Irene Bloemraad, eds. 2008. *Civic Hopes and Political Realities: Immigrants, Community Organizations, and Political Engagement.* New York: Russell Sage Foundation.

Ramakrishnan, S. Karthick, and Thomas J. Espenshade. 2001. "Immigrant Incorporation and Political Participation in the United States." *International Migration Review* 35(3): 870–910.

Ramakrishnan, S. Karthick, Jane Junn, Taeku Lee, and Janelle Wong. 2011. *2008 National Asian American Survey,* 2008 [computer file]. ICPSR31481-V1. Ann Arbor, Mich.: Inter-university Consortium for Political and Social Research [distributor], 2011-08-12. doi:10.3886/ICPSR31481.

Ramakrishnan, S. Karthick, and Celia Viramontes. 2006. *Civic Inequalitites: Immigrant Volunteerism and Community Organizations in California.* San Francisco: Public Policy Institute of California.

———. 2010. "Civic Spaces: Mexican Hometown Associations and Immigrant Participation." *Journal of Social Issues* 66(1): 155–73.

Ramakrishnan, S. Karthick, Janelle Wong, Taeku Lee, and Jane Junn. 2009. "Race-Based Considerations and the Obama Vote." *Du Bois Review: Social Science Research on Race* 6(1): 219–38.

Ramirez, Ricardo, and Janelle Wong. 2006. "Nonpartisan Latino and Asian American Contactability and Voter Mobilization." In *Transforming Politics, Transforming America: The Political and Civic Incorporation of Immigrants in the United States*, edited by Taeku Lee, Karthick Ramakrishnan, and Ricardo Ramírez. Charlottesville: University of Virginia Press.

Reed-Danahay, Deborah, and Caroline Brettell, eds. 2008. *Citizenship, Political Engagement, and Belonging: Immigrants in Europe and the United States*. New Brunswick, N.J.: Rutgers University Press.

Rim, Kathy. 2009. "The Social and Political Consequences of Asian American Panethnicity." Presented at the annual meeting of the American Political Science Association, Toronto, Canada (September 3–6).

Roccas, Sonia, and Marilynn B. Brewer. 2002. "Social Identity Complexity." *Personality and Social Psychology Review* 6(2): 88–106.

Rogers, Reuel Reuben. 2006. *Afro-Caribbean Immigrants and the Politics of Incorporation: Ethnicity, Exception, or Exit*. New York: Cambridge University Press.

Rosenstone, Steven J., and John Mark Hansen. 1993. *Mobilization, Participation, and Democracy in America*. New York: Macmillan.

Rosenstone, Steven J., and Raymond E. Wolfinger. 1978. "The Effect of Registration Laws on Voter Turnout." *American Political Science Review* 72(1): 22–45.

Rumbaut, Rubén G. 1995. "Vietnamese, Laotian, and Cambodian Americans." In *Asian Americans: Contemporary Trends and Issues*, edited by Pyong Gap Min. Thousand Oaks, Calif.: Sage Publications.

———. 2008. "The Coming of the Second Generation: Immigration and Ethnic Mobility in Southern California." *Annals of the American Academy of Political and Social Science* 620(1): 196–236.

Rusk, Jerrold G. 1976. "Review: Political Participation in America: A Review Essay." *American Political Science Review* 70(2): 583–91.

Sahagun, Louis, and My-Thuan Tran. 2009. "Vietnamese Americans Protest Art Exhibit in Santa Ana." *Los Angeles Times*, January 18.

Saito, Leland T. 1998. *Race and Politics: Asian Americans, Latinos, and Whites in a Los Angeles Suburb*. Urbana: University of Illinois Press.

Sakamoto, Arthur, Kimberly A. Goyette, and ChangHwan Kim. 2009. "Socioeconomic Attainments of Asian Americans." *Annual Review of Sociology* 35: 255–76.

Sampson, Robert J. 2008. "Moving to Inequality: Neighborhood Effects and Experiments Meet Social Structure." *American Journal of Sociology* 114(1): 189–231.

Sampson, Robert J., Jeffrey D. Morenoff, and Thomas Gannon-Rowley. 2002. "Assessing 'Neighborhood Effects': Social Processes and New Directions in Research." *Annual Review of Sociology* 28: 443–78.

Sanchez, Gabriel R. 2006. "The Role of Group Consciousness in Political Participation Among Latinos in the United States." *American Politics Research* 34(4): 427–50.

Sanders, Jimy M., and Victor Nee. 1987. "Limits of Ethnic Solidarity in the Enclave Economy." *American Sociological Review* 52(6): 745–73.

Schaffner, Brian F., and Matthew Streb. 2002. "The Partisan Heuristic in Low-Information Elections." *Public Opinion Quarterly* 66(4): 559–81.

Schaffner, Brian F., Matthew Streb, and Gerald Wright. 2001. "Teams Without Uniforms: The Nonpartisan Ballot in State and Local Elections." *Political Research Quarterly* 54(1): 7–30.

Schattschneider, E. E. 1960. *The Semisovereign People: A Realist's View of Democracy in America*. New York: Holt, Rinehart, and Winston.

Schier, Steven E. 2002. "From Melting Pot to Centrifuge: Immigrants and American Politics." *Brookings Review* 20(1): 16–20.

Segura, Gary M., and Helena Alves Rodrigues. 2006. "Comparative Ethnic Politics in the United States: Beyond Black and White." *Annual Review of Political Science* 9(1): 375–95.

Segura, Gary M., Harry Pachon, and Nathan D. Woods. 2001. "Hispanics, Social Capital, and Civic Engagement." *National Civic Review* 90(1): 85–96.

Shachar, Ron, and Barry Nalebuff. 1999. "Follow the Leader: Theory and Evidence on Political Participation." *American Economic Review* 89(3): 525–47.

Shankar, Lavina Dhingra, and Rajini Srikanth, eds. 1998. *A Part, Yet Apart: South Asians in Asian America*. Philadelphia: Temple University Press.

Sheth, Manju. 1995. "Asian Indian Americans." In *Asian Americans: Contemporary Trends and Issues*, edited by Pyong Gap Min. Thousand Oaks, Calif.: Sage Publications.

Shingles, Richard D. 1981. "Black Consciousness and Political Participation: The Missing Link." *American Political Science Review* 75(1): 76–91.

Sigel, Roberta S. 1970. *Learning About Politics: A Reader in Political Socialization*. New York: Random House.

Singer, Audrey, Susan Wiley Hardwick, and Caroline Brettell. 2008. *Twenty-First Century Gateways: Immigrant Incorporation in Suburban America*. Washington, D.C.: Brookings Institution Press.

Skocpol, Theda, and Morris P. Fiorina, eds. 1999a. *Civic Engagement in American Democracy*. Washington, D.C.: Brookings Institution Press.

———. 1999b. "Making Sense of the Civic Engagement Debate." In *Civic Engagement in American Democracy*, edited by Theda Skocpol and Morris P. Fiorina. Washington, D.C.: Brookings Institution Press.

Smith, Aaron. 2009. *The Internet's Role in Campaign 2008*. Washington, D.C.: Pew Internet & American Life Project.

Smith, Daniel A., and Caroline J. Tolbert. 2004. *Educated by Initiative: The Effects of Direct Democracy on Citizens and Political Organizations in the American States*. Ann Arbor: University of Michigan Press.

———. 2007. "The Instrumental and Educative Effects of Ballot Measures: Research on Direct Democracy in the American States." *State Politics and Policy Quarterly* 7(4): 416–45.

Smith, Gregory, and Allison Pond. 2008. *Pew Forum: A Slight but Steady Majority Favors Keeping Abortion Legal.* Washington, D.C.: Pew Forum on Religion & Public Life.

Smith, Michael, and Joe R. Feagin, eds. 1995. *The Bubbling Cauldron: Race, Ethnicity, and the Urban Crisis.* Minneapolis: University of Minnesota Press.

Smith, Michael P., and Luis Guarnizo. 1998. *Transnationalism from Below.* New Brunswick, N.J.: Transaction Publishers.

Somashekhar, Sandhya. 2002. "Many Asian Americans Prefer Road Less Traveled in Politics." *The Daily Review,* November 3: local,1.

Somers, Margaret R. 1994. "The Narrative Constitution of Identity: A Relational and Network Approach." *Theory and Society* 23(5): 605–49.

Spickard, Paul. 2001. "Whither the Asian American Coalition?" *Pacific Historical Review* 76(4): 585–604.

Stephens, Matt. 2011. "Hindu Temple of the Woodlands to Open in June." *Woodlands Villager,* May 4. Available at: http://www.yourhoustonnews.com/woodlands/news/article_17e1008e-e9c1-5fcb-9c44-fc77fdb0d354.html (accessed March 29, 2011).

Sterne, Evelyn Savidge. 2001. "Beyond the Boss: Immigration and American Political Culture from 1880 to 1940." In *E Pluribus Unum? Contemporary and Historical Perspectives on Immigrant Political Incorporation.* New York: Russell Sage Foundation.

Stokes, Atiya Kai. 2003. "Latino Group Consciousness and Political Participation." *American Politics Research* 31(4): 361–78.

Stoll, Michael A. 2001. "Race, Neighborhood Poverty, and Participation in Voluntary Associations." *Sociological Forum* 16(3): 529–57.

Stoll, Michael A., and Janelle Wong. 2007. "Immigration and Civic Participation in a Multiracial and Multiethnic Context." *International Migration Review* 41(4): 880–908.

Strolovitch, Dara Z. 2007. *Affirmative Advocacy: Race, Class, and Gender in Interest Group Politics.* Chicago: University of Chicago Press.

Stryker, Sheldon, Timothy J. Owens, and Robert W. White, eds. 2000. *Self, Identity, and Social Movements.* Minneapolis: University of Minnesota Press.

Sundeen, Richard A., Cristina Garcia, and Lili Wang. 2007. "Volunteer Behavior among Asian American Groups in the United States." *Journal of Asian American Studies* 10(3): 243–81.

Suro, Roberto, Richard Fry, and Jeffrey Passel. 2005. *Hispanics and the 2004 Election: Population, Electorate and Voters.* Washington, D.C.: Pew Hispanic Center.

Tajfel, Henri. 1978. *Differentiation Between Social Groups: Studies in the Social Psychology of Intergroup Relations.* London: Academic Press.

Tajfel, Henri, and John C. Turner. 2004. "The Social Identity Theory of Intergroup Behavior." In *Political Psychology: Key Readings*, edited by John T. Jost and Jim Sidanius. New York: Psychology Press.

Takagi, Dana Y. 1998. *The Retreat from Race: Asian-American Admissions and Racial Politics*. New Brunswick, N.J.: Rutgers University Press.

Takaki, Ronald T. 1989. *Strangers from a Different Shore: A History of Asian Americans*. Boston: Little, Brown.

———. 1995. *Strangers at the Gates Again: Asian American Immigration after 1965*. New York: Chelsea House Publishers.

Takezawa, Yasuko. 2000. "Children of Inmates: The Effects of the Redress Movement among Third-Generation Japanese Americans." In *Contemporary Asian America*, edited by Zhou Min and James V. Gatewood. New York: New York University Press.

Talev, Margaret. 2010. "Indian Americans a Growing Political Force in Both Parties." *Mclatchydc.com*. Available at: www.mclatchydc.com/2010/10/27/102703/indian-americans-a-growing-political.html (accessed March 29, 2011).

Tate, Katherine. 1993. *From Protest to Politics: The New Black Voters in American Elections*. New York: Russell Sage Foundation.

Toji, Dean. 2003. "Japanese: Rise of a Nikkei Generation." In *The New Face of Asian Pacific America: Numbers, Diversity & Change in the 21st Century*. San Francisco: AsianWeek and UCLA Asian American Studies Center Press.

Tolbert, Caroline J., and Daniel A. Smith. 2005. "The Educative Effects of Ballot Initiatives on Voter Turnout." *American Politics Research* 33(2): 283–309.

Tollison, Robert D., and Thomas D. Willett. 1973. "Some Simple Economics of Voting and Not Voting." *Public Choice* 16(1): 59–71.

Toner, Robin, and Janet Elder. 2007. "Most Support U.S. Guarantee of Health Care." *New York Times*, March 2.

Toyota, Tritia. 2010. *Envisioning America: New Chinese Americans and the Politics of Belonging*. Palo Alto, Calif: Stanford University Press.

Tran, My-Thuan. 2008. "Vietnam Echoes in City Feud: Vietnam Echoes in City Feud; Selecting a Name for a District in San Jose Exposes a Rift Among Immigrants and Tests a Young Politician." *Los Angeles Times*, March 22, 1.

Trounstine, Jessica. 2006. "Dominant Regimes and the Demise of Urban Democracy." *Journal of Politics* 68(04): 879–93.

Tuan, Mia. 1998. *Forever Foreigners or Honorary Whites? The Asian Ethnic Experience Today*. New Brunswick, N.J.: Rutgers University Press.

Tuchman, Gary. 2008. "Anderson Cooper 360 Degrees: The Asian American Vote." *CNN.com - Transcripts*. Available at: http://transcripts.cnn.com/TRANSCRIPTS/0802/08/acd.01.html (accessed December 8, 2007).

Turner, John C., ed. 1987. *Rediscovering the Social Group: A Self-Categorization Theory*. Oxford: Blackwell.

Turner, Jonathan H. 1987. "Toward a Sociological Theory of Motivation." *American Sociological Review* 52(1): 15–27.

Uba, Laura. 1992. "Cultural Barriers to Health Care for Southeast Asian Refugees." *Public Health Reports* 107(5): 544–48.

Uecker, Jeremy E., Mark Regnerus, and Margaret L. Vaaler. 2007. "Losing My Religion: The Social Sources of Religious Decline in Early Adulthood." *Social Forces* 85(4): 1667–92.

Uhlaner, Carole J., and F. Chris Garcia. 2002. "Latino Public Opinion." In *Understanding Public Opinion*, edited by Barbara Norrander and Clyde Wilcox. Washington, D.C: CQ Press.

Uhlaner, Carole J., Bruce E. Cain, and Roderick D. Kiewiet. 1989. "Political Participation of Ethnic Minorities in the 1980s." *Political Behavior* 11(3): 195–231.

U.S. Census Bureau. 2000. *Census 2000 Summary File 1 (SF1) 100 Percent Data* [dataset]. Available at: http://factfinder.census.gov (March 29, 2011).

———. 2002. "Voting Rights Act Amendments of 1992, Determinations Under Section 203." Washington: Government Printing Office. Available at: http://www.justice.gov/crt/voting/sec_203/fedreg_July.php (accessed February 2, 2010).

———. 2004. *2000 Census of Population and Housing: United States Summary, 2000.* Washington: U.S. Census Bureau.

———. 2008a. *2008 American Community Survey 1-Year Estimates* [dataset]. Available at: http://factfinder.census.gov (March 29, 2011).

———. 2008b. *Current Population Survey Voter Registration Supplement 2008*, November 2008 [dataset]. Available at: http://www.icpsr.umich.edu/icpsrweb/RCMD/studies/25643 (accessed March 29, 2011).

———. 2008c. *2006–2008 American Community Survey 3-Year Estimates, Public Use Microdata* [dataset]. Available at: http://factfinder.census.gov (March 29, 2011).

U.S. Citizenship and Immigration Services. 2009a. *Characteristics of Specialty Occupation Workers (H-1B): Fiscal Year 2008, Annual Report.* Washington: Department of Homeland Security.

———. 2009b. *Yearbook of Immigration Statistics: 2008.* Washington: Department of Homeland Security, Office of Immigration Statistics.

U.S. Department of Justice. 2010. "The Attorney General's Language Minority Guidelines 28 C.F.R. Part 55." Available at: http://www.justice.gov/crt/voting/28cfr/55/28cfr55.htm (accessed February 1, 2010).

U.S. General Accounting Office (GAO). 2000. *H-1B Foreign Workers: Better Controls Needed to Help Employers and Protect Workers.* Washington: Government Printing Office.

Uslaner, Eric M., and Richard S. Conley. 2003. "Civic Engagement and Particularized Trust: The Ties that Bind People to their Ethnic Communities." *American Politics Research* 31(4): 331–60.

U.S. News and World Report. 1966. "Success Story of One Minority Group in U.S." *U.S. News and World Report* 93: 73–76.

Varadarajan, Tunku. 1999. "A Patel Motel Cartel?" *The New York Times*, July 4.

Verba, Sidney. 2003. "Would the Dream of Political Equality Turn out to Be a Nightmare?." *Perspectives on Politics* 1(4): 663–79.

Verba, Sidney, and Norman H. Nie. 1972. *Participation in America: Political Democracy and Social Equality*. New York: Harper & Row.

Verba, Sidney, Norman H. Nie, and Jae-On Kim. 1978. *Participation and Political Equality*. Cambridge: Cambridge University Press.

Verba, Sidney, Kay Lehman Schlozman, and Henry E. Brady. 1995. *Voice and Equality: Civic Voluntarism in American Politics*. Cambridge, Mass.: Harvard University Press.

Võ, Linda Trinh, and Rick Bonus, eds. 2002. *Contemporary Asian American Communities: Intersections and Divergences*. Philadelphia: Temple University Press.

Voss, Kim, and Irene Bloemraad, eds. 2010. *Rallying for Immigrant Rights*. Berkeley: University of California Press.

Wald, Kenneth D., and Allison Calhoun-Brown. 2010. *Religion and Politics in the United States*, 6th ed. Lanham, Md.: Rowman & Littlefield.

Wang, Xinyang. 2001. *Surviving the City: The Chinese Immigrant Experience in New York City, 1890–1970*. Lanham, Md.: Rowman & Littlefield.

Warner, Stephen. 1993. "Work in Progress Toward a New Paradigm for the Sociological Study of Religion in the United States." *American Journal of Sociology* 98(5): 1044–93.

Warner, R. Stephen, and Judith G. Wittner, eds. 1998. *Gatherings in Diaspora: Religious Communities and the New Immigration*. Philadelphia: Temple University Press.

Waters, Mary C. 1990. *Ethnic Options: Choosing Identities in America*. Berkeley: University of California Press.

Wei, William. 1993. *The Asian American Movement*. Philadelphia: Temple University Press.

Weisberg, Herbert F. 1980. "A Multidimensional Conceptualization of Party Identification." *Political Behavior* 2(1): 33–60.

———. 1983. "A New Scale of Partisanship." *Political Behavior* 5(4): 363–76.

Welch, Susan, Lee Sigelman, Timothy Bledsoe, and Michael Combs. 2001. *Race and Place*. New York: Cambridge University Press.

Wolfinger, Raymond E. 1965. "The Development and Persistence of Ethnic Voting." *American Political Science Review* 59(4): 896–908.

Wolfinger, Raymond E., and Steven Rosenstone. 1980. *Who Votes?* New Haven, Conn.: Yale University Press.

Wong, Janelle S. 2000. "The Effects of Age and Political Exposure on the Development of Party Identification Among Asian American and Latino Immigrants in the U.S." *Political Behavior* 22(4): 341–71.

———. 2005. "Mobilizing Asian American Voters: A Field Experiment." *Annals of the American Academy of Political and Social Science* 601(1): 102–14.

———. 2006. *Democracy's Promise: Immigrants and American Civic Institutions.* Ann Arbor: University of Michigan Press.

———. 2007. "Two Steps Forward, One Step Back . . . The Slow and Steady March of Immigrant Political Incorporation." *DuBois Review* 4(2): 457–67.

Wong, Janelle S., and Jane Naomi Iwamura. 2007. "Religion, Civic Engagement, and Immigrant Politics. The Moral Minority: Race, Religion, and Conservative Politics in Asian America." In *Religion and Social Justice for Immigrants,* edited by Pierrette Hondagneu-Sotelo. New Brunswick, N.J.: Rutgers University Press.

Wong, Janelle S., Pei-Te Lien, and M. Margaret Conway. 2005. "The Role of Group-Based Resources in the Political Participation of Asian Americans." *American Politics Research* 33(4): 545–76.

Wong, Janelle S., Kathy Rim, and Haven Perez. 2008. "Protestant Churches and Conservative Politics: Latinos and Asians in the United States." In *Civic Hopes and Political Realities: Immigrants, Community Organizations, and Political Engagement.* New York: Russell Sage Foundation.

Wright, Gerald C. 2008. "Charles Adrian and the Study of Nonpartisan Elections." *Political Research Quarterly* 61(1): 13–16.

Wu, Frank H. 2002. *Yellow: Race in America Beyond Black and White.* New York: Basic Books.

Wuthnow, Robert. 1999. "Mobilizing Civic Engagement: The Changing Impact of Religious Involvement." In *Civic Engagement in American Democracy,* edited by Theda Skocpol and Morris Fiorina. Washington, D.C.: Brookings Institution Press.

Yang, Fenggang. 1998. "Chinese Conversion to Evangelical Christianity: The Importance of Social and Cultural Context." *Sociology of Religion* 59(3): 237–57.

———. 2000. "The Growing Literature of Asian American Religions: A Review of the Field, with Special Attention to Three New Books." *Journal of Asian American Studies* 3(2): 251–56.

Yang, Fenggang, and Helen Rose Ebaugh. 2001. "Transformations in New Immigrant Religions and their Global Implications." *American Sociological Review* 66(2): 269–88.

Yang, Elizabeth M., and Kristi Gaines. 2008. "Ensuring Access to the Ballot Box: Voting Rights in the United States." *Social Education* 72(5): 223–29.

Yang, K. Y. 2004. "Southeast Asian American Children: Not the 'Model Minority.'" *The Future of Children* 14(2): 127–34.

Yang, Phillip Q. 1994. "Examining Immigrant Naturalization." *International Migration Review* 28(3): 449–77.

Yonemoto, Karen. 2009. "Sacred Changes: Multiracial Alliances and Community Transformation Among Asian American Churches in the U.S." Ph.D. Diss., University of Southern California.

Yoo, David K., ed. 1999. *New Spiritual Homes: Religion and Asian Americans*. Honolulu: University of Hawaii Press.

Yu, Eui-Young. 1977. "Koreans in America: An Emerging Ethnic Minority." *Amerasia Journal* 4(1): 117–31.

Zhou, Min, and Carl L. Bankston III. 1998. *Growing Up American: How Vietnamese Children Adapt to Life in the United States*. New York: Russell Sage Foundation.

Zhou, Min, and James V. Gatewood, eds. 2000. *Contemporary Asian America: A Multidisciplinary Reader*. New York: New York University Press.

Zhou, Min, and Yang Sao Xiong. 2005. "The Multifaceted American Experiences of the Children of Asian Immigrants: Lessons for Segmented Assimilation." *Ethnic and Racial Studies* 28(6): 1119–52.

Zia, Helen. 2001. *Asian American Dreams: The Emergence of an American People*. New York: Farrar, Straus and Giroux.

Index

Boldface numbers refer to figures and tables.